Atmospheric Justice

Atmospheric Justice

A Political Theory of Climate Change

STEVE VANDERHEIDEN

OXFORD
UNIVERSITY PRESS

OXFORD
UNIVERSITY PRESS

Oxford University Press, Inc., publishes works that further
Oxford University's objective of excellence
in research, scholarship, and education.

Oxford   New York
Auckland   Cape Town   Dar es Salaam   Hong Kong   Karachi
Kuala Lumpur   Madrid   Melbourne   Mexico City   Nairobi
New Delhi   Shanghai   Taipei   Toronto

With offices in
Argentina   Austria   Brazil   Chile   Czech Republic   France   Greece
Guatemala   Hungary   Italy   Japan   Poland   Portugal   Singapore
South Korea   Switzerland   Thailand   Turkey   Ukraine   Vietnam

Copyright © 2008 by Oxford University Press, Inc.

Published by Oxford University Press, Inc.
198 Madison Avenue, New York, New York 10016

www.oup.com

First issued as an Oxford University Press paperback, 2009

Library of Congress Cataloging-in-Publication Data
Vanderheiden, Steve.
Atmospheric justice : a political theory of climate change / Steve Vanderheiden.
   p.   cm.
Includes bibliographical references.
ISBN 978-0-19-973312-5
   1. Climatic changes—Political aspects.   2. Climatic changes—Environmental
aspects.   3. Environmental justice.   4. Greenhouse gases—Environmental
aspects.   I. Title.
QC981.8.C5V355   2008
363.738'74—dc22   2007029916

9 8 7 6 5 4 3 2 1

Printed in the United States of America
on acid-free paper

Acknowledgments

This book could not have been completed without the generous help of a great many people. I thank all those who helped me either think about or work on this project or the issues it treats, as well as those who facilitated its completion, and apologize to anyone that I forget to mention here. All of the credit but none of the blame for my current thinking about equity and responsibility owes to those under whom I've had the privilege to study political theory, especially Peter Diamond, Bruce Landesman, Cindy Stark, Tom Reed, Leslie Francis, Patrick Riley, Bernie Yack, Marion Smiley, Harry Brighouse, Eric Olin Wright, Claudia Card, Allen Buchanan, Booth Fowler, and Charlie Anderson. Thanks also to Dale Murray, David Schlosberg, Terence Ball, Robyn Eckersley, Joel Kassiola, Tim Luke, Peter Cannavo, Harlan Wilson, Joe Bowersox, John Meyer, Bill Chaloupka, Sheri Breen, John Barry, David Mapel, and Michaele Ferguson either for their helpful insights into this project or for general guidance in exploring the field of environmental political theory. I'm indebted to David McBride at Oxford University Press for his patience and careful oversight with the manuscript, and to the two anonymous reviewers at OUP for their invaluable constructive criticism.

In addition, I'd like to acknowledge the University of Minnesota for granting me a semester's leave to complete the draft version of the manuscript, and to Natalie Holstad at Taylor & Francis, Nicholas

Rescher at *Public Affairs Quarterly*, and Michael DePaul at the *Journal of Philosophical Research* for granting me permission to adapt previously published ideas in new ways. Most of all, I thank my partner Janet Donavan, without whose humor, support, and infinite patience I could never have hoped to finish this project.

Contents

Introduction

In the aftermath of Hurricane Katrina's devastating effects on the
U.S. Gulf Coast, the storm, which was a category 4 hurricane when it
hit New Orleans in August 2005, breaching Louisiana's levy system
and rendering most of the city uninhabitable, became a set piece in a
highly adversarial international war of words over what is widely
perceived to be U.S. intransigence against meaningful global climate
policy development. In contrast with two other high-profile natural
disasters occurring during the same period—the Indonesian tsunami
of December 2004 and the Pakistani earthquake of October 2005—
Katrina was seen by some critics of U.S. climate policy as a direct
consequence of increasing atmospheric concentrations of greenhouse
gases (GHGs) and the climatic changes that are expected to result
from them. While the United States was victimized by the hurricane,
it was seen by some as partially responsible for causing it, unlike those
genuinely "natural" (because in no way anthropogenic) disasters in
Indonesia and Pakistan. Most countries sent aid to Katrina's victims—
many of whom owned no automobiles and so were among those
Americans least responsible for contributing to climate change through
fossil fuel combustion—but some also included pointed criticism in
the process, alluding to the U.S. withdrawal from the Kyoto Protocol
and ongoing obstructionism in further climate policy efforts. For
example, British Royal Commission on Environmental Pollution Chairman Sir John Lawton noted that the increasing intensity of hurricanes,
of which Katrina

was a manifestation, is "very likely due to global warming" and blasted those climate skeptics dominating American climate policy and political institutions by remarking: "If this makes the climate loonies in the States realize that we've got a problem, some good will come out of a truly awful situation."[1]

It remains to be seen whether Lawton's expressed wish will come true, but the causal connection to which he alludes is not without substance. Relying upon satellite records of tropical cyclone activity dating back to 1970, a team of scientists from Georgia Tech and the National Center for Atmospheric Research (NCAR) reported in a September 2005 issue of *Science*, published one week before Lawton's comments, that the most intense hurricanes (those reaching category 4 and 5) had increased by 80 percent worldwide since 1970, consistent with the hypothesized relationship between observed sea-surface temperature warming and hurricane intensity. They conclude that "global data indicate a 30-year trend toward more frequent and intense hurricanes," with an expected near doubling of category 4 and 5 hurricanes, which now comprise 35 percent of such storms, in a trend that "is not inconsistent with recent climate model simulations that a doubling of CO_2 may increase the frequency of the most intense cyclones."[2] As Richard Kerr explains:

> Global warming and tropical cyclones are naturally linked by the storms' appetite for heat. Tropical storms are heat engines that draw their energy upward from warm ocean water to drive their winds before expelling waste heat to the upper atmosphere. So warming the tropical oceans—in effect throwing more wood on the fire—might be expected to spawn more frequent or more intense tropical cyclones.[3]

Though it would surely be tendentious to conclude that Hurricane Katrina or any other single storm was caused by oceanic warming resulting from human emission of GHGs, much less that the United States was itself responsible for causing the storm, Lawton was right to suggest that the increasingly intense hurricanes observed by climatologists and dreaded by disaster planners in New Orleans for decades are themselves likely to be due to global warming.

Intense hurricanes are not the only deadly manifestation of the global warming that accompanies climate change[4]—heat waves are another, and perhaps the 2005 hurricane season in the United States, which also saw category 4 Rita hit Texas and category 4 Wilma sweep across Florida, may yet become the agenda-setting visible public display of the consequences of a destabilized climate that the 2003 heat wave was for much of Europe, increasing issue salience and public pressure upon policy makers to take action to avert further damage. The link between anthropogenic climate change and heat waves is also well established: Gerald Meehl and Claudia Tebaldi of NCAR, relying on a global coupled climate model, found that heat waves would likewise very likely increase in frequency and duration in the twenty-first century, given current GHG emission trends. Choosing illustrative grid points of Chicago and Paris, which suffered deadly heat waves in 1995 and 2003, respectively, Meehl and Tebaldi predicted more frequent (by 25 and 31 percent for Chicago and Paris), more intense, and longer (by 3–4 days per event) heat waves over the course of this century.[5] Other adverse ecological consequences are predicted for those industrialized nations that have thus far controlled global climate policy development, although the bulk of climate-related harm is expected to be suffered by residents of developing nations, so the warnings that have steadily been issued by scientists for the past 15 years should become less hypothetical and more urgent to those publics with the power to force effective action to mitigate harm of climate change.

Indeed, the human threat posed by global climate change has not gone unnoticed by the insurance industry, which Evan Mills describes as "a lightning rod, serving as a global integrator of impacts across all sectors of the economy, and messenger of these impacts through the terms and price signals it projects to its customers."[6] The industry, which evaluates risk and spreads it across time and geographic areas, cannot—unlike those industries responsible for bankrolling the climate skeptics that deny human causes of climate change—afford to ignore the evidence about the increasing damage caused by climate-related events such as hurricanes, floods, droughts, or other catastrophes. As Stephen Schneider and Kristin Kuntz-Duriseti note:

> The financial service sector has taken particular note of the potential losses from climate change. Losses from weather-related disasters in the 1990s were eight times higher than in the 1960s. Although there is no clear evidence that hurricane frequency has changed over the past few decades (or will change in the next few decades), there is overwhelming data that damage has increased astronomically.[7]

Since weather-related property damage accounts for 90 percent of all insured catastrophe losses, the insurance industry is a significant stakeholder in global climate policy efforts. While it might guard against climate-related liquidity threats through traditional means (higher premiums and deductibles, new exclusions, etc.), it may also, as Mills suggests, "become more proactive in formalizing social solidarity to prevent and, when necessary, endure and adapt to extreme events that individuals cannot manage independently." Insurers might, he writes, "extend their self-chosen historical role in addressing root causes (as founders of the first fire departments, building codes, and auto safety testing protocols)" to urge climate-related loss prevention.[8]

Insofar as the private insurance industry does not become the powerful advocate for effective global climate change mitigation policies, or as long as such policies remain elusive, the risks posed by climate change will remain but will become far more difficult for the victims of climate change to absorb. Risk pooling could be taken over by governments rather than private insurers, insuring against property losses, crop losses, or perhaps, in some cases, loss of individual lives or of entire communities that result from extreme weather events and litigating against responsible industries in order to recover damages, but governments ultimately will be exposed to the same liquidity problems as are private insurers. Either significant parts of the world's population can be left entirely exposed to risk, as disaster fatigue begins to take its toll upon private charity efforts for catastrophe victims, or steps can be taken to reduce that risk and thereby to maintain those institutions that now protect against it. Given the widespread nature of the predicted harm of climate change, in which a great many persons stand to be significantly and adversely affected, the first option appears unacceptable, since it leaves huge populations vulnerable to total ruin, and others with potential environmental refugee crises as a result. The second option, on the other hand, requires the acknowledgment that we are all in this together—this is the ethos of risk pooling—with the policy responses that such an acknowledgment entails.

At some point, the mounting evidence that humans are indeed changing the climate will become impossible to ignore, even for those domestic social and political institutions that are now habitually inclined to protect the fossil-fuel–based industries that oppose, for narrowly self-interested reasons, the regulation of GHGs, which comprises an essential component of any effective climate policy. Whether or not that point will come in time to spare the planet irreparable ecological damage, however, is another question entirely, as Lawton's guarded comment indicates. Whether those affected populations will take adequate steps to preserve or extend the social institutions that guard against the arbitrariness of climate-related disasters, maintaining society's ability to protect its vulnerable members against climate-related risk, likewise remains an open question. Although any single climate-related catastrophe cannot with any certainty be definitively attributed to anthropogenic climate change, given the highly complex nature of climate and its multifarious drivers, what is certain is that as long as such weather events continue to wreak their destructive force upon human settlements and populations, global climate change will remain on the public's agenda, even if it continues to be largely excluded from the U.S. government's policy agenda. However, effectively addressing the problem of anthropogenic climate change requires more than simply the self-interested acknowledgment of its deleterious effects. It also requires a commitment to fairness, as much of this book attempts to explicate.

Aims of the Book

A purely self-interested national strategy for coping with increasing risk of environmental harm would be for those less vulnerable to climate-related damage to refuse to pool risk with those who are more vulnerable—a strategy similar to the cherry-picking of the healthiest persons by health insurance schemes—since this would minimize expected losses, with risk itself held constant. In the context of global climate, industrialized nations might, insofar as they pursue a purely self-interested climate policy strategy, elect to insure against climate-related losses through adaptation rather than mitigation, doing little to reduce their GHG emissions and instead devoting funds that might be used to reduce domestic GHG emissions to assisting those affected by climate change in adapting to changing climatic conditions, likely limiting this adaptation assistance to their own citizens. The incentives toward such an isolationist policy may be especially strong given the collective action problems plaguing nonglobal climate policy efforts. Unless other nations likewise take proactive steps to reduce their GHG emissions, the beneficial effects of strong domestic actions will be undermined, since the ecological effects of increased atmospheric GHG concentrations are global in nature, producing similar effects upon local climate regardless of their source. While self-interested worries about climate change may be sufficient to thrust the issue onto the public agenda, they are unlikely to provide sufficient motive for accepting the costs of a genuinely effective global climate regime, given what the costs to industrialized nations may entail, especially because many of the benefits of such efforts to avert climatic destabilization accrue to others, including residents of developing countries and future generations.

Because anthropogenic climate change is caused primarily by fossil fuel combustion and deforestation, residents of industrialized nations are responsible for the vast majority of the accumulated GHGs that cause climate-related harm. In this sense, climate change is a byproduct of the affluence of the world's most advantaged nations and persons. Yet, as the Intergovernmental Panel on Climate Change (IPCC) predicts, "the impacts of climate change will fall disproportionately upon developing countries and poor persons within all countries, and thereby exacerbate inequities in health status and access to adequate food, clean water, and other resources."[9] The net effect of these two apparent facts is a shifting of the ecological costs of the high consumption rates of the world's affluent to those who can least afford to bear them and are also least responsible for the phenomenon that generates them. Aside from presenting a genuinely global environmental problem, then, anthropogenic climate change also presents a unique case of global injustice, where the ongoing failure to adequately address the problem exacerbates the global inequity that is part and parcel of the problem itself.

For this reason, ideals of fairness were from the inception of the 1992 *United Nations Framework Convention on Climate Change (UNFCCC)* made a central component of the nascent global climate regime's mission, which called upon the world's nations to "protect the climate system for the benefit of present and future generations of humankind, on the basis of equity and in accordance with their common but differentiated responsibilities and respective capabilities." The imperative to address climate change in a manner that promotes fairness—based on the ideals of equity and national responsibility—has both a practical and a principled justification. Insofar as the problem of anthropogenic climate change is also a problem of global injustice, that problem cannot be meaningfully addressed without also taking the promotion of justice as a central aim of global climate policy efforts. Given the fact that a global climate regime would require both an international cooperative scheme and significantly expanded domestic institutions charged with implementing its assigned targets, those institutions ought to embody what John Rawls has described as "the first virtue of social institutions."[10] For a global climate regime to be effective, universal participation will eventually be necessary, even if the industrialized nations may be required to bear the initial burdens of climate change mitigation, and such universal participation would be practically impossible under unfair terms of cooperation. Not only must the assignment of costs be fair, but procedural fairness ought also to be a central aim of the climate regime, in order to engender the trust necessary for compliance and to help ensure that the terms of the agreement are genuinely fair to all.

Climate change policy, then, offers a unique case for the normative analysis of public policy issues in several respects. Since climate change is a fully global environmental problem, it defies nonglobal policy responses and necessitates international cooperation in a manner unlike other environmental issues that can be addressed by the actions of a limited number of states or other actors. Moreover, its global nature defies conventional assumptions about state sovereignty and the geographically bounded nature of principles of justice (as discussed in chapter 3). By the nature of individual GHG emissions, the conventional assumptions regarding moral and legal responsibility are complicated by the complex causal chain and aggregative nature of climate-related harm, again challenging the conventions of applied ethics and political theory.

Because of its unique international and intergenerational redistributive effects, as well as its *intra*national and *intra*generational effects, climate change challenges prevailing egalitarian theories of justice in their explicit rejection of cosmopolitan justice and inability to articulate a defensible account of intergenerational justice (subjects of chapters 3 and 4). Among current public policy issues, climate change presents a problem for which a critical analysis in terms of justice and fairness is most needed, as perhaps the paradigm case in which an environmental problem is inseparable from a problem of injustice, and can also be the most illuminating. This is so because it applies normative concepts and theories to real-world problems, revealing the essential issues of fairness that comprise those problems, and making evident several difficulties in those concepts and theories in their translation from the theoretical to the applied.

Therefore, this book aims not only to cast the light of applied ethics and political theory to a pressing contemporary environmental problem, which I hope illuminates the aspects of justice and responsibility that the design of a fair and effective global climate regime must consider in the process, but also to use a public policy issue to shed some light upon several contemporary theoretical problems that exist within contemporary theories of justice and responsibility. In this sense, I intend the book as a project in both theory (ethical and political) and applied theory, with problems that arise for both and are treated in the course of its seven chapters. Climate change challenges conventional normative analysis of public policy in a number of interesting ways, and conventional normative theory likewise challenges both existing and proposed responses to the problem of global climate change in ways that are equally interesting. For the observer of climate change with a nascent interest in its normative analysis, or to the scholar of normative theory with a cursory interest in the application of theories and concepts to concrete policy issues, I hope that what follows will be of value, but its greatest value I expect will be for those who are genuinely interested in the sophisticated theoretical analysis of climate policy, at that point—crucial for both theorists and informed practitioners—where theory and application meet. For this reason, I have deliberately eschewed the superficial theoretical analysis that typically afflicts the applied theory literature written for nontheorists, while attempting to maintain the accessibility to theoretical controversies for nonspecialists and grounding the arguments and analysis in historical context and empirical fact where possible. An underlying premise of this book is that normative theory can actually be valuable for the analysis of public policy, and that application to real-world public policy issues can provide an equally valuable critical tool for theorists, and it is my sincere hope that the text achieves this difficult harmony between theory and practice, and might thereby further the worthy endeavor of the sophisticated normative analysis of public policy issues.

Plan of the Book

Chapter 1 begins with a short history of climate change as a policy issue, beginning with the first theoretical articulation of what would later be called the "greenhouse effect" and through the nascent development of global climate policy under the rubric of the *UNFCCC*. Because this book's primary objective is to suggest how normative concepts from political theory and philosophy might inform the design of a fair and effective global climate regime, some contrast with actual policy development processes is instructive. As the current global regime was being developed through a series of scheduled conferences, two main rifts began to widen over the scope and direction of that regime. The first was between the United States and Europe, with the former resisting mandatory GHG reduction targets and the latter pressing for stronger national commitments, and the second was between the industrialized nations of the North and the developing nations of the South, where the former (albeit not unequivocally) has largely led climate policy development while the latter, with some justified complaint for this exclusion, has largely been reduced to the role of ratifying or ineffectively resisting policies proposed by the former. Since both of these disagreements have been articulated in the language of justice— rightly so, for they very much involve justice—they are briefly presented in their historical context first, and then examined more theoretically later in the book. Also introduced in chapter 1 is the orchestrated anti-Kyoto campaign in the United States, where climate skeptics—those denying the existence of anthropogenic climate change, often as part of a conscious political strategy— began calling into question the scientific basis of climate change as part of an effort to defeat or forestall regulatory action, introducing problems of knowledge and uncertainty that are further examined in chapter 6. Finally, and in contrast with the relatively open, inclusive, and fair global policy-making process, chapter 1 examines the domestic energy policy process exemplified by the secretive Cheney energy task force, which effectively set the George W. Bush administration's climate and energy policy for its two terms.

Chapter 2 examines the concept of justice—as conceived by philosophers, relying largely on the account of *liberal egalitarian justice* articulated by John Rawls, Ronald Dworkin, and others—as a normative ideal that captures part of the offense of anthropogenic climate change, as the world's relatively affluent disproportionately are causing, through the deleterious effects upon global climate of their high rates of resource consumption, an environmental hazard that is expected to impose its greatest costs upon the world's poor. Besides the problem for justice presented by climate change itself, the ideal of justice offers a normative basis for a remedial global climate regime, which aims both to reduce the problem's causes and to rectify its damaging effects through compensation and adaptation transfers. The crucial role of justice was aptly identified within the text of the *UNFCCC*, which called for the allocation of the various costs of global climate change mitigation "in accordance with equity and the common but differentiated responsibilities and respective capabilities" of the world's nations. This phrase, which has been oft-repeated and to which subsequent chapters pay a good deal of attention, introduces the two primary models of fairness upon which the design of a normatively defensible climate regime must be based: It ought to promote *equity* among nations and between generations, and it ought to take account of the concept of *responsibility* in doing so. Since the discussion of responsibility is the main subject of chapters 5 and 6, this chapter sets the groundwork for chapters 3 and 4 by introducing the egalitarian theory of justice, sketching its essential features and the manner in which it is intended to be applied, background that must be considered in light of the various difficulties in applying the ideal to problems of cosmopolitan and intergenerational justice that the analysis of climate change entails.

Chapter 3 examines the idea of *cosmopolitan justice*, or the application of egalitarian principles of justice to relations between nations, such as those affected by global climate policy. In this chapter, three primary challenges to the international application of egalitarian justice principles are considered: (1) the doctrine of *state sovereignty* in international law and political theory, which holds that the internal affairs of states ought to be the exclusive prerogative of national governments, further implying that global intervention in those affairs in order to promote justice is therefore a violation of that doctrine; (2) the theory of *political realism*, which denies the existence of valid normative ideals within international relations, maintaining instead that the advancement of national interests are the only defensible aims in policy such as that affecting climate, again undermining the claim that the ideal of justice requires a remedial global climate regime; and (3) the anti-cosmopolitanism of Rawls himself (along with some allies), which urges that principles of justice can apply only within societies, and then only in some societies such as those already liberal and pluralist, denying that the aggregate global effects of anthropogenic climate change raise any distinctive problems for justice itself. Since the third challenge is the most serious of the three to the case for a global climate regime informed by the ideals of justice, chapter 3 examines both the Rawlsian case against the international application of his difference principle and the important challenge to that limitation and defense of cosmopolitan justice by Charles Beitz. Here, the case for cosmopolitan justice is examined, paying particular attention to its application to the problems of global climate, which seem to involve the sort of conditions to which justice theory may validly apply.

In chapter 4, the extension of egalitarian justice theory to relations between generations (or intergenerational justice) is considered, as climate change likewise has effects upon future generations that are commonly regarded as giving rise to claims of intergenerational justice. As is the case with cosmopolitan justice, the extension of justice theory across generations is beset by several obstacles, including several endemic to the Rawlsian theory. In addition to the difficulty associated with redistributing resources over time, which is structurally distinct from the way in which they may be distributed within or between contemporary persons or societies, several other problems afflict intergenerational justice, and these together are known as the *future generations problem*. In chapter 4, two main challenges to defending a global climate regime as essential for meeting intergenerational obligations are examined: (1) the fact that egalitarian principles of distributive justice cannot be used to make interpersonal comparisons among noncontemporaries and so cannot justify intergenerational obligations from the argument for distributive justice; and (2) the fact that it is apparently impossible for current policy decisions to harm specific persons in the future, given the effects of various policy choices upon the identities of future persons. However we regard our obligations to futurity—whether in terms of rights or duties, and whether based in justice or the avoidance of harm—we must establish them upon some philosophical foundation that defines their nature and scope, and in chapter 4 I argue for such a foundation that might undergird climate-related obligations in a way that is susceptible to neither the problems inherent in the argument for just savings, which serves as the intergenerational justice component in Rawls, nor those of Derek Parfit's nonidentity problem, by appealing to the idea of *foresight*, which allows persons to reasonably predict the future effects of current actions, and thereby to account for them ethically.

While chapters 3 and 4 are principally concerned with equity, chapters 5 and 6 examine several problems in applying the normative concept of responsibility to issues surrounding anthropogenic climate change. Chapter 5 begins by introducing the normative *principle of responsibility*, which defines the responsibility-based model of fairness, and then surveys several relevant distinctions within the concept of responsibility (causal vs. moral, positive vs. negative) along with some degrees of responsibility (fault, liability, moral blame), and applies these to problems analogous to the climate case. Three distinct problems for attributing responsibility for climate change are examined in chapter 5: (1) what Thomas Nagel terms *moral luck*, in which otherwise similar acts may be evaluated differently according to factors that lie outside of the agent's control, apparently violating the principle of responsibility; (2) the difficulty in establishing causation for harm that results from the aggregate effects of many similar acts or the multifarious individual point sources of GHG emissions, which confounds conventional ethical analysis; and (3) the attribution of *collective responsibility* to nations—as a global climate regime appears to entail, in that it assigns liability to nations rather than persons—which defies the individualistic assumptions of the principle of responsibility, because it mistakenly appears to hold some persons morally responsible for harm to which they did not contribute, and for which they are not at fault. Though all three problems are serious ones, and might otherwise undermine the case for basing a global climate regime upon the idea of responsibility, as the climate convention urges, I argue in chapter 5 that they do not in fact do so. Rather, the mistakes that lead to these objections illuminate the proper manner in which persons and nations can be held responsible for climate-related harm and how a climate regime might assign remedial liability on that basis.

Chapter 6 is also concerned with responsibility, but in the problems raised by some of the conditions that are often assumed to be necessary for its proper attribution. Three primary issues are addressed here: (1) persons are largely ignorant of the effects of those acts that contribute to climate change and so cannot intend them, complicating assessments of moral responsibility for those actions; (2) there remains some uncertainty concerning the scientific basis of those predicted effects, although its degree is often wildly exaggerated by climate skeptics, which further muddies the attribution of responsibility for acts or consequences about which persons may be ignorant; (3) the evident deception behind at least some widely disseminated climate skepticism—in what appears to be a deliberate strategy to achieve a policy result through the sort of disinformation campaigns considered in chapter 1—further complicates the attribution of causal responsibility for ongoing GHG emissions, because those engaged in deception often must share fault and liability with those committing the harmful acts in question. In all three cases, the common assumptions that knowledge about and intentions toward some harmful consequence are necessary epistemic conditions for assessments of fault and liability are called into question. Rather, I argue, agents can be held responsible for those consequences that they should have anticipated, regardless of whether or not they in fact anticipate or intend those consequences. Unreasonable ignorance, in all three above cases, cannot exonerate agents from culpability. As applied to the design of a global climate regime, this standard entails that nations be held liable for their historical emissions dating back to the first IPCC assessment report, but not for those GHGs emitted before then. Finally, chapter 6 presents a defensible public policy strategy for issues (e.g., climate change) that are plagued by problems of uncertainty, endorsing the precautionary principle, which shifts the burden of proof in some cases involving large-scale predicted harm, as well as a means of "managing" uncertainty.

Following these chapters that consider the variety of theoretical issues surrounding the application of the normative concepts of justice and responsibility to the design of a global climate regime—the two models of fairness upon which the climate convention is to be based—chapter 7 incorporates these arguments and observations into a case for a modified version of the *equal shares* approach, in which nations are assigned roughly equal per capita emissions shares and then allowed to engage in limited trading and other forms of compliance with these targets, contrasting this approach with the *equal burdens* model, in which the costs of mitigation and adaptation are assigned roughly equally among nations. In chapter 7, a case is made against several versions of the equal burdens approach, including its incarnation in the Kyoto Protocol as well as in the Bush administration's emissions intensity proposal, as being unfair, or in violation of both equity and responsibility. The equal shares approach, suitably modified to take account of both historical ignorance and a distinction between survival and luxury emissions, is defended against several anticipated objections. In addition, chapter 7 makes the case for instantiating the equal basic access to the earth's atmospheric services as a moral and legal environmental right, drawing upon Henry Shue's distinction between basic and nonbasic rights, and comparing this right with the claimed right to develop, urged by developing nations at climate conferences and implied but not guaranteed by the equal shares approach. Finally, chapter 7 makes the case for procedural fairness in future global climate policy development, urging the recognition of democratic norms for both principled and practical reasons.

Atmospheric Justice

I

The Politics of Climate Change Mitigation

In 1896, the Nobel Prize–winning Swedish chemist Svante Arrhenius formulated the first theoretical model for estimating the effects on global temperature of increasing atmospheric concentrations of carbon dioxide, estimating that a doubling of CO_2 concentrations would result in an average temperature increase of 5–6°C (or 9–11°F), describing the heat-trapping properties of atmospheric CO_2 as a "hothouse" and identifying what would later be termed the "greenhouse effect."[1] Nearly a century before the world's policy makers would begin to pay serious attention to the causal links between human activities, increases in atmospheric concentrations of CO_2, and their consequences for global climate, Arrhenius not only described these effects theoretically, but also published estimates of temperature variation resulting from various levels of atmospheric CO_2 stabilization that come remarkably close to those representing the near-consensus view of current climate science. His climate research fell into obscurity, however, not least because of his own mistaken estimate that it would take another three millennia of burning fossil fuels to double atmospheric CO_2 concentrations— now expected to take place by the middle of the twenty-first century— and his optimistic prediction to the Swedish Academy that climate change will "allow all our descendents, even if they only be those of a distant future, to live under a warmer sky and in a less harsh environment than we were granted."[2]

Most of the twentieth century would elapse before the potential negative consequences of this greenhouse effect on global climate became widely appreciated. For the first half-century, most scientists assumed that rising production of CO_2 from fossil fuel combustion was being absorbed into the oceans rather than accumulating in the atmosphere. In a 1957 paper, the oceanographers Roger Revelle and Hans Suess described this process in dramatic terms, absent any predictions of deleterious climatic consequences, noting of this shock to the carbon cycle: "Within a few centuries we are returning to the atmosphere and oceans the concentrated organic carbon stored in sedimentary rocks over hundreds of millions of years."[3] Revelle and Suess based this theory on their failure to find evidence in support of the alternative hypothesis that atmospheric CO_2 levels had indeed been increasing, but chemist Charles Keeling, relying on data collected by manometers placed atop a Hawaiian volcano—far from any contaminated air that might be carried by trade winds, skewing the measurements—would soon provide definitive evidence to the contrary. From the Mauna Loa Observatory, Keeling regularly measured atmospheric CO_2 concentrations and plotted them along a time-series graph, producing the famous "Keeling curve" that conclusively shows the steady increase in atmospheric CO_2 concentrations from 315 parts per million (ppm) in 1958 to 383 ppm in 2007. At this rate, the doubling of atmospheric CO_2 from its preindustrial level of 280 ppm—which analyses of polar ice core samples demonstrate to have remained in a remarkably stable equilibrium for more than 10,000 years—will occur less than three centuries after the Industrial Revolution rather than taking the several millennia that Arrhenius had estimated.

Keeling's findings would revive interest in climate change among the world's scientific community, leading to a series of scientific meetings and initiatives organized under the auspices of the United Nations, contributing the important observation that gases other than CO_2 also affect global climate (methane and nitrous oxide, e.g.), eventually yielding the term "greenhouse gases" (or GHGs) as the standard reference to the heat-trapping properties of those gases released into the atmosphere as a result of human activities. The term "greenhouse effect" soon entered the popular lexicon, illustratively capturing the process originally described by Arrhenius by which these gases would collect in the atmosphere, letting in direct solar radiation but trapping heat-causing thermal radiation reflected from the earth's surface, in effect acting as a giant greenhouse enclosing the planet, and scientists and advocacy groups began identifying some of the likely adverse effects of such profound and widespread climatic changes. Nonetheless, the world's policy-making community largely ignored these findings, despite their implications for the global ecological consequences of ongoing practices.

Not until 1988—then the warmest year on record and with the southern and midwestern United States in the midst of a severe drought—would the "greenhouse effect" emerge as a major political issue. In a hearing that summer organized by Senator Timothy Wirth (D-CO), who had been unsuccessfully attempting to draw attention to the issue for several years, the tipping point came with the testimony of the director of NASA's Institute for Space Studies, James E. Hanson, who claimed to be 99 percent certain that atmospheric GHG concentrations were increasing as a consequence of human activities, not natural variation. Hanson declared, in what would provide crucial momentum to the climate policy-making process: "It is time to stop waffling so much and say the evidence is pretty strong that the greenhouse effect is here." As resource economist J.W. Anderson notes, Hanson's testimony had "unusual force" since he was "the first scientist of his stature to declare flatly that the rising temperatures were related to burning fuel."[4] Less than a week later, the Toronto Conference on the Changing Atmosphere, attended by scientists and politicians from 48 nations, called for a 20 percent reduction in GHG emissions by 2005, and later that year the U.N. General Assembly authorized the formation of the Intergovernmental Panel on Climate Change (IPCC), ushering in a new era for climate change policy and politics.

The IPCC—an international consortium of climate experts impaneled by the World Meteorological Organization and the U.N. Environment Programme—would become the world's preeminent source of climatological expertise, collecting and assessing existing data and theoretical models in climate science and disseminating its findings to policy makers. Though the IPCC does not conduct its own scientific studies, it provides a thorough peer-review process for both unpublished and published work from throughout the world, issuing periodic assessment reports (of which there have been four so far), special reports, and technical papers. The panel is divided into three substantive areas known as working groups, producing technical documents intended for scientific experts as well as summaries for policy makers. In its assessment reports, the IPCC states its specific findings on nine policy-related questions, summarizes their scientific bases or evidentiary support, and estimates the degree of certainty associated with each finding. The first IPCC assessment report was issued in 1990, with subsequent reports released in 1996, 2001, and 2007, confirming the scientific basis for the existence of anthropogenic climate change and urging the world's policy-making community to take action in order to reduce GHG emissions. This report paved the way for the 1992 *United Nations Framework Convention on Climate Change (UNFCCC)*, negotiated in preparation for the 1992 U.N.

Conference on Environment and Development (or "Earth Summit") in Rio de Janeiro.

Climate Science Today

Before continuing our examination of global climate policy development, we might briefly examine the current state of scientific knowledge as assessed and disseminated by the first four IPCC assessment reports, laying out the basics of what we now know about the causes and likely consequences of anthropogenic climate change. The primary controversies within climate science today concern not the existence of what Arrhenius called the "hothouse"—the heat-trapping effects of atmospheric GHGs and the anthropogenic causes of their increased atmospheric concentrations are no longer genuine controversies—but instead what the various effects of higher atmospheric concentrations of the various GHGs are likely to be. I examine some of those predicted effects below, and later consider in greater detail the proper role played by the remaining scientific uncertainty surrounding some of those effects, but first I briefly review the current state of scientific knowledge about the problem.

Carbon is one of the basic building blocks of life on the planet earth, with CO_2 the dominant means by which carbon is transmitted between natural carbon sinks, including living things. In an exchange known as the *carbon cycle*, humans and other animals take in oxygen through respiration and exhale CO_2, while plants absorb and store CO_2, emitting oxygen and keeping terrestrial life in balance. All of the planet's energy originates from the sun and is converted into plant-based food and fiber through photosynthesis, in addition to the direct solar effects of producing heat and light. Fossil fuels, then, represent underground storehouses of CO_2, absorbed from the atmosphere and then stored as the plants fossilized, as well as solar energy, so fossil fuel combustion—which oxidizes carbon-based fuels into CO_2, returning stored carbon to the atmosphere—may therefore be seen as both a withdrawal from the planet's finite account of stored solar energy and a release into the atmosphere of CO_2 that had long been sequestered underground. When thousands of years' worth of stored solar energy is consumed in a matter of decades, as has been regularly occurring since industrialization, the planet's stored energy supply is depleted far more rapidly than it can be replenished, and its carbon cycle is dramatically disrupted. Both of these present significant problems for humans in the long term because neither is sustainable, but it is the latter problem than concerns us here.

The two gases comprising the bulk of the earth's atmosphere—nitrogen and oxygen—produce no greenhouse effects, since neither absorbs nor emits thermal radiation. Those gases that scientists have identified as having greenhouse properties, including water vapor and CO_2, occur naturally in the atmosphere and keep the planet approximately 34°C warmer than it would be without any atmospheric absorption of infrared solar radiation. Without these critical gases, which provide an atmospheric blanketing known as the *natural greenhouse effect*, the earth would be inhospitable to human life. While some life might be possible to sustain within a small range of temperature variability beyond that seen since the last Ice Age, the climatic equilibrium produced by 10,000 years of GHG stability is responsible for developing and maintaining the ecosystemic balances that have fostered the development of all terrestrial life, and even tiny changes from that equilibrium could throw those ecosystems dramatically out of balance. The *enhanced greenhouse effect* of anthropogenic climate change has already raised the earth's average surface temperatures by an estimated 0.6°C and warmed its arctic regions by more than 5°C during the twentieth century, threatening to cause significant ecological disruption, as increasing atmospheric concentrations of GHGs have begun what scientists believe will be an unprecedented period of warming, with current estimates ranging from 1.4°C to 5.8°C of average global surface temperature increases by the year 2100.

Although atmospheric CO_2 occurs naturally, human activities have contributed to the significant increases in CO_2 concentrations over the previous century, as the preindustrial equilibrium of 280 ppm increased to 383 ppm by 2007, with the concentration now rising by a rate of roughly 1.5 ppm each year and accelerating in its rate of increase. Likewise, the several other minor GHGs (methane, nitrous oxide, and fluorinated gases) have also seen increasing atmospheric concentrations over recent decades as the result of human activities. The "greenhouse effect" originally described by Arrhenius refers to what is known as "positive radiative forcing," as increasing amounts of thermal radiation are now being trapped in the earth's atmosphere rather than being dissipated into space, warming the planet's surface. CO_2 produced by the combustion of coal, oil, and natural gas—fuels that have been combusted at unprecedented and increasing rates since the Industrial Revolution—is by itself responsible for more than 60 percent of the enhanced greenhouse effect, while roughly a third results from deforestation, which eliminates sinks that act as large reservoirs for absorbing and storing CO_2, and the remainder is due to increasing concentrations of other GHGs.

This positive radiative forcing is partially offset by negative radiative forcing, where other pollutants released into the atmosphere from human activities (especially sulfur compounds from fossil fuel combustion) accumulate, blocking incoming infrared radiation and consequently producing a cooling effect on surface temperatures, similar to that produced by large-scale volcanic eruptions. Since the aerosols involved in negative radiative forcing are produced by many of the same processes that also cause positive forcing, a central controversy in climate science concerns the extent to which negative forcings might offset positive ones. Given that the atmospheric lifetimes of aerosols, which fall to the planet's surface in the form of acid rain, are much shorter than those of GHGs, the cooling effect of current fossil fuel combustion is expected to partially offset its warming effect in the short term, but observed surface warming is likely to significantly increase as this offsetting negative forcing diminishes. Also, the cooling effect of aerosols is often localized in a way that the warming effect of GHGs is not, so accurate measurement of surface temperature variations is complicated by aerosol hot spots.

According to the IPCC's third assessment report,[5] "human activities have increased atmospheric concentrations of GHGs and aerosols since the preindustrial era," with methane (CH_4) concentrations up from 700 to 1,750 ppm and nitrous oxide (N_2O) rising from 270 to 316 during the same period, and tropospheric ozone increasing by an average of 35 percent over that time, with variation by region, in addition to the above-noted increases in atmospheric CO_2. The result of these increasing concentrations of GHGs was, according to the IPCC, a clear warming trend over the past century: "Globally it is very likely that the 1990s was the warmest decade, and 1998 the warmest year, in the instrumental record (1861–2000)." Aside from the temperature records, evidence of warming can be observed in increasing (by 1–2 mm per year) global mean sea levels, shorter (by two weeks) ice cover of rivers and lakes, thinning (by 40 percent in thickness and 10–15 percent in extent) arctic sea ice, widespread retreat of nonpolar glaciers, decreased (by 10 percent) snow cover and permafrost, longer (by 1–4 days) growing seasons, and poleward and upward shifts in plant and animal ranges, as well as earlier plant flowering, bird arrival breeding seasons, and emergence of insects and increasingly frequent coral reef bleaching. In addition to these ecological effects, inflation-adjusted weather-related economic losses increased by an order of magnitude over the past 40 years as a consequence of more frequent episodes of increasingly severe weather.

What are the predicted consequences of these climatic changes? Although the magnitude of specific effects is likely to vary according to a number of factors that determine the point at which atmospheric GHG concentrations are stabilized, the IPCC bases its predictions on six different modeling scenarios, in which CO_2 concentrations stabilize by the year 2100 at between 540 and 970 ppm, resulting in a projected average surface temperature increase of 1.4°C to 5.8°C between 1990 and 2100, which is between 2 and 10 times the observed rate of warming over the past century and is "without precedent for at least the last 10,000 years, based on paleoclimate data."[6] Globally, average precipitation is projected to increase but with wide regional variation, including increases and decreases of between 5 and 20 percent; glaciers are expected to continue their retreat, and sea levels are expected to rise by 0.09–0.88 mm, with significant regional variation. The consequences of continuing habitat alterations and sea level rises are expected to exacerbate current threats to biodiversity, "with an increased risk of extinction of some vulnerable species."

While anthropogenic climate change is expected to visit significant and in some cases catastrophic harm on the planet's nonhuman species, the focus of the IPCC reports, which I follow here, is on the planet's human habitats and populations. According to the IPCC, "climate change is projected to increase threats to human health, particularly in lower income populations, predominantly within tropical and subtropical countries." These threats occur both directly, from heat and cold stress, loss of life in floods and storms, and so on, and indirectly, from changes in ranges for disease vectors and water-borne pathogens, decreased air and water quality, and the like. In addition, ecological productivity including food production is likely to be diminished by climate change and sea level rise, with possible increases in some cereal crop yields in temperate regions with small increases in temperature but with larger decreases as temperature increases further, and with decreases in potential crop yields projected with all temperature increases in most tropical and subtropical regions. Furthermore, the IPCC predicts, climate change "will exacerbate water shortages in many water scarce areas of the world" as hydrological cycles are altered, and "populations that inhabit small islands and/or low-lying coastal areas are at particular risk of severe social and economic effects from sea level rise and storm surges." Of its general effects on humanity, the report predicts: "The impacts of climate change will fall disproportionately upon developing countries and the poor persons within all countries, and thereby exacerbate inequities in health status and access to adequate food, clean water, and other resources."[7]

From Rio to Kyoto

With the formation of the IPCC, formal recognition of the seriousness of anthropogenic climate change had finally been granted. Although it conducts no original scientific research, the panel is composed of an international blue ribbon collection of scientific experts charged with reviewing available data and examining existing climate models, and it employs a rigorous peer-review process in order to ensure that its assessments represent the consensus of the world's climate experts. In charging the IPCC not only with its scientific mission but also with the responsibility for producing a policy maker's report on climate impact estimates and mitigation opportunities, its creation and empowerment also imply a commitment to policy formulation based on the best available scientific evidence; and the selection of the panel's members and its procedural commitments to scientific integrity imply a commitment to apolitical science, where the available evidence shapes the appropriate political response, rather than manipulating science in order to serve the needs of political actors. Although slow in coming, the decision to charge the IPCC with advising the world's policy makers on how best to address the problem of climate change initially represented a rare and ambitious commitment to what Charles Lindblom calls a "rational-comprehensive" approach to the policy-making process.[8] As Lindblom predicts, successful real-world examples of such rational-comprehensive processes are exceedingly rare, and the climate regime policy-making process would prove no exception.

At the G7 summit the year following the Toronto conference, the leaders of the world's seven main industrial powers called for a "framework convention" charged with limiting global GHG emissions. Through a series of negotiating sessions among delegates from the G7 nations, the political divisions that continue to plague ongoing international climate change mitigation efforts began to form. Western European nations wanted to move quickly and to adopt binding GHG emission reduction targets, while the United States pressed for more time for research and nonbinding voluntary targets. At this time, the coal, oil, and automobile industries—concerned about the economic consequences of a climate convention with mandatory GHG emission caps for their carbon-intensive business interests—began to lobby governments against any binding targets and to question the scientific basis of existing climate research. Despite the release of the IPCC's first assessment report in 1990, revealing a consensus among the world's scientific experts that global warming was very likely both under way and human caused, the weight of this verified evidence did little to affect the bargaining positions of the various political actors. The Europeans pointed to the report's main conclusions to underscore their urgency to undertake meaningful regulatory action, while the United States identified the various uncertainties noted within the report as a justification for its refusal to commit to any binding emission limits. The carbon-intensive industries, meanwhile, began preparing their strategy to discredit and undermine the report's scientific findings in order to defeat or forestall any GHG regulatory regime that might emerge from these meetings.

Released with much fanfare at the June 1992 Earth Summit in Rio de Janeiro, the *UNFCCC* embodied these international divisions. The convention declares anthropogenic climate change to be a "common concern of mankind" and resolves to take all necessary steps in order to prevent "dangerous anthropogenic interference with the climate system." Noting the primary contributors to climate change in a way that set the stage for a mitigation framework that would eventually be embodied within the Kyoto Protocol, the *UNFCCC* acknowledges that "the largest share of historical and current global emissions of greenhouse gases has originated in developed countries." All 192 national signatories to the treaty pledged to freeze emissions at 1990 levels by the year 2000 and, pending future study and through future international action, to "protect the climate system for the benefit of present and future generations of mankind, on the basis of equity and in accordance with their common but differentiated responsibilities and respective capacities." It was for these latter two explicitly noted reasons—that industrialized countries were primarily responsible for causing the problem and were uniquely capable of its mitigation—that concerns for "equity" required that "the developed countries take the lead in combating climate change and the adverse effects thereof."[9] Equity would be the *UNFCCC*'s noblest aspiration and most difficult obstacle, as the finer points of implementation would soon begin to threaten the guarded optimism generated by this early international agreement.

The *UNFCCC* contained no binding emissions limits or enforcement mechanisms, but the decision by the United States to sign and ratify the treaty nonetheless marked a significant concession to the Europeans' eagerness for at least a declared commitment to meaningful future action. Although a compromise product of a then-intractable political divide between the United States and Europe over how to proceed, and one that has not diminished since, the treaty marked the beginning of a period during which the various parties could at least agree to disagree. This minimal level of international cooperation, with the United States publicly declaring its commitment to formulating and implementing a workable agreement based in *UNFCCC* principles even while attempting to weaken or undermine such efforts behind the scenes, would not last the decade.

In addition to the nonbinding pledge to freeze GHG emissions at 1990 levels pending further policy development, the *UNFCCC* also instituted a series of regular meetings to assess progress toward implementing an effective climate change mitigation regime, setting seven formal negotiating sessions, called Conferences of the Parties (COPs), to follow the Earth Summit. The first of these (COP-1) was held in Berlin in March 1995, where participating nations agreed to the Berlin Mandate, acknowledging that the *UNFCCC*'s voluntary approach had failed to check the growth of global GHG emissions and calling for enforceable "quantified reductions" within specified time frames and according to the "common but differentiated responsibilities" model enshrined within the *UNFCCC*. The following year, at COP-2 in Geneva, with the U.S. announcement that it would support legally binding targets and timetables and call to other industrialized nations to do the same, more than 100 nations signed the Geneva Declaration, pledging a commitment to establishing a global climate regime. The following year, however, fractures in the coalition began to widen. At an interim negotiating session in Bonn during March 1997, the European Union proposed that industrialized nations be required to reduce GHG emissions by 15 percent from 1990 levels by 2010, while the new British Labor government had vowed to lead the world by supporting a 20 percent reduction from that baseline. Support for aggressive efforts within the United States, however, was flagging, and national delegates instead pressed for an international regime in emissions trading allowances, resisting the call for mandatory GHG reductions.

By this time, the organized resistance to emissions reduction targets had attained a critical mass in the United States, with carbon-intensive industries having deployed a powerful lobbying and public relations campaign against U.S. participation in any kind of binding climate change mitigation regime, and with several American labor unions likewise publicly declaring their opposition to a climate treaty. Against this backdrop and with the Monica Lewinsky scandal and subsequent impeachment hearings still fresh in the public's mind, President Clinton declared in an address to the U.N. General Assembly in June 1997 that "the science is clear and compelling. We humans are changing the global climate."[10] At a July 24 White House conference designed to increase public awareness of the problems of climate change, president announced that "we see the train coming, but most Americans in their daily lives can't hear the whistle blowing." It may have been Clinton that didn't hear the train coming, though, as the U.S. Senate, by an overwhelming 95–0 vote, approved the Byrd-Hagel Resolution the very next day, threatening rejection of any treaty binding the United States to mandatory emission caps unless developing nations were also included within such a GHG abatement regime and as long as participation would have adverse effects on the domestic economy. The resolution was a stinging rejection of the emerging Kyoto Protocol, and its message was heard beyond the halls of power in Washington.

Despite this palpable threat from an institution with the power to veto U.S. participation in any climate regime—which in effect threatened the entire global effort, since no regime could be effective without the participation of the world's largest GHG polluter—global negotiations toward binding emissions caps continued as planned. COP-3 was held in Kyoto in December 1997, and at its conclusion more than 150 nations had signed the Kyoto Protocol, committing all the world's industrialized nations to legally binding reductions on emissions of six GHGs: carbon dioxide, methane, nitrous oxide, hydrofluorocarbons, perfluorocarbons, and sulfur hexafluoride. Again citing the "common but differentiated responsibilities and respective capabilities" model, the industrialized nations (called Annex B countries) were bound to an average of a 5 percent reduction in GHG emissions from 1990 baseline levels, to be achieved by the compliance period of 2008–2012. These mandatory emissions caps ranged from a prescribed 8 percent reduction for the European Union (with its "bubble" cap for all member countries, with individual country targets ranging from a 28 percent reduction by Luxemburg to a 27 percent increase by Greece) to a 10 percent allowed emissions increase for Iceland. The United States was assigned a 7 percent reduction and Japan a 6 percent cut, while Russia, Ukraine, and New Zealand were required to freeze at 1990 levels and Australia was assigned a target 8 percent above its 1990 baseline. Caps were also applied to the nations of Eastern Europe and of the former Soviet Union ranging from 5 to 8 percent below 1990 emission levels. Altogether, caps were applied to all 38 of what were then the world's industrialized nations, which together accounted for 75 percent of global emissions, and the prescribed cuts would, if followed, result in a 5.2 percent decrease in GHG emissions from the 1990 baseline by 2012.

Largely at the insistence of U.S. delegates to the negotiations, the Kyoto Protocol adopted several market-based implementation "flexibility" mechanisms, allowing participating nations to meet part of their assigned reduction burdens without reducing domestic emissions. The Clean Development Mechanism (CDM) allows Annex B nations to meet part of their assigned emission reductions by investing in projects that reduce emissions in developing nations, which were excluded from mandatory caps under the treaty. Developing countries must opt into nonbinding emissions caps in order to be eligible to undertake such projects under the agreement, although the United States unsuccessfully pressed for a proposal to allow developing countries to voluntarily accept mandatory caps as a condition for receipt of CDM investments but was opposed by Saudi Arabia, China, and India, which saw this as an attempt to cap their economic development through "sustainable development" projects.

Similarly, a provision called Joint Implementation allows Annex B nations to fulfill part of their assigned reductions by investing in emission-reducing projects in other participating industrialized nations, generally understood at the time to include countries of Eastern Europe and the former Soviet Union. Also at the insistence of the United States, a marketable emissions permit trading system was adopted that would provide yet another "flexibility" mechanism for industrialized nations to meet their reduction burdens without reductions in domestic emissions, since they would be allowed to meet their obligations by purchasing unused emission shares from countries exceeding their prescribed reductions. Finally, and also in a concession to the United States in order to secure its participation, parties agreed to count net rather than gross emissions, allowing nations to take into account land use changes in calculating their total emissions, counting toward compliance the effects of reforestation projects that increase a carbon sinks as equivalent to GHG emission reductions, reducing compliance costs for nations with relatively abundant forests like the United States and Canada.

Not included within the initial round of binding emissions reductions were mandatory emission caps for the world's developing nations, including China, India, and Brazil, where per capita emissions were a tiny fraction of those of the industrialized nations but where annual emission growth rates were among the world's highest. Given the Senate's threatened rejection of any treaty that did not bind these fast-growing economies, to which Senators feared losing business if not included within mandatory caps, the prospects for U.S. ratification of the treaty appeared dim. Observers realized at the time that the rejection of the protocol by the world's largest source of GHG emissions would effectively undermine the efficacy of the global effort, and that it would give a significant economic advantage to the United States to allow that nation to escape caps that its competitors had accepted. Nonetheless, the implementation measures adopted at the conference held that the protocol would go into effect once ratified by 55 countries representing 55 percent of the world's GHG emissions. While the U.S. responsibility for 25 percent of world GHG emissions was sufficient to undermine the efficacy of the protocol, its opposition could not block the treaty from going into effect.

While COP-3 was the most productive of the scheduled negotiating sessions, others were scheduled for each year to follow. COP-4 was held in Buenos Aires in November 1998—the first meeting held in a developing nation—but little was accomplished. COP-5 was again held in Bonn in October 1999 and was marked by the bold challenge by German Chancellor Helmut Schroeder for industrialized countries to ratify the Kyoto Protocol by 2002, or "Rio +10," to mark the tenth anniversary of the Earth Summit. Europe made some concessions to the United States on emissions trading, the Clinton administration's negotiating team dropped its insistence that COP-6 be delayed until after the 2000 presidential elections, and several developing nations hinted at accepting binding GHG limits in the future. When COP-6 was held in The Hague in November 2000, the United States, with a lame duck president and mired in a contested election, reversed its conciliatory tone from Bonn, pushing hard for maximum allowances for both emissions trading and carbon sinks in a desperate bid to complete a deal before the presidential transition period. Although joined by Japan, Canada, and Australia in its demand for greater credit toward compliance with Kyoto targets for its productive forests, resistance from the European Union caused the negotiations to collapse. In March 2001, reversing a campaign pledge to regulate CO_2, the newly elected President George W. Bush formally withdrew the United States from the Kyoto Protocol, promising to develop a domestic climate change mitigation proposal in its place. While likely a moot point given the Senate's continued refusal to consider ratifying the protocol, the U.S. decision brought scathing criticism from the rest of the world, widening the rifts that had opened under the more internationally cooperative Clinton administration.

With unfinished business following the collapse of negations in The Hague, a July 2001 meeting in Bonn—four months after the Bush administration announced its withdrawal from the Kyoto Protocol—saw the European Union nations show unprecedented flexibility on carbon sinks, emissions trading, and penalties for noncompliance, all in an effort to convince a sufficient number of nations to participate in order to bring the treaty into force against continued U.S. intransigence. Negotiations at COP-7 during October 2001 in Marrakesh, Morocco, produced an agreement known as the "Marrakesh Accords," reassuring developing nations that emissions trading and CDM implementation measures would not grant Annex B nations a "right, title, or entitlement" to emit GHGs and requiring that domestic emission reductions constitute a "significant element" of mandatory GHG caps that would be "conducive to narrowing per capita differences" in emission between developed and developing nations, and established a fund designated for support of technology transfer to developing nations. By May 2002, the required 55 nations had ratified, but the treaty still required the participation of nations responsible for 55 percent of 1990 GHG emissions. When Russia ratified the treaty in November 2004, adding its 17 percent of global emissions toward the required 55 percent after years of false starts, the ratification threshold was finally met, and the treaty entered into force on February 16, 2005. In November 2005, the COP-11 meeting in Montreal was thus also the first Meeting of the Parties to the Kyoto Protocol (MOP-1). As of May 2007, 170 nations representing 61.6 percent of global emissions had ratified the treaty,[11] including all Annex B nations but the United States and Australia.

Climate Policy in the United States

Although Australia, given its status as the world's largest exporter of coal, has also refused to sign the Kyoto Protocol, the U.S. government remains the primary obstacle blocking the empowerment of an effective global climate regime, but it is hardly the only obstacle. The George W. Bush administration remained steadfastly opposed to any mandatory caps or timetables through the G8 meetings in June 2007, at which European leaders again unsuccessfully implored the United States to drop its intransigent opposition to meaningful international climate action, but several other domestic climate policy developments warrant a brief mention in qualification of this assertion. The unanimous congressional opposition to mandatory caps on display in the Byrd-Hagel Resolution had softened by 2003, when the McCain-Lieberman Climate Stewardship Act, which aimed to cap post-2010 industrial emissions at year 2000 levels, garnered considerable support while being rejected 43–55. The bill was reintroduced in 2005, where it was defeated 38–60, and again in 2007, gaining the co-sponsorship of presidential hopeful Senator Barack Obama (D-IL).

Nonbinding declarations of sentiments have been more successful, as the Senate did pass a resolution following its 2005 defeat of McCain-Lieberman declaring: "Congress should enact a comprehensive and effective national program of mandatory, market-based limits and incentives on emissions of GHGs that slow, stop, and reverse the growth of such emissions," and the Bush administration, after spurning German Chancellor Angela Merkel's call at the 2007 G8 meetings for a 50 percent emissions reduction by 2050, reluctantly agreed to "take seriously" the need to reduce global emissions. Prior to the G8 meeting but after reiterating its unswerving opposition to mandatory caps and timetables, the administration announced that it would organize climate policy development meetings among the world's 15 biggest greenhouse polluters to "contribute to the important dialogue that will take place in Germany next week," albeit in a move that critics charge was intended to derail impending G8 talks. This proposal followed Bush's 2005 Asia-Pacific Partnership on Clean Development and Climate, which likewise aimed to include China and India in talks but produced no binding commitments, and was described by Senator John McCain (R-AZ) as "nothing more than a nice little public relations ploy."[12]

To provide the necessary background in climate politics for the examination of several theoretical problems in the following chapters, here I examine the roles both of the U.S. government and of private industry in opposing the Kyoto Protocol, as well as other efforts to curb global GHG emissions, whether at the global, national, state, or local level. The point of this examination is not simply to criticize the U.S. government and private fossil fuel industries for their ongoing intransigence against all attempts to control the growth of global GHG emissions and for their disingenuous attacks on climate science— although both of these themes feature in this examination for reasons relevant to the larger inquiry—but rather to establish what continues to plague effective climate policy development and to set up discussions about the nature of uncertainty and responsibility in climate politics and policy, as well as about the proper design of just climate policy institutions and procedures. Pointed criticism of these main antagonists to the goal of effectively addressing anthropogenic climate change is not gratuitous, but rather is intended to provide illustrative contrasts with the sort of policy process that might, in a world in which democracy and justice were more abundantly available, stand a better chance of shaping a normatively defensible global climate regime.

Since reversing his 2000 campaign pledge to regulate CO_2 soon after assuming office, President George W. Bush has been unwavering in his opposition to all efforts to impose mandatory limits on GHG emissions within the United States. His administration has successfully blocked efforts toward effective climate policy at the national level and has opposed and obstructed ongoing global efforts to carry out the mandate of the *UNFCCC* as well as those by state and local governments to fill the policy void left by the federal government's refusal to act on the issue. Throughout, the three basic themes of his administration's position remained unchanged: (1) it maintained that there remains too much scientific uncertainty about the causes and effects of climate change to warrant mandatory emissions caps, (2) that it would be unfair to the United States to accept binding caps and timetables unless large developing nations like India and China also did, and (3) that reducing the nation's GHG emissions would be too expensive for the expected domestic benefits. These were, not coincidentally, the main themes of the fossil fuel industry's anti-Kyoto lobbying and public relations effort (examined below), forming the cornerstone of the public–private partnership that emerged between government and industry in opposition to meaningful action to stabilize atmospheric GHG concentrations.

The president's public case against mandatory emissions caps is instructive. In his 2002 *Economic Report of the President,* Bush defended his decision to abandon the Kyoto Protocol by accusing the treaty of focusing too much on "unreasonable, infeasible targets" in requiring mandatory caps and timetables. In support of the claim that a 7 percent reduction from 1990 emissions by 2012 was unreasonable and infeasible, the report cites an unidentified estimate that compliance could cost "up to 4 percent of GDP in 2010—a staggering sum when there is no scientific basis for believing this target is preferable to one less costly."[13] In fact, most scientists maintain that emissions reductions far greater than those mandated under the Kyoto Protocol will be necessary in order to meet the goal of avoiding "dangerous anthropogenic interference with the climate system," and any "less costly" mitigation plan than Kyoto's would plainly fail to meet this stated aim. No reference is given for the 4 percent GDP figure, but it is well above the high end of the range of economic estimates reviewed by the IPCC in its 2001 third assessment report and so constitutes an implausible outlier among cost estimate studies. Counting only the direct costs of emissions reductions and not the ancillary economic and noneconomic benefits of decreased fossil fuel consumption and its associated health and environmental consequences, and not counting emission reduction credits from carbon sinks or CDM projects that were included in the protocol but are not reflected in most economic models—both of which would significantly reduce its costs—compliance with the Kyoto targets is projected to cost the United States between 0.24 and 0.91 percent of GDP, with 0.52 percent identified as the best estimate.[14] Given the ancillary benefits that follow from decreased fossil fuel combustion—cleaner air and water, better health, decreased dependence on nonrenewable energy and imported oil, and so on—these costs are neither unreasonable nor infeasible and can be accomplished with existing technologies.[15]

President Bush's report is particularly critical of the proposed regulation of CO_2, which, unlike such pollutants as sulfur dioxide and nitrogen oxides that can be controlled through the addition of end-of-pipe equipment to existing facilities, "can only be reduced by either reducing energy use or replacing fossil fuel facilities, equipment, and transportation fleets with ones that use fuels with lower or zero emissions." As discussed below, Bush never wavered from opposing any proposal that either reduces consumer demand for fossil fuels or requires a conversion from the current fossil-fuel–based energy economy to one based in cleaner renewable energy sources, despite the fact that CO_2 emissions are responsible for more than 60 percent of the enhanced greenhouse effect. Carbon regulation, which directly affects demand for fossil fuels and indirectly affects fossil fuel industry profits, would for this reason be "vastly more expensive" than regulation of other GHGs and additionally "raises concerns about fuel diversity, national security, and the ability to sustain our economic strength and quality of life."[16] The report does not elaborate the bases for these concerns, and so it is difficult to assess the validity of the claims that reduced energy use or the conversion from high-emission, high-pollution, nonrenewable, and mostly imported fossil fuels to low-emission, less polluting, and largely domestically produced renewable energy sources would harm either "fuel diversity" or national security, although the most plausible effect is precisely the opposite.[17] The "economic strength" and "quality of life" claims are both references to economic growth (though dubious ones),[18] and so depend on the administration's core premise that GHG emissions produce no offsetting harmful effects against which GHG abatement costs might be compared, and its implied claim that modernization of the nation's fossil-fuel–based energy and transportation infrastructure to reflect the demands of environmental sustainability confers no economic benefits. Neither of these claims is supported by the available evidence, so it would seem that even the president's economic growth argument depends on the outright rejection of the reality of anthropogenic climate change.

Some have suggested that the most efficient U.S. response to climate change may be for the country to continue pursuing its high-growth and high-emissions economic path, reserve some significant share of the proceeds from that growth, and use that accumulated wealth to compensate the victims of climate change.[19] Since this approach would concede the reality of climate change—a point of ideological resistance for President Bush—the report instead proposes another connection between economic growth and environmental protection. Rather than focusing national policy directly on improving environmental practices through enforceable standards, it envisions public pressure for a "cleaner and safer environment" inevitably resulting from society's rising affluence and, presumably, by stimulating consumer demand for sustainable goods rather than for governmental regulation, and solving the problem through some "invisible hand" of the market.

> Prosperity also allows us to commit ever-increasing resources to environmental protection and to the development of science and technology that will lead to both future growth and a better environment. Indeed, empirical evidence suggests that growth eventually goes hand in hand with environmental improvements.[20]

While the general claim that rising national affluence correlates with increasing public demands for environmental protection may be nominally true, its implication is misleading, and it fails to make the case against mandatory GHG emissions caps. Wealthy nations, like wealthy persons, have more disposable income to spend on luxury items such as parks or other recreational spaces, and for this reason have generally done a better job with some forms of environmental protection than have poor ones. However, economic growth also increases national emissions—recall the report's claim that compliance with the Kyoto Protocol would stifle economic growth—and no "empirical evidence" exists to support the contrary claim that is implied, if not explicitly stated, here. Although economic growth often leads to reduced "emissions intensity" (a connection examined below), it does not reduce GHG emissions themselves. Absent some further link in the causal chain—for example, by economic growth leading voters to elect a different president and Congress—the above claim, if intended to establish a negative correlation between economic growth and aggregate national emissions as part of a case against mandatory caps and timetables, is plainly false.

The relation between economic growth and GHG emissions that would eventually form the cornerstone of the Bush administration's long-promised Kyoto "alternative" involves not aggregate national emissions but rather "emissions intensity," or total emissions divided by gross domestic product. In the early stages of industrialization, nations generally experience sharply increasing rates of emissions intensity as economic growth is largely the product of fossil-fuel–intensive industrialization and deforestation. More advanced industrialized and postindustrial nations see their emissions intensity rates decline as service industries contribute a greater share toward GDP than does high-emissions manufacturing. Thus, developing nations like Brazil, China, and India now have emissions intensity levels that are three to four times those of industrialized nations. When the president finally announced his climate "policy" proposal to reduce the nation's GHG emissions intensity between 2002 and the Kyoto compliance year of 2012—with no binding emissions caps or enforceable standards and with no required change from "business as usual" emissions growth projections for the United States—it was widely dismissed as a nonstarter. Carl Pope of the Sierra Club called it a "sweetheart deal to the corporate polluters that funded his campaign," and the *Economist* dismissed it as "utterly inadequate" and "all hat and no cattle."[21] According to an analysis by the Pew Center on Global Climate Change, the Bush plan would allow emissions to increase 14 percent above 2000 levels and 30 percent above 1990 levels by 2010, far in excess of the 7 percent reduction from 1990 levels assigned under the Kyoto Protocol for which the Bush plan was billed as an "alternative," or the voluntary stabilization at 1990 levels mandated by the Rio Declaration, to which the United States remains committed.[22]

The Bush administration's case against participating in a global climate regime, then, comes down to two claims: (1) the empirical claim either that anthropogenic climate change is not occurring or that we cannot be sufficiently certain about its causes or effects, and (2) the normative claim that the Kyoto Protocol is unfair in requiring the United States to reduce its emissions when India and China are not required to do so. Although a third claim is often made concerning the protocol's economic costs, this claim cannot stand on its own and may instead by folded into the other two. The cost–benefit claim implied within the Byrd-Hagel Resolution and the 2002 *Economic Report of the President*, for example, notes that the GHG emissions cuts mandated by the protocol would entail domestic compliance costs, but acknowledges neither the various economic benefits of compliance that might be compared with those costs nor that global benefits are expected to exceed them. Thus, the Bush administration's arguments rely either on the dismissal of climate-related harm altogether or else on some normative argument about fairness, that is, that it is unfair to require the United States to bear compliance costs when it is not the exclusive beneficiary of those expenditures or when others are exempted from mandatory caps. The empirical case, as I show below, is easily refuted by the available evidence, so the best case against the U.S. participation within a global climate regime must be based in some argument about fairness, from which we might infer that the United States would willing to participate in such a regime if only it could be designed in a manner that was indeed fair, underscoring the importance of this inquiry's primary aim.

Climate Policy Opposition

If there are any internal divisions between the policy aims of the fossil fuel industry and those of the Bush administration, they have yet to surface in public. The various ties between the administration and the coal and oil industries have been sufficiently observed elsewhere, as has the relentlessness with which both have proceeded in dismantling or weakening the nation's environmental protection laws and halting or reversing enforcement actions against polluters and other environmental despoilers.[23] Whether this overt hostility to environmental protection laws and sustainable energy and transportation policies is driven by ideological zealotry or simply by economic-interest–based politics makes little difference, since it has become a de facto point of unity among the various factions of the contemporary American political right. Observers have pointed to each of these two hypotheses, evidence exists to support both.

Bill McKibben, for example, doubts that the administration's anti-environmentalism is "inspired by a grand ideological vision" like its foreign policy. Rather, he suspects that it is simply "institutionalized corruption: a steady payback to the logging, mining, corporate farming, fossil fuel, and other industries that contributed heavily to put Bush in power."[24] On the other hand, Bill Moyers suspects a deeper ideological basis for the current hostility to both climate science and policy, noting of the two main factions comprising Bush's electoral base that "a powerful current connects the administration's multinational corporate cronies who regard the environment as ripe for the picking and a hard-core constituency of fundamentalists who regard the environment as fuel for the fire that is coming."[25] This current, which serves as an ideological bridge between corporate libertarians and religious fundamentalists, is disdain for environmental regulation, Moyers suggests, with one camp motivated by economic gain from environmental exploitation and the other by a combination of apocalyptic millennialism and a perverted version of the doctrine that humans are to have dominion over the earth.[26] Whether for ideological reasons or from a corruption of democratic processes, the solidarity among contemporary American conservatives in virulent opposition to any mandatory caps or timelines on climate change has thus far proved a sufficient obstacle to meaningful policy development.

In some circles, this anti-environmentalism appears to be highly ideological, displaying many of the characteristics first described by the historian Richard Hofstadter as the "paranoid style" of the contemporary American right wing, in which reactionary politics are justified by a dominant belief that the nation has been "dispossessed" by those bent on subverting its values and therefore stands in dire need of repossession. He writes:

> The old American virtues have already been eaten away by
> cosmopolitans and intellectuals; the old competitive capitalism has
> been gradually undermined by socialistic and communistic
> schemers; the old national security and independence have been
> destroyed by treasonous plots, having as their most powerful agents
> not merely outsiders and foreigners as of old but major statesmen
> who are at the very centers of American power.[27]

Characterized by the latent distrust that was transferred from McCarthyism to a distrust of the United Nations and international law, this paranoid style—which encourages its true believers to distrust official facts such as those of climate science as part of a plot to subject the nation to outside tyranny—trades on a currency of unseen enemies and organized conspiracies, feeding on popular resentment by blaming sinister others for domestic economic and cultural decline. In this ideologically charged and insular subculture, it comes as little surprise that global climate change, with its combination of multilateralism, reliance on scientific expertise, concern for the foreign and nonwhite victims of U.S. industrialism, and prescription for global cooperation in order to promote environmental sustainability, would attract such ire.

Nowhere is this paranoid style more prominently displayed than in the occasional rants against the scientific basis of climate change by U.S. Senator James Inhofe (R-OK), who on the Senate floor has called it "the greatest hoax ever perpetrated on the American people." Inhofe has delivered a series of Senate speeches on this hoax hypothesis, some on technical scientific issues about which he has no training, but most on what he sees as its political basis, alleging an international conspiracy whereby "environmental extremists exploit the issue for fundraising purposes" and, in contradiction with the accusation of environmentalists propagating known falsehoods in its invocation of irrational belief, that

> man-induced global warming is an article of religious faith to the
> radical far left alarmists. Therefore, contending that its central tenets

are flawed to them is heresy and of the most despicable kind. Furthermore, scientists who challenge its tenets are attacked sometimes personally for blindly ignoring the so-called scientific consensus.

Inhofe's theory has other aspects, including a European Union conspiracy to gain competitive advantage over the United States: "People have to understand that the economic destruction of our country is something that would inure to the benefit of the European Union and many others who are in competition with us. We have to understand that there is an economic motive behind it which one would have to seriously consider."[28]

Whatever the cause, unflinching opposition to mandatory GHG emissions caps has been a feature of official Republican policy since at least a year prior to the negotiation of the Kyoto Protocol, with the party's 1996 platform anticipating and rejecting calls for the nation to participate in a global climate regime with mandatory emissions caps. As the strongly worded climate plank reads: "Republicans deplore the arbitrary and premature abandonment of the previous policy of voluntary reductions of GHG emissions. We further deplore ceding U.S. sovereignty on environmental issues to international bureaucrats and our foreign economic competitors."[29] Democrats in Congress have done little better, as evidenced by the unanimous and preemptive rejection of the protocol through the Byrd-Hagel Resolution. Insofar as climate policy hostility is ideological, it hasn't been overly divisive within the legislative branch.

While it may not matter for the future of global climate whether opponents of GHG regulation are ideologically motivated or merely repaying their industry patrons, it might matter for our assessment of their culpability for contributing to climate change. As considered further in chapters 5 and 6, citizens may be held responsible for the policies of their government insofar as it is democratically responsive to their expressed preferences, but cannot be held responsible for their government's actions when they are detached from such democratic mechanisms. Both the ideological and economic explanations for the root cause of current climate policy opposition posit a kind of disconnect between government and those whose interests it is supposed to reflect, and the truth likely lies somewhere in between. However, the possibility that "institutionalized corruption" drives U.S. climate policy opponents is the more disturbing of the two, for it implies that the public interest in maintaining a climatic stability may be subverted not from mere irrational beliefs or ideological blinders, but rather knowingly and in the pursuit of selfish interests. No more serious charge can be made against a government, given the magnitude of the interests at stake.

The Cheney Energy Task Force

Whereas crusaders and conspiracy buffs like Inhofe suggest an ideological basis for the anti-environmental zealotry in contemporary American politics, the more pragmatic political and economic opportunism displayed by Bush administration insiders in crafting those policies relevant to climate change offer support for McKibben's thesis: While ideology may play a role in driving the administration's continued opposition to the climate convention, patronage considerations appear to play the dominant role. Since the selfish desire for economic gain at the expense of others entails a more insidious motive than found in tenaciously held but irrational ideological convictions, it is worth exploring the plausible bases for the Bush administration's climate policies as a precursor to upcoming explorations of fault and liability in chapters 5 and 6. In addition, these policies are worth exploring in order to see the myriad ways in which democratic procedures can be subverted or circumvented, with defensible policy goals and processes undermined and indefensible ones used in their place, providing an illustrative lesson in policy process design that can be put to use in chapter 7. Finally, this examination of the Bush administration's climate policy strategy reveals the ways in which several distinct policy areas are related, and how a unified campaign against GHG regulation has shaped the nation's energy, environmental, and transportation policies.

Shortly after taking office in 2001, President George W. Bush established the National Energy Policy Development Group (NEPDG), with Vice President Dick Cheney named as chair. Charged with developing a national energy policy to "promote dependable, affordable, and environmentally sound production and distribution of energy," the NEPDG solicited input from hundreds of corporations, organizations, and individuals, amassing more than 12,000 pages of documents. In May 2001, it released its final report, *Reliable, Affordable, and Environmentally Sound Energy for America's Future*, issuing a set of recommendations for developing a comprehensive national energy policy. Soon after the report was released, both the process and product of the task force would be roundly criticized as little more than an energy industry wish list, replete with unwarranted subsidies and "regulatory relief" but containing no substantive efforts toward energy conservation and based on a deeply flawed process that effectively excluded nonindustry representatives. Cheney, who mockingly described energy conservation as perhaps a "sign of personal virtue" but "not a sufficient basis for a sound, comprehensive energy policy"[30] several weeks before the task force's report was to be released, focused the task force's initial recommendations exclusively on increasing energy supply, belatedly adding several small-scale energy efficiency proposals after his ridicule of conservation created a public relations problem. The report, which was mired in controversy from its inception, nonetheless formed the blueprint for the administration's energy position, much of which was incorporated into policy.

The report, which the Natural Resources Defense Council (NRDC) calls "a throwback to the days when energy barons pursued oil, coal and other natural resources without a care for their impact on our land, air or water,"[31] proposed building 1,300 new electric power plants over the next 20 years—most of them powered by coal, which is the most carbon-intensive energy source—along with new regulatory concessions for existing coal-fired plants and oil refineries to significantly expand operations without their having to meet the stricter air quality standards that apply to modern plants and refineries. Along with further entrenching the nation's reliance on coal for its electrical power generation, the NEPDG recommended a $2 billion subsidy for so-called "clean coal" technologies and called for opening up the Arctic National Wildlife Refuge and other currently protected federal lands to oil drilling and increasing oil exploration on the Outer Continental Shelf. If the task force represents a vision for the future of energy policy, as is suggested by the image of Cheney printed on the report's cover, gazing off into the distance as if divining the future, the future looks much like the past, only more so—dominated by fossil fuels.

Rejecting the Bush campaign promise to regulate CO_2 as a pollutant, the Cheney task force recommended a "three-pollutant" (sulfur dioxide, nitrogen oxides, and mercury) regulatory approach to air pollution that would later be adopted by Congress as part of the Bush administration's "Clear Skies" proposal, weakening existing air quality standards and lengthening the compliance periods for reducing these three pollutants, and making adherence to standards voluntary rather than regulatory. No explicit mention of climate change or of any national strategy for slowing or reversing the growth of GHG emissions found its way into the report. Though unmentioned, the task force's recommendation for dramatically expanding both coal production and oil drilling obviously bodes ill not only for current efforts to reduce the human impact on global climate but also for such efforts in the future. Given the three-decade life cycle of new coal-fired power plants, the Cheney proposal to further entrench the nation in a carbon-based energy economy would substantially delay the conversion to cleaner sources of energy and raise the future costs of compliance with GHG emissions targets. The omission of any reference to GHGs or to anthropogenic climate change was telling: The report simply maintained the Bush administration's discredited claim that energy policy is unrelated to climate policy.

This is not to say that the Cheney task force report did not issue proposals that would shape the nation's climate policy for years to come: It did, but mostly through its omissions rather than its recommendations. Aside from its above-noted proposals to significantly increase coal and oil production and its rejection of calls to regulate CO_2 as a pollutant, despite requests from its own U.S. Environmental Protection Agency (EPA) to do so, the report contains several high-profile missed opportunities, which together could have reduced domestic energy use that, in per capita terms, is now more than double that of energy demand in Western Europe[32] by the equivalent of more than two-thirds of the 1,300 new power plants that it proposes. The report declined to recommend increasing corporate average fuel economy standards for automobiles—a conservation measure with the potential to reduce domestic oil consumption by 1.9 million barrels per day through 2012 by using existing technologies alone[33]—and left in place the "light truck loophole" that allows the increasingly popular minivans and SUVs to emit 30 percent more GHGs than passenger cars. Although proposing expansion of the government's Energy Star product labeling and consumer education programs for household appliances in an attempt to calm the unrest caused by Cheney's public mocking of energy conservation, the task force opted against proposing to increase efficiency standards for such appliances, and the administration cut in half the Department of Energy's budget for setting new efficiency standards and significantly weakened existing air conditioner efficiency standards prior to the report's release; policy decisions that, according to the NRDC, "will force construction of at least 40 more power plants by 2020, cost consumers as much as $900 million in higher electric bills in that year, and generate 180 million more tons of carbon dioxide emissions over the next three decades."[34]

According to the Department of Energy's own estimates,[35] energy efficiency measures alone could reduce the nation's energy demand by the equivalent of 610 of the proposed 1,300 new 300-megawatt power plants, and implementation of existing renewable energy technologies could save the equivalent of another 180 plants. More significantly, these conservation and renewable energy efforts, far from harming either "fuel diversity" or national security, would save more than $30 billion annually in energy costs and cut CO_2 emissions from power plants by a third, compared with the NEPDG's proposed 1,300 new power plants that would increase those emissions by 35 percent. With Cheney's revealed predisposition toward regarding energy conservation as an insufficient basis for the nation's energy policy, further reflected in his choice of policy "advisors" as well as the task force's substantive recommendations, the report focused nearly entirely on increasing energy supply to the virtual neglect of demand-side measures, and issued essentially the same set of recommendations that would have been included had the report been authored directly by representatives from the oil, coal, automobile, and nuclear industries. In other words, the report expressed the same disdain for energy conservation as did Cheney himself with his ill-chosen sound bite used to introduce it, demonstrated the same concern with GHG emissions as did the Bush administration's fossil fuel industry patrons, and reflected the lopsidedness of the process by which it was produced; a reflection that was not obscured by the success with which Cheney managed to keep many of the details of that process secret.

Following the release of the report—which funded its $135,615 printing costs from the Department of Energy's solar, renewables, and energy conservation budget—the Sierra Club and Judicial Watch sued the NEPDG and Cheney, seeking the release of documents under the Federal Advisory Committee Act (FACA), a government transparency law mandating that advisory committees hold open meetings and make records publicly available, as well as requiring that they "be fairly balanced in terms of the points of view represented" and "not be inappropriately influenced by the appointing authority or by any special interest." Cheney continued to withhold requested records, citing executive privilege and claiming that industry representatives were not technically members of the NEPDG and so were not subject to FACA disclosure requirements. Both the federal District Court and the D.C. Circuit Court of Appeals found against the vice president in *Judicial Watch v. NEPDG* (2002), but their ruling was reversed on appeal to the U.S. Supreme Court, which (in *Cheney v. District Court*, 2004) cited separation of powers issues as the legal basis for its refusal to require the executive branch to comply with blanket requests to hand over documents to the those nongovernmental organizations as well as the U.S. General Accounting Office (GAO), which also sought documents. The case was remanded for further review to the D.C. Circuit Court, which dismissed the suit in April 2005 on grounds that FACA only requires transparency for meetings in which outsiders have the power to vote on or veto advisory committee recommendations.

Based on the available evidence, the emerging picture of the task force's internal procedures closely matches the widespread criticism that it effectively excluded consumer and environmental groups from input into the final recommendations. Energy Secretary Spencer Abraham met with more than 100 industry representatives during the report's drafting phase, but both he and Cheney repeatedly denied requests from environmentalists for meetings prior to the report's release. After the public relations fiasco created by Cheney's "personal virtue" comments, task force staff director Andrew Lundquist met in April 2001 with representatives from 14 environmental groups, though the meeting came after the completion of the draft report, lasted less than an hour, and, according to a NRDC account, "much of the time was taken up by introductions."[36]

He met with environmental group representatives twice more in May, and he sent his deputy, Patricio Silva, to meet with NRDC representatives once in March. Cheney did meet with representatives from the NRDC, the Sierra Club, the Union of Concerned Scientists, and U.S. PIRG (U.S. Public Interest Research Group, a federation of state PIRGs) on June 5—two weeks after the report was released—calling that meeting, according to the NRDC, "to discuss his false claim that the task force report included 11 of 12 Sierra Club recommendations" rather than to solicit input into or accept feedback about the report's substantive policy recommendations.

Although the Department of Energy claimed in a prepublication press release that the task force had "actively sought all viewpoints," subsequently released evidence from Department of Energy records suggest otherwise. According to more than 12,000 pages of documents released by the agency in 2002, the NEPDG met extensively with energy industry representatives, including 19 contacts with the Nuclear Energy Institute, 15 with the Bonneville Power Administration, 14 with the Edison Electric Institute (a coal industry group), 12 with the U.S. Enrichment Corporation, 11 with the North American Electric Reliability Council, 9 each with the National Mining Association and Westinghouse, and 8 each with the American Gas Association, the Electric Power Research Institute, and CMS Energy. The task force had four contacts with Enron, in addition to six documented meetings between corporate representatives and Vice President Cheney. In all, the released documents show 714 contacts between task force representatives in which Department of Energy staff were present—contacts with Cheney alone are not included because the White House continues to withhold the relevant documents—compared to 29 contacts with nonindustry representatives.[37] Subsequently released documents reveal maps of Iraqi oil fields, lists of foreign clients for Iraqi oil, and other documents suggesting the comprehensive nature of the task force's blueprint for the Bush administration's subsequent energy policies.

According to a GAO investigative report on NEPDG processes, the report "was the product of a centralized, top-down, short-term, and labor-intensive process" in which task force officials "met with, solicited input from, or received information and advice from nonfederal energy stakeholders, principally petroleum, coal, nuclear, natural gas, and electricity industry representatives and lobbyists." How much impact these meetings had on the final product remains unknown, although the task force's substantive recommendations provide the basis for reasonable inferences about those impacts, since "the Office of the Vice President's (OVP) unwillingness to provide the NEPDG records or other related information precluded GAO from fully achieving its objectives and substantially limited GAO's ability to comprehensively analyze the NEPDG process."

Since the GAO study had been requested by Congress, its final report admits defeat in its mission of promoting "accountability, integrity, reliability" in government, chastising the White House for its secrecy surrounding the processes by which the report was produced:

> From the outset, OVP did not respond to our request for information, including descriptive information on the process by which the *National Energy Policy* report was developed, asserting that we lacked statutory authority to examine NEPDG activities. We were also denied the opportunity to interview staff assisting the Vice President on the NEPDG effort. As a result, throughout the spring and summer of 2001, we engaged in extensive attempts to reach an agreement with OVP on our information request in an effort to fulfill our statutory responsibilities in a manner that accommodated the Vice President's asserted need to protect certain executive deliberations. Importantly, we significantly narrowed the scope of our review by, among other things, withdrawing our initial request for minutes of NEPDG meetings. We also offered flexibility in how we would access certain documents. Despite our concerted efforts to reach a reasonable accommodation, the Vice President denied us access to virtually all requested information, with the exception of a few documents purportedly related to NEPDG costs that OVP provided to us. The Vice President's denial of access challenged GAO's fundamental authority to evaluate the process by which NEPDG had developed a national energy policy and to obtain access to records that would shed light on that process.[38]

As a result of the shroud of secrecy protecting many of the records concerning the processes by which the Cheney energy task force's report was produced, the public may never know the extent of influence exercised over the report's final recommendations. This much, however, is clear: The report's content reflects an overriding concern for the interests of the energy industry, with little or no attention to energy conservation or the environmental consequences of rising domestic demands for energy. In further entrenching fossil fuel combustion within the nation's energy infrastructure, the task force demonstrated no concern for reducing the nation's GHG emissions or for any of the other costs associated with fossil fuels. Despite this successful effort to withhold the most damning evidence documenting the Bush administration's lack of concern for such problems, the policy recommendations issued by the NEPDG clearly resulted from a deeply flawed process built on overt hostility to meaningful stakeholder participation, transparency, and public accountability. The process, then, contains a valuable negative lesson on how not to make good climate policy that all those sincerely interested in designing a "reliable, affordable, and environmentally sound energy policy for America's future" would do well to learn.

The entire Cheney energy policy reads like a wish list of the energy industry, largely because it is a set of policy recommendations that was apparently authored by lobbyists from those industries with no balancing public or environmental interest group representation, but perhaps the most egregious component of the policy that emerged from the NEPDG was the retroactive legal immunity proposed for manufacturers of methyl tertiary-butyl ether (MBTE), a gasoline additive that is a known pollutant and suspected carcinogen. According to a study by staffers for Representative Henry Waxman (D-CA), "this waiver is worth billions to energy companies; the major beneficiaries would be Exxon, which, according to the Center for Responsive Politics, contributed $942,717 to candidates in the last election cycle; Valero Energy, $841,375; Lyondell Chemical, $342,775; and Halliburton, $243,946."[39] Aside from the apparent corruption that such a proposal represents, allowing polluters to purchase legal immunity from consumer lawsuits through their campaign contributions, this proposal shows a blatant disregard for public health without any discernable energy-related justification in its rush to reward and protect some of the government's biggest patrons. A regulatory agency is said to be *captured* when it becomes overly dependent on the industry that it was designed to regulate and so becomes unable to effectively carry out its adversarial mission in defense of the public interest. The Cheney task force report offers a case in which an entire government appears to have been captured by an industry sector, albeit one that it never intended to regulate.

The Campaign against Climate Science

From the beginning, the global effort to develop an effective climate change mitigation regime was closely paralleled by an industry effort to defeat it. In 1991, following the release of the IPCC's first assessment report but before the Rio Earth Summit, a lobbying and public relations campaign was inaugurated on behalf of what Jeremy Leggett calls the "Carbon Club," including oil and coal industries as well as automobile manufacturers and chemical companies, which ardently opposed any regulations limiting GHG emissions.[40] Since emissions caps would limit demand for both coal and oil as well as for the most fuel-inefficient automobiles—on which the American auto industry had staked its future—this multi-industry coalition sought to block the progress of all efforts at GHG regulation in order to protect their corporate bottom lines.

One of the first disinformation efforts of this campaign saw the formation of an industry group named the Information Council on the Environment (ICE), which designed a lobbying and public relations campaign that would feature climate skeptics[41] Robert Balling, Pat Michaels, and Sherwood Idso in an effort to "reposition global warming as theory rather than fact."[42] Following a strategy that remains dominant among industry-orchestrated anti-Kyoto campaigns, modeled on the successful tobacco industry effort to discredit the scientific link between smoking and cancer, the ICE aimed to discredit the scientific basis of climate change research with the general public, running television and newspaper advertisements in electoral districts that get their electricity from coal and claiming that climate change predictions were nothing more than a hoax perpetuated by environmental groups using fear-mongering as a fundraising technique, and asserting that GHG abatement efforts would raise gas prices by more than a dollar per gallon and cripple the domestic economy.

Before the ICE campaign was exposed as an industry front by environmentalists—it was funded by Western Fuels Association, a $400 million coal mining operation—it produced a video titled *The Greening of Planet Earth*, narrated by Idso and featuring skeptic Richard Lindzen, that made the rounds in Washington, D.C., and was reputed to be a favorite of John Sununu, President George H.W. Bush's chief of staff, quickly gaining adherents to the industry's antiregulatory cause by trumpeting the potentially beneficial effects of global warming. The video's core message, which acknowledged the reality of anthropocentric climate change while ICE was also denying it, is described by Ross Gelbspan:

> In near-evangelical tones, it promises that a new age of agricultural abundance will result from the doubling of the atmospheric concentration of carbon dioxide. It shows plant biologists predicting that yields of soybeans, cotton, wheat, and other crops will increase by 30 to 60 percent—enough to feed and clothe the earth's expanding population. The video portrays a world where vast areas of deserts are replaced by grasslands, where today's grass- and scrublands are transformed by a new cover of bushes and trees, and where today's diminishing forests are replenished by new growth as a result of a nourishing atmosphere of enhanced carbon dioxide.[43]

The theory being advanced by the video did not need to be scientifically sound, nor did the campaign even need to be internally coherent in its position on whether anthropogenic climate change was indeed occurring. It was sufficient for those already inclined to oppose GHG regulation for ideological reasons or from political debts to identify more publicly palatable alternative explanations for their policy positions against meaningful mitigation efforts.

Another part of this ICE campaign was the creation of an industry-funded climate journal, *World Climate Review*, edited by University of Virginia climatologist and prominent climate skeptic Pat Michaels, who would later dissociate himself from what he called the ICE's "blatant dishonesty" but remain on as editor of the journal, renamed the *World Climate Report*. These two "journals"—which employ no processes of peer review and are essentially outlets for coal industry propaganda that attempt to confer legitimacy on climate skepticism—served as the source of most of the published climate skeptic "research" that has been cited by opponents of climate change mitigation policy as counterpoint to the consensus-based processes of the IPCC and the voluminous legitimate peer-reviewed scientific literature on the subject. Written for an audience that includes policy makers and not scientists, they make no attempt to mimic in style or content legitimate scientific journals or to follow norms of basic research ethics. While employing credentialed scientists as editor and contributors, the content of these "journals," reflecting the interests of their patrons and scientific knowledge base and prevailing prejudices of their intended audience, is unequivocally one of political advocacy and not credible scientific research, advancing conspiracy theories about the insidious motives of environmental groups and a tyrannical U.N.-based world government rather than engaging in any serious debates about the genuine uncertainties existing in climate science.

In anticipation of the 1995 COP meetings in Berlin, a second industry lobbying and public relations effort was initiated in 1994, this time called the Global Climate Coalition (GCC), which spent more than $1 million during both 1994 and 1995 in an effort to discredit the findings and impeach the credibility of the IPCC, which was due to publish its second assessment report in 1996. The coordinated campaign of the GCC, led by Exxon and funded by 54 fossil fuel and chemical industry opponents of carbon taxes or regulation, added to the considerable budgets of those separate industry lobbying and public relations efforts that had been ongoing since the demise of ICE. The American Petroleum Institute alone spent $1.8 million in 1993 to one public relations firm (Burson-Marsteller) in opposition to a short-lived Clinton-proposed U.S. carbon tax. Before it was disbanded following the triumph of its anti-Kyoto campaign in the United States and some bad publicity over the group's tactics, the GCC would enjoy tremendous influence over U.S. climate policy, and a third industry-orchestrated campaign (this time called the Cooler Heads Coalition) would take its place after its eventual demise. A similar industry-led campaign was initiated in Europe in March 1996, named the European Science and Environment Forum.

The demise of the GCC is instructive for what it was able to accomplish and for what eventually caused it to unravel. Having successfully blocked

Senate ratification of the Kyoto Protocol and with some of its members facing increasing public criticism for their role in scuttling the climate convention, the organization began to see several high-profile defections in 1997. DuPont was the first company to bolt from the GCC, and later that year British-based BP Amoco withdrew from the coalition after revelations surfaced about the company's involvement in undermining the treaty, fearing that the negative public relations implications might hurt its bottom line. In a speech announcing his company's decision to pull out, BP chairman John Browne remarked: "The time to consider the policy dimensions of climate change is not when the link between GHGs and climate change is conclusively proven, but when the possibility cannot be discounted and is taken seriously by the society of which we are part. We in BP have reached that point." Likewise, when Ford Motor Company withdrew from the coalition in 1999, CEO William Clay Ford, Jr., denounced the contrived skepticism that had become the GCC's calling card, claiming: "The present risk is clear. The climate appears to be changing, the changes appear to be outside natural variation, and the likely consequences will be serious. From a business planning point of view, that issue is settled. Anyone who disagrees is, in my view, still in denial."[44] Following BP's lead, Royal Dutch Shell withdrew in 1998, and DaimlerChrysler, General Motors, and Texaco all left the coalition in early 2000.

As can be expected with corporate decision making generally, these defections from the GCC and its increasingly negative public image were largely based in the rational fear that a company's association with such a sinister organization, particularly once its primary aim had already been realized, might harm its financial bottom line. Not only might member companies face boycotts and other bad publicity, but as an Earth Policy Institute history of the GCC points out, "to deny that Earth is getting warmer in the face of such compelling evidence is to risk a loss of credibility, something that corporations cannot readily afford."[45] In part to repair their tainted public images, several former GCC member companies (including BP Amoco, Shell, and DuPont) joined the Business Environmental Leadership Council, a group founded by the Pew Center on Global Climate Change that claims in its mission statement: "We accept the views of most scientists that enough is known about the science and environmental impacts of climate change for us to take actions to address its consequences."[46]

Faced with declining corporate membership and the legitimacy crisis that this rush to dissociate from the group entailed, the GCC announced in March 2000 that it was undergoing a "strategic restructuring" in which individual companies would no longer be asked to contribute, reserving membership instead for trade associations such as the American Petroleum Institute, which insulate member companies from public criticism while allowing them to continue supporting the group's anti-Kyoto efforts, in order to "bring the focus of the climate debate back to the real issues." In reality, the many high-profile defections from the group had left ExxonMobil standing virtually alone and exposed. Following President George W. Bush's announcement that the United States was abandoning the "fatally flawed" Kyoto Protocol—a phrase taken verbatim from GCC anti-Kyoto literature—the group disbanded altogether in 2002, explaining that it "has served its purpose by contributing to a new national approach to global warming. The Bush administration will soon announce a climate policy that is expected to rely on the development of new technologies to reduce greenhouse emissions, a concept strongly supported by the GCC."[47] These "new technologies" would turn out to be the "clean coal" program promoted by the Cheney task force and the president's hydrogen fuel cell research initiative, which is widely viewed as a pretext for postponing any further increases in automobile fuel efficiency standards and political cover for those domestic auto companies that have neglected current fuel efficiency technologies.

Although the GCC has gone away, ExxonMobil's campaigns against climate science and effective climate policies have not diminished, as the company continues to pour money into a host of anti-environmental efforts, funding at least 40 organizations devoted to opposing climate policy, including conservative think tanks, quasi-journalistic Internet public relations firms, a FoxNews.com columnist (climate skeptic Steven Milloy), and religious and civil rights groups.[48] The Competitive Enterprise Institute alone received $1.38 million from ExxonMobil between 2000 and 2003—including $60,000 annually for "legal activities" that included two lawsuits against the federal government attempting to block the dissemination of government documents that acknowledge the existence of anthropogenic climate change—the American Enterprise Institute received $960,000, and the George C. Marshall Institute (where the skeptics Willie Soon and Sallie Baliunas are employed as "senior scientists") $310,000.[49] Chris Mooney notes of such "think tanks" that their purpose is to "provide both intellectual cover for those who reject what the best science currently tells us, and ammunition for conservative policy makers" like Inhofe and Dana Rohrabacher (R-CA).

In addition, the company has spent more than $55 million directly on lobbying activities in the past seven years, and in 2001 pledged $100 million over 10 years to fund Stanford's Global Climate and Energy Project. While this research grant might be taken to imply that ExxonMobil is serious about advancing knowledge about global climate change, it must be taken in context: By contrast, Shell has spent more than $1.5 billion on research and development of renewable energy sources, and BP more than $500 million, so ExxonMobil's research budget—which aims to advance carbon sequestration technologies so that the world can continue its reliance on oil for energy—is comparatively small for its status as the world's largest energy company and most profitable corporation, amounting to just two days' earnings. Moreover, ExxonMobil, which openly predicts that solar and wind energy will provide less than 1 percent of world energy supply by the end of the century, plans to spend more than $100 billion on oil exploration over the lifetime of the Global Climate and Energy Project grant, so it plans to devote 1,000 times the resources to finding new oil supplies to exploit than it has committed toward advancing human knowledge of climate. The grant also provided some much-needed damage control for its public image, as the company touts its Stanford partnership in a recent ad campaign. Whether ExxonMobil has, like many of its competitors, been chastened by the growing public scorn for its anti-environmental record or whether, by contrast, it is merely seeking to "buy" some legitimacy for the climate skepticism that it has bankrolled for over a decade remains to be seen.

Perhaps the most infamous—and, among the anti-Kyoto crowd, influential—document to have emerged from ExxonMobil's sponsorship of think-tank "research" is the Soon and Baliunas review article, published in a 2003 issue of *Climate Research* and claiming without any original research that "the twentieth century is probably not the warmest nor a uniquely extreme climatic period of the last millennium."[50] Although the authors' methods and conclusions were quickly discredited, the article garnered the attention of politicians seeking to confer legitimacy on their rejection of the climate convention. In order to increase its visibility, a second version of the article was published, this time with the skeptics Craig Idso, Sherwood Idso, and David Legates as co-authors. Calling it a "powerful new work of science," Inhofe devoted half of a Senate hearing to the article, boasting that it fully refutes the scientific consensus that climate change is real. Meanwhile, *Climate Research* editor Hans Von Storch resigned the day before Inhofe's hearing in protest of editorial policies that had allowed the article's publication without sufficient peer review, calling it a "flawed paper" and claiming that he was pressured to publish the paper and not allowed to publish a rebuttal repudiating the authors' conclusions. Von Storch told the *Chronicle of Higher Education* that the climate skeptics "had identified *Climate Research* as a journal where some editors were not as rigorous in the review process as is otherwise common." Another editor at the journal, Clare Goodess, also resigned in protest following the events.[51] Nonetheless, the article retained its luster among those for whom the article's conclusions are more important than its scientific integrity. As the *Wall Street Journal* notes, "since being published last January in *Climate Research*, the paper has been widely promoted by Washington think tanks and cited by the White House in revisions made to a recent Environmental Protection Agency report."[52] Despite its thoroughly repudiated claims,[53] the article has been widely championed by opponents of GHG regulation who point to its publication in what is ordinarily a peer-reviewed journal as evidence of scientific dissensus over climate change.

ExxonMobil's sponsorship of skeptical climate "research" is not limited to the United States. In November 2004, the British-based and Exxon-funded International Policy Network released a report calling climate change a "myth," the mainstream science that supports it "fatally flawed," and Britain's chief scientist "an embarrassment" for believing in it, claiming that sea level increases will not exceed 20 cm over the next century and that this will actually benefit fish stocks.[54] Nor has the company confined its anti-Kyoto efforts to disinformation campaigns directed at misleading the public: Although the company has publicly denied lobbying any governments over climate policy,[55] documents obtained by Greenpeace under the Freedom of Information Act from a series of State Department climate policy meetings between 2001 and 2004 show the administration thanking Exxon executives for their "active involvement" in developing climate policy, seeking advice from the company on future policies, and instructing Undersecretary of State Paula Dobriansky to consult with it on developing Kyoto alternatives. In one released document, President Bush is said to have "rejected Kyoto in part because of input from you [the GCC]."[56]

Such skepticism well suited the prevailing political climate in the United States, which after the 1994 takeover of Congress by conservative ideologues became committed to a political agenda of deregulation and to a general offensive on the scientific basis for the nation's environmental policies. Following the symbolically significant act by the 101st Congress of abolishing the nonpartisan Office of Technology Assessment, which was charged with reviewing the scientific basis of public policy, in 1995 the House Science Subcommittee on Energy and the Environment initiated a series of coordinated attacks on the nation's environmental regulations under the rubric of congressional hearings ironically titled "Scientific Integrity and the Public Trust," in which previously settled issues such as the nation's participation in the Montreal Protocol on the phasing out of ozone-depleting chemicals were reopened, with subcommittee chair Rohrabacher describing the scientific consensus behind the ozone treaty as a "sky-is-falling cry from an environmental Chicken Little" bent on "scaremongering" the public in order to "intimidate and repress rational discussion."[57] A central objective of these hearings was to forestall or undermine the ongoing negotiations toward establishing a global climate regime, and to that end the skeptic Pat Michaels was given top billing in the hearings, testifying against several of the nation's leading climate experts. Describing climate change as based on "junk science"—a favorite term of anti-environmental ideo-logues, used in reference to any credible scientific research that finds domestic industry or consumption patterns to cause adverse environmental conse-quences—the central strategy of these hearings was to call into question the integrity of mainstream science, and thereby to discredit the empirical bases of the nation's environmental policies.

Despite the emphasis paid to the persistent claims by climate skeptics that continuing scientific uncertainty could not justify any mandatory caps or time-tables, which implies the need for further research in order to reduce these uncertainties, at the subcommittee's recommendation the House elected to terminate the $1.2 billion Global Change Research Program. Rohrabacher accused that program, which is the primary government research effort into the causes and consequences of climate change, of being nothing more than the product of Vice President Al Gore's "environmental fanaticism,"[58] and later defunded the EPA's global monitoring program, which assesses ecosystem vulnerability to climate change. In December 2004, buried in a 3,000-page omnibus spending bill, Congress eliminated funding for the Climate Reference Network, which supports the climate monitoring system operated by the National Oceanic and Atmospheric Administration and consists of 110 obser-vation stations, including Keeling's original site on Mauna Loa. According to Kevin Trenberth, head climate analyst as the National Center for Atmospheric Research, the $3 million cut, which was ostensibly justified by budget woes and not intended as an attack on climate science, carried a clear message nonethe-less: "It's almost as though some people don't want to know how the climate is changing. Maybe they prefer uncertainty, so that they can avoid taking action."[59]

In general, the U.S. government has since 1990 displayed little interest in supporting the sort of research that its repeated references to scientific uncer-tainty imply is necessary for informed climate policy formulation. According to a 2005 investigation by the GAO, none of the 21 climate change studies that the administration plans to publish by 2007 complied with the 1990 Global Change Research Act, which require reports to Congress every four years on the poten-tial effects of global climate change on agriculture, energy, water resources, and biodiversity. Of nine studies due to be published by September 2005, only one is currently on schedule, with the consequence that (according to the GAO report) "it may be difficult for the Congress and others to use this information effectively as the basis for making decisions on climate policy."[60] This apparent reluctance to contribute to the advancement of atmospheric science is under-standable insofar as credible scientific research undermines the policy aims of Kyoto opponents. Those government-funded studies that the administration has been unable to defund, delay, or suppress have all confirmed the reality of anthropogenic climate change, leading the George W. Bush administration to contrive several ethically dubious schemes to block their dissemination to the public.

Manufacturing Uncertainty

By the time George W. Bush took office in early 2001, the existence of anthropogenic climate change was acknowledged by broad scientific consensus. The IPCC had released three assessment reports, with each report scrupulously documenting the levels of certainty that attached to each of its findings. Nonetheless, President Bush in 2001 requested that the National Academy of Sciences (NAS) review the IPCC's findings, and the NAS confirmed them.[61] So also did the American Geophysical Union,[62] which likewise strongly urged President Bush to take action to avert the hazards of climate change. Moreover, according to an analysis by Naomi Oreskes of 928 abstracts of articles published in refereed scientific journals between 1993 and 2003 (the year of the infamous Soon and Baliunas review article), not a single published scientific research paper disagreed with the existence of anthropogenic climate change. As she cautions, "the scientific consensus might, of course, be wrong," but this striking evidence from peer-reviewed climate science strongly supports the existence of such a consensus. Insofar as the processes of peer review on which legitimate scientific research is based represent the standard for establishing credible scientific knowledge, this clear case of consensus must be regarded as demonstrating the factual nonexistence of genuine scientific controversies surrounding anthropogenic climate change that are alleged by climate skeptics and other opponents of GHG regulations. As Oreskes notes of this consensus, "politicians, economists, journalists, and others may have the impression of confusion, disagreement, or discord among climate scientists, but that impression is incorrect."[63]

Nonetheless, when a U.S. State Department report to the United Nations in May 2002 acknowledged that human activities were indeed causing climate change,[64] the president distanced himself from its findings, ridiculing it as "a report put out by the bureaucracy."[65] In September of that year, he ordered the removal of the climate section of the EPA's annual air pollution report,[66] though it had been a regular part of the report in previous years, and in June 2003 attempted to substantively alter the climate change findings in the EPA's annual *Report on the Environment*[67] when the draft report acknowledged anthropogenic climate change.[68] According to a Union of Concerned Scientists report and based on an internal EPA memo and interviews with current and former

EPA staff, the White House Council for Environmental Quality (CEQ), the Bush administration's main climate science censor, demanded the following changes to the draft report:

- The deletion of temperature data in order to, according to the EPA memo, emphasize "a recent, limited analysis [that] supports the administration's favored message."
- The removal of any reference to the 2003 National Academy of Science review (requested by the White House) confirming that human activity causes climate change.
- The elimination of the summary statement acknowledging that "climate change has global consequences for human health and the environment."
- According to the EPA memo, the CEQ demanded so many qualifying words (e.g., "potentially" and "may") that it implied "uncertainty… where there is essentially none."[69]

In the final version of the report that was released to the public, the entire section on climate change was deleted. According to the Union of Concerned Scientists report, EPA staffers "chose this path rather than compromising their credibility by misrepresenting the scientific consensus." EPA head Christine Whitman, who would later describe the political environment at the agency as "brutal," resigned shortly thereafter, and several long-time staffers also quit in protest.

The CEQ is the executive branch office responsible for devising and promoting the administration's environmental policies, and on taking office in 2001, Bush appointed Philip Cooney, a former oil industry lobbyist and "climate team leader" for the American Petroleum Institute, as chief of staff at the CEQ. According to documents obtained by the New York Times through the Government Accountability Project, Cooney "repeatedly edited government climate reports in ways that play down links between such [GHG] emissions and global warming."[70] Cooney, who has a bachelor's degree in economics and no formal scientific training, altered the scientific conclusions of government climate reports by altering texts to exaggerate uncertainties in climate science and deleting references to projected climatic effects, even after the documents had been approved by other White House officials. Other administration appointees to scientific posts have displayed similar patterns of behavior in suppressing climate science and promoting their skepticism. In an October 2002 memo, for example, the State Department's chief climate negotiator "strongly" urged the deletion of references to the scientific findings of either the NAS climate panel or the IPCC, claiming that their official summaries "do not include an appropriate recognition of the underlying uncertainties and the tentative nature of some of their findings."[71]

This practice of suppressing scientific research and intimidating or harassing researchers when their findings oppose some predetermined political agenda is not limited to the executive branch. Alongside the anti-Kyoto diatribes of such science-bashing legislators as Inhofe and Rohrabacher, several other members of Congress who oppose action to limit GHG emissions took their ironically named "sound science" crusade a step further. When the National Academy of Science released its 2003 report confirming the existence of anthropogenic climate change, Senate Commerce Committee Chair Ted Stevens (R-AK) threatened to subpoena those members of the academy who had contributed to the study. "He was threatening the academy," remarked NAS panel chairman Gordon Orians about the incident. "We are seeing, at present, an attempt to suppress science when its findings are not congenial with what policymakers want to do."[72]

Similarly, House Energy and Commerce Committee Chair Joe Barton (R-TX), infuriated by the 1998 publication in *Nature* of a study of historical temperature records that demonstrate significant global warming over the course of the twentieth century, demanded of researchers Michael Mann, Ray Bradley, and Malcolm Hughes that they turn over to Barton a detailed list of all financial support they have ever received, a list of all conditions attached to every federal and private grants received by the scientists, the "exact computer code" used to generate the findings in *Nature*, and a detailed account of the scientists' contributions to the work of the IPCC that included a "detailed narrative explanation" of errors alleged by Barton.[73] In response, 20 prominent U.S. climate scientists sent an open letter to Barton, noting that such an unreasonable request "can be seen as intimidation—intentional or not—and thereby risks compromising the independence of scientific opinion that is vital to the preeminence of American science as well as to the flow of objective advice to the government." Senator McCain and University of Arizona President Peter Likins condemned Barton's actions as "political retribution" and "intimidation" that "threatens the relationship between science and public policy."[74]

The lengths to which the opponents of GHG regulation have gone to manipulate and suppress scientific evidence that conflicts with their political goals are well documented and highly disturbing. They do not suggest a regime with a genuine concern for ensuring scientific certainty in the policy process, but rather one bent on suppressing any information that might contradict its public protests against the need to reduce GHG emissions and with little regard for either facts or scientific integrity. In its campaign to restore scientific integrity in policy making, the Union of Concerned Scientists circulated a statement, signed by more than 6,000 scientists, including 47 Nobel laureates, declaring that: "The distortion of scientific knowledge for partisan political ends must cease if the public is to be properly informed about issues central to its well being, and the nation is to benefit fully from its heavy investment in scientific research and education." Although its call for a "government return to the ethic and code of conduct which once fostered independent and objective scientific input into policy formation" and "legislative, regulatory and administrative reforms that would ensure the acquisition and dissemination of independent and objective scientific analysis and advice" have thus far generated no concrete results, the scientific community has at least begun to defend its integrity and independence in the face of threats issuing from a state that seeks to use science not for the sake of advancing knowledge, but for the sake of advancing its political agenda.

The attempt to manipulate science for political ends is hardly a new phenomenon, even if the intensity with which George W. Bush administration officials have pressured scientists, threatened or intimidated agencies, and substantively altered or suppressed scientific reports surpasses that of earlier administrations. Nor are such campaigns confined to government officials, as some of the first and most successful efforts to manipulate the public's perception of scientific facts were conducted by industry—especially the tobacco and chemical industries, against the scientific evidence linking health problems to smoking and exposure to industrial chemicals—and such industry disinformation campaigns continue. Epidemiologist and former Assistant Secretary of Energy David Michaels describes the process by which industry groups deliberately attempt to obscure the findings of independent scientists in order to prevent regulation of their products as "manufactured uncertainty," summarizing it as follows:

> If, for example, studies show that a company is exposing its workers
> to dangerous levels of a certain chemical, the business typically
> responds by hiring its own researchers to cast doubt on the studies.
> Or if a pharmaceutical firm faces questions about the safety of one of
> its drugs, its executives trumpet company sponsored trials that show
> no significant health risks while ignoring or hiding other studies that
> are much less reassuring. The vilification of threatening research as
> "junk science" and the corresponding sanctification of industry-
> commissioned research as "sound science" has become nothing less
> than the standard operating procedure in some parts of corporate
> America.[75]

This industry pattern of challenging independent scientific findings has become so routine, Michaels suggests, that "it is now unusual for the science behind any proposed public health or environmental regulation not to be challenged, no matter how powerful the evidence."

It is increasingly difficult to introduce independent scientific evidence into public policy processes, Michaels suggests. Given the deregulatory climate at the U.S. Food and Drug Administration and the EPA, "civil lawsuits have become the primary means for protecting the public from unsafe drugs and chemicals," but the manufacturers have succeeded in blocking the introduction of much independent science from those tort trials. While these industry attempts to manipulate the public perception of scientific facts and levels of uncertainty are hardly new, Michaels suggests that "it is fair to say that never in our history have corporate interests been as successful as they are today in shaping science policies to their desires." He notes, for example, the Bush administration's decision to remake a committee advising the Centers for Disease Control and Prevention on childhood lead poisoning in order to replace independent scientists with industry-friendly skeptics willing to oppose stronger federal standards, despite clear evidence connecting lead exposure to impaired childhood development.

This ironically named "sound science" campaign has been aided and abetted by the U.S. government, which has allowed industry to successfully call for the suppression of scientific data supporting conclusions that call for further regulation or establish the requisite causal links between industrial activities and adverse health consequences that might support tort lawsuits. In a 2001 midnight appropriations rider, without hearings or debate, Congress adopted a provision called the Data Quality Act, which ostensibly aims to ensure "the quality, objectivity, utility, and integrity of information" used in legislation and administrative rule making, but has in practice been used primarily by industry groups in order "to slow or stop attempts at regulation by undercutting scientific reports" and provides industry "an established procedure for killing or altering government documents with which they do not agree."

In perhaps the most notable use of the Data Quality Act by industry, the Exxon-financed Competitive Enterprise Institute (CEI) in 2003 sued the White House Office of Science and Technology Policy in order to force government agencies to stop using the 2000 *National Assessment of the Potential Consequences of Climate Variability and Change*,[76] a climate change report commissioned by Congress in 1990 to assess region-by-region impacts of global warming, alleging that the report (which acknowledges climatic changes) is inaccurate and biased.[77] Allegedly at the request of the Bush administration, which was named a party in the suit, the CEI lawsuit also sought to suppress the EPA's 2002 *U.S. Climate Action Report*, a document that the agency is required to publish under the 1992 Rio treaty. This, despite the fact that the EPA report had already been bowdlerized by CEQ pressures to water down its language, downplaying any links between human activity and climate change and exaggerating the extent to which the report's findings were uncertain, leading EPA scientists to charge that the amended report "no longer accurately represents scientific consensus."

Based on documents obtained by the attorneys general from Maine and Connecticut through a Freedom of Information Act request, the CEQ apparently solicited the CEI lawsuit in order to suppress the report's acknowledgments of global warming. In an email from CEI executive and head of the Cooler Heads Coalition Myron Ebell to Cooney—who would later resign in the wake of political fallout from his clandestine editing work on various government-sponsored scientific reports—Ebell thanks Cooney for "calling and asking for our help" on the matter and recommends blaming a "fall guy (or gal)...as high up as possible" in the EPA for the report, further noting that CEI might call for the firing of EPA head Whitman. The two state attorneys general unsuccessfully called on U.S. Attorney General John Ashcroft to investigate the matter, noting in their request that "the idea that the Bush Administration may have invited a lawsuit from a special interest group in order to undermine the federal government's own work under an international treaty is very troubling."[78] While troubling, this was hardly an isolated incident in a well-coordinated campaign by government and industry to manufacture uncertainty and thereby forestall passage of effective GHG-limiting legislation, and only part of a larger strategy to avoid GHG regulation. And it should be disturbing not just in its policy implications, but also in its reflection of the governmental processes that allowed it.

Conclusions

From this analysis of climate change policy development, several prominent themes emerge. While the global effort to design an effective global climate regime began as an effort toward rational-comprehensive policy making—where policy is constructed on the basis of the available scientific facts and where the overriding imperative is to address the identified problem in the fairest and most effective manner possible—several obstacles would prevent that from happening. Most prominently, the politicization of science by industry opponents of global climate policy efforts, together with sympathetic representatives in government, has stymied the development of fair and effective climate policy through a coordinated public relations and lobbying campaign designed to undermine the scientific basis of climate change, and thereby to convince the public that no mandatory action is needed. Thus far, this campaign has enjoyed tremendous success, scoring a major victory with the election of George W. Bush in 2000 (and again in 2004), essentially assuring continued U.S. opposition to all meaningful climate policy efforts, both foreign and domestic. In the meantime, industry influence on the policy process—on dramatic display in the Cheney energy task force—continued to subvert efforts to reduce the nation's GHG emissions and succeeded in further entrenching the nation in a carbon-based energy economy for decades to come.

Why did this happen? One obvious lesson, again on display in the Cheney energy task force, as elsewhere, is that bad process begets bad policy. Although the international process for developing climate policy under the *UNFCCC* may not contain the same democratic deficits that plague the U.S. government, its efforts toward the allowance for and inclusion of meaningful participation by developing nations deserves some criticism. Another lesson concerns the crucial need for independent science: Since the early 1990s, the public has been deliberately and systematically misled by industry efforts to undermine the scientific basis for global climate policy. These campaigns include massive public relations efforts, the bankrolling of climate skeptics as well as media (mass media outlets, quasi-scholarly journals, think tanks, research programs at credible universities) to disseminate their message, and a highly effective political lobbying effort that succeeded in mobilizing latent conservative fears of world government against participation in the Kyoto Protocol and latent distrust of science against the further study of the problem. We cannot adequately address global environmental problems that we do not fully understand, but we cannot understand them properly, much less address them effectively, when ideologues and corporate lobbyists succeed in subverting, suppressing, and misrepresenting scientific knowledge to suit their own narrowly construed political agendas. Finally, and related to the first two lessons, the policy process depends on openness and accountability, the sincere search for truth and for solutions to common problems, and the representation of the interests of all citizens, and the case study of climate policy development presented in this chapter offers an indictment of all of these essential democratic norms. If a global climate regime is to be both fair and effective, it must find a way to strengthen its democratic commitments and to resist the antidemocratic influences that currently plague U.S. politics and government.

2

Climate Change, Fairness, and Equity

Anthropogenic climate change presents an issue in global politics that is inherently and centrally concerned with justice and fairness—normative concepts examined in some detail in this chapter. First, however, let us briefly observe some of the known causes and predicted effects of anthropogenic climate change. The increase in atmospheric concentrations of greenhouse gases (GHGs) that scientists first noticed in the twentieth century and that continues unabated in the twenty-first century is caused primarily by industrialization and the human combustion of fossil fuels, which has thus far largely reflected the world's existing economic disparities, with the world's affluent contributing the bulk those GHGs now accumulated in the atmosphere and the world's poor relatively little. According to the Intergovernmental Panel on Climate Change (IPCC), the global poor, despite their disproportionately small share of responsibility for causing the problem and their receiving little or no benefit from those activities that contribute toward climatic instability, are nonetheless expected to suffer disproportionate harm from a changing climate. Thus, the predicted consequences of unabated GHG emissions include the shifting of the ecological costs of the high-consumption lifestyle of the world's affluent onto those who can least afford to bear them, are least responsible for producing them, and have received the least advantage from them.

Hence, anthropogenic climate change presents a case of the world's affluent benefiting at the expense of the world's poor in a relationship that can plausibly be described as exploitation. Alan Wertheimer defines exploitation as a relationship in which "*A* exploits *B* when *A* takes unfair advantage of *B*"—that is, *A* (the exploiter) benefits from an involuntary exchange by which *B* (the exploitee) is made worse off.[1] What makes this kind of exploitation particularly objectionable, according to Wertheimer, is its involuntary character. By both Marxist and libertarian accounts of exploitation, *B* may voluntarily and harmlessly accept costs that serve to benefit *A*, in effect redistributing welfare to *A*, but when this redistribution is coerced or otherwise involuntary, then *B* is wrongfully exploited by it. Although typically applied to economic relationships rather than instances of environmental harm, the redistribution of the costs and benefits of fossil fuel combustion between the world's poor and affluent displays the salient characteristics of *B* being forced to suffer some costs from an activity that benefits *A*. One might object at this point to this characterization of unabated GHG emissions by the world's affluent as exploitation:

> But the rich aren't literally using the poor in the way that exploiters typically use exploitees in economic relationships, because they aren't extracting something directly from them. Rather, the affluent are using the atmosphere's GHG absorptive capacity in a way that largely benefits them and disproportionately harms the poor, but inanimate objects or natural capacities are not the kind of things that can suffer from exploitation.

This objection is unsatisfactory in two respects: First, it is common to speak of natural resources as being exploited, which is generally taken to mean not that some inanimate object is harmed but that some persons benefit by the overuse of the resource and at the expense of others who might otherwise have access to it, and the atmosphere is a natural resource that can be overused in this way. Second, the atmosphere is a common and finite resource that all must share, so the overuse of the atmospheric commons by one group necessarily entails harm to others, whether by forcing other groups to accept smaller shares of the resource as a consequence of its overuse, or by causing them to suffer the adverse consequences of resource degradation that results from patterns of overuse from which they did not benefit. Because this is essentially the choice now faced by the world's poor, one may therefore say that they are being exploited, at least insofar as their involuntary loss is another's gain. A Marxist account of justice applied to climate issues, which I do not pursue any further here, would take this exploitation to play as fundamental a role as equity and responsibility do in the inquiry that follows.[2]

The upshot of this argument about exploitation is an observation about fairness: There appears to be something that is fundamentally unfair—or rather, as I describe this sort of unfairness in this and the next two chapters, something unjust—about the way in which overuse of the planet's atmosphere by one group has the apparent effect of visiting significant and undeserved harm on another. Indeed, philosophers and political theorists have developed the concept of distributive justice to analyze and describe the kinds of allocation of benefits and harm that are on display in this climate change example. This chapter analyzes the concept of distributive justice as it might be applied to the climate case, in its known causes and predicted effects, as well as in the design of a remedial global climate regime that aims to mitigate those injustices and compensate for those that remain, paying particular attention to the manner in which climate change entails distributive or redistributive effects and the extent to which these effects may be justified or deserved. Later, I also examine retributive justice and restorative justice, which also play prominent roles, through the principle of responsibility, in the design of just institutions such as a remedial climate regime.

Chapters 3 and 4 examine two special and controversial applications of principles of distributive justice to problems of global climate change. Chapter 3 examines the problems with and potential for applying the concept of distributive justice across national borders in what is known as *cosmopolitan justice*, the global redistributive effects of anthropogenic climate change, and what obligations such effects might entail. Chapter 4 considers the application of the concept of distributive justice over time, examining whether and how obligations toward future generations might arise from such considerations. First, however, let us consider the nature of justice as it has been developed within contemporary political theory and philosophy, paying particular attention to theories of distributive justice as they might apply to the climate case. With that foundation in justice theory, I proceed to examine how, throughout the process of negotiation and in the major agreements of the climate convention, the discourse of justice and fairness manifests in climate politics, underscoring the nature of climate change as itself a problem of justice, as are the international mitigation efforts proposed to address its problems and the processes used to generate them, and highlighting the critical importance of these normative concerns to designing workable agreements.

What Is Justice?

Since chapters 3 and 4 examine two different extensions of the concept of justice—across national borders and over time—let me first identify and briefly describe that concept as it is currently understood within the dominant tradition in political philosophy. In ordinary language, as well as academic discourse, justice is concerned with four related concepts: equality, distribution, desert, and responsibility. For example, the "justice system" of legal trials and punishments is charged with treating all citizens equally, other things being equal. Treating persons as equals entails that it would be wrong to arbitrarily punish any person in the absence of a morally relevant difference—guilt, for example—between them and others, and it would also be wrong to reward persons in the absence of such relevant differences between them and others. Criminal punishment involves the state distribution of a *bad*—something that persons aim to avoid—and so can be justified only by something that the accused has voluntarily done in order to become deserving of punishment, thereby allowing the state to hold that person responsible for his or her criminal act. The same applies to justice in the distribution of goods: In order to treat persons as equals, we often reserve the prerogative to award larger shares of goods to persons displaying some relevant characteristic—a meritorious action, a unique talent, or an unusual need—that distinguishes them from others and that therefore makes them uniquely deserving of the good. By so rewarding them for this characteristic, we attribute responsibility to them for it.

Philosophers and political theorists also rely on these four concepts in defining justice but use them more specifically and apply their resulting conceptions of justice more broadly, often inclusive of any social or political relation in which the distribution of either goods or bads is involved. As a philosophical concept, justice applies to a large set of relations, many of which are simply not relevant to the subject of this book, and so I focus instead on *social justice*, which is concerned with the way that social and political institutions distribute both goods and bads among their constituent members—a distribution that tends to be based in *equity* more than *responsibility*, although both play a role. Hence, cosmopolitan justice and intergenerational justice immediately appear as marginal cases of social justice, since international justice involves matters of the distribution of goods and bads among different societies—unless it can be said, and it probably cannot, that there exists some cohesive global society—and intergenerational justice involves such distribution among persons who may be part of a single society but who do not exist as contemporaries and so cannot obviously acknowledge each other as such. Whether these marginal cases properly belong inside or outside the borders of social justice theory is a problem taken up in chapters 3 and 4, but for now I defer that question and refer instead to the more popular scholarly term for the same thing by talking about distributive justice.

As John Rawls opens his landmark *A Theory of Justice*, "Justice is the first virtue of social institutions." Justice, in other words, is to social institutions what moral goodness is to individual persons: that normative ideal which serves to distinguish between good and bad outcomes or states of affairs, to inform present and future acts and choices, and to evaluate proposed and past actions. Whether its relevant power is legal, political, or economic, the virtuous social institution is one that uses its power justly and in pursuit of justice. Understanding justice, then, is as important to social and political philosophy as understanding moral goodness is to ethics, and Rawls's theory of justice—comprehensively presented in his 1971 magnum opus and further developed through a series of published books and papers since then (along with a cottage industry of Rawls interpretation and criticism)—has focused attention on the nature of justice for both academic followers and critics in the decades since. Enough has already been written about the Rawlsian account of justice that I undertake only the briefest summary of it here, for what concerns us in this inquiry are not so much the general controversies within justice theory between Rawlsians and their critics but rather the more specific questions about whether or not and how the normative concept of distributive justice may defensibly be applied to the international and intergenerational issues surrounding climate change.

Since the Rawlsian theory of justice depends on a set of arguments for its foundation that are also the subject of debates about international and inter-generational justice, it is worth briefly surveying the case Rawls makes in its defense. Recall that justice is related to equality, and this typically takes the form of a premise that all persons are morally equal—an assumption that does not entail that they be assumed equal in other respects. Some persons are stronger, smarter, or cleverer than others, and the assumption of moral equality acknowledges this factual inequality. Instead, it is based on the attribution of equal *value* to all persons, in which no person's life or interests are treated as intrinsically more valuable than another's, a premise that does not depend on any matter of fact about particular persons and that holds regardless of whether or not persons are similar to others in other respects. Assuming that persons are moral equals further entails that, ceteris paribus, no person should be better or worse off than any other. While inequality is not necessarily bad—some persons, after all, *deserve* to be better or worse off than others—*arbitrary* or undeserved inequality in outcomes is taken to be unjust. Of course, other things are often not equal, so some may deserve better or worse outcomes than others based on voluntary acts or choices that they have made, for which they can therefore be held responsible. As an egalitarian, Rawls works from the premise that no person, merely by virtue of "accidents of birth," deserves more or fewer resources or opportunities than any other. Insofar as persons are to enjoy qualitatively better or worse lives, these differential outcomes ought to be based on morally relevant differences between persons and not those variables for which persons cannot be held responsible, however influential such variables are in actual societies.

This summary may initially appear to conflate two contrasting types of equality: equality of outcomes, where all persons experience a similar level of welfare, and equality of opportunity, where all begin with similar resources but may end up with widely disparate levels of welfare. While Rawls is sometimes mistakenly identified as advocating equality of outcomes, his theory plainly is concerned with ensuring equality of opportunity. As a variety of *liberal egalitarianism* (a genus that also includes Ronald Dworkin's theory of justice, examined below), Rawlsian justice does not demand that all persons be equally happy or experience equal levels of utility, nor does it prescribe certain ways of life for persons to follow. These, while essential to ensuring equality of outcomes, would constitute an unwarranted interference in individual liberty and so would be illiberal. Instead, it is tolerant of a wide range of "conceptions of the good" or plans of life, subject only to the limitations that one person's version of the good life not involve harming others and that they be held responsible for their choice of life plans. Recall that Rawls assumes persons to be both free and equal, and the capacity to form, revise, and pursue one's "conception of the good" is taken as the quintessential individual freedom.

In order to allow persons an approximately equal chance of realizing their particular conceptions of the good, liberal egalitarian justice seeks to equalize opportunities within society. Rawls casts these opportunities as "primary goods"—defined as "things that every rational man is presumed to want" and that "normally have a use whatever a person's rational plan of life," including personal "rights and liberties, powers and opportunities, income and wealth" and "the social bases of self-respect"[3]—while other liberal egalitarians offer various other names for the set of opportunities to be subject to principles of distributive justice. The basic idea, though, is that persons are treated as moral equals insofar as all begin with a roughly equal opportunity to realize their chosen life plans, on which their welfare depends, but that they may deserve varying levels of happiness or welfare based on their voluntary acts or choices or the manner in which they manage their resources and opportunities. Implicit in this focus on opportunities rather than outcomes is an assumption concerning the value of authenticity in the choosing of life plans, where each person is presumed to be the best judge of his or her own welfare and so is given ultimate authority over the manner in which he or she may choose to deploy resources.

Hence, the apparent conflation of outcome and opportunity equality vanishes. It can be simultaneously true that no persons deserve better or worse outcomes merely because of who they are rather than what they've done or chosen *and* that persons may deserve better or worse outcomes as a consequence of their voluntary acts and choices. Insofar as persons may be held responsible for the way in which they convert opportunities into welfare, they deserve only equal opportunities and not equal outcomes. Persons with expensive tastes are not entitled to extra resources in order to realize an equal level of welfare as persons who choose life plans that are more easily satisfied—an unequal distribution of opportunities required by equality of outcomes—and awarding them larger shares would fail to hold them responsible for the voluntary nature of such a preference. Similarly, someone choosing hard work and deferred gratification over leisure and instant gratification deserves greater accumulation of resources, because these decisions are likewise voluntary ones over which agents have control. Persons deserve to enjoy a range of outcomes from the starting point of equality of opportunity but are held as a matter of justice to deserve only those inequalities for which they are responsible through their acts and choices.

Among liberal egalitarians, several controversies remain over what constitute deserved advantages and disadvantages, but in general, it is widely assumed that persons deserve only those advantages and disadvantages that result from their voluntary choices for which they may be held responsible, and not those arising from luck alone—a claim explored in greater detail in chapter 5. Since income and wealth are resources of which some deserve more or less than others, a *distributive principle* offers a formula for when inequality is deserved and when it is not. One influential way of parsing this distinction that owes to Dworkin[4] is to identify the advantages and disadvantages that result from inborn natural endowments (or *endowment-sensitive* inequality) and those that follow from different levels of ambition among persons (or *ambition-sensitive* inequality). Since persons are, in some sense, responsible for their ambition, which manifests in their acts and choices, in a way that they cannot be held responsible for their native endowments, Dworkin's version of liberal egalitarian justice maintains that persons be entitled to their ambition-sensitive inequalities, which they can be said to deserve, but not their endowment-sensitive inequalities, which they cannot be said to deserve, since they cannot justifiably be held responsible for them. For Dworkin, justice is simply the realization of desert.

Rawlsian Distributive Justice

This does not yet provide a philosophical defense of the distinction—except by way of the theory of responsibility that features in chapters 5 and 6, which is undeveloped here—although Dworkin assumes rough agreement with the more famous defense of egalitarian justice given by Rawls. Being naturally selfish and rather shortsighted, Rawls assumes, each of us is likely to identify our own advantages as resulting from our ambition, while we see the similar advantages of others as resulting from luck alone. Thus, we would have a difficult time in coming up with an unbiased account of which advantages are deserved and which are undeserved. All of us think that we deserve our advantages and not our disadvantages, while we think precisely the opposite of others. If required to deliberate with others about the proper allocation of advantages and disadvantages across all of society, making sure to allocate to each person exactly the advantages and disadvantages he or she deserves, each of us would be tempted to award the most advantage to ourselves—or, if formulating a rule that applies generally, then to those most like ourselves—and the fewest to others or those least like ourselves. A moment's reflection on this quandary should tell us two things: that none of us would be able to justify our selfishly determined allocations as fair, as we surely must recognize that they serve our advantage to the detriment of others, and that a multitude of selfish allocation claims is unlikely to generate consensus over how society's primary goods ought to be allocated.

For Rawls, the solution to this problem comes via the thought experiment of what he calls the *original position*, where persons are thought to privately reason about what is both rational and fair, constructing principles of justice or general rules about how society's primary goods are to be allocated, which in turn establishes standards for which primary goods persons do and do not deserve. In order to avoid the problem of many selfish allocations, the original position has us deliberate about which principles of justice to endorse from behind a *veil of ignorance*, where competing principles are evaluated in contrived ignorance of one's own race, gender, socioeconomic status, religious predilections, and most other ascriptive and chosen attributes that make people different in the real world. Behind the veil of ignorance, we may still attempt to choose principles that serve our self-interest, but we are deprived of the relevant knowledge about our particular interests that might allow us to bias the rules in our favor. Behind the veil of ignorance, then, we can choose principles that are fair for all, since each person in effect takes on the position of all.

In such a position, what principles of justice would a rational person, aiming to maximize his or her share of society's primary goods, choose? One further stipulation about the original position is worth mentioning: Rawls assumes that persons are risk averse and so would choose principles of justice that maximize the primary goods of the least advantaged—because they may find themselves among that group, for all they know—rather than gambling on the probability that they might wind up among society's more advantaged. Though some members of society may be more risk tolerant than others, in fact, the assumption of risk aversion models the requisite equal respect and concern to which all are entitled, for reasons that are explored further in chapter 6. Behind the veil of ignorance, self-interested but risk-averse persons would not choose an equal allocation of primary goods within society if some unequal alternative existed where all were better off than under equality, because such a preference would be irrational. Being risk averse, they would not choose arrangements under which most but not all were better off than under equality, even if significantly so, since that would be to wager that they would not end up among society's least advantaged, for whom equality would be better. Rational parties, Rawls suggests, would choose to maximize the expected benefits of the least advantaged, which as far as they know they may be.

Representing this claim numerically, all would prefer a society of (12, 10, 9, 8, 6) over one of (5, 5, 5, 5, 5), since all social positions in the first set are preferable to their counterparts in the second. That is, all would prefer an unequal distribution of goods only on the condition that no other possible allocation could improve the conditions of the worst off. A society of (10, 8, 5) is not better than (5, 5, 5) and is worse than (7, 7, 7), despite being better than either at both the mean and median. Were persons assumed to be risk tolerant rather than risk averse, persons might prefer a society of (12, 11, 10, 9, 3) over (7, 7, 7, 7, 7) on the 80 percent chance of winding up better off in the former than in the latter, but Rawls disallows this risk tolerance in the interest of taking seriously the plight of the disadvantaged as well as the advantaged, which is required by the premise of moral equality. This assumption of risk aversion is also consistent with our understanding of justice as developed thus far. Those losing the gamble of the "natural lottery" by wagering that they would be among the top 80 percent but winding up in the bottom quintile, and who are worse off as a consequence, would then suffer as a result of their bad luck rather than as the result of any voluntary choices. A society like one based on slavery that is prosperous on average but that has a small minority that is desperately poor through no fault of their own cannot therefore be said to be a just society, at least as long as some alternative arrangement would allow the least advantaged to be better off, even if this results in lower average prosperity. Because the conditions of choice in the original position require maximizing the shares of goods allocated to the least advantaged (or the *minimum*), this Rawlsian distributive principle is often called *maximin*.

The idea that inequalities in primary goods are unjustified unless they benefit society's least advantaged (also known as the *difference principle*) comprises only part of the Rawlsian principles of justice, though it is the most widely applicable and most discussed part. It is worth noting at this point that the difference principle is not, as some critics have suggested,[5] a "time slice" standard for evaluating a given distribution of wealth in society at a fixed point in time, where the existence of inequalities in wealth among citizens necessarily requires justification in reference to its effects on the disadvantaged, but rather is meant as a principle to be applied only to the basic structure of society rather than to each instance of socioeconomic inequality. Beyond this, as Rawls would later clarify, the difference principle requires only that "however great the inequalities in wealth and income may be, and however willing people are to work to earn their greater shares of output, existing inequalities must contribute effectively to the benefit of the least advantaged."[6] Persons can acquire more than others through hard work and deferred gratification and retain these unequal shares of primary goods without injustice, as long as their gains follow from legitimate expectations based in a just basic structure and social institutions; egalitarian justice does not (as is sometimes alleged) require continuous economic leveling, and so is much closer to an equality of opportunity theory than one based in equality of outcomes.

Although considerable controversy remains within liberal egalitarian justice theory over the nature of the goods to be distributed and the precise formula to be used in such distribution, equality remains a powerful ideal within philosophical accounts of justice, and departures from equal treatment, resources, or opportunity can be justified only by morally relevant differences between persons. Only then can one person be said to deserve more or less than another. Where inequality is justified, it must be based on some voluntarily chosen and socially desirable characteristics of persons—for example, their willingness to work harder or to defer gratification, to innovate or take entrepreneurial risks, or to otherwise display qualities that warrant reward—or else some elective and socially undesirable characteristic, such as laziness, frivolousness, offense against others, or other qualities or choices that warrant social sanction. Less important than the minor differences between them are the major points of consensus among egalitarians: Despite their inborn differences, no persons deserve to be better or worse off as the result of factors beyond their control, so justice demands that all be given an equal chance to realize their conceptions of the good. What is most fundamentally unjust about our own society and world is that the life chances of persons vary enormously, and for reasons other than those that any reflective person could plausibly describe as deserved.

Fairness, Equity, and the Climate Convention

The centrality of justice issues in both the human causes and international response to climate change is evident in the prominence with which these normative concepts are included in the main international treaties, communiqués, and resolutions (hereafter collectively referred to as the *climate convention*) that acknowledge the global problem or attempt to address it through remedial action. While global climate change is not unique among contemporary environmental issues in raising such normative concerns—treaties on biodiversity and governing the shared use of the oceans likewise invoke the language of justice—it does uniquely pose both a fully global set of international justice problems along with considerable intergenerational justice concerns, providing an exemplary case for the application of these normative concepts to the development and analysis of public policy. Moreover, the costs that are expected to follow from a changing global climate present a clear and compelling case for intervention and mitigation, and both practical and principled reasons weigh in favor of a global climate regime that is designed with such justice concerns explicitly in mind.

Many legal and political documents express normative ideals in order to declare a commitment to some high-minded aspirations alongside the much less lofty workings out of the inevitable power struggles and compromises that are essential to gaining assent to the final product, and the climate convention is no exception. As the product of diplomatic negotiation and power politics, the convention's language reflects political expedience as much as reasoned philosophical reflection, and the occasional declaration of normative ideals should not be taken out of context from the legal framework in which those ideals are either realized through concrete measures or else included as a kind of window dressing with little palpable support within the document's formal provisions. Nonetheless, these normative declarations serve some function even if they represent no binding policy provisions, and parties to the convention are often as much concerned with the language and ideals expressed within the document—a concern that is reflected in the often acrimonious battles over wording—as its concrete provisions.

Where policy development takes place over time, further refinements of some initial agreement may be seen as striving toward the ideals expressed in early political documents and then gradually worked out through subsequent negotiations and other revisions. The body of constitutional law that has gradually expanded individual rights and liberties, as well as given shape and direction to such ideals as liberty and equality, serves as one illustration of the role of such early declarations of commitment to normative ideals prior to their full support within law and policy. Another may be seen in the rational incentives constraining legislators, given a primary motive of securing reelection, in which each prefers to avoid the complex and conflictive process of designing the specific rules and procedures necessary for implementing policy, so all delegate these responsibilities to professional administrators with the necessary expertise and insulation from electoral politics to accomplish the job. Legislators instead concern themselves with issuing general directives or setting goals toward which those charged with implementing policy are to aim, reserving oversight power and the prerogative to revisit that legislation as necessary in the future. In consequence, they are in a unique position to declare commitments to sets of ideals, even if early attempts to realize them through specific rules and procedures fall short of realizing them, in a way that can give substance and direction to future policy development.

Accordingly, the climate convention document containing the most explicitly normative language is both the first important treaty to emerge from international climate negotiations and the one with the least substantive content: the 1992 *United Nations Framework Convention on Climate Change* (or *UNFCCC*). The *UNFCCC* contains no binding commitments, and signatory nations agreed only to a nonbinding pledge to freeze GHG emissions at 1990 levels pending further study, but its symbolic importance in recognizing the importance of the issue and in initiating international political action to address climate change cannot be overstated. Additionally, the treaty set most of the normative ideals that continue to guide development and evaluation of the fairness of ongoing climate policy negotiations and development. Its declared commitment to equity in both its process and substantive policy outputs, though subsequent agreements display significant deficits in both of these regards, nonetheless remains the foundational ideal of climate policy development, and its normative language continues to serve as the basis for efforts to design a climate regime that realizes these goals.

Most central to the treaty's expressed normative commitments is its declaration that "the Parties should protect the climate system for the benefit basis of present and future generations of humankind, on the basis of equity and in accordance with their common but differentiated responsibilities and respective capabilities" (Article 3.1). Here, the fundamental roles of both intergenerational and international (or cosmopolitan) justice are explicitly identified as guiding ideals for future policy development, with the latter defined in terms of both "equity" and the "common but differentiated responsibilities and respective capabilities" of national participants. I explore all three of these ideals further below, but note that equity here refers to distributive justice, and "responsibilities" and "capabilities" refer to the differential national levels of historical GHG emissions and respective national abilities to reduce present levels of national emissions, and are offered in conjunction with equity as criteria for assigning remedial responsibility among nations for climate change. It is for these explicit reasons of fairness that the *UNFCCC* directs the developed nations to "take the lead" in the initial phase of climate policy development, assigning emission caps first to those nations that are the largest current and historical GHG polluters and primary beneficiaries of industrialization and postponing the assignment of binding caps to developing nations until the second phase of policy development, following the Kyoto Protocol's compliance period in 2012.

In addition to these expressed normative commitments, the *UNFCCC* contains several other notable references to justice or fairness. In accordance with the decision to exempt developing nations from the initial round of GHG emissions caps, it declares that "the Parties have a right to, and should, promote sustainable development" (Article 3.4), implicitly linking climate policy with existing development efforts and instantiating claims for higher allowable emissions shares by developing countries in the discourse of rights, in the only invocation of rights made within the convention. Binding emissions caps on developing nations, if set at per capita levels much lower than those in industrialized nations as if based on some historical baseline such as the 1990 emissions used in the Kyoto Protocol, would effectively prevent those nations from industrializing, so this language expresses the ideal of reducing existing inequalities in per capita emissions between industrialized and developing nations as the developing nations industrialize, linking climate policy to an existing discourse of sustainability in which inequality and cosmopolitan justice play significant roles.[7]

In order to accommodate this interest in development, with its principled concern for international fairness and practical need to gain the assent of large developing nations such as India and China, the goal of *sustainable development*—industrialization based on energy-efficient technologies that might minimize the growth of GHG emissions, generally assumed to be a means of raising living standards within developing nations without significantly increasing the ecological stress that accompanies economic growth—is expressed as both a right, which would presumably be violated if emissions caps were assigned to these nations at levels well below those of their industrialized cohorts, and a duty incumbent upon the industrialized nations toward developing countries. Moreover, this right to develop requires that the climate regime give "full consideration" to the "specific needs and special circumstances" of developing nations (Article 3.2), making further reference to the differential capacities for reducing GHG emissions between developed and developing nations.

Although comparatively little attention has been paid to issues of procedural fairness in the development of international climate policy, the *UNFCCC* nonetheless declares that "the financial mechanism shall have an equitable and balanced representation of all Parties within a transparent system of governance" (Article 11.2). Such normative commitments to equitable representation within policy-making bodies and to transparency in governance are again both principled and pragmatic: Developing country participation is essential to the long-term efficacy of any mitigation effort, and this participation in turn depends on their inclusion within fair procedures of democratic decision making; such procedural fairness likewise helps guarantee that substantive policy outputs reflect fair allocations of emissions reductions burdens rather than unfair allocations that match the world's existing economic hierarchy. Thus far, procedures in development of the climate convention have fallen far short of this ideal, but the declaration of a commitment to procedural fairness is nonetheless worth remarking. If nothing else, the treaty's normative language serves as a point of critique against which the actual policies and practices of the climate convention may be assessed.

Why Be Concerned with Fairness?

A cynic might read the text of the *UNFCCC* and wonder why its framers bothered with such high-minded but ultimately empty rhetoric. After all, our cynic might reason, treaties set the terms governing power relations in international politics, and negotiators aim merely to achieve the best possible advantage for the nations they were sent to represent. Nobody really wants to see a fair treaty, for this would entail foreswearing the aim of seeking advantage, so representatives employ the rhetoric of fairness only insofar as they think that it might result in their interests being advanced more effectively. This claim, which assumes a doctrine of *realism* examined in chapter 3, holds that normative ideals such as justice and equity cannot validly be applied to relations between nations, and so offers a tempting explanation for the presence of such terms in the framework convention. If the treaty's framers were so concerned with fairness, our cynic might further speculate, why was it drafted by representatives of only a small group of affluent nations and then brought to the Earth Summit to be signed by other nations that were largely excluded from the process by which it was given shape? Why, in other words, were the framers not more attentive to issues of procedural fairness, if fairness itself was some kind of goal? Had they been more inclusive in the treaty's framing phase, they might have been forced to make more substantive concessions to those nations that were expected to be most harmed by climate change rather than winning their acquiescence through flowery language and ultimately empty gestures at true international cooperation.

While our cynic may be right in identifying the likely motives of those national delegates charged with authoring the *UNFCCC*, we can nonetheless identify two distinct reasons why these delegates as well as the polities that they represent should be concerned with designing a climate regime that at least approximates the ideals of fairness and equity expressed in the treaty. The first is pragmatic: Given the costs inherent in implementing an effective global climate change mitigation regime, a necessary but insufficient condition for the willing participation of relevant parties is its perceived fairness in allocating burdens. Given the absence of a strong and centralized international regulatory regime capable of effectively monitoring and enforcing the terms of a global climate regime, the manner in which the agreement allocates burdens and responsibilities for GHG abatement must be widely seen as fair in order to be accepted, implemented, and enforced by participating parties. The prospect of an international executive authority capable of coercing unwilling cooperation with a global emission reduction program not only is practically implausible but also would be objectionable on other bases. In order to be effective, moreover, participation in a global climate regime must be universal, or it risks GHG "leakage" to nonparticipating nations and displays collective action problems. Here, the perception of fairness—where costs and benefits of participation are seen as fairly allocated—is the best guarantor of the willing universal participation, and genuine fairness is usually the most reliable way of bringing about its perception.

This is not to say that participation must be without costs to participants, because reducing GHG emissions to a level at which stabilization avoids dangerous climatic disruptions is likely to be expensive and to require lifestyle changes for many in the industrialized world. The primary task of the climate convention is to allocate these costs fairly, and participants in cooperative schemes are often more willing to endure greater individual sacrifices in the effort to generate a collective benefit or avoid a collective calamity if they regard those sacrifices as having been allocated fairly, and less willing to endure such burdens while convinced that these have been unfairly assigned. Most cooperative schemes are difficult enough to maintain against incentives to defect or free ride—self-interested motives can overwhelm one's sense of fairness—when each participant is allocated their fair share to contribute, but they become far more difficult when these assigned shares are seen as being unfairly assigned. While all delegates to the climate convention may, as our cynic suggests, simply aim to achieve the best possible terms for the nations they represent, they will be limited in this desire by the need to propose terms that are widely regarded as being fair to all, rather than transparently advantageous to a powerful few.

The need for fairness in a global climate regime is not only a pragmatic one designed to ensure the willing cooperation of all participants, but ought also to be based on a commitment to employing only justified coercion. Concerns about universal participation alone may not be sufficiently robust to prevent powerful nations from taking unfair advantage of the powerless, should the goal of the exercise be understood as merely obtaining consent to some allocation of burdens and not necessarily achieving a fair allocation. Moreover, the assigned emissions caps that comprise a necessary component of a global climate regime require sufficient enforcement power—part of willing cooperation in a cooperative scheme entails assurance that others do not defect from it—and this power can be justified only if being used to advance justice. Insofar as a climate regime creates and wields coercive power to enforce upon humanity an unfair allocation of emission reduction burdens, even if this allocation was sufficient to reduce global emissions below some identified aggregate global threshold, then one problem of international justice (the unfairness of the status quo) would merely be replaced by another. Insofar as the status quo presents in part a problem of injustice, the proper remedy must replace the unjust system with a just one; no other remedy will do. Not only must justice be done as an outcome, providing a remedy to the injustice of climate change, but it must also be reflected in the means used to realize that outcome. The second reason for being concerned with fairness, then, is that stabilizing climate is only an intermediate goal in this cooperative endeavor; we must be concerned with the ultimate goal of advancing justice for its own sake, as well.

Assessing the Fairness of the Climate Convention

While the approved text of the climate convention frequently declares commitments to justice, equity, and procedural fairness, its policy provisions and the procedures used to generate them often fall far short of realizing these ideals. Here, our cynic might once again prod us with a challenge to the assumptions that we have been making about fairness:

> Why should we assume that ideals expressed in a document like the
> UNFCCC will ever be realized in the way that a climate regime is
> implemented? Once other nations are brought on board, where is the
> incentive for the powerful to compromise with the powerless in order
> to realize fair terms of cooperation? If delegates to the climate
> conferences see their job as promoting their national interests at the
> outset, giving just enough ground in order to bring other nations on

board but only to serve those interests, why would they suddenly
become motivated by fairness down the road?

The ideals expressed in the climate convention may ultimately turn out to be
empty rhetoric rather than guiding norms toward which future policy developments may aspire, especially if delegates aim only to advance national interests
rather than securing a genuinely fair agreement. Paraphrasing Thomas
Hobbes, ideals without binding legal provisions to instantiate them in policy
are but words.

Our cynic aptly identifies what may safely be assumed as the motivation of
participants in a global climate regime: While persons can occasionally be motivated by genuine concerns for justice rather than self-interest—especially when
acting as free agents, less so when acting as proxies charged with advancing the
interests of another person or group—a more powerful motive will be the desire
to advance their self-interests or those of the group they represent. In those
cases where the requirements of justice run contrary to individuals' self-interest
or those of their group, we may hope that they will subordinate their own interests to the demands of justice, but it is perilous to rely on such naive optimism
without mechanisms in place for discouraging self-interested behavior and
encouraging cooperation. As James Madison famously notes in *Federalist 51*,
neither internal nor external checks on the climate policy process would be necessary if we could be certain that delegates to the climate conference were motivated only by justice, but we cannot rely on such universal altruism. A better
approach would be to ensure that we get the process right first so that we can
approximate the just outcome by virtue of the inherent fairness of the processes
by which it is generated, even if participants are individually motivated not by
justice but rather by a desire to advance some set of partial interests.

While all participants may understand the practical necessity of avoiding
the appearance of unfairness, they will nonetheless by motivated toward securing for the parties they represent the most favorable possible arrangements.
How can the procedural elements of the climate policy process contribute
toward checking self-interest and guiding participants toward a fair solution?
The answer, and a solution to the problem identified by the cynic, is that the
procedures used during the course of climate policy development must themselves be designed with fairness in mind. If some are allowed to dominate the
process by which policy is formulated, whether by excluding opposing parties
from meaningful participation altogether or by allocating power unequally—
monopolizing leadership posts in order to control the agenda, with weighted
voting schemes designed to stifle opposing proposals, by maintaining a veto
threat against unfavorable legislation, through procedural rules designed to

block amendments or limit debate, by using outside force or influence against opponents to coerce or manipulate policy outcomes, or by generally refusing to treat all parties as equal partners in the policy-making process—one can expect the policy outputs to reflect the unfairness of the process used to generate them. The best guarantee of a fair policy is a fair policy-making process, an observation that is easily stated but extraordinarily difficult to achieve in practice. Its practical elusiveness, however, should not be used as a reason not to take all realistic steps to approximate this ideal of political equality.

There are several difficulties in achieving political equality in theory as well as practice, since such international negotiations as the climate talks defy democratic norms that have developed around national and subnational polities. Taking political equality as an ideal for representation, it remains unclear on what basis power in the legislative process ought to be apportioned. Should all nations be given equal power through an equal number of representatives or votes, regardless of their population sizes? On the other hand, should representation be proportional to population, with larger nations receiving more power than smaller ones? Should nations that have higher per capita emission rates and are therefore more responsible for causing climate change, or those that are more affluent and thus with greater capacity for reducing emissions, be given more power in order to entice their participation, without which the regime cannot be effective? Conversely, should those nations that stand to be most adversely affected be given greater power, based on the intensity of their interests in an effective solution? Should national governments choose all of their national delegates, or might some be selected by opposition parties or minority groups residing within national borders? Should industry sectors or individual corporations be given representation of their own, as multinational organizations with interests but no clear national affiliation? Should nonindustry nongovernmental organizations—environmental groups, consumer advocates, or social justice organizations—be given a role in legislation? Given predicted effects of climate change on biodiversity and future generations, should advocates for future people or nonhuman animals be granted representation at climate talks?

None of these questions is easily answered. Some, such as the proposal to give the big polluters more influence, are normatively unpalatable but may be practically necessary in order to ensure sufficient participation to address the problem. Others, like the proposal to somehow represent future people and nonhuman animals, are normatively appealing but are extraordinarily difficult to institutionalize in practice.[8] Still others, such as the questions of whether national representation should be equal per nation or proportional by population and whether industry or nongovernmental organizations ought also to be represented, have no clear answers in democratic theory and would pose significant practical difficulties, as well. Despite these quandaries, however, several questions about the proper procedures to employ in climate talks designed to produce fair and equitable policy outputs are considerably less controversial. Allowing the industrialized nations of the G8 to utterly dominate all facets of the policy-making process to the exclusion of any meaningful participation by the world's other nations, which contain the vast majority of the world's population, including most of those expected to be most adversely affected by climate change, plainly violates any defensible version of political equality. Allowing the United States to hold the entire process hostage, based on its status as the biggest GHG polluter and unchallenged global hegemon, can likewise be condemned as a gross violation of procedural equality without any theoretical controversy. Democratic theory may not yield all of the answers needed to get the process right, but the violations of democratic norms that are most likely to undermine the chances of producing a fair agreement are easily identified, if difficult to avoid.

Chapter 7 pays further attention to some of these problems surrounding the attainment of procedural fairness in the policy-making processes used to set the terms for a global climate regime. For now, note the significant obstacles to satisfying those norms of democratic deliberation used to guide the design of smaller scale policy-making processes, and that we can only hope to approximate norms of political equality and fair and effective representation of all relevant interests, if more proximately than has thus far been the case with the climate conferences. For this reason, I do not believe we should rely on *pure procedural justice*, which holds that just policy outcomes are by definition those that result from perfectly fair processes, rather than being defined by independent criteria such as principles of justice. By this account, given a climate policy process in which procedural ideals were fully met, there would be no need to speculate about which outcomes were required as a matter of justice, for *whatever* outcome was selected as the result of that process would be just by definition. Rather, we should rely on the idea of *imperfect procedural justice*, defining the just policy outcome in terms of independent criteria in principles of distributive justice, acknowledging (unlike *perfect procedural justice*) that the process we employ does not guarantee an independently defined just outcome, but aims for an approximately fair process in order to minimize injustice in policy.

Is the Kyoto Protocol Unfair?

The primary case made by U.S. critics against the Kyoto Protocol as an unfair agreement is based on the protocol's exemption of developing nations from the first round of mandatory emissions caps. This exemption, which dates back to the 1992 *UNFCCC* declaration that the industrialized countries should "take the lead" in accepting the first round of emissions caps in any climate regime and was explicitly reaffirmed with the 1995 Berlin Mandate, has been repeatedly cited by Congress and the George W. Bush administration in opposition to the protocol and, by extension, to the *UNFCCC* process itself. For example, the Byrd-Hagel Resolution justifies its threatened rejection of the treaty by claiming that "the proposals under negotiation, because of the disparity of treatment between Annex B Parties and Developing Countries and the level of required emission reductions, could result in serious harm to the United States economy." Bush, elaborating on these reasons but framing them explicitly in terms of fairness, explains his 2001 decision to formally withdraw from participation in the protocol, claiming:

> I oppose the Kyoto Protocol because it exempts 80 percent of the world, including major population centers such as China and India, from compliance, and would cause serious harm to the U.S. economy. The Senate's vote, 95–0, shows that there is a clear consensus that the Kyoto Protocol is an unfair and ineffective means of addressing global climate change concerns.[9]

Both the Senate resolution, in its reference to the "disparity of treatment" between developing and industrialized nations, and the president's stated justification for withdrawal invoke the treaty's unfairness as a primary objection. But is this exemption, as its critics charge, unfair? It would clearly be unwise and ultimately self-defeating for a global climate regime to permanently exempt developing countries from mandatory emissions caps. The IPCC estimates that leakage—GHG-producing activities migrating from Annex B to non-Annex B nations—would range from 5 to 20 percent with developing country exemptions, meaning that if Annex B nations achieved the mandatory 5 percent emissions decrease from the 1990 baseline, these gains would be offset through leakage with between 0.25 and 1 percent increases from non-Annex B countries. In addition, those developing countries that were initially exempted from binding emissions caps are also those with the highest current rates of emissions intensity as well as some of the world's highest rates of emissions growth. While emissions in the industrialized nations have grown by an average of 1.2 percent per year since 1990, they are increasing at three times that rate in non-Annex B nations. At projected rates of increase, total emissions from developing nations will surpass those of industrialized ones in coming decades. Developing nations will eventually need to be brought under a global cap, and controls on emissions increases in the near term will make compliance with that cap more tenable in the longer term. Without emissions caps placed on such populous countries as India and China, any gains from proactive efforts within industrialized countries could be offset by corresponding emissions increases from those nations without caps.

Those nations that had accepted binding caps would be required to impose significant limits on allowable emissions for those GHG-producing industries doing business within their borders, significantly raising the costs of their operations and thereby creating incentives for those industries to relocate from nations with binding caps into those developing nations without them, a phenomenon known as "the race to the bottom" for its disincentives against enforcement of costly labor and environmental standards. Not only would such a permanent exemption cause industrialized nations to lose more manufacturing jobs and revenue to developing countries, such as China and India, but it would also miss the opportunity to require these industries to adopt the kinds of modern, low-emissions technologies that might ultimately reduce global emissions, instead causing GHG leakage from countries with emissions caps to ones without them and producing no net benefit for climate. The only effective way to ensure that high-emissions industries do not simply migrate to those nations without emission caps is to require universal participation in a regime of mandatory caps. If this is what is meant by those objecting to the developing country exemptions that were granted under the Kyoto Protocol, then those critics would have a point, though not one about fairness.

The objection sketched above and cited by Congress and the president as implicating the treaty's fairness has to do with the regime's efficacy, not its fairness. While the exemptions may *also* be unfair, the above analysis provides no reasons for thinking so. More likely, what is meant by those critics is a different kind of claim: "These exemptions, with the incentives they create for our domestic industry to relocate overseas, are bad *for us* and so we cannot support them," an objection that has to do with neither fairness nor the overall efficacy of the treaty, and that is found alongside the fairness claim in both the Senate resolution and the president's justification for withdrawal. Though such sentiments featured less prominently in congressional debates over NAFTA, CAFTA, and U.S. membership in the World Trade Organization—all of which likewise encouraged industry migration overseas—the debates leading up to Byrd-Hagel, in which business migration to India and China was repeatedly expressed as a major concern, suggest that this worry about losing the nation's manufacturing base and not some broader concerns with fairness or cosmopolitan justice was behind the objection, and the language of fairness was merely a superfluous embellishment.

Both of these are valid concerns—legislators should be interested in the adverse effects of treaties on the domestic economy as well as the effects of GHG leakage on the efficacy of a global climate regime—but neither directly indicts those exemptions as unfair. Some mitigation costs are inevitable if a climate regime is to be effective, and the United States would be required to bear considerable abatement and adaptation costs in any global regime that was genuinely fair, so in this way the economic costs argument runs directly contrary to the fairness claim. Critics cannot simultaneously demand that the climate treaty be fair, effective, and inexpensive to the United States, for a fair treaty must allocate costs in proportion to national responsibility and capability or must advance cosmopolitan justice, all of which require the United States to bear a significant share of costs. As already observed, the climate convention, if it is to enjoy requisite international support, must be fair as well as effective, and these two goals are mutually reinforcing: Its fairness is necessary to ensure its efficacy, by promoting the willing participation of those bound by the regime's terms, and it must be effective in order to avoid unfairness, by mitigating the projected effects of climate change. Economic impacts must be considered within these terms; they are acceptable insofar as they are necessary for sufficiently reducing emissions, and they must allocate the costs of emissions abatement fairly. Given the importance of fairness in a workable climate regime, let us next consider whether the decision to assign mandatory emissions caps only to the world's industrialized countries is indeed, as its critics have alleged, unfair.

A Developing Country Perspective on Fairness

In response the Bush administration's allegations of unfairness, advocates of developing nations have aptly pointed out the significant gaps between those industrialized nations assigned binding caps under the Kyoto Protocol and those developing nations exempted from them in their respective per capita GHG emissions as well as their widely disparate national standards of living, which comprise the two factors justifying differential treatment under the *UNFCCC*'s "common but differentiated responsibilities and respective capabilities" model. In a response by the Delhi-based Centre for Science and Environment to Bush's claims of unfairness from his speech announcing withdrawal from the Kyoto Protocol, these global disparities are highlighted as being morally relevant:

> The total carbon dioxide emissions from one U.S. citizen in 1996
> were 19 times the emissions of one Indian. U.S. emissions in total

are still more than double those from China. At a time when a large
part of India's population does not even have access to electricity,
Bush would like this country to stem its "survival emissions," so that
industrialized countries like the U.S. can continue to have high
"luxury emissions." *This amounts to demanding a freeze on global
inequity, where rich countries stay rich, and poor countries stay poor, since
carbon dioxide emissions are closely linked to GDP growth.*[10]

Several normative claims are presented here, and they are worth considering
with some care, because they have implications for the design of a fair or just
climate regime. First, it is claimed that the high per capita emissions rates of
industrialized nations constitute a morally relevant difference between them
and developing nations such as India that warrant differential mitigation burdens; and that those high emissions are causally responsible for climate change
and therefore connote moral responsibility for addressing it through assigned
GHG emissions reductions. Second, the above reply distinguishes between a
basic minimum level of GHG emissions that all need in order to survive ("survival emissions") and those that go beyond this threshold, instead resulting
from activities usually associated with affluence ("luxury emissions"), arguing
that the former ought to be given priority over the latter, and that Bush's objection fails to adequately recognize that priority. Finally, it asserts a right for
nations such as India to develop, increasing their national and per capita GHG
emissions at the same time that those industrialized nations that were assigned
emissions caps under the protocol are required to decrease theirs.

In the first claim, justice is seen as requiring remedial responsibility or liability to be assigned in proportion to causal responsibility, measured by the
degree to which various nations have contributed to the increasing concentrations of atmospheric GHGs that cause the harm associated with climate change.
Generally referred to as the *polluter pays* principle—a standard that is usually
based in strict liability, though it need not be—this claim is well established in
both philosophy and law, even if increasingly unpopular in U.S. public policy.
Similar to *retributive justice*, where punishment of offenders is justified on the
theory that crime creates an imbalance against society that can be redressed
only by the imposition of some kind of penalty that is proportionate to the
offense, and to *restorative justice*, which instead treats offense as primarily
wronging the victim rather than the state and so requires restitution to be paid
by the offender to the victim as a matter of justice, the polluter pays principle is
also distinct from both. Since it is concerned only with liability and not with the
finding of fault—a distinction explored further in chapter 5—the requirement
that polluters pay for damage that they cause need not be seen as actual

punishment, which requires moral blame as well as attributions of fault, nor is it exactly restorative since the costs to be assumed by the polluter need not necessarily reimburse the victims for harm they suffer as a consequence of the polluter's actions. The polluter pays principle is, though, here being treated as a requirement of justice.

In addition, the above rebuttal to Bush claims that, in assessing causal responsibility for climate change, national average per capita emissions (which controls for national population size) and not aggregate national emissions (which does not) ought to be the standard used for determining national liability. Even if India, which has a much larger population than does the United States, was to produce the same total emissions (which it does not), this standard would recommend attributing much more causal responsibility, and therefore also more liability, to the United States than to India, because the former has per capita emissions rates 19 times higher than the latter. The rebuttal asserts a right to a basic minimum level of per capita GHGs ("survival emissions"), below which nations cannot be held responsible for causing climate change and so do not deserve the be assigned liability for its mitigation, but above which (with "luxury emissions") they begin to incur liability for their role in causing climate change. India, therefore, cannot be faulted or assigned liability for causing climate change, since its average citizen produces only survival emissions (or so, at least, is implied), but the United States can and must be faulted for causing the problem, so must pay the costs of its mitigation. This idea that persons have a right to emit some minimum level of survival emissions has much to recommend it, and this is considered further below, but first let us consider the third claim from the above rebuttal. It likewise asserts a kind of right—one to development, held by developing nations such as India—though one with more extensive implications for assigning national emissions caps.

If we suppose that such nations as India have a right to develop, then we must also suppose that they have a right to emit GHGs at a per capita level considerably above the level of survival emissions, and one much closer to those granted to industrialized nations. The claim made on behalf of such a right, and a recurrent one within the climate convention, invokes the normative ideal of equity, which is to be applied either to living standards or to GHG emissions, or both. When so applied, it becomes clear what this claim is asserting: that the current worldwide distribution of wealth is highly inequitable and is reflected in highly unequal national emissions rates, that justice demands these inequities be reduced, and that imposing emissions caps on developing nations such as India at levels that are too low to allow for industrialization and other forms of development would in effect freeze the world's nations in their present state of development, allowing rich countries to continue producing per capita emissions at rates far higher than those in developing nations, reserving the benefits of high emissions for those nations that are currently among the world's affluent, and preventing their spread elsewhere.

Emissions Caps and the "Right to Develop"

As Thomas Athanasiou and Paul Baer point out, assigning fair and equitable emissions caps to developing nations need not be justified on principled grounds alone, though these are also important, since "a climate treaty that indefinitely restricts a Chinese (or Indian) to lower emissions than an American (or European) will not be accepted as fair and, finally, will not be accepted at all."[11] Neither India nor China would or should accept any climate convention that assigns them per capita emissions caps that are too low to allow for industrialization or higher consumption rates, since these would effectively constitute a barrier to development. On the other hand, no climate regime that excludes India and China from all GHG emission limits stands a chance of arresting the current growth in global emission rates. Normative concerns based in the "common but differentiated responsibilities and respective capabilities" model may have been the stated justification for the decision to exempt developing nations from mandatory caps during the first compliance period, but also significant was the desire on the part of the Annex B countries to defer discussion of the incendiary question of how high or low to set any assigned per capita GHG caps in India and China if they were to be included under the first round of binding caps. Resolving this problem to the satisfaction of both industrialized and developing nations would have been far more difficult than simply deferring the question entirely, as was accomplished by exempting the latter from any mandatory caps, since basing future caps for China or India on their 1990 baseline emissions would have raised valid objections about denying rights to develop.

Developing countries would not have accepted caps that represented per capita emissions rates that amount to a mere fraction of the emissions allowed within industrialized nations, as in basing them on the 1990 baseline, but neither could they be assigned caps set at levels allowed for Europe and Japan, let alone the United States, for this would allow for significant increases in worldwide emissions even with Annex B nations meeting their assigned targets. In China, where there are eight motor vehicles for every 1,000 people, or in India where there are seven, emission caps comparable to those assigned to the United States—where there are 767 increasingly inefficient automobiles for every 1,000 people—would obviously be unfair. As Athanasiou and Baer note: "We cannot hope to find justice in a world where the poor come to live as the rich do today, for there is not world enough. There will have to be some other kind of solution. There will, indeed, have to be new dreams on all sides, and the rich, in particular, will have to make those dreams possible by learning to share."[12] Limits on the absorptive capacity of the atmosphere require that increases in allowable per capita emissions from developing nations such as India and China be accompanied by even larger decreases in allowable per capita emissions in the industrialized nations, given their smaller populations, in order simply to freeze global emissions levels, to say nothing of significantly reducing them, which is seen as necessary to fulfill the *UNFCCC*'s mandate of avoiding dangerous interference with the planet's climate system.

Denying developing countries sufficient emissions allowances for their development would have been hugely unfair and unacceptable to them, but adjusting the assigned emissions allowances within the industrialized nations to reflect significant per capita increases in India and China while allowing the same global aggregate emissions levels would have been tremendously unpopular and even less likely to be accepted by the relevant parties. Opening up the question of developing country emissions caps would have forced the participants attending the convention to at least consider the "contraction and convergence" scenario urged by many climate activists, requiring the industrialized nations to significantly reduce their emissions (the *contraction*, with reductions much steeper than those prescribed under the Kyoto Protocol) in order for developing nations to eventually be allowed per capita emissions caps equal to those in industrialized nations (the *convergence*). As Athanasiou and Baer note, ecological limits will not allow for convergence without contraction, and the former is a demand for equity that is inseparable from the demands of efficacy contained in the latter. At the climate conferences, temporarily exempting developing nations from emissions caps seemed a superior strategy to trying to convince either developing countries to accept limits on development or industrialized ones to accept contraction.

Exempting developing countries from the initial round of binding GHG emissions caps may have been politically expedient, but is it unfair to industrialized countries such as the United States, as the George W. Bush administration has alleged? Here, it is helpful to view a climate regime as essentially a decision about how to allocate mitigation and compensation costs, and to rely on theories of justice and responsibility for assistance in determining their fair distribution. As noted above, the polluter pays principle offers a responsibility-based account of the proper distribution of costs: Those who are responsible for causing the problem through their historical emissions are the ones that should pay, and in proportion to those historical emissions. While home to 40 percent of the planet's population, China and India have together contributed only 9 percent of accumulated anthropogenic GHGs, compared with more than 30 percent by the United States, which has less than 5 percent of world population. By a strict liability version of the polluter pays principle, the United States should bear 30 percent of total mitigation costs and China and India a combined 9 percent. As the *UNFCCC* acknowledges, the world's industrialized countries, which are together responsible for more than 75 percent of historical emissions though comprising only 20 percent of the world's population, bear primary responsible for causing global climate change and so, by this principle, ought to be assigned primary liability for its remedy. But should they accept *all* of the responsibility and liability for the problem, presuming this to be the effect of exempting developing country emissions from caps? Though the average Indian produces significantly less climate-changing gas than does the average American, they contribute *some* GHGs into the atmosphere. Doesn't justice demand that India accepts *some* costs, proportional to its historical emissions?

It may or it may not, depending on which version of the "survival emissions" claim is most defensible. A weak version of this claim holds Indians significantly *less* responsible, but still responsible, for causing climate change, therefore requiring them as a matter of justice to bear *some* of the costs of its remedy, while a strong version (and the one implied by the rebuttal) would maintain that Indians are not responsible at all for causing climate change, and therefore ought to be assigned *no* remedial burdens. The argument for the weak version is based on a strict liability version of the polluter pays principle, where liability is assigned in proportion to historical GHG emissions, but how might a defense of the strong version be formulated? The answer is implied by the distinction between "survival" and "luxury" emissions: It posits some basic minimum level of emissions that each person may emit without being assessed liability, and assigns national liability based on the total amount of historical emissions emitted above this minimum. It claims that mitigation costs should be assigned to each nation based on its historical share of total luxury emissions, exempting survival emissions from this formula. If the rebuttal's implication that such developing countries as India and China have historically produced only survival emissions and not luxury emissions is true, then they would bear no responsibility for causing climate change, and hence can be attributed no liability. At minimum, their share of liability would be significantly less by this fault-based standard than under strict liability.

How might this minimum be calculated, and on what basis should we suppose that India's per capita emissions fall below it? One method would be to determine the total annual GHG emissions that could be safely absorbed by the planet's carbon sinks and divide that sum by global population, yielding a per capita emissions rate that all persons could safely produce without causing any adverse climate-related effects and so necessitating no liability. Here, per capita emissions beyond this point could be identified as those responsible for caus-ing climate change, while those below the threshold could be treated as benign. The distinction between survival and luxury emissions implies a slightly differ-ent approach, however. Here, the basic minimum is calculated by a determina-tion of how much a person must be allowed to emit in order to meet their basic human needs and to which all persons would therefore be entitled as a matter of basic rights, even if the world's population producing GHGs at this rate would still contribute to the increasing atmospheric concentrations that cause climate change. Can this strong version of the claim be defended, and if so, which of these two methods of calculating a basic minimum below which emis-sions confer no liability best approximates ideals of justice?

Under a fault-based standard, it would be difficult to justify attaching liabil-ity to persons that are responsible only for some minimal quantum of survival emissions, without which they could not meet their basic needs and would not survive. No person can be faulted for acts that are necessary for survival, because they cannot plausibly be expected to refrain from committing them, or as Kant famously put the same point, *"ought* implies *can."* Fault cannot plausibly be assigned to persons producing only survival emissions, and they would also lack the necessary remedial capacity for being assigned liability without fault, since they cannot reduce their emissions any further. These observations do not yet specify what the basic minimum threshold emission level ought to be and so cannot yet release the average Indian from possible liability for climate change mitigation burdens altogether, but they do weigh in favor of the strong version of the claim about the relevance of average national per capita emis-sions to assessments of national liability, urging a fault-based standard of liabil-ity rather than the strict liability that is commonly associated with the polluter pays principle. Liability should be assigned in proportion to causal responsibil-ity modified by a determination of how much of a nation's total emissions are above some per capita basic minimum, rather than above absolute zero per capita emissions.

These assessments of the fairness of the Kyoto Protocol have thus far relied on the polluter pays principle, but there are several other considerations that weigh against its straightforward application to the climate case. As considered further in chapter 5, assigning mitigation burdens based on a nation's histori-cal emissions appears to hold some persons responsible for the actions of oth-ers, as contemporaries are faulted for the emissions-producing acts of those born earlier. Either individual persons in such cases are being held vicariously liable—or liable for the fault of others—or else entire nations are being held collectively responsible for some set of acts, both of which raise philosophical problems that require further examination before we can accept them. Chapter 6 considers the roles played by knowledge and ignorance in assessments of responsibility—whether, for example, we can hold persons or nations responsible for emissions if they are unaware of any harmful consequences that might follow from them—which may limit our use of those historical emissions that were released prior to the first IPCC assessment report or some other point at which all should know the harmful effects of such actions. Before we consider these problems, however, we must consider several other criteria that have been proposed as the basis for assessing national GHG emissions.

The *UNFCCC* proposes a hybrid standard by which liability is assigned according to three criteria: equity, historical responsibility, and the respective capabilities of nations to reduce their emissions, where the latter is a function of national wealth, current GHG emission patterns, and potential for improvement in energy and transportation infrastructure. Similarly, Eileen Claussen and Lisa McNeilly of the Pew Center on Global Climate Change propose a hybrid standard based on responsibility for emissions, ability to pay for mitigation, and opportunity to reduce emissions, where nations ranked higher on all three criteria are assigned the first and most stringent emissions caps, while those scoring lower are gradually brought under caps later.[13] Equity is discussed in more detail below, but the focus on capacity for improvement deserves some mention here. Attributions of liability do not always entail fault, and sometimes the liable parties are other than the ones responsible for causing some injury for which liability is assessed, merely because they are in the best position to assist. For example, liability for famine relief may be assigned to affluent nations that are most able to help, even if they are in no way responsible for causing the problem, which might instead owe to the actions of the corrupt government of an impoverished country. Responsibility and capability often identify different liable parties, so the differences between these two standards warrant some further examination.

Responsibility versus Capability as the Criterion of Liability

The "capabilities" model has much to recommend it, though its value is based on neither the ideals of responsibility nor equity, and it has indirect implications for distributive justice. What makes one nation more capable of reducing its emissions than another? One measure is relative wealth, since an affluent nation has more economic resources to spare, with fewer of its resources spent on providing essential goods, so this surplus wealth could be deployed on GHG-reducing technologies or on reducing its consumption with fewer welfare losses than in a poorer country. Another measure is the relative efficiency of its energy and transportation infrastructure, since the costs of upgrading an already-efficient system are likely to be higher per unit of GHG reductions than in a nation with a relatively inefficient system. Finally and causally related to the first two measures, a nation with high current per capita emissions is likely to be more capable of reducing its emissions than one with currently low emissions, in terms of costs per unit of GHG reduction.

Hypothetically, at least, a capabilities-based approach promotes efficiency, achieving the greatest results at the lowest cost, since it gives priority to those emissions reduction projects that can be achieved most cheaply and easily, and efficiency is an instrumental value for promoting a climate regime's efficacy, if not its fairness. However, the flexible compliance measures that were included in the Kyoto Protocol—Joint Implementation, the Clean Development Mechanism, and emissions trading—already promote efficiency by allowing nations to meet part of their assigned emissions cuts by investing in GHG-reducing projects elsewhere or by transferring resources to those with unused emissions credits. With these measures in place, basing national emissions shares on indices of unequal relative national capabilities offers no unique efficiency advantage, because the flexibility measures already provide for efficiency aims. What matters for efficiency is which emission reduction projects are undertaken, not who is required to pay for them. The capabilities criterion may prioritize projects in terms of their relative efficiency in reducing emissions, but it provides no independent ground for assigning those nations found to be most capable of reducing their emissions the costs of doing so.

The main value served by basing the assignment of national mitigation burdens on capabilities rather than responsibility, then, is not efficiency but political expedience: In order to produce the necessary assent to the terms of the agreement, costs needed to be dispersed among nations more equally than might have been required by considerations of responsibility alone, minimizing the objections of those nations bearing the largest share of causal responsibility, which must be brought on board if the regime is to be effective. Hence, the Kyoto Protocol assigned all of the relatively affluent industrialized nations reduction targets based on 1990 baseline emissions, with variation in assigned percentage reductions based loosely on respective national capabilities, and exempted developing countries from such burdens altogether, also based partly in capabilities and partly on fairness. Insofar as the capabilities approach bases assigned emissions reductions on relative levels of national wealth, given that more affluent nations can more easily afford to undertake GHG reduction projects than can poorer ones even if these projects are not the most efficient ones available, it can indirectly promote equity through the climate regime by allocating greater mitigation burdens to the affluent and fewer to the poor.

In order to highlight the contrasting views of fairness embodied within the responsibility-based model and that within an equity-based model, consider two hypothetical countries: "Pollutia" and "Efficistan." Pollutia is heavily industrialized, has far higher per capita GHG emission rates, but is nonetheless poorer than its neighbor Efficistan, whose information economy and high-efficiency infrastructure have allowed it to keep its per capita GHG emissions significantly lower at the same time that its citizens enjoy higher levels of economic prosperity. The responsibility model would base a climate regime on their respective historical emissions, assigning Pollutia steeper cuts, and therefore greater mitigation costs, on account of its greater causal responsibility. By coincidence (though this need not necessarily be the case), efficiency considerations would recommend the same, for the most cost-effective GHG reduction opportunities would also be found in Pollutia, with Efficistan having already undertaken GHG-minimizing projects. On the other hand, equity considerations would demand that Efficistan be assigned higher mitigation costs than its neighbor, as would a capabilities standard, not because it is more responsible for causing the problem but because assigning costs in this way would reduce the inequality between these two countries and allocate the costs of climate change mitigation in a manner that benefits the least advantaged rather than "aggravate existing disparities" between the two countries. In order for Efficistan to most efficiently reduce its combined GHG emission, it might be allowed to meet its targets by investing in ecological modernization projects in Pollutia as well as within its borders.

Which of the two models generates the fairer outcome? In both cases, emissions would be reduced by the same amount and would involve largely the same projects (undertaken in Pollutia). To the extent that we see the climate regime as applying principles of retributive justice—assigning mitigation burdens as a kind of punishment for bad behavior—we would favor the responsibility model, though its allocation on the basis of causal responsibility need not imply any moral blame on the part of Pollutians nor be overtly punitive. Instead, if we view the respective development paths taken by the two countries as faultless—until recently, let's say, no one knew that Pollutia's high emissions caused any problems—our support for the responsibility model diminishes. Should we learn that Efficistan's relatively low emissions were the result of pure luck rather than any sort of deliberate choices made by past or current citizens—suppose its low emissions and high wealth were the consequence of abundant hydropower and mineral resources that it exploited without sharing with its neighbor while Pollutia was forced to rely on coal for its energy and heavy manufacturing in order to create commodities to trade for needed mineral resources, so that the average person born in Efficistan faced much more favorable life prospects than his or her counterpart born across the border through no personal accomplishment or merit nor from the fault of anyone else—the equity model appears more appropriate. The main difference in outcome between the two models involves neither total emissions rates nor the specific projects undertaken in order to achieve them, but the effect of the climate regime on the initial economic inequality between the two nations. The responsibility model would widen this inequality by placing greater burdens on the poorer nation, while the distributive justice model would narrow it by doing the opposite.

Based largely on political expedience but due also in part to some valid concerns about holding nations morally responsible for their historical emissions, the hybrid system of basing national liability on "equity and their common but differentiated responsibilities and respective capabilities" was adopted under the *UNFCCC*. In practice, distinguishing between those GHGs resulting from a nation's intentional acts and choices, thus recommending the responsibility-based model, and those that result from luck alone, weighing in favor of an equity model, would be extraordinarily difficult, and the *UNFCCC* text provides little guidance as to the weight to be given to these three separate criteria in allocating national GHG mitigation burdens. The Claussen and McNeilly proposal offers only a rough scale, where the three criteria are added together and the world's nations are grouped into three broad categories, indicating the priority with which they are required to reduce emissions. As discussed above, the capabilities criterion has little independent value to recommend it once the efficiency-promoting "flexibility" measures are included, but the other two criteria must be balanced in some way, because they often lead to divergent prescriptions for the allocation of mitigation costs. As discussed in chapters 5 and 6, several problems surrounding holding nations responsible for their GHG emissions may affect the extent to which we may validly base such assignments on responsibility, and the problems surrounding the concept of cosmopolitan justice examined in chapter 3 may affect the extent to which principles of distributive justice may validly be applied to global inequities. For now, though, we may simply observe that a fair climate regime is one that appropriately combines these two models of fairness.

Returning to the question of whether or not it was unfair to exempt developing countries such as India and China from the first round of binding emission caps, neither responsibility nor equity considerations generate much of an argument that a temporary exemption would be unfair—nor, for that matter, would the capabilities criterion—since these countries are responsible for only a small fraction of world historical emissions, with much of these consisting of survival emissions, and with these nations enjoying considerably lower standards of living than those Annex B nations that were assigned binding caps under the Kyoto Protocol. The reasons for adopting this two-tiered system, in which only industrialized countries initially accept binding emissions caps in the initial implementation period while developing countries are resolved to be brought under a global cap at some unspecified future point, are compelling enough: The former have disproportionately contributed to the problem and partly as a result have adequate resources for mitigating it. They emitted an average of 3.2 metric tons of carbon per capita in 1990 (among them, the United States was highest at 6.0 metric tons), while non-Annex B nations averaged 0.4 metric tons.[14] By contrast, gross domestic product in the industrialized nations of the Organization for Economic Co-operation and Development averaged $22,020 per capita in 1999, compared with $3,530 in developing nations.[15] If a fair allocation is to be based on either equity or the UNFCCC's "common but differentiated responsibilities and respective capabilities" model of fairness, then the industrialized nations of the North must shoulder nearly the entire mitigation burden, at least in the initial phase.

Contrary to the assertion of Kyoto critics, there appears to be nothing unfair to the United States or to other industrialized countries in assigning the initial round of mandatory emissions caps only among those nations with the highest historical and current per capita emissions, whether fairness is conceived in terms of either responsibility or capabilities (or, as discussed below, equity). Such an exemption of developing countries from mandatory caps would, if permanent, be clearly imprudent and would very likely undermine the climate regime's efficacy in the long run, as such developing nations as India and China industrialize and in doing so increase their national GHG emissions without legal limits. Assigning fair per capita emissions caps for these countries may prove to be the biggest challenge to be faced by the global climate regime, however, for the main arguments against equal per capita emissions shares—considered in chapter 7—all fail, but the "contraction and convergence" scenario of equal per capita emissions quotas would require the world's affluent nations to reduce their emissions far below the levels set under the Kyoto Protocol if the UNFCCC's mandate of avoiding dangerous interference in the planet's climatic system is to be met. This requirement would constitute a significant burden on such nations as the United States, but the fact of its high costs does not impugn its fairness. As Athanasiou and

Baer summarize their responsibility- and capability-based case for equal per capita emissions shares:

> In 1990, the industrialized countries were responsible for 75 percent of all CO_2 emissions, as well as 79 percent of the CO_2 still in the air and 88 percent of the human-caused warming. They must pay as well because their riches trace back to a past in which the world was open. And they must pay because only they can, and because if they don't, the warming will quite certainly prove unstoppable.[16]

Conclusions

From the distinction between deserved and undeserved inequality in egalitarian justice theory, along with the aspirations toward justice embodied within the climate convention, we might posit several preliminary observations concerning the justice and injustice of climate change. Persons are now being born into a world of enormous and widening socioeconomic inequality, where the vast majority of the disparity in advantage and disadvantage among the world's persons can be traced to the morally arbitrary "accidents of birth" that constitute undeserved endowment-sensitive inequality. A world that allows this, we might say, is highly unjust, but this does not yet say anything of interest to the climate debate for it does not tell us what to do to remedy this injustice. From this highly unequal and unjust initial distribution of goods and bads in the world, the projected consequences of global climate change threaten to "aggravate existing disparities" (to borrow a phrase from the IPCC) by worsening the conditions and opportunities of the world's poor, in both absolute terms and relative to the world's affluent. First, then, we might observe that climate change takes an already unjust global distribution and exacerbates its undeserved inequality to the detriment of the least advantaged. Second, while climate change does result from voluntary acts and choices—things for which persons may be held responsible—those persons most responsible for causing the problem are expected to suffer the least climate-related harm, while those least causally responsible are expected to suffer the most damage. Third, those acts that are largely responsible for causing climate change—fossil fuel combustion and deforestation—simultaneously benefit those already affluent and harm the poor, in effect transferring welfare from poor to rich, and again aggravating existing disparities.

Aside from the objectionable global inequality that currently stands to be exacerbated unless the world can design and implement a fair and effective

GHG abatement regime, the primary distributive problem involves the alloca-tion of the earth's atmospheric capacity to absorb GHGs among the world's nations or citizens. The global atmosphere is a finite good that, unlike Rawlsian primary goods, cannot be increased by allowances for unequal shares, and one that may appropriately be considered as a global primary good. The critical importance of its capacity to produce a stable climate cannot be underesti-mated, because it is absolutely vital for the continuance of life on this planet and instrumental to human flourishing. While the atmosphere itself is not something that can be parceled into shares and allocated among the world's people—there is, after all, only one atmosphere, which must be shared among all the planet's inhabitants—its capacity to absorb GHGs (a function that is technically performed by terrestrial carbon sinks, which provide the planet's respiratory functions of absorbing carbon and emitting oxygen, but which for parsimony are called here *atmospheric absorptive capacity*) is something that can at least conceptually be so divided in the form of GHG emissions caps. One central task of a global climate regime is to allocate this capacity, and a just regime must do so according to principles of distributive justice.

Since national GHG emission rates are closely correlated with industrial development and national wealth, if imperfectly so, we may assume that nations all prefer higher allowable emissions rather than lower ones, especially as lower caps divert resources from other welfare-enhancing projects and toward com-pliance with emissions limits. Moreover, the atmosphere is, of all planetary natural resources, the one that comes closest to being a pure public good in that GHGs released anywhere have similar effects, making it a common as well as an essential resource. Like all finite resources, it is possible to overallocate the planet's atmosphere by releasing excessive aggregate levels of emissions, at least for a limited time. Since more GHGs are currently being emitted in a given year than the atmosphere can absorb, atmospheric concentrations are consequently increasing, as they have since the beginning of the Industrial Revolution. While it is too late to even contemplate returning to the preindus-trial equilibrium of 280 ppm of atmospheric CO_2, there remains a pressing need to stabilize atmospheric GHG concentrations at some level at which the most serious harm of climate change can be avoided, and this entails some global limits on annual emissions. The first task for a global climate regime is to determine the total amount of annual emissions that can be safely produced each year—a problem for which justice theory offers little direct guidance, even if indirect imperatives can be found in considerations of intergenerational justice—and only then must it allocate shares of that total among the world's nations, a problem for which justice theory is well suited.

3

Climate Change and International Justice

As discussed in chapter 2, anthropogenic climate change is, in its causes and effects, unavoidably an international issue. Greenhouse gases (GHGs) produced anywhere in the world accumulate in the planet's atmosphere, producing the same heat-trapping effect regardless of their geographic origin. Once atmospheric GHG concentrations increase, their effects can be felt throughout the world, although these effects are expected to vary considerably among nations. According to the Intergovernmental Panel on Climate Change (IPCC), "the impacts of climate change will fall disproportionately upon developing countries and poor persons within all countries, and thereby exacerbate inequities in health status and access to adequate food, clean water, and other resources."[1] For the most part, the nations and peoples that are expected to bear the brunt of climate-related damage are among those least responsible for the GHG pollution causing climatic problems, and those that are the most responsible for current and historical GHG emissions are expected to suffer the least damage. If the *UNFCCC*'s mandate of avoiding dangerous interference with the planet's climatic system is to be met, the global politics of GHG abatement efforts will require international cooperation in order to set and enforce fair and effective national emissions caps and prevent cross-border leakage from undermining the efforts of those nations now undertaking significant emission reduction projects. All the world's nations and citizens are stakeholders and participants in what must be a fully global effort if the worst effects of what could be humanity's most pressing global threat are to be avoided.

Aside from the current lack of strong institutions of international governance for implementing and enforcing global environmental regulations such as those of the Kyoto Protocol, the primary political difficulties plaguing the international politics of climate change involve normative challenges posed by three main inequities involved in the causes and effects of climate change. The first concerns the relative causal responsibility of nations: Due to significantly varying levels of industrialization, urbanization, and other variables related to current and historical per capita GHG emissions among the world's nations, some nations are far more responsible than are others for contributing to climate change, but formally acknowledging this fact and instantiating it in policy have proven politically difficult. Many carbon-intensive activities that are associated with national affluence, such as industrialization and high rates of consumption, now stand to make poor nations even poorer by forcing them to bear the economic costs of climate change. Second, those nations that bear greater causal responsibility for anthropogenic climate change also tend to possess greater economic capabilities to undertake large-scale GHG reduction projects, marking a second kind of international inequity. The third inequity concerns the predicted harmful effects of climate change, which by IPCC estimates will be borne primarily by developing nations, which are far less causally responsible and economically able to undertake mitigation projects. Cooperative efforts to solve collective problems are easiest when all parties are equally responsible for causing the problem, stand to be equally affected by it, and are equally capable of solving it. With global climate change, significant inequality exists in all three of these areas, complicating the design and implementation of a fair and effective global climate regime considerably.

Taken together, these three kinds of inequity suggest that an analysis of climate change through the lens of egalitarian justice may provide the requisite conceptual framework for diagnosing the justice issues in global climate change and incorporating standards of justice into the design of a fair and effective global climate regime. As observed in chapter 2, egalitarian justice theory provides two conceptions of fairness to which the *UNFCCC* has aptly committed itself, with a responsibility-based model addressing historical or backward-looking assessments for those cases in which some kinds of inequality may be justified, such as attributions of liability for causing climate change, and an equity-based analysis that examines current distributions of goods in a manner that is more appropriate for allocating scarce resources independent of historical responsibility considerations, as in the assignment of national emissions caps. Taken together, these two normative models of fairness may be applied to climate policy issues in order to prescribe remedies to the global inequities that are part and parcel of the injustice of anthropogenic climate change, and to address the unequal levels of responsibility among nations for contributing to the problem. This chapter and the next examine several theoretical problems surrounding the distributive justice model in its liberal egalitarian form, and chapters 5 and 6 examine those surrounding the responsibility model.

If the principles of justice examined in chapter 2 could be applied to relations between nations or to interpersonal comparisons among all the world's people, then the resulting theory of *cosmopolitan justice* would assist in applying those fairness and equity ideals declared in the climate convention to the design of a just global climate regime. It would allow us, that is, to apply the premise of moral equality that underlies egalitarian justice theory to all the world's persons, rather than merely to all members of some society. Before we can validly apply egalitarian principles of justice to global climate policy, however, we must consider several theoretical challenges to the very existence of cosmopolitan justice: (1) the concept of state sovereignty a longstanding principle in international law and politics; (2) political realism, a school of thought in political science that maintains that the application of such normative ideals as justice to relations between nations is misguided; and (3) most formidable, a claim by the leading exponent of justice theory, John Rawls, that his principles apply only to the internal affairs within nations and cannot be extended to apply either to relations between nations or among all of the world's persons. Together, we can refer to these various challenges as *global justice skepticism*, since they share in common a rejection of cosmopolitan justice, if for quite different reasons and with distinct implications.

The first skeptical challenge involves the principle of *state sovereignty*, which weighs against the imposition of coercive international standards onto domestic political institutions, and which has historically been a fundamental principle of international law and politics. Although sovereignty enjoys a complicated current status, it nonetheless remains a powerful norm within both politics and philosophy and poses some difficulties for overcoming the resistance it implies to institutions of international governance and cooperation. The concept is examined further below, but note for now that it has the status of a prima facie case against interference by one nation, or a multinational organization such as the United Nations, in the internal affairs of another. Given that emissions caps, when assigned and enforced by a global regime—even when subsequently ratified by such domestic legislative bodies as the U.S. Senate— are considered by many to violate this principle, the achievement of international justice through an equity-based climate regime is likely to be frustrated unless sovereignty-based objections can be addressed. Moreover, the philosophical case for maintaining a strong version of state sovereignty in international politics, which rests on several distinct forms of communitarianism, objects to applying normative ideals to international issues such as climate policy, and we must consider these objections.

The second skeptical challenge involves the doctrine of *political realism*, especially as developed by contemporary neorealists, which straightforwardly rejects the application of normative principles such as justice to relations between nations—not overriding those ideals with a more powerful claim, as in the sovereignty objection, but denying that such ideals have any weight at all—claiming instead that the only legitimate aims underlying foreign policy or international law are the advancement of national economic or strategic interests. Realists that regard normative concerns as unjustified fictions in international politics have developed and disseminated a deep skepticism regarding such ideals as global justice, which are disparagingly relegated to naive idealists or else cynically wielded by realists when thought to serve national interests, and this rejection of the genuine reliance on normative ideals in international politics has influenced the way that political theorists and philosophers regard the application of such criteria to international affairs. We must consider the arguments for the realist variety of global justice skepticism, and consider whether it provides a decisive case against cosmopolitan justice.

Finally, a third skeptical challenge poses another obstacle to the international application of the norms of distributive justice, this time by the rejection of cosmopolitan justice by Rawls himself, in a set of arguments against cosmopolitan justice that were implied in his early work but made explicit in his 1999 *The Law of Peoples*. In adopting distributive justice as a guiding ideal for the design of a climate regime, the climate convention declares its commitment to treating all persons or peoples as equals, with none being regarded as intrinsically more or less important than others. This assumption about the moral equality of all humans, while compelling in its denial of unjustified discrimination and similar to the presumption of equality on which egalitarian justice theory is based, may export culturally specific moral standards, expand the justice community beyond its proper boundaries, and strain the motives that are necessary for recognizing and acting on obligations of justice. These limits on a justice community, with their implications for extending egalitarian assumptions across national borders, comprise the third problem in applying cosmopolitan justice to the design of a global climate regime.

State Sovereignty

Within international law, the concept of sovereignty has held since the 1648 Treaty of Westphalia that each nation's internal affairs ought to be the exclusive concern of its government and citizens, and that no other state may legitimately interfere with them. The principle of state sovereignty has a similarly long history in political thought, dating back at least to the Hobbesian claim that a singular and recognized common political authority is a necessary condition for the establishment of legal order as well as the basis on which conventional norms of justice might be formed. Although the argument from *Leviathan* is also taken as the basis for the doctrine of realism, its necessary association between a recognized common sovereign authority and binding normative standards likewise weighs against intervention within another state for the purpose of establishing or maintaining institutions of justice, a practice known as humanitarian intervention. The Hobbesian argument supports a version of sovereignty like that established at Westphalia: It holds that a sovereign ought to have exclusive authority over its own territory, wherein it alone may establish and enforce terms of justice. Since justice is assumed to have no independent existence outside of the standards created and enforced by an effective sovereign, there can be no justification for one state interfering with the internal affairs of another. The idea that one or more states may legitimately interfere in the affairs of others for the purpose of establishing cosmopolitan justice or promoting human rights is a much more recently conceived notion, and one that opposes both the legal principle of state sovereignty and its theoretical basis.

The principle of sovereignty, along with its counterpart principle of territorial integrity, is not without its current advocates and defenses, including, as Allen Buchanan notes, the practical necessity of a recognized state with effective jurisdiction over a bounded territory in order to establish and protect individual rights. Where competing claims to jurisdiction over the same territory exist, Buchanan observes, that conflict can undermine the incumbent political authority charged with protecting the rights of citizens, so any authority whose sovereignty over some territory was contested—as, for example, with another state interfering in its internal affairs and thereby challenging its claim of a monopoly over legitimate coercion—would encounter both legitimacy and enforcement problems, with the protection of rights a likely casualty. Because recognized internal political control of a nation-state's territory and social institutions is vital in establishing an effective legal order, which in turn is necessary for protecting individual rights and stabilizing expectations, territorial integrity allows a sovereign government unchallenged authority over its territory and hence "gives citizens an incentive to invest themselves sincerely and cooperatively in the existing political processes" and thus constitutes an essential condition for effective political participation.[2]

Building on such pragmatic concerns for maintaining the requisite social and political conditions for maintaining a just and well-ordered society, liberal nationalists[3] suggest that state sovereignty is essential for maintaining a distinct national identity as instrumental for developing individual autonomy. Undermining sovereignty or violating territorial integrity thus undermines the bases for citizenship and autonomy, about which justice is centrally concerned. Such liberal premises yield equivocal views about sovereignty and territorial integrity, as Buchanan notes, because these principles are subject to abuse by states attempting to resist external attempts to promote legitimate governments or protect threatened citizens. Buchanan rejects what he terms absolutist versions of the principles, which do not distinguish between legitimate and illegitimate states, in favor of progressive versions of sovereignty and territorial integrity that apply only to legitimate states. Similarly, while Rawls denies that principles of distributive justice apply across national borders, he rejects the absolutist version of sovereignty in favor of one that applies only to decent states, including illiberal ones, reserving the option to intervene in serious rights-abusing cases.[4]

How far might such a progressive interpretation go in justifying intervention by one state into the affairs of another? Two crucial distinctions set the boundaries for the application of these principles. Relying on Buchanan's progressive interpretation, we might define a legitimate state as one that generally recognizes and protects the human rights of its citizens and resident aliens, so that humanitarian intervention may be justified in cases where a state may not be threatening its neighbors but is nonetheless engaged in objectionable internal actions. More pertinent to the issue of sovereignty over climate policy, however, is the distinction between what is purely an internal affair within a given nation that ought therefore to be left to the exclusive control of that nation's legitimate government and what, on the other hand, constitutes an issue with sufficient external effects to justify outside interference. Climate policy, it would seem, cannot justifiably be described as purely an internal matter, because GHGs emitted anywhere have the same effects regardless of their geographic origin and therefore have the potential to harm those residing outside the nation-state's borders. This "spillover" effect turns what might otherwise be an issue of exclusively domestic concern into one in which other states become justifiably interested parties. Although few such transboundary issues existed at the time of the peace of Westphalia, the idea of sovereignty it spawned would not deny one state the prerogative to interfere with another if the first was somehow being threatened—whether directly, as through military force, or indirectly, through common resource-related scarcity—by the second.

Nonetheless, the principle of sovereignty poses a conceptual obstacle to the application of principles of cosmopolitan justice, since even Buchanan's progressive version denies that justice applies across borders, claiming instead that only serious violations of human rights, not merely violations of the norms of cosmopolitan justice, justify humanitarian intervention or secession. The global reach of climate change may defeat claims of sovereignty in principle, since national climate policy cannot validly be described as purely an internal matter subject to the exclusive authority of national governments rather than the coercive influence of a global regime, but the theoretical case for sovereignty sketched above nonetheless calls into question the validity of principles of cosmopolitan justice. Hobbesian sovereignty locates the origin of justice in social conventions, making the terms of justice culturally relative rather than universal, while moral cosmopolitanism claims justice to be the product of abstract reason, making its reach necessarily universal. As discussed further below, cosmopolitanism need not depend on an ethical universalism grounded in abstract reason and can instead arise from democratic norms applied to transboundary issues that transcend the borders and authority of nation-states. However, such skeptical challenges to the global reach of principles of egalitarian justice significantly limit the aims and scope of international institutions such as a global climate regime, since they regard justice as a normative concept that applies only within and not across national borders, preventing such a regime from taking the promotion of justice as among its objectives. Since this theoretical foundation for state sovereignty is substantially similar to the argument for realism, the two are considered together below. First, however, we must consider the claim that the principle of sovereignty may undermine the enforcement of international environmental standards such as those necessary to mitigate the adverse effects of global climate change.

Transboundary Problems and State Sovereignty

The principle of state sovereignty maintains that the internal affairs of a sovereign nation ought to be decided within that political community, presumably by members of the community (though sovereignty need not entail democracy), free from outside interference. While the most common critique against this principle relies on the existence of a set of universal human rights that no state may legitimately violate—justifying outside intervention in the interest of protecting those rights if it does—this is not the avenue pursued here. Instead, the focus is on the distinction between what can and cannot be justifiably insulated from outside interference by this principle. Specifically, I address the question of whether a nation's GHG emissions ought to be recognized as an exclusively internal policy issue to which the principle of state sovereignty might apply, or whether it presents an example of the sort of problem that necessitates international cooperation and thus defeats the case against interference.

The initial design of the U.S. federal system contained something like the principle of state sovereignty applied to the various formerly autonomous states in the union. The national government in the early decades of the republic was weak, with states given near-complete sovereignty over their internal affairs, but this arrangement soon proved unworkable. Goods produced, taxed, and regulated within one state would be sold in another state, generating conflicts over which states properly had authority over them. Two states might share a river as a common border, and disputes would arise over which state rightfully had jurisdiction over the management of the river. The solution to these problems, pragmatically worked out through a long series of judicial decisions, was to make an increasing proportion of rules at the national level and apply them uniformly across all states, leaving to the states all those matters not subject to the authority of the national government.

The most common occasion for the federal government limiting state sovereignty in this way involved *transboundary* problems, where some action or legislation in one state caused deleterious consequences in another. When air and water pollution flow across political borders, they displace the costs of one political jurisdiction's polluting activities, from which the first polity benefits, onto another, leading to what economists term an *externality*, but leading also to conflicts between states over the spillover effects of one state's lax regulatory standards onto another state, which suffers uncompensated costs of the first state's activities. The evolution of American federalism has been driven in part by the need to adequately respond to such problems.

In the development of U.S. antipollution laws, it has been primarily for this reason that federal standards have been adopted to ensure a minimum level below which states cannot sink in competition with one another for industrial development. When separate political jurisdictions are forced to compete for the economic benefits of industry by undercutting the economic and environmental regulations of neighboring jurisdictions, allowing industry to shop among various potential sites for those that allow for the lowest labor costs and require the lowest regulatory standards, the inevitable effect has been to encourage the sort of deregulation that benefits industry at the expense of its hosts. In those areas most desperate for economic development, "regulatory relief" and tax holiday packages are often made so generous in order to attract industrialization that the state and local governments offering them lose economically as well as environmentally, but are nonetheless so attracted by the desire to demonstrate some immediate results that they continue to offer them anyway. Curtailing transboundary problems to ensure that pollution leakage across borders does not undermine regulatory goals and to protect state and local authorities against the perverse incentives of this "race to the bottom," the federal government assumed regulatory responsibility for setting uniform national standards on most environmental issues—climate policy being a striking counterexample that has invited recent lawsuits to remedy[5]—and did this against the gravitational pull of state sovereignty and the force of precedent in constitutional law.

In addition to such practical concerns for regulatory uniformity, democratic theorists have suggested a model that partially incorporates the principle of state sovereignty but defines the appropriate jurisdiction for policy issues in terms of the stakeholders that they affect. David Held defends what he terms a "cosmopolitan project" from such a standard, for example, claiming that democratic norms no longer support sovereignty that coincides with the borders of nation-states:

> The idea of a political community of fate—of a self-determining collectivity—can no longer be meaningfully located within the boundaries of a single nation-state alone, as it could more reasonably be when nation-states were being forged. Some of the most fundamental forces and processes that determine the nature of life chances within and across political communities are now beyond the reach of individual nation-states.[6]

Held suggests that transboundary problems such as global climate change, where the policies of one state have profound effects on the welfare of those in others, create "overlapping communities of fate" that require new institutions of cosmopolitan democracy, globalizing governance along with the various welfare-affecting forces that are increasingly globalized. An illustration of political authority evolving to coincide with the scope of the problems it aims to govern can be found in the development of American federalism, which is less the product of deliberate design based on how best to govern and more the result of concrete historical circumstances and the occasional need to change existing arrangements. As previously noted, the powers of the national government were initially made subservient to those of the states, but over time, more and more public policy problems revealed themselves as national in scope, therefore requiring the reach and uniformity that is possible only through national policy and governance. Based largely on the multistate locus and scope of various problems and the problems this created, the evolution of American federalism has consisted, save for several recent exceptions, in a general trend toward the nationalization of regulatory policy. As a practical problem for governance, the governmental authority charged with setting public policy on a particular issue has generally evolved to coincide with the scope of that issue, where national government has claimed control over those issues that are national in scope, state governments have retained control over those issues that are limited to individual states, and local governments have been assigned those issues that are local in scope.

Behind these practical concerns, though, lies a democratic principle regarding the proper political jurisdiction for public policy problems: Problems that affect some group of persons ought to be decided by those persons, either directly or through their representatives. Not only does this fundamental principle of democracy capture the essence of democratic governance, but it looms large in all democratization efforts and suggests one tentative conclusion when it comes to considering political responses to climate change. In designing a political regime in order to address a policy issue such as climate, that regime must operate at the same level as the problem it aims to address, or it risks being undermined in its practical efficacy and democratic legitimacy by the transboundary problems noted above. Insofar as the rules issued by a regime require at least the assent of those bound by them, some participation by affected populations or their representatives becomes both practically necessary as well as a matter of procedural fairness, since enforcement of rules through force alone is often impractical and always objectionable on normative grounds. As already discussed, the problem of climate change is truly a global one; although the effects of climate change are expected to be uneven globally, no one is expected to be unaffected altogether. The proper political jurisdiction for an effective climate regime, then, must be international. Nations cannot opt out of participation in a climate regime, since they cannot refrain from causing climate change or from suffering climate-related harm.

The principle of state sovereignty is largely a relic of a bygone era in which significant transboundary issues did not exist, so the appropriate locus of decision-making authority rarely stretched beyond the nation-state, or the city-state before it. Now that such transboundary issues feature much more prominently in international politics, the original justification for state sovereignty—that some recognized common authority was necessary for establishing such norms as justice within some territory, and that conflicts among levels of governance would undermine such norms—must for practical and theoretical reasons give way to universal standards that apply across national boundaries and that require global political authorities.

Along with transboundary problems, the notion that all persons possess a common set of rights, regardless of whether these are recognized or protected by their governments—as most prominently expressed in the 1948 U.N. Declaration of Human Rights along with its subsequent extensions and clarifications—has likewise weakened the legitimacy of strong versions of the principle of state sovereignty. Incorporating these objections, we are left with a much weaker claim: that legitimate, rights-respecting nation-states ought to enjoy exclusive authority over policy issues that are entirely contained within their national borders. Because state sovereignty rests on the premise that the policy in question affects only residents of that territory with no spillover effects on others, and this premise fails to hold when it comes to climate change, the principle of sovereignty runs into direct conflict with the notion upon which it originated: that the proper authority for a problem includes all those affected by it. Regarded in this way, the sort of cosmopolitanism necessary for justifying a global climate regime need not rest on the moral universalism eschewed by communitarians or deny that national identity plays a crucial role in citizenship, as it shares a foundation with the principle of sovereignty in democratic norms that grant persons control over matters that coincide with communities of which they are a part. As such, it cannot indict efforts to design and implement a fair and effective global climate regime, for the main issues addressed by such a regime are international in scope and so transcend the exclusive jurisdiction of national governments, justifying a political response corresponding with the global scope of the problem.

Is Realist Skepticism Philosophically Defensible?

Insofar as it recognizes only the advancement of national interests as valid aims of political actors in international relations, realism necessarily rejects the consideration of such ideals as justice or the protection of human rights in foreign policy, except insofar as these might affect national interests. A realist might, for example, be concerned with the consequence of a policy that exacerbates global poverty if it proceeds to cause some persons residing among impoverished populations to become politically radicalized and hence to volunteer to act as suicide bombers against those nations they see as responsible for that poverty, but the concern would be motivated by those security threats rather than by any injustice endemic to global poverty in itself. Likewise, a realist might prefer to see climate talks produce a treaty with mandatory caps and timelines if national interests would be better served with a treaty than without one, but this preference would be based on a calculation only of the respective national costs and benefits of having versus not having a climate treaty in place, rather than by wider concerns about global justice. Adverse effects on other nations, whether of compliance with the treaty's terms or the climate-related costs of the failure to produce an agreement to limit GHG emissions, would not be included within the calculation. Only an *idealist* would define good or bad foreign policy in terms of its consequences for other nations, and this primary reliance on normative criteria is what realists unequivocally reject. A realist, then, acts in advancing national interests in the same manner as does an egoist in advancing self-interest; neither regards the interests of others as relevant considerations in choosing a course of action.

Many persons are, in fact, egoists. That is to say, they concern themselves only with their own selfish interests in deciding between alternative acts, disregarding as irrelevant to their choice the negative effects of alternative acts for others. As a result, they are entirely unmoved by appeals to fairness, which necessarily accounts for the interests of others, though they might invoke normative ideals if they believe that this would advance their own interests. An even higher percentage of delegates to international negotiations such as climate conferences are probably realists than are egoists within the general population, because several factors lend toward the appointment of realists to such positions. First, they are appointed by national governments, and they may consequently regard themselves as trustees of the nation-state with a duty to advance its interests first and foremost, and perhaps exclusively. Should they not feel so compelled to act as trustees from a sense of duty, they may either be directly elected or else have an indirect electoral connection as an appointee of an elected government, and so feel compelled to advance national interests not from a sense of duty but from a desire to secure reelection for themselves or for the party or administration they represent. Similarly, they may subscribe to the adversarial model of deliberation (or *pluralism*), where advocates of various opposing interests represent only their partial interests in a political forum, trusting that the policy that best serves the good of all emerges from this competition among partial interests, acting as egoists even if also motivated by concerns for others.

The evident fact that there are egoists in the world does not rule out the existence of justice or fairness between persons, and the likelihood that realists dominate climate talks cannot rule out the validity of applying such normative concepts to international affairs. The question here is not whether actual persons have certain beliefs or convictions; it is instead whether the realist skepticism about the validity of such normative concepts in international affairs can be justified, which is quite a different question. People can have all sorts of unjustified beliefs, and even act on them, but this does nothing to increase the validity of those beliefs, which must be supported by defensible reasons or arguments. Hence we ask: Can we *justifiably* apply normative criteria to international affairs such as anthropogenic climate change or to the design of a global climate change regime, or are realists justified in rejecting such criteria in international politics? In entertaining this question, let us start by examining the negative case against recognizing such ideals as valid terms for evaluating relations between nations, and then consider the positive case for their application.

The Hobbesian Foundation of Realism

When realists seek a scholarly foundation for their skepticism about the validity of normative ideals in international politics, they usually seek to ground their claims in the work of Thomas Hobbes. After all, the defining feature of the state of nature that Hobbes describes in *Leviathan* is that, in the absence of a recognized common authority, justice and injustice simply do not exist. In such a condition, where each is at war with every other, Hobbes counsels all to narrow their concerns to the egoistic pursuit of self-interest, free from any moral limits on action:

> To this war of every man against every man, this is also consequent;
> that nothing can be Unjust. The notions of Right and Wrong, Justice
> and Injustice have there no place. Where there is no common power
> there is no Law: where no Law, no Injustice. Force, and Fraud, are in
> war the two Cardinal virtues. Justice, and Injustice are none of the
> faculties neither of the Body, nor Mind. If they were, they might be in
> a man that were alone in the world, as well as his Senses, and
> Passions. They are Qualities, that relate to men in Society, not in
> Solitude.[7]

As Hobbes describes, the moral concepts of right and wrong and political concepts of justice and injustice wholly disappear in the context of war, giving way to mere advantage and disadvantage. Realists claim that international politics is, in effect, a state of nature or of anarchy, with no recognized "common power" and thus no law, no justice or injustice, and no possibility for cooperation. Hence, concern for self-interest—transformed into national interest in international relations—is paramount, and pure egoism, whether at the individual or national level, is best served by effectively wielding whatever instruments of power are available, which explains why "force and fraud" become virtues rather than vices in this natural condition.

This passage is widely cited by realists as justification for their rejection of normative concerns in international politics, and is often mistakenly taken as an endorsement by Hobbes of the unrestrained exercise of national power and disregard for other-regarding ideals such as justice in international affairs.

Articulating the intellectual foundation for contemporary realist antipathy toward institutions of international law and governance, Robert Kagan casts the disagreement between the United States and continental Europe over the 2003 Iraq war in terms of the latter's preferred vision of a Kantian republic of laws dedicated to eternal peace and the former's contrasting vision of a Hobbesian state of nature in which might makes right; or, as his sound-bite synopsis of the argument puts it, "Americans are from Mars and Europeans are from Venus."

> Europe is turning away from power, or to put it a little differently, it
> is moving beyond power into a self-contained world of laws and rules
> and transnational negotiation and cooperation. It is entering a post-
> historical paradise of peace and relative prosperity, the realization of
> Kant's "Perpetual Peace." The United States, meanwhile, remains
> mired in history, exercising power in the anarchic Hobbesian world
> where international laws and rules are unreliable and where true
> security and the defense and promotion of a liberal order still depend
> on the possession and use of military might.[8]

Kagan's account of the clash between American realism and European ideal-ism could just as easily be a description of their differences over the Kyoto Protocol as their disagreements over the necessity of the Iraq war, for it cap-tures the U.S. rejection of international law, the authority of the United Nations, and the Kantian goals of peace and global cooperation in either case. This "Hobbesian world" preferred by realists, in which international anarchy reigns and the world's nations are engaged in a constant struggle to advance national interests at the expense of others, cannot be justified simply by invoking Hobbes without taking his claims in context. Indeed, Kagan's enlistment of Hobbes as a champion of realism could not be more ironic, since the most basic argument of *Leviathan* is that no person could rationally prefer the anar-chic state of nature to civil society under an effective sovereign government.

The Hobbesian argument supposes that normative ideals ("justice and injustice") are only conventions that can be recognized and enforced within a society, or between societies that recognize a common sovereign, and during peacetime. They are not, as Kant would later argue, products of reason alone that can exist among men "in Solitude" but that lose all force during war, since they rely on a common authority to adjudicate disputes between contending parties. Likewise, moral limits on national conduct have no force in the absence of a recognized international authority capable of monitoring and enforcing compliance with agreed-upon terms of peace and cooperation. When one person attacks another without provocation and goes unpunished, we might follow Hobbes in declaring that right and wrong have ceased to exist, as injustice was allowed. But Hobbes makes clear that a state of nature is something to be avoided; *Leviathan* is above all a plea for peace and a condemnation of the scourge of war. In claiming that all rational persons desire peace and that natural law commands them to seek it by forfeiting their power over others, submitting to a common authority in order to secure the requisite conditions for "commodious living," and establishing conventions of justice and injustice, Hobbes is hardly the anarchist that realists portray. As Charles Beitz points out, "if international relations is a state of nature, it follows that no state has an obligation to comply with regulative principles analogous to the laws of nature. But it also follows that widespread compliance with such principles would be desirable from the point of view of each state."[9] A more plausible application of Hobbes to international affairs would urge rather than reject the "international laws and rules" that Kagan derides.

An alternative foundation for realism can be found in psychological egoism—the claim that all persons are in fact motivated exclusively by a concern to advance their own interests—where realist assumptions about human motives derive from a view of human psychology. By this account, the fact of egoism renders the pursuit of altruistic motives dangerously naive. Hans Morgenthau's influential 1962 *Politics Among Nations*, for example, defends realism by claiming that "power politics" permeates domestic politics and even family relations, and is a ubiquitous fact of life that political actors must not only accept but embrace, disabusing themselves of contrary motives such as those based in the unselfish pursuit of ideals. Although Morgenthau's famous defense of realism has been highly influential, it rests on two logical mistakes. It commits the naturalistic fallacy by inferring a normative prescription from what is claimed as an empirical fact, invalidly deriving an *ought* from an *is*; even if all persons really are egoists at heart, this does not make it right or proper for nations to disregard ideals such as justice. In addition, as Marshall Cohen points out, "showing that all relations are infected with power politics in this sense shows that international relations do not present a unique problem or an impassable terrain for ethical conduct or ethical judgment."[10]

Against this view, Richard Ned Lebow suggests that Morgenthau's classical realism be read not as an endorsement of a Machiavellian power politics that eschews ethical considerations altogether, as contemporary neorealism maintains, but rather as a pragmatic skepticism toward institutionalizing normative principles that Morgenthau himself would later disavow. Despite his rejection of Wilsonian idealism, Lebow notes, Morgenthau retained the view that "state actions had to conform to higher interests" and was "adamant" that morality "should limit both the ends that power seeks or the means employed to seek those ends."[11] This interpretative problem need not concern us here as we assess the realist rejection on empirical grounds of the normative foundations for international terms and institutions of justice. As Cohen suggests, either Morgenthau's empirical claims justify a more sweeping skepticism against ethical ideals in any setting and not merely in international relations—in which case, realism makes no unique case against cosmopolitan justice—or they merely offer one way of viewing human behavior from which nothing follows. Selfish motives may be readily seen in nearly all human action if one is inclined to spot them, but this cannot impugn the existence or normative force of global justice, even if it does accurately predict that such ideals may be difficult to establish in practice.

In short, neither the doctrine of state sovereignty nor the school of realism provides a valid philosophical case against cosmopolitan justice, nor does either attempt to justify an alternative normative theory. Sovereignty is a longstanding norm within international law and politics that has slowly yielded its absolute prohibitions on interference in domestic affairs to modern notions about human rights and other cosmopolitan ideals, pragmatically evolving to allow for such interference when concerned with such issues as global climate change that transcend national boundaries. Realism is an influential school of thought in international relations, but its claimed foundations in either Hobbesian political thought or premises of psychological egoism fall far short of providing any kind of philosophical defense of global justice skepticism. Like other empirical premises on which social scientific theories are often based, the realist rejection of normative ideals in international politics has the status of an assumption on which further conjectures about institutions and actions may be constructed, but it lacks noncircular proofs for that assumption. Cosmopolitan justice may still have some weight in designing a global climate regime, though we have yet to consider its most difficult challenge.

The Rawlsian Case against Cosmopolitan Justice

If the standard realist argument for skepticism about cosmopolitan justice in international relations comes from Hobbes, global justice skeptics in political theory most often ground their rejection of international justice in Rawls, whose *The Law of Peoples* expressly limits egalitarian principles of justice to internal rather than external relations of nations. In brief, justice is held by Rawls to be a normative ideal that applies only within bounded political communities that share a common political culture, since the communal solidarity and reciprocity that justice requires depend on the kind of interpersonal ties among citizens and sense of shared fate that can exist only among a people or within a nation-state, not between them. As David Miller characterizes the source of Rawlsian skepticism about cosmopolitan justice:

> Now although in the contemporary world there are clearly forms of interaction and cooperation occurring at the global level—the international economy provides the most obvious example, but there are also many forms of political cooperation, ranging from defense treaties through to environmental protection agreements—these are not sufficient to constitute a global community. They do not by themselves create either a shared sense of identity or a common ethos. And above all there is no common institutional structure that would justify us in describing unequal outcomes as forms of unequal treatment.[12]

Following Rawls, Miller's primary worry is that the sense of community necessary for persons to see others as recipients of justice duties is stretched too thin if the justice community is extended beyond national borders. When persons cooperate in a common endeavor such as citizenship in a nation, they express a commitment to the group itself that entails recognition of the fundamental injustice of undeserved inequality. Not only does the international community lack the "common institutional structure" necessary to remedy undeserved inequality among persons, but according to Miller it also lacks the psychological bases for treating others as equal participants in a common project.

What would it take for all of humanity to see itself as bound up in a common endeavor such that cosmopolitan justice might be possible? Andrew Hurrell argues that the basic "political prerequisites for a meaningful justice community," presumably including a global climate regime concerned with advancing justice while averting catastrophic climate change, include

> some acceptance of equality of status, of respect, and of consideration; some commitment to reciprocity and to the public justification of one's actions; some capacity for autonomous decision making on the basis of reasonable information; a degree of uncoerced willingness to participate; a situation in which the most disadvantaged perceive themselves as having some stake in the system; and some institutional processes by which the weak and disadvantaged are able to make their voice heard and to express claims about unjust treatment.[13]

Unlike Miller and Rawls, however, Hurrell is more optimistic about the development of a global justice community and finds the essential elements of one in the discourse of universal economic and social human rights. While the rights framework initiated by the U.N. Declaration of Human Rights has not been fully translated into the legal and political framework necessary for realizing such rights, Hurrell notes that it has set widely recognized "social expectations against which the suffering engendered by the current distribution of economic goods represents a staggering injustice," so has at least begun forging a wider set of moral bonds based in common humanity.

According to Hurrell, the policy areas in which global political community remains most conspicuously absent are in antipoverty efforts and economic development, where concerns for global economic justice in North/South development debates surfaced briefly in the 1970s, but vanished in the 1980s with "a blanket denial on the part of the international financial institutions and of Northern governments that the international system was in any way responsible for underdevelopment" and concomitant resistance on the part of affluent states to even characterize global economic inequality as an issue of cosmopolitan justice, let alone seriously attempt to reduce that inequality. On the other hand, he notes, the discourse of cosmopolitan justice has prominently featured in several environmental debates, in which "Northern civil society groups mobilized successfully and incorporated some justice concerns because of their broader interest in sustainability"—as, for example, in the sustainable development movement as well as in global climate policy development. On such global environmental issues, Hurrell observes, "the poor matter to the rich," and as a result, "concessions have had to be made in the interest of creating new cooperative regimes." The contrast between environmental debates in which concerns for global justice have played a central role and economic debates from which it has been excluded, with their contrasting endorsement of global cooperation, "reinforces the claim that a meaningful justice community requires some degree of equality of power."[14] Even if the rhetoric of attaining North/South equality and recognizing interdependence within climate policy development has been largely symbolic and has failed to manifest in genuine procedural fairness, the fact that both sides have endorsed the discourse of global justice within the climate convention represents a significant advance from earlier policy regimes and contributes toward forming the sort of global community that is a necessary condition for the meaningful existence of cosmopolitan justice.

Nonetheless, Rawls has resisted the call to internationalize his original position and thus to treat national origin as a morally irrelevant "accident of birth" in a way that would broaden his liberal egalitarianism into a cosmopolitan theory of justice. Much of his resistance owes to the contractarian tradition in which his argument is situated. In this tradition, and as noted above, it is commonly assumed that the members of a political community are uniquely bound by its terms and that the obligations accepted as elements of the contract apply only within that community's borders. The justification for contractarian principles of justice, then, rests on the idea that the citizens of a given state would endorse its terms, whether or not they have done so in fact, and this kind of justification seems to preclude the extension of principles beyond the peoples that hypothetically endorse them. As Beitz notes, contractarian theories "usually rest on the relations in which people stand in a national community united by common acceptance of a conception of justice," thereby limiting their scope to relations within and not between nations, such that "it is not obvious that contractarian principles with such a justification support any redistributive obligations between persons situated in different national societies."[15] The Rawlsian original position, following the contractarian tradition of modeling rational consent on an imagined bargaining situation among citizens, assumes that parties share a common nationality and choose principles that only apply within the nation itself but cannot be extended beyond its borders.

Although there exists no real deliberation and no one actually "chooses" anything in the original position, persons are required to reflect on the generally accepted ideals of justice latent in their society's political culture and on other specific features of their own societies—including economic arrangements, levels of development, and so on—in their endorsement of principles of justice. The upshot of Rawlsian contractarianism is that the principles derived from the thought experiment of the original position are valid only for societies that closely resemble the political culture of the contemporary United States or United Kingdom, so apply only to the internal arrangements of these societies, not to their external affairs or foreign policy. Hence, whereas the difference principle applies to public policy issues that affect the distribution of resources *within* society, by the Rawlsian account it remains silent on issues that concern the distribution of similar resources *between* societies. Redistributive taxation for the purpose of improving the condition of society's poor may be justified as a matter of justice, but redistributive taxation in order to benefit the poor from other societies, even if they are significantly worse off than society's own least advantaged, cannot be justified by Rawlsian justice theory, at least in its standard interpretation.

The Case for Cosmopolitan Justice

Beitz challenges this standard interpretation by arguing that the logic of Rawlsian contractarianism requires that at least some distributive issues be based on an international rather than strictly a national original position, where the veil of ignorance also obscures one's nationality. Consider, he suggests, the global distribution of natural resources: Although these plainly affect the welfare opportunities of those who are able to control the resources around them, their natural distribution cannot be the product of any sort of deserved inequality among peoples since it does not result from any voluntary acts or choices. Natural resource wealth is a significant determinant of national prosperity, but its natural distribution across the globe is neither equal nor a reflection of morally relevant differences among peoples inhabiting various territories, even if the conservation of those resources can be attributed to voluntary choices. Thus, Beitz argues that natural resource wealth ought to be treated as morally arbitrary, in much the same way that Rawls treats the distribution of natural talents in society. In the "natural lottery" of birth, Rawls notes, persons are born into highly disparate situations of advantage and disadvantage—with unequal talents, initial resources, and so on—and this inequality can be attributed only to luck and not to the sort of conscious acts and choices that result in deserved inequality among persons. About this kind of natural inequality, but equally applicable to the distribution of natural resources among nations, Rawls writes: "These are simply natural facts. What is just and unjust is the way that institutions deal with these facts."[16]

When it comes to the "natural facts" of unequally distributed natural talents, the Rawlsian principles of justice recommend a redistribution of social resources to those born disadvantaged in their native endowments in order to compensate for their lesser opportunities, treating society's overall stock of talent in effect as a common resource. Although talents themselves (or *natural primary goods*) cannot be redistributed within society, social primary goods are subject to redistribution, and egalitarian imperatives therefore weigh in favor of equalizing starting points by giving those with lesser natural primary goods a greater share of social primary goods. Positing that persons deserve their talents entails the further claim that persons are entitled to the unequal share of social goods that might follow from them, and for Rawls this would amount to an endorsement of significant inequality. In weighing alternative distributive arrangements in society, persons in the original position must consider the possibility that they may be born among the least advantaged, in their natural talents, parental wealth, and so on, and in doing so opt for arrangements that maximize opportunities for those with the least. Can egalitarians, Beitz asks rhetorically, accept the inequalities that result from unequally distributed natural resources when justice demands that we mitigate the effects of unequally distributed natural talents? From the logic of the original position, it would seem that they cannot, at least insofar as persons are held to be no more responsible for the natural resources that lie within their national borders than they are for their own natural talents. As Beitz argues, "The fact that someone happens to be located advantageously with respect to natural resources does not provide a reason why he or she should be entitled to exclude others from the benefits that might derive from them."[17]

In simple terms, it seems no less fair that some have the tremendous advantages that come from ready access to bounteous natural resources, while others suffer from disadvantages in this regard, than it is that some are born with social advantages over others. If egalitarian justice is concerned with reducing such undeserved sources of inequality, then it must be as concerned with natural resources as it is with the natural primary goods. In the model of the original position, however, Rawls requires that persons choose principles of justice in ignorance of their personal attributes of natural primary goods, but with full knowledge of their relative national share of the world's natural resources. Their chosen principles thus reflect the fairness concerns of unequal shares of natural primary goods but not those associated with unequal access to natural resources, another "natural fact" about which Rawls remains silent. Beitz persuasively argues against this position as logically inconsistent, and in favor of an international original position in which the principles of justice derived apply to relations among as well as within nations.

In the context of deliberation over principles of justice governing the distribution of the world's natural resources, Beitz argues that the original position must obscure one's nationality and hence national share of global resources behind the veil of ignorance, thereby generating principles that would apply to the global distribution of such resources. In this international original position, parties

> would know that resources are unevenly distributed with respect to population, that adequate access to resources is a prerequisite for successful operation of (domestic) cooperative schemes, and that resources are scarce. They would view that natural distribution of resources as arbitrary in the sense that no one has a natural prima facie claim to the resources that happen to be under one's feet.[18]

In view of this ignorance, he suggests, "parties would agree on a resource redistribution principle that would give each society a fair chance to develop just political institutions and an economy capable of satisfying its members' basic needs." Whereas Rawls argues for a much more limited "duty of assistance" in The Law of Peoples—where affluent nations have a duty to help other states develop institutions of justice and become well ordered but need not redistribute wealth across borders beyond what is minimally required for this aim—Beitz suggests that a "resource redistribution principle" follows the maximin logic of the difference principle, so that "each person has an equal prima facie claim to a share of the total available resources, but departures from this initial standard could be justified (analogously to the operation of the difference principle) if the resulting inequalities were to the greatest benefit of those least advantaged by the inequality."

Unsatisfied with this limited critical claim that natural resource distribution be treated as morally arbitrary within the original position and thus be recognized as an undeserved source of inequality to be redressed through principles of justice, Beitz aims for a wider critique against the Rawlsian limits on the scope of principles of distributive justice, and thus to provide a defense of full cosmopolitan justice. Against the premise that nation-states are independent and self-sufficient and thus are not part of a global justice community, he points out that in fact "states participate in complex economic, political, and cultural relationships that suggest the existence of a global scheme of social cooperation."[19] This interdependence, exemplified by reduced trade barriers in regimes of economic globalization, can be mutually beneficial, he suggests, but it also widens the political and economic gap between rich and poor nations, in many cases undermining domestic sovereignty by shifting power away from governments and toward economic actors. In recognition of the growing economic interdependence among nations, Beitz observes, complex international forms of governance have developed in recent decades, and "these institutions and practices can be considered as the constitutional structure of the world economy; their activities have important distributive implications."[20] Insofar as justice is the primary virtue of social institutions, he argues that it ought to guide these international institutions as well as domestic ones. Given the development of "a global scheme of social cooperation" based in the recognition of increasing global economic and political interdependence, "we should not view national boundaries as having fundamental moral significance. Since boundaries are not coextensive with the scope of social cooperation, they do not mark the limits of social obligations."[21]

Although Rawls and others have replied to Beitz's case for cosmopolitan justice, I do not attempt to summarize their remaining points of contention here. Since Beitz's argument for the resource redistribution principle and not his wider cosmopolitanism would provide sufficient justification for a global resource regime that applies principles of distributive justice to the allocation of atmospheric absorptive capacity, Rawls's unpersuasive reply to that proposed principle shall suffice here. Acknowledging that Beitz "believes that the wealthier countries are so because of the greater resources available to them," Rawls takes no issue with the normative argument that such advantages connote duties to others, instead rejecting on empirical grounds the causal links between natural resource wealth, national prosperity, and a nation's opportunity to become well ordered. He suggests, in rejecting the claim of inconsistency in the original position's treatment of one source of natural inequality as relevant to justice but another as irrelevant, and essentially reiterating his earlier premise that cross-border obligations are limited to a duty of assistance and not of justice, that since "the crucial element in how a country fares is its political culture—its members' political and civic virtues—and not the level of its resources, the arbitrariness of the distribution of natural resources causes no difficulty."[22]

One need not be a natural resource determinist to see the critical role played by natural resource wealth in patterns of national development. While Rawls may be correct in suggesting that even the resource-poorest peoples—with the possible exception of Eskimos, he notes—could become decent and well ordered, it is surely invalid to infer from this that resource wealth, and the economic prosperity that often if not always follows from it, plays no role in the development of just institutions. As Adam Przeworski and colleagues have shown, democracy—an essential condition for developing a decent and well-ordered society—is more likely to flourish in wealthy countries than in poor ones,[23] a point that Rawls essentially concedes with his duty of assistance. Even if political culture is also a significant variable, Rawls is mistaken in discounting altogether the role played by resource wealth, and so underestimates its importance to justice.

Moreover, one need not endorse Beitz's resource redistribution principle in order to see why principles of distributive justice must guide the allocation of shares of the atmosphere's absorptive capacity in the form of national emissions caps. Insofar as some nations are now rich as a consequence of their abundant resources, Beitz argues for the redistribution of that wealth in order to reduce global economic inequality, from the claim that such a distribution is morally arbitrary. While conventional property rights claims might be wielded against the resource redistribution principle, since it opposes granting entitlement to natural resource based on their location within political borders, no such territorial property claims apply to the climate case. Unlike most other natural resources, there is no natural "distribution" of atmospheric space, so climate defies conventional theories of property by presenting a case of a pure public good that is fully international, as well as being vital to human flourishing and currently overallocated.

Although persons or nations make claims on the atmosphere as theirs to use when they emit GHGs, these claims cannot draw on existing theories of entitlement to property, since the resource transcends political borders and is not the sort of good that can be appropriated from the commons by being improved, as through a Lockean labor theory of value. No resource redistribution principle is needed in order to acknowledge the lack of valid claims to unequal shares of the atmosphere, despite the current existence of highly unequal de facto claims on the resource. Insofar as a justice community develops around issues on which peoples are interdependent and so must find defensible means of allocating scarce goods, global climate change presents a case in which the various arguments against cosmopolitan justice cease to apply. All depend on a stable climate for their well-being, all are potentially affected by the actions or policies of others, and none can fully opt out of the cooperative scheme, even if they eschew its necessary limits on action. Climate change mitigation therefore becomes an issue of cosmopolitan justice by its very nature as an essential public good, so it is to the analysis of such goods that I now turn.

Atmospheric Absorptive Capacity as a Common Resource

The planet's atmosphere is a common good that provides vital climatic services to all the world's persons, with its absorptive capacity allowing for a finite quantity of GHG emissions before heat-trapping gases begin to accumulate in the atmosphere, destabilizing those climatic services and causing harm to persons and peoples. When viewed in this way, several problems for cosmopolitan justice are revealed, and a powerful claim for recognizing the terms of justice applied among the world's nations and persons becomes more apparent. In this section, I examine the atmosphere's status as both a shared good to which multiple parties have competing claims, demanding adjudication under the terms of justice, and a public good subject to free rider problems, requiring binding terms of cooperation to which all must be able to assent.

All of the world's nations and peoples need and want to emit GHGs; they need to emit survival emissions if their members are to meet basic human needs, and they want to emit luxury emissions so that those members can enjoy aspects of the good life that go beyond mere survival. These needs and wants can be thought of as claims to shares of atmospheric absorptive capacity, and through their current emissions levels all nations now make de facto claims on this capacity. Such claims cannot be infinite, given the atmosphere's finite capacity to absorb GHGs and satisfy those claims, and its capacity to sustainably do so is already being exceeded. These overall claims on the atmosphere must now be reduced if we are to avoid catastrophic climate change in the future, so the task for justice is to articulate and justify a distributive principle by which we may limit overall atmospheric claims in a manner that is fair to all nations and peoples, and to allocate those emissions shares in a manner that is likewise fair to all. Justice makes both intergenerational and international demands in this regard; if we fail in the first objective, we will cause catastrophic climate change, harming untold millions of current and future persons as well as other life on this planet, while failure in the second objective may produce the same result, because any system of unfairly assigned atmospheric shares may undermine the international cooperation necessary for sustainably managing the common resource and enjoying its services.

The world's nations and peoples, both present and future, depend on this scheme of cooperation for their continued access to the vital services provides by climatic stability, and so are part of an interdependent global justice community. While Rawls may be right to hold that such interdependence does not arise among nations with most goods subject to redistribution, he would surely be wrong to hold that nations are not interdependent in their common reliance on the services provided by the earth's atmosphere. If the cooperative scheme is to be effective and the common resource maintained, all must agree to abide by its terms. Defection by even one nation can undermine the climate regime's efficacy, not only through carbon leakage across borders but also through the incentives for further defection caused by this initial defection through a global "race to the bottom" in climate policy. Cooperation is necessary but must be based on terms that are fair, for both principled and practical reasons.

An instructive analogy to the issues surrounding the atmospheric commons for both international and intergenerational justice is offered by the shared use of a fishing commons, which displays many of the same features as the shared atmosphere. Suppose a fishing village shares a common lake, where overfishing during any one season leads to the gradual depletion of fish stocks for future seasons. In order to ensure that the existing fish populations are not depleted, all must agree to limit their annual catches, even though each may individually prefer to catch more fish in a given year than allowed under these limits. Moreover, limits must be fairly assigned among villagers, or some will justifiably refuse to participate, jeopardizing the entire scheme. If those sharing the lake can agree on a fair allocation of the total number of fish to be caught in a given year—where no one's share is unjustly large or small, relative to the others that year—but the total annual catch is beyond the regenerative capacity of the fish stock to replace fish harvested during the year, then limits are unfairly assigned within the community, because future resources are sacrificed for present ones. Should this dimension of justice be neglected, future catches will decline until the fish population is depleted. Even though no one takes more than his or her fair share of the total, the community will have taken too much in a given year and will predictably suffer in the future. Only when resource shares are fairly assigned along both dimensions will a genuinely fair and effective solution have been reached.

Aside from these issues of justice in the allocation of emission shares, several other difficulties arise from the atmosphere's status as a *public good*; that is, its climate-stabilizing services are both nonrivalrous in that one person's enjoyment of the good does not diminish its enjoyment by others, and non-excludable in that, once produced, access to the good cannot be prevented. These services are jeopardized by the overuse of the atmospheric sink as excessive emissions of heat-trapping gases threaten to disrupt the planet's climatic system, due largely to collective action problems of the sort described here by Derek Parfit:

> It can be true of each person that, if he helps, he will add to the sum of benefits, or expected benefits. But only a very small portion of the benefit he adds will come back to him. Since his share of what he adds will be very small, it may not repay his contribution. It may thus be better for each if he does not contribute. This can be so whatever others do. But it will be worse for each if fewer others contribute. And if none contribute this will be worse for each than if all do.[24]

Insofar as public goods rely on voluntary contributions in order to be produced or maintained, and since such goods can be enjoyed by all regardless of their personal contribution to the good's provision, they are subject to the free rider problem, which economists describe as a form of market failure resulting from the unremunerated positive externalities that such goods provide, but which might more simply be described as problem of incentives: Economically rational persons have no incentive to pay for any good that they can enjoy for free. As a result, public goods cannot be produced for profit and so cannot be provided by markets alone.

The standard solutions to such problems include privatizing the goods in question, which makes them excludable so that free riding becomes impossible, and state provision, which relies on compulsory rather than voluntary contributions. The first option is unavailable in cases involving pure public goods such as climate, which by definition produce goods from which none can be excluded, because either all enjoy a stable climatic system or none do, regardless of individual contribution to its protection or depletion. The second option involves compulsory contribution, which in this case involves the negative contribution of accepting mandatory caps on their GHG emissions, requiring justification given its coercive nature. Since all rationally prefer to avoid contributing and instead free ride on the efforts of others, and since none can rationally agree to accept the costs of contribution without the assurance that all others will likewise contribute their fair shares, the cooperative solution requires all to accept mandatory contributions of their fair emissions limits in a system that is transparent and fair, so that none is tempted to defect because disgruntled from unfair treatment or suspicious of others shirking their assigned burdens. As Paul Baer notes: "To protect the resource and to protect themselves, the parties must grant each other the right to a fair share, and accept enforcement of a mutually agreed limit."[25]

As described above, national contributions toward a cooperative scheme maintaining climatic stability entail the acceptance of some cap on national emissions, and these can therefore be equal contributions when national per capita emissions caps are also equal. Insofar as all nations equally enjoy climatic stability, egalitarian justice demands that their required contributions be assigned equally, as well. But what if the enjoyment of the common good is *not* equal? As the IPCC predicts, climate change is expected to harm developing nations more than industrialized ones, and from this one might infer that the former benefit more from climatic stability than do the latter. Following the principle of equity, then, each person might be assigned as their fair share toward the provision of a public good that proportion of overall benefits that they receive in return. Where some benefit more by some public good, they owe more toward its provision, and those enjoying it less consequently owe less. A lighthouse is a kind of public good, but some users plainly benefit more by its existence while others benefit less by it. Justice cannot demand that all contribute equally toward the lighthouse's maintenance, for this would be to redistribute from some to others without justification; in the lighthouse case, it seems unfair to tax mariners and landlubbers equally for its provision, even if the latter are not technically prohibited from enjoying its externality effects. Fair shares, therefore, are not necessarily equal shares, because equity demands that persons contribute unequally toward the provision or maintenance of public goods from which they will benefit unequally, and equally to those from which they benefit equally.

The likely fact that some parties stand to be harmed more than others by climate change poses an interesting theoretical question for justice: Does this justify unequal contributions toward either the avoidance of the public bad of climate change or the public good of climatic stability though the assignment of unequal national per capita emissions caps? Reference to the Rawlsian original position may be instructive on this point. Insofar as individual GHG emissions provide a rough measure of personal welfare (or "luxury"), it would be unjust to assign some persons lower caps based on the morally arbitrary fact of their national residence. None can be said to deserve lower levels of welfare merely because they were born in ecologically vulnerable nations or regions, so in this sense it would be unjust to restrict their emissions more than others are restricted. However, equal emissions do not necessarily correspond with equal opportunities for welfare. For example, those residing in cold regions require more energy in order to meet their basic needs and so may have higher "survival emissions" than those living in temperate regions, justifying higher emissions limits in order to have equal welfare opportunities. Since those expected to suffer the most harm from climate change are primarily located in warm or temperate regions, these two considerations offset. Other offsetting considerations might also be factored into the assignment of fair national emissions shares, but these are likely to coalesce around a rough equality in per capita emissions, and they certainly cannot endorse the significant inequality on display in current national rates.

While these observations may not yet identify the precise emissions shares that ought to be assigned to each nation as a matter of justice, they should give shape to the general problem that egalitarian justice theory aims to address in designing a fair and effective climate regime. From egalitarian assumptions about moral equality, we can see how difficult the current de facto claims on the atmosphere are to defend. No persons, merely by virtue of their national identity, geographic residence, prior use patterns, or command of wealth or power, deserve to be awarded a much larger share of the planet's atmosphere than do any others. Even if some may defensibly be allowed to emit slightly more than others based on considerations such as those examined above, this cannot justify the radical inequality on display in current claims on the planet's atmospheric capacity. Where distributions of valuable resources are highly unequal, as is so of current shares of the atmosphere, egalitarian justice demands that this inequality be justified or rectified, and here no such justification is possible.

Since the atmosphere's capacity to absorb GHGs without producing the public bad of climate change is finite, allowing Annex B nations to contribute far less toward avoiding this public bad by assigning them higher emission caps necessarily entails that developing countries will be forced to accept lower caps in the zero-sum game of reducing global emissions, violating what many see as their "right to develop" as rising emissions necessarily accompany industrialization and rising standards of living. Moreover, the current scarcity that forces such choices will only increase in the future, as global emissions are expected to increase by 69 percent between 1995 and 2020, fueled by a 66 percent increase in world energy demand during that period,[26] while the IPCC estimates that global emissions must be reduced by 50 percent from current rates if atmospheric concentrations are to be stabilized during this century.

Insofar as the industrialized nations continue to resist contributing their fair share toward avoiding the public bad of climate change, they will continue to transfer costs to residents of developing countries and to future generations, both of whom will thereby be required to make significantly greater sacrifices as a result. Inadequate contributions by Annex B nations toward a solution, as manifest in their excessive current claims on atmospheric space, have the dual consequence of enabling the public bad of climate change to wreak its predicted damage while at the same time forcing others to contribute more toward averting the public bad than would otherwise be required, even while suffering damage from that avoidable public bad.

Conclusions

The normative construct of liberal egalitarian justice offers a powerful diagnostic tool for assessing several of the main problems surrounding anthropogenic climate change, as well as useful criteria for designing a global climate regime that meets the *UNFCCC*'s mandate of being fair and effective. Once we overcome the limitations that have been placed on the application of liberal egalitarian principles of justice, we can readily apply them to some of the distributive problems in the design of a climate regime, such as the allocation of national emissions shares. As described above, the thought experiment of the original position, when combined with egalitarian assumptions concerning the moral equality of persons, yields a powerful argument for assigning roughly equal per capita emissions shares, a conclusion examined further in chapter 7. Even without accepting full cosmopolitan justice, Beitz's resource redistribution principle—when applied in allocating the common resource of atmospheric absorptive capacity—demonstrates that the variety of claims now being made for unequal shares of that resource are based on morally arbitrary "accidents of birth," including national residence, historical use patterns, and relative national affluence and power. No person or people can be said to have a valid claim to much more of that shared resource than others can be permitted, and none deserves the larger shares to which some nations now lay claim through their current GHG emission patterns. Justice is the primary virtue of such institutions as a global climate regime, and justice requires that it be subject to defensible distributive principles in the manner in which it assigns costs and secures benefits.

4

Climate Change and Intergenerational Justice

Suppose that all of the world's nations were to endorse, implement, and enforce a set of greenhouse gas (GHG) emissions caps that met those standards of international distributive justice discussed in chapter 3, and all were able to comply with their assigned caps. The atmospheric capacity to absorb GHGs, in this case, would be allocated in such a way that each nation was allowed to emit exactly its share of some agreed-upon global annual amount of heat-trapping gases, and no nation could make a valid complaint that their share had been unfairly assigned or that another's was unfairly high. Such a feat of international policy development would indeed be an extraordinary rare accomplishment, for it would mean that all those nations that could have used some outside sources of unequal power in negotiations to produce a more favorable deal for themselves, or could have undermined a fair agreement in its implementation or enforcement phases, declined to do so in the interest of international justice. But would such an agreement be enough? If the standards of international justice could somehow be met, could we say that the climate convention truly realized justice itself, embodying what John Rawls calls "the first virtue of social institutions" in its policy assignments?

This scenario, however unlikely, would not necessarily be enough to meet the demands of justice. If the agreed-upon total annual GHG limit was set too high, then the world's human population would be allowed to cause significant climate-related damage in the future. Even if such effects did not by themselves violate the terms of international justice, they could cause sufficient harm to future persons that would, in consequence of current climate policy decisions, inhabit a planet on which their welfare opportunities were sufficiently diminished that we may conclude that the current generation failed in its duties with respect to them. Not only must we pay attention to principles of international justice in allocating shares of atmospheric absorptive capacity, then, but we must likewise follow standards of intergenerational justice in determining the total amount of allowable GHG emissions to allocate among the world's nations in the form of emissions caps. Observing principles of justice in one of these dimensions does not guarantee consistency with principles of justice in the other. Both must work together to inform our design of a global climate regime if it is to be truly just.

The *UNFCCC* declares that we have a duty to protect the planet's climate system for the benefit of "future generations of humankind," and most people would probably agree that their generation has at least some kind of moral obligation toward those generations to come in the future, but what is the nature of this widely assumed duty? Upon what basis do we owe people of the future costly constraints on our own actions of the kind required to reduce our total current emissions? Insofar as doing so entails some forgone welfare now, reducing current consumption and directing more of our resources toward upgrading our energy and transit infrastructure, how much sacrifice of current welfare interests is required in order to meet our obligation to future generations? How much must we know about the future in order to recognize such obligations? Must we know what future people will be like, or what kinds of activities or lives they will prefer to pursue? Must we know what technologies will be developed in the future? Does it matter whether or not we can expect future people to inhabit a world roughly similar to our own, or will the differences that the future brings disconnect present generations from the future? Does it make a difference whether people in the future will be more prosperous than we are, either on average or between their respective places in the socioeconomic hierarchies of each generation?

These are some of the difficult questions that must be faced when pondering the nature and extent of our—that is, those of the present generation of humans—obligations toward future generations. Despite the intuitive implausibility of the claim that we have *no* duties with respect to future persons, admitting that we ought to pay *some* attention to the consequences of our actions for those who will later inhabit our world does not go very far in answering the question of *how much* we owe future people, nor does it provide any reason *why* we might be obligated to assume potentially high costs for the benefit of persons whom we will never meet and about which we may know very little.

The problem of intergenerational justice is central in current debates over the normative basis for global climate policy. For example, the *Stern Review*—a 2006 economic analysis of climate change that was commissioned by the British government—concludes that

> if we don't act, the overall costs and risks of climate change will be equivalent to losing at least 5% of global GDP each year, now and forever. If a wider range of risks and impacts is taken into account, the estimates of damage could rise to 20% of GDP or more. In contrast, the costs of action—reducing greenhouse gas emissions to avoid the worst impacts of climate change—can be limited to around 1% of global GDP each year.[1]

While the report unequivocally endorses as economically rational a climate policy capable of stabilizing emissions at 550 ppm, it controversially refuses to discount the welfare of future generations in calculating the costs of current inaction. Unlike economic models that apply a discount rate to future welfare in order to arrive at a present value to compare against current consumption, the review treats future persons as having moral claims on current policy equal to those of present ones, discounting future costs of climate change only for various uncertainties and not for the "pure time preference" often used to justify future discount rates and noting that climate change will be seen as "much less of a problem" as less weight is "placed on prospects for the long-run future."[2] The economic analysis of climate change, then, depends on the ethical claim that we must consider the welfare of future generations. Absent some theoretical basis for this claim, the justification for accepting potentially high current costs in return for averted future harm rests on perilous ground.

Contemporary debates about environmental issues such as climate change, in which present policy choices predictably affect those conditions under which future persons will live, usually take at least some obligation toward future persons as a bedrock assumption,[3] with relatively few observers paying serious note of the difficulties surrounding the claim that we owe something to future persons. Unless we can establish that we owe future generations something, such as the ability to inhabit a planet with a stable climatic system, the predicted hazards of climate change may be significant for their redistributive effects within this generation but would be far less compelling overall, and the notion that persons should now undergo costly processes of social transformation so that future persons can enjoy the climatic stability that is now being threatened by some current acts loses much of its normative force. This chapter, then, examines the nature and extent of our duty of intergenerational justice, with an emphasis on the way in which these are affected by or might inform issues surrounding climate change.

Intergenerational Egalitarianism and Just Savings

One possible solution to the problem of what and why the current generation of humans owes future generations might be drawn from the ideals of distributive justice examined in the preceding chapters. If we can extend the notion of egalitarian justice to relations between nations, given previously observed obstacles, can we not likewise extend it to include relations between generations, where depriving future persons of their fair share of essential goods may be seen as a distributive injustice? After all, a person's time of birth is also part of the "natural lottery" over which they have no control and thus bear no responsibility, so it seems straightforwardly unfair for those born in the future to be made worse off by consequence of current choices than those alive today. In order to model the moral arbitrariness of the stages of national development in which persons live, Rawls holds that the parties in the original position "do not know to which generation they belong"[4] but know that they all belong to the same generation. Hence, none can endorse principles that inhibit development or otherwise sacrifice one generation's welfare for the sake of another. However, the distribution of resources across generational lines is not an issue of egalitarian justice for Rawls, for reasons explored below. If the difference principle could be applied across generations, it would instruct us to make current policy decisions with regard to the possibility that our choices might cause future generations to be among the least advantaged, and to act now accordingly. Given its long-term effects, climate policy would seem to involve intergenerational justice, provided that such obligations exist.

Rawls does not reject intergenerational obligations altogether but denies that the thought experiment of the original position can be used to generate them. He instead grounds intergenerational obligations in the duty to assist others in establishing and maintaining institutions of justice, but this proposal falls short of establishing egalitarian norms of intergenerational justice for reasons equivalent to those noted above concerning his international duty of assistance. Recall also that the motivational force of the original position relies on persons viewing themselves as part of a shared justice community, which requires a substantial degree of interdependence and at least the possibility of reciprocity in order to produce the bonds of solidarity necessary for persons to accept terms of cooperation such as those embodied within principles of justice.

Although we might be able to posit a kind of interdependent global community within the context of anthropogenic climate change since the actions of each affect all other humans, albeit in small ways, we cannot posit a similarly interdependent intertemporal justice community, even within a single society. While our actions now can beneficially or adversely affect future people in that we can do a better or worse job as environmental stewards in ways that may significantly affect their prospects, the same cannot be said of the effects of their actions on us. While they may be dependent on us, we are not dependent on them, so an intertemporal community cannot be truly interdependent and thus lacks the requisite basis for social solidarity.

Moreover, social resources such as primary goods cannot be redistributed over time in the same way as they can within contemporary society, so the difference principle cannot so readily provide a justification for unequal allocations of resources over time. If the least advantaged members of a given society existed in the past and are now deceased, nothing can be done now to improve their conditions. Likewise, if they will exist in the distant future, nothing can be done now to redistribute current resources to improve their material conditions, even if unsustainable policies adopted now will frustrate future conservation efforts. Based on such considerations, Rawls specifies that parties in the original position know themselves to be contemporaries rather than members of different generations, who might then be required to allocate society's primary goods across generational lines. A self-interested group of delegates from a single generation lacks motive for selecting principles that do not privilege their own generation's welfare at the expense of others, since they need not persuade members of other generations to accept them.

Within a single generation, the fact that society's social primary goods *can* be readily redistributed makes their unequal allocation something that requires justification, but unequal allocations over time need no similar defense. It is not obviously unjust that members of the current generation enjoy greater shares of primary goods than did those of previous ones, and we cannot opt for policies that benefit futurity on Rawlsian distributive justice grounds unless we can know that those to whom we defer our own welfare will be less advantaged than we are and that the deferred primary goods will actually accrue to them. The maximin rule of the difference principle cannot be applied across generations in the same way as it can among contemporaries, since we can neither reliably identify the least advantaged generation nor ensure that our current policies will actually redistribute resources in a way that benefits them. At most, we can ensure that current policies do not frivolously squander our inherited stock of primary goods, but it remains far from obvious how this prudential aim depends on principles of egalitarian justice.

Hence, intergenerational egalitarian justice is distinct from justice within generations in two crucial senses: Its egalitarianism is concerned with the allocation of aggregate natural and social resources to entire generations within society rather than to individual persons, and the egalitarian principle that guides this allocation is not the maximin rule of the difference principle but is rather a standard of economic savings and resource conservation whereby a nondeclining stock of natural and social primary goods is to be transmitted across generations, leaving each successive generation no worse off than the previous one. According to Rawls, each generation must ensure that society in the future will have access to the requisite resources for maintaining just institutions, but not those needed in order to equalize primary goods across generational lines. Its focus is on maintaining some baseline level of natural and social resources, which requires only that aggregate resources do not significantly diminish over time, makes Rawlsian intergenerational obligation based not in egalitarian justice but rather in a just savings principle.

Societies, Rawls argues, have an obligation to equitably allocate their resources over time, requiring of generations that "each receives from its predecessors and does its fair share for those which come later."[5] While this "fair share" is never precisely defined, he does suggest that no generation should deliberately waste society's resources, because each generation has a duty to leave for later generations "a fair equivalent in real capital" that "enables the later ones to enjoy a better life in a more just society."[6] By this he is presumed to mean some combination of human-made and natural capital, including a productive natural environment capable of yielding stocks of natural resources, rather than primary goods themselves, as both human capital and natural capital constitute the means by which future primary goods are produced. But when we examine the just savings principle and its justification more closely, it turns out not to offer the strong obligation for the egalitarian allocation of resources over time implied by references to a generation's "fair share." Persons in the present are not required to treat the welfare of future persons as equal to those in the present and so have no obligation to ensure that future persons have equal primary goods. From the just savings principle, a different kind of duty to others is articulated.

This intergenerational obligation does not depend on the thought experiment of the original position and is not subject to the difference principle. Instead, the just savings rate is based on duties to maintain existing institutions of justice and to establish them where they do not exist, since "saving is demanded as a condition of bringing about the full realization of just institutions and the fair value of liberty." Within a society that is not well ordered, Rawls argues, a positive savings rate is required in order to bring about the requisite material conditions for society to become well ordered and for the institutions of justice to be established. Once society becomes well ordered and institutions of justice have been established, additional net saving is unnecessary. In fact, Rawls notes, saving beyond this threshold "is more likely to be a positive hindrance, a meaningless distraction at best if not a temptation to indulgence and emptiness."[7] This duty is not based in the egalitarian premises that motivate his principles of justice, where society's allocation of primary goods aims to ensure that all its members have a roughly equal chance of living good lives, and it does not require the equitable distribution of primary goods over time. Rather, the duty to conserve social and natural resources originates in the "natural duty" to "further just arrangements not yet established, at least when this can be done without too much cost to ourselves,"[8] which provides an insufficient basis for this generation to undertake costly measures necessary to avoid causing future climatic instability.

The obligation to save, then, has little to do with equality between persons, or obligations to individual persons in the future. Rather, this duty is "an understanding between generations to carry their fair share of the burden of realizing and preserving a just society."[9] If our own society was neither just nor well ordered, we would have a duty to save as instrumental to attaining just institutions and a well-ordered society in the future; if it was already is just and well ordered, our obligation to save is based only on the duty to preserve such institutions, presumably requiring lower savings rates, and permitting even negative ones. Our obligations are not to persons, then, nor are they particularly extensive. The minimal nature of such obligations can most clearly be seen in the contrast that Rawls later draws between the duty of assistance to other nations and cosmopolitan justice. Since the former only aims to help a society to establish just institutions, he writes, "once that end is reached" and the duty has been fulfilled, there remains no further duty "to raise the standard of living beyond what is necessary to sustain those institutions," nor is there any reason from justice "for further reduction of material inequalities among societies," as between the present and future in a single society. Cosmopolitan justice, by contrast, has as its "ultimate concern" the "well-being of individuals and not the justice of societies."[10]

Hence, just savings is part of a general duty of assistance, is of a roughly similar nature to the duties that Rawls holds are owed to other nations as explored in chapter 3, and lies outside of the theoretical confines of distributive justice itself. As such, anything further than a positive duty to ensure the basic conditions for establishing or maintaining just institutions is seen by Rawls as entailing unwarranted interference in the prerogative of a distinct society for self-determination, whether this interference is with other states or earlier incarnations of the same state. To this positive duty, we may add the negative obligation not to cause harm—though Rawls does not mentions such a duty, and as discussed below, this intuitive standard is more difficult to establish than it may appear—but no one is obligated to equalize primary goods across generational lines or national borders, and concerns for the overall stocks of primary goods available within other nations or to futurity are based only in these two duties. Application of egalitarian justice standards such as the difference principle is rejected in those cases involving distinct justice communities, whether separated by national boundaries or time, that lack the necessary interdependence or basis for reciprocity.

While the just savings rate may provide some normative foundation for a global climate regime designed to mitigate future climate-related harm, Rawls has difficulty explaining the motivation for parties accepting the principle of just savings in the original position, and his own account of the basis for such a norm fails to make a persuasive case for intergenerational justice. Obligations among persons typically rely on reciprocity, where I obey moral rules with respect to my treatment of you because I expect you to do the same for me, but future people cannot reciprocate acts of their predecessors. Should we now adopt a just savings principle, the savings rates of past generations would be unaffected, and this one-sidedness is so of each generation's decision to save or squander its resources. As a substitute for the motivational force of norms of reciprocity, which cannot apply over time, Rawls originally suggested that parties in the original position regard themselves as heads of households, bound to adjacent generations out of paternal sentiment, where "they are to ascertain how much they should set aside for their sons by noting what they would believe themselves entitled to claim of their fathers."[11]

Rawls later amends this standard (calling it "defective") by noting that obligations to other generations come not merely as a result of paternalistic sentiments, but by the consideration that whatever savings principle those in the original position choose, "they must want all *previous* generations to have followed it." He elaborates: "Thus, the correct principle is that which the members of any generation (and so all generations) would adopt as the one their generation is to follow and as the principle they would want preceding generations to have followed (and later generations to follow), no matter how far back (or forward) in time."[12] This consideration, he writes, preserves the "time of entry interpretation" of the original position, where "parties do not know to which civilization they belong or, what comes to the same thing, the stage of civilization of their society,"[13] but are aware that they are contemporaries. Insofar as parties in the original position all belong to the same generation, they must be given a *reason* for cooperating with past and future generations, or they will be insufficiently motivated to do so, given the costs of savings to the present generation in forgone consumption. However, no such reason is provided in this amended version of intergenerational motivation, where Rawls's unfounded demand for reciprocity replaces his objectionable sentiment of paternalism. Behind the veil of ignorance, rational persons are unlikely to endorse a savings principle that requires each generation to significantly forgo consumption in the interest of the next generation, to which none are worried that they might belong. Ultimately, he cannot justify his own truncated principle.

Missing is an account of why the premise of moral equality requires each generation to save and conserve in the interest of future generations. In denying that the difference principle applies to intergenerational justice, Rawls undercuts the foundation of a more thoroughgoing egalitarian allocation of resources over time, significantly limiting the scope and extent of intergenerational obligations. Savings—or, by extension, the maintenance of stable environmental conditions—becomes a duty incumbent upon present persons based only in the duty to establish or maintain institutions of justice in society, and then only requires us to act insofar as this can be done "without too much cost to ourselves." A more robust foundation for intergenerational obligations is needed if the significant costs necessary for reducing our GHG emissions are to be justified in the interest of fulfilling duties to future generations.

Why should parties in the original position endorse a principle of justice that requires the present generation to limit its current acts that have deleterious effects on the natural environment, when the adverse effects of such acts will manifest only in the future? Here, the counterfactual nature of Rawls's revised motive for parties in the original position reveals its shortcomings: Ignorant of the stage of national development in which they will live, no persons could endorse a standard of zero emissions growth, for this would impose a cap on development for those societies in the early stages of industrialization. Moreover, they cannot now agree to such a standard on grounds that they would have wanted all previous generations to follow it, for this implies a desire that society to have forgone industrialization entirely. The motive for capping national emissions in the interest of future generations cannot therefore be based in the Rawlsian thought experiment, which supposes this generation to be part of a cooperative scheme with past and future generations where all accept common limits in the interest of all. Past generations accepted no such limits, because such limits were unnecessary for most of human history, so there is no sense in which current adherence to the terms of a fair and effective global climate regime could be justified in this way.

In addition, parties in the original position, if ignorant of their national residence and stage of development, face a difficult wager in defining the terms of the principles of justice as they might apply to climate policy. As noted above, they cannot endorse very low per capita emissions on the Rawlsian grounds that they would have desired that all previous generations followed that rule, for that would be to forgo the economic and social benefits of development. Neither, though, could they endorse very high GHG emissions caps, for this would be to endorse climate change. Although parties in the original position might be averse to ecological hazards such as climate change, they could not endorse strict emissions caps within their own nations of residence unless they could be assured that other nations would also endorse them, lest they risk competitive disadvantage in development. Likewise, they could not endorse highly unequal national per capita emissions caps, for these would prevent development of poorer nations in which, for all they know behind the veil of ignorance, they might reside. Parties in an intergenerational original position may opt to endorse a global climate regime sufficiently empowered to enforce emissions regulations in a manner that would prevent the buildup of atmospheric GHGs over time, but it remains unclear what motive might support such a regime within the original position of contemporaries that Rawls insists on.

In short, Rawls initiates a discussion of intergenerational justice that yields a mechanism in which resource conservation issues such as climate change mitigation might be addressed through his just savings principle, but much more theoretical work is needed before such aims may be regarded as matters of justice. Problems of motivation in agreements between generations plague the defense of such duties, given the apparent impossibility of intertemporal reciprocity. Unless intergenerational cooperation of the sort required for a more egalitarian allocation of resources over time can be demonstrated to be rationally justified—as being the object of present duties based in concerns for justice, where securing the conditions necessary for maintaining the welfare of future persons can be shown to be required of those in the present—then the prospect of grounding duties of environmental protection in intergenerational obligations cannot be fully realized. Before unpacking a possible justification for intergenerational cooperation, however, we must confront two other conceptual obstacles to the defense of duties to future generations sufficient for justifying costly commitments to maintaining climatic stability.

The Future Generations Problem

Thus far, we have simply assumed that our present actions may beneficially or adversely affect the welfare of future generations, so this inquiry has focused on the theoretical problem of whether and why such interests might connote claims by future persons on present actions or policies. If the *UNFCCC*'s mandate of preventing dangerous anthropogenic interference with the planet's climatic system is a duty of justice, then we must owe future persons something; at minimum, we must be able to think of them as being able to make claims on our present decisions such that we are prohibited from engaging in acts or adopting policies that cause them harm. Such claims may assert rights that can be violated by policies that do not adequately guard against environmental degradation or they may posit interests that stand to be affected and so deserve to be considered by current policy-making processes. If future persons have a right to a stable climate, then we in the present have a duty toward those future persons to recognize and protect that right, which requires us to limit our overall GHG emissions, accepting some costs now for their benefit later. Moreover, we would have this duty regardless of whether any persons in existence at the time of our decisions were benefited or harmed by them, since our duty is to future persons, even if we also have duties to persons alive now. If future persons do not have such a right, it remains unclear whether or why we should now be concerned with the long-term consequences of our present actions.

For reasons examined in the next section, we cannot suppose that future generations of persons have any rights that are binding on us now, since persons cannot acquire rights until they come into existence. Should we continue on our current emissions trajectory, raising atmospheric concentrations of heat-trapping gases to dangerous levels and seriously destabilizing climate for well over a century, we cannot violate the currently existing rights of any future persons. Neither, as examined below, can we obviously harm future persons by our present actions. Not only do future persons lack currently binding negative rights against harm, but it may be impossible for us to harm any particular future persons through our current policy decisions. Taken together, we can refer to this disjunction between present actions and either harm to or rights of future persons as the *future generations problem*. Although the idea that we in the present may affect the rights or interests of future persons seems obvious, the causal connection between current policies and the rights or interests of future persons is more difficult to establish than it may seem. We can go no further unless we can first defend the notion that our actions now can benefit or harm future generations. Absent this basic premise, we can have no obligations of justice toward them.

The chief argument against basing intergenerational obligations on either the rights or interests of future persons comes from what Derek Parfit calls the *nonidentity problem*, an objection involving the causal chain connecting present acts to the identities of future persons. Insofar as the different policy choices we make today may differently affect reproductive patterns into the future—for example, by changing the time at which parents conceive—the identities of those who exist as future persons depend in some measure on these choices. As Parfit claims:

> It is in fact true of everyone that, if he had not been conceived within a month of the time when he was in fact conceived, he would never have existed. Because this is true, we can easily affect the identities of future people, or *who* the people are who will later live. If a choice between two social policies will affect the standard of living or the quality of life for about a century, it will affect the details of all the lives that, in our community, are later lived. As a result, some of those who later live will owe their existence to our choice of one of these two policies. After one or two centuries, this will be true of everyone in our community.[14]

When we embark on significant policy paths, where the future world would be quite different had we chosen an alternative path, much in the possible world generated by one policy would be different from the possible world of the other policy, including the people who reside in it. Given our choice between policies that Parfit calls "Conservation" and "Depletion"—options that can be taken to represent effective and ineffective climate policy—and the different levels of material prosperity that are likely to result from either option, the identities of future persons turn on our present decisions. The future world that results from a current choice of conservation would in a century or two be inhabited by an entirely different set of humans than those who would exist had we instead chosen depletion.

As a result of choosing a high-growth, high-consumption, and high-pollution path, the planet's future capacity to fulfill human wants and needs will likely be significantly diminished by environmental degradation and climatic instability, worsening conditions for those inhabiting the future world. While we can reliably predict these adverse consequences for those who *would* live in a polluted and depleted future world, Parfit argues that we cannot validly say that our present policy choice actually harms any future person. How can this be? According to the nonidentity problem, we can say that our choice of depletion will cause increasing resource scarcity and pollution and that such conditions are averse to the welfare of future persons, but we cannot say that our choice harms any *particular* individuals, since "if we had chosen Conservation, this would not have benefited these people, since they would never have existed."[15] No future person whose existence depends on our present choice of depletion could regret our having made that choice, so cannot claim to be harmed by it. Had we chosen otherwise, they would never exist.

Assuming their lives to be worth living, it would be better *for them* to be born into a world of scarce resources and low prosperity than never to be born at all. Choosing conservation today is, in effect, a choice to deny one set of possible persons the chance to be born, and this must be worse for them than any possible harm that might befall them once born, including conditions of severe resource scarcity. Unless the present policy choice causes them to exist *and* causes them some harm relative to alternative policy scenarios in which they would also exist, which Parfit calls "Same-People Choices," that policy cannot be bad *for them*, and thus cannot be the object of current obligations. The claim that we have a duty to maintain environmental conditions beyond the lifetimes of those persons currently in existence entails either some identifiable set of persons to whom that duty is owed or at least a causal chain that connects our current policy decisions to the welfare of future persons. No persons born as the result of a policy of depletion could validly complain of our having harmed them, since their very existence owes to our current choice. Since our choice neither benefits nor harms any particular future person, the only way in which we can presently affect future generations is to cause one set of persons to be born rather than another, but this neither harms nor benefits either. Or so, at least, it would seem.

Given the apparent impossibility of our present policy choices directly harming particular future persons, it appears that we cannot have any duties with respect to them, including negative duties not to harm them and positive duties to assist them, since neither is possible, at least insofar as these obligations are to persons. Of course, this assumes an individualist ontology in which obligations are owed by individuals to other individuals, and such objections cannot impugn moral systems based in webs of communal relationships or other collectivist ontologies, but it does challenge the egalitarian justice theories through which the climate convention's expressed ideals of equity and responsibility are to be realized. We can compare possible worlds resulting from conservation and depletion, by this account, but each would be inhabited by an entirely different set of persons, making average welfare comparisons possible but attributions of fault or offense for current actions difficult and interpersonal comparisons impossible. We can predict that average future persons born under conservation would enjoy more abundant resources, less pollution, and a more stable climate, but as Parfit points out, such a policy would probably lead to considerably fewer future persons than would exist under depletion, since sustainable policies limit population growth while unsustainable ones allow for higher growth rates.

Hence, comparisons between these two possible worlds is further complicated by what Parfit calls "Different-Number Choices," where the larger number of persons existing from depletion policies offsets the higher average utility enjoyed by the smaller number resulting from policies of conservation, making depletion the policy alternative that yields greater total utility over time.[16] We must prefer the greater total utility of depletion over the greater average utility of conservation, Parfit suggests, or be logically committed to culling the world's least advantaged in order to raise averages. But this commits us not only to depletion but also to maximizing population up to that point where additional persons have lives that are barely worth living, as each additional birth adds to total utility up to that point, an implication he calls the "Repugnant Conclusion" but nonetheless finds inescapable.

Combined with the uncertainty surrounding the needs and preferences of future persons, these observations have confounded efforts to justify moral duties toward future generations of the kind asserted by the climate convention, which depend on the premise that our present actions can either harm or protect the interests of future persons. Unless we can show that some policy choice that we make now—opting for a fair and effective global climate regime rather than the status quo, for example—will benefit future persons or that its alternative will harm them, we cannot justify the expense to the current generation entailed by such a policy. If, as is supposed by the climate convention, we have some duty toward future generations to maintain climatic stability, then it must at least be possible for us to harm future persons by our present actions. It is simply incoherent to suppose that we have a duty that it is either impossible to discharge or impossible to fail to do so; to say that we ought to do something implies not only that we can, but also that we can be bereft in our duties. Parfit's argument casts doubt on that possibility and with it the notion that we have obligations toward future generations of any kind.

One possible strategy for avoiding this conclusion is to dispense with the individualistic basis of ethics altogether—where duties can be owed only to individual persons—distinguishing instead between actions that make conditions worse for future generations taken as a whole and those that merely have an effect on the identity of specific persons. Here, as in the Rawlsian just savings principle, moral duties are seen as being owed to entire generations rather than specific individuals, so effects on the identity (though not the number) of future persons are treated as irrelevant.[17] Unless the welfare of future generations somehow reduces to the welfare of its particular individual members, this approach encounters some of the problems of attributing collective responsibility examined further in chapter 5. Another strategy accepts that moral duties are owed only to individuals but denies that individual acts of environmental degradation affect the identities of *all* future persons, even if some are affected, causally linking present acts with future harm to at least some specific persons.[18]

For example, my decision to drive to work rather than walking or taking public transit adds marginally to future pollution and resource scarcity, but surely my act leaves unchanged the identities of most future persons for whom that marginally greater scarcity constitutes a burden.

Both approaches, however, encounter similar problems in disaggregating individual from aggregate effects. The first entirely subsumes the individual within the collectivity by its focus on whole generations, which are not moral agents and so cannot have the rights, interests, preferences, or welfare associated with persons, in treating generations rather than persons as the objects of harm and therefore recipients of obligations, whereas the second erroneously assumes that individual contributions to epiphenomena such as climate change can be distinguished on the basis of whether each particular act affects the identities of future persons or merely harms them, thereby isolating discrete instances of environmental degradation that cause harm but do not affect the number or identity of future persons. Both, as Parfit notes, rely on a version of the principle of beneficence that "will not appeal to what is good or bad for those people whom our acts affect,"[19] and here the future generations problem returns. Absent identifiable parties that can lodge a valid claim against the present generation to limit its consumption in the interest of avoiding harm to them, or at least parties whose interests can be demonstrably and adversely affected by our present patterns of resource use, there would appear to be no defensible basis for the claim that we ought to manage our resources for the benefit of as-yet nonexistent persons. If depletion is morally wrong, it is unclear who is *wronged* by it.

Environmental Rights

One possible way around the future generations problem involves the recognition of environmental rights. If future generations have interests that can be adversely affected by climate change, then they may be able to make moral claims against the present generation that seek to ensure that current policies do not damage the planet's climatic system. Regarded in this way, such claims might be based in moral rights, and our duties toward future generations based on their right to climatic stability, rather than grounded in distributive justice or based in the adverse effects of current policy on particular future persons. Intergenerational justice, then, would be a matter of assuring equal rights for all, including future persons, and respecting those rights through current choices. But do future generations have a right to a stable climate system? Would this generation violate the rights of future persons if we allowed excessive concentrations of GHGs to collect in the atmosphere, causing the range of effects predicted in the assessment reports of the Intergovernmental Panel on Climate Change? More basically, can future generations as collectives or future persons as individuals have rights at all? What would it mean to attribute a right to either a person or a group that does not now exist and whose existence is merely possible? Thinking about duties to future generations in terms of rights rather than distributive justice or Parfit's person-affecting utilitarianism offers several advantages, evident from our examination of the two main alternatives above, but a rights approach contains several problems and challenges of its own, which we now examine.

We might begin by distinguishing moral from legal rights. Both are structurally similar in that a rights holder has a valid claim against anyone who might violate that right. Moral rights are based in ethics, and the violation of this kind of right is a moral offense; it is *wrong* to violate a person's moral rights, and such violations may in principle be remedied through compensation or defeated by the assertion of a more primary right that "trumps" it in cases of conflict. Since rights claims entail correlative duties, others have a moral duty to respect my moral rights and a legal duty to respect my legal rights. Asserting a moral right connotes that the right ought to be recognized, whether by the state or by other people, and that others are under some obligation to respect that right. Most legal rights, then, are based in moral rights, but legal rights are formally recognized by the legal and political authority of a given state, allowing rights holders to press for a legal remedy if their rights are violated. When we ask whether there ought to be a right to a stable climate, our question concerns both kinds of rights; if a moral right can be justified, then there is a strong case for recognizing a legal right, as well.

Rights can be either positive or negative, and environmental rights such as one to climatic stability display features of both. In the case of negative rights, where persons are protected against certain kinds of acts by others—for example, the rights not to be harmed or deprived of free speech—claims are made against those specific persons or governments that attempt to violate those rights, while positive rights—for example, the right to an education or to economic security—require provision and so are made more generally on a state or society. Negative rights are violated only by the acts of others, then, whereas positive rights can be violated by their failures to act. As observed in chapter 7, both positive and negative rights can protect either basic or nonbasic interests, because all rights aim to protect or advance some set of valuable agreed-upon human interests. Finally, most rights are defeasible; there are some cases in which the violation of a right may be justified, morally and legally, so the claim for redress that is entailed by the possession of a right is only prima facie valid. The most common occasion in which a right is overridden involves direct conflict with another right that has priority over it—for example, you have the right to move about freely, but not to enter my home uninvited.

Here we examine moral rights, although these arguments generally contain the normative implication that states should also recognize them as legal rights. If future persons have a right to a stable climate system, then the moral disapprobation available from purely moral rights may be insufficient to prevent the current generation from violating that right, so transforming the moral right into a legal one, on which persons can seek legal relief from the state, may add the enforcement power necessary to fully realize the interest at stake. Indeed, this right is considered in chapter 7 as a possible legal right, and one that might serve to enforce the normative aims of the climate convention. Since we are concerned with the question of whether anthropogenic climate change violates the rights of future persons, we have three main questions to consider before such a case can be made: (1) Can there be anything like a right to a stable climate system? (2) Can rights be held by persons who do not yet exist and so are not actual people? And (3) can groups such as future generations be the holders of rights, which are normally reserved for individual persons?

The third question is the easiest to dismiss as an objection to the rights approach, since it collapses into the second one. Although we often speak of future generations as having rights as a collectivity, we may reduce those rights to individual ones such that only future persons and not groups hold rights that may be violated by our present acts. Since Rawls assumes through his just savings principle that the current generation has a duty to entire generations rather than to specific persons within it, we might infer that he has in mind collective rather than individual rights as the basis for those duties, but his "duty of assistance" (of which just savings is a part) is not based in rights—no persons or societies have a right to our assistance, even if we have an obligation of justice to provide it—making his just savings principle an inadequate foundation for defending the rights of future persons. If future individuals have rights, then nothing is added by supposing that the entire future generation of which they are part also has rights for or against the same things or that they have rights as a group rather than as individuals. It is more parsimonious to speak of entire generations rather than particular individuals, but we may without difficulty treat references to the rights of future generations as a kind of shorthand for rights held by the individual persons making up those generations. If future persons may have rights as individuals, then groups of them can, too.

The second question is slightly more difficult, because we cannot without difficulty say that merely possible persons have rights, since nonexistent persons now have no interests of the kind that rights protect. In order to dissociate this problem from the contentious metaphysical question of when a fertilized human egg becomes a person, let us consider as a "future person" only those whose existence may begin more than a year from now. Perhaps the most basic right of all is the right to exist, but can merely possible future persons have a right to exist? Suppose that they did. Counting all the possible sperm–egg pairings in one of my political theory courses, there are a great many possible persons whose right to exist stands to be violated by the failure of various combinations of students to bring them about. Can we say that some possible person has been wronged, in this case? Were this a legal as well as a moral right, should the state redress it by forcing some particular pairing? Since it would be physically impossible for all possible persons from my class to be brought into existence, do my students have some obligation to bring as many possible persons into existence as they can? Plainly, it would be absurd to suppose that all possible persons have rights, even those as basic as the right to exist, but this does not mean that future persons do not have rights. Only *actual* future persons, when they come to exist, and not merely all those *possible* future persons, have rights of this kind. Lacking current interests, however, actual future persons can only have rights in the future, once they become persons and so acquire interests, although these future rights may in the future be violated by actions committed in the present.

A second problem with attributing rights to future persons concerns the uncertainty not only about their identities but also about their tastes and preferences. Since rights are intended to protect or advance a person's interests, can we attribute rights to them in the absence of specific knowledge about those things that they would include among their interests? Joel Feinberg thinks that we can, as long as future persons have the kinds of interests that can now be identified and represented by proxies. In what he terms the "interest principle," he argues that both nonhuman animals and future persons have interests that can be advanced or frustrated, from which it follows that they may at least in principle have rights, because "a right holder must be capable of being represented and it is impossible to represent a being that has no interests," and "because a right holder must be capable of being a beneficiary in his own person, and a being without interests is a being that is incapable of being harmed or benefited, having no good or 'sake' of its own."[20] Insofar as rights exist in order to protect interests, being the sort of thing that has interests is a necessary but insufficient condition for having a right. Duties based in rights are essentially duties to advance, or to refrain from interfering with, certain kinds of interests.

Feinberg's sights are set lower than at defending actual duties to future persons that might bear on present actions or policies. Rather, he aims to discredit the notion that future persons cannot even in principle make rights claims that entail correlative duties. In response to an identity objection like Parfit's, Feinberg suggests that the fact that we can reasonably predict that our present actions will affect the interests of future persons, which are likely to be fairly similar to our own regardless of what specific genetic information those future persons contain, ought to be enough "to certify the coherence of present talk about their rights."[21] Uncertainties about future persons aside, he writes, "the vagueness of the human future does not weaken its claim on us that it will, after all, be human."[22] We may not know their specific identities, nor can we know much about the conditions in which they will live—whether, for example, new technologies will be available for reducing the costs of adapting to climatic changes—but we can know which basic human interests future persons will have and, in general, how our present policies may affect those interests. Feinberg, however, stops short of making the stronger claim that there are any such rights; his claim is merely that they are possible. While it is true that we can now conceive of some of those interests that future persons are likely to have—they will have basic needs similar to ours, including needs for food, clean air and water, and so on—"yet there are no actual interests, presently existent, that future generations, presently nonexistent, have now."[23]

While this allows Feinberg to avoid the absurd conclusion that every missed reproductive opportunity violates the rights of some possible future DNA sequence, the limitations his interest principle must overcome are serious ones for intergenerational justice. He maintains only that future persons will, once they come to exist, have interests that give rise to rights, but not that we now have any duties with respect to those interests. Moreover, representing the interests of future persons by proxies is complicated by the fact that we cannot know the circumstances in which future persons will live, so we cannot know for certain which of our current actions might later violate the rights of persons who come to exist in the future. Feinberg, that is, shows that we can identify some interests that are likely to arise in the future, at which point they will connote duties, but does not show how these interests now entail claims on current acts or policies.

Feinberg's discussion, despite its pessimistic conclusion about grounding present climate policies in the rights of future persons, may actually give us some traction in connecting current policies with future harm to persons. While we cannot harm the interests of a person that does not yet exist, and such potential persons can thus have no current rights based in those interests, our current policies can degrade the material or environmental conditions in which future persons will reside, and these conditions can be made worse in their ability to satisfy basic needs than alternative conditions produced by more environmentally sound policies. While we may not have any duties now incumbent on us that correlate with rights of future persons—at present, then, future persons can make no rights claims against us on behalf of these future interests—we may have duties now associated with the future effects of our policies on persons who will exist in the future. The key point is that we can presently talk about the future rights of actual persons—that is, persons who will come to exist and at that point have rights—because we can reasonably speculate about their needs and interests, even if those rights and their correlative duties do not presently exist.

As long as we can assume that the basic interests of future persons will be similar to ours, we can safely assume that we would be quite likely to harm those interests if we cause them to be deprived of goods or resources that are critical to our interests. Since we know that people will need clean water to drink in the future, we know that a policy choice now that causes all water to become too polluted to drink in a century will harm the interests of those living a hundred years hence. Though we may not violate the rights of future persons at the time that we make that policy choice, our choice would be almost assured of violating the rights of actual persons in the future, barring the intervention of some unforeseen technological solution to the problem developed between now and then. If persons in 2107 have rights to clean water, those future rights will be violated by our current policies insofar as these policies cause water supplies to be polluted in the future; though there are no binding rights or correlative duties in 2007, decisions made now can affect the interests protected by rights in the future and can therefore violate those rights. The mere possibility of water purification technology coming on line before then might avert those rights violations, but this kind of technological optimism cannot reduce our current responsibilities and does nothing to diminish the fault inherent in our polluting acts even if it manages to avoid blame for them.

To repeat what has been observed thus far: When others have moral rights, we have moral duties to respect those rights. It would be wrong for us to act in ways that cause someone's rights to be violated, whether those rights are violated immediately or at some point in the future. The lag time between the harmful act and its consequence appears to be morally irrelevant because such delays between cause and effect do not ordinarily defeat prima facie claims originating in rights. Although future persons are the sorts of things that can have moral or legal rights in that they have interests that can be estimated and represented, they can have no rights until they actually come to exist, connoting no duties until that point. Some policy choices we make today may violate the rights of persons in the future, even though the persons they come to affect do not exist today. This policy choice, therefore, may not be wrong today because it violates future persons' future rights—having no rights now, they can make no claim on behalf of those rights today—but the policy may *become* wrong in the future, once it violates those rights, if it does. If the policy is not wrong now for violating some persons' rights, even if it becomes wrong in the future for this reason, does this make the policy morally permissible today? There are other moral duties than those associated with rights, so do we have some other kind of ethical reasons not to choose the policy that apply to us now?

Parfit provides a useful analogy for thinking about the effects of our actions on future persons. Imagine, he suggests, shooting an arrow into a distant wood where it comes down, out of sight, and wounds some person. "If I should have known that there might be someone in this wood," Parfit claims, "I am guilty of gross negligence."[24] My act plainly caused the harm in question, and if I should have anticipated this possibility, then I acted negligently. The fact that I did not know the victim, or that she was far away in space, makes no moral difference. As Parfit argues, "remoteness in time has, in itself, no more significance than remoteness in space." Had my arrow been shot so high that it long remained in the air, finally coming down one year later and again wounding some person, then I would again be negligent insofar as I should have anticipated this outcome. Since negligence attaches to acts rather than outcomes—hence findings of negligence even when the act in question has not yet caused any harm—the negligence must attach to my act at the time that it was committed, not one year later when the harm eventually obtains. Ordinarily, negligence occurs much closer in time to the harm it risks, but there is no reason why this need necessarily be the case, and the determination of negligence need not wait until the harm is actually suffered. For this reason, persons may be guilty of negligence even if their risky behavior *never* causes harm.

The concept of negligence suggests something about the scope of our negative duties toward others when risk rather than actual harm is at stake. Not only must it be wrong to harm a person and a violation of their rights, but it must also be wrong to act in such a way that it becomes highly likely that a person will be harmed sometime in the future. The wrongness of negligence lies in the exposure of persons to risk of harm, and not only in the actual harm itself. As further considered in chapter 5, the actual occurrence of harm resulting from some person's having been exposed to risk by another's negligent act is largely a matter of luck, and we cannot justifiably distinguish between a negligent act that results in harm and one that, by luck alone, does not. The wrongness of a negligent act begins at the time of the act itself and is neither increased nor diminished by contingent facts or events that cannot have been anticipated by the agent in question, because negligence is defined in part by the risks that an agent should have anticipated causing. If we adopt the polluting policy today and some future technology prevents its adversely affecting persons a century from now, that policy is nonetheless wrong at the time we adopt it insofar as we can anticipate its harmful effects. It may not violate the rights of future persons, or violate the future rights of persons who come to exist in the future, but is wrong nonetheless, with respect to our duties toward future persons. It is faulty because it culpably exposes others to risk, and is no less so merely because that risk fails to manifest in harm.

The question of whether persons might have a right to a stable climate is taken up in chapter 7, where it can be distinguished from the problems associated with attributing rights to future generations. If currently existing persons can be said to have such a right, then the same right can be applied to future persons, so our acts in the present may in the future violate the rights of actual persons if these acts destabilize climate, even if they violate no such rights now. Unlike the right of future persons against being harmed, however, the right to climatic stability would prevent our acting now in a manner that caused climatic instability, since these actions would presumably also violate the rights of currently existing persons who suffer the earlier effects of the same acts. The problem with grounding duties to future generations is not in this right, however. Rather, it lies in the apparent impossibility of our violating any actual rights of future persons by our current actions at the time we must decide whether or not to allow them, which significantly weakens the claim that we have any present duties toward future generations that our choices of climate policies might now violate. In order to establish the stronger claim that we have duties toward future generations that require us as a matter of justice to exercise restraint on our GHG-emitting actions, it must be shown that we harm them, violate their rights, or deprive them of some good to which they have a valid claim by failing to do so.

Sustainability as an Obligation

Underlying the policy options for addressing the looming crisis of global climate change in theory and practice is the idea of sustainability. As a contested concept, its precise meaning has come to be the focus of scholarly debates, but those finer points of contention need not concern us here. Put simply, sustainability requires that present natural resources be consumed no more quickly than they can be replaced, so that, given stable rates of use and replenishment, they will continue to exist in perpetuity. Or more generally, the sustainable management of the environment allows for the maintenance of constant levels of welfare over time, as the capacity to yield the resources instrumental for welfare is not diminished. Since atmospheric absorptive capacity is a natural resource that can be used either sustainably, by releasing no more GHGs than can be safely absorbed in carbon sinks, or unsustainably, resulting in increasing atmospheric concentrations of GHGs, we may treat the imperative not to upset the planet's climatic stability as one for the conservation of a renewable resource. Like other renewable resource conservation issues, humans can use the atmosphere's absorptive capacity up to some point, but beyond this threshold the stability of the system is compromised and its future capacity to yield its current benefits is diminished. At issue in climate change, then, is whether and why there exists a moral obligation to manage the atmosphere in a manner consistent with its sustainable use. If there is an obligation to maintain climatic stability, there must be a related one not to exceed atmospheric absorptive capacity. But what is this duty, and why is it incumbent on us?

Although this discussion has not yet found a foundation for rights-based obligations to future persons, we may be able to defend one, in a form suitable for supporting the declared futurity aims of the climate convention, through a duty of resource conservation. Two key features of such a rights-based duty reveal themselves through consideration of the nature of environmental harms. First, for conservation to be effective, a steady commitment to its imperatives over time is required. A law that mandated sustainable forestry practices on every day but Sunday would obviously be ineffective in maintaining a sustainable forest. Second, conservation prescriptions and proscriptions must be binding on all, not merely on particular persons or organizations. To prohibit some but not all nations from unlimited emissions would be ineffective in guarding against the predicted hazards of climate change. Conservation practices, in other words, must be generally binding along two dimensions: over time and across borders or populations.

Not only must its imperatives be binding over time, but the prescriptions and prohibitions generated by a duty of conservation must allow for causal chains connecting actions with their consequences that stretch over time. If dumping toxic waste into a river is banned today for its deleterious effects on others, then so must be the storage of that same waste in containers that are expected to start leaking into the river a year from now. In both cases, the offense in question involves the intentional release of harmful pollutants into the water, which predictably increases risks of harm to others. Claiming that the harm obtaining next year is somehow less relevant to current decisions is to make a temporal cut that cannot bear careful scrutiny. As in the case of negligence, the offense in causing environmental harm with delayed effects is not diminished by the time lag between the negligent act and its resulting harm, as indeed some time lag is almost always present in harm from negligence, and the relevant fact about the victims of unsustainable environmental practices is not that they exist at the time of the negligent act but that they exist at the time when they are harmed. If the current generation is bound by a duty of conservation, then all must be bound by it and for their entire lifetimes, and the duties associated with it must ensure that critical resources continue to be available into the future. No temporal statute of limitations may excuse future harm that results from present acts as long as those harmful consequences may reasonably be predicted, and no spatial immunity may allow those harmful acts to transpire.

As Brian Barry notes, the idea of discrete generations is an abstraction in that it implies that one entire group of persons departs as another arrives on the scene, with no overlap. Since human population replacement is continuous and ongoing, a "prudent provision for the welfare of all those currently alive therefore entails some considerable regard for the future."[25] Because the harms that obtain from depleting or despoiling natural resources often have a delayed-release effect or a lag time before the offending act and the manifestation of the resultant harm, limiting culpability to harm affecting currently existing persons cannot be justified. If toxics from my underground storage tank leak into the groundwater and poison my next-door neighbor, then my act is no more pernicious than if my neighbor's infant daughter, born next week, is poisoned by them. To absolve a polluter of harm to persons born after some initial act that sets in motion the polluting process is to fail to take seriously the nature of pollution, which often functions like a time bomb on those who are later exposed to its hazards. Likewise with the atmosphere: Damage done to it at one point in time will continue to adversely affect persons long after, including some persons born well after the initial act. If rights to climatic stability entail negative duties on the part of others to refrain from causing climate change, then those duties must take into account the lag time between the initial emissions, the point at which harm begins to obtain, and the much later point when those emissions cease producing their adverse climatic effects.

None of these observations, though, yet defends a duty of conservation, although they do begin to sketch the outlines of one. As Parfit suggests, the relationship between generations is a kind of prisoner's dilemma, where the policy option that leads to the best overall outcome when considering the welfare of multiple generations is conservation, because slightly lower welfare for the current generation is traded for considerably higher welfare for future generations, but it is also true that each generation would be better off with depletion, because the costs of conservation are born by the current generation while most of its benefits will obtain in the future. No generation can rationally endorse conservation unless all generations are bound by it, but each generation needs a justification for accepting a coercive policy option that adversely affects current consumption in favor of long-term sustainability. On what grounds, then, may persons be rationally compelled to choose conservation rather than depletion?

The solution to the problem need not require knowing the identities or preferences of the future persons, or even the material conditions in which they will live, as long as current persons can rationally recognize that the present choice of depletion will make it impossible to recognize and protect the rights and related interests that each generation can affirm as basic to human flourishing. Insofar as we can identify existing persons who might later be harmed by our current actions, or delayed effects of our present actions that will very likely cause deleterious effects to persons who predictably will come to exist, then those adverse effects are just as binding on our actions as if our policy of depletion immediately violated the rights of existing persons. To suppose otherwise requires either the willful ignorance of the likely harmful effects of actions or policies, or the devaluation of the interests of future persons. Thus, we may justify environmental rights, which connote a duty of conservation, through an individualist ontology and egalitarian premises conjoined with a basic harm principle.[26] Recall that the first Rawlsian principle of justice argues from the thought experiment of the original position for the most extensive set of rights and liberties compatible with equal rights or liberties for all. Since treating persons as moral equals entails an equal concern for their welfare—whether that welfare is to be enjoyed now or in the future is irrelevant and to suppose otherwise is to rely on an unjustified time preference—egalitarian premises can justify a set of obligations to future persons based in rights as long as it can somehow be demonstrated how future rights of merely possible persons might be binding on present decisions.

Since the recognition of rights entails correlative duties, these duties can include claims on behalf of future persons as long as we can grant that future persons *will* have rights equivalent to those accorded to actual persons once they come to exist, and that our present actions and policies can affect the future protection of those rights along with the interests they aim to protect. If a right to climatic stability will in the future be threatened by policy decisions made today, then our ability to connect those policy decisions with future rights violations must inform our current decisions. Moreover, our duties of justice to future persons may be built on our duties to existing persons. Recall that the nature of environmental harm requires that duties related to it be binding across persons and over time, and that the logic of the intergenerational prisoner's dilemma requires some assurance that agreed-upon limitations will continue to be binding into the future in order to guard against each genera-tion's incentive to free ride. If we in the present have an obligation to refrain from excessive GHG emissions—met by, for example, stabilizing atmospheric GHG concentrations at some agreed-upon level—then this duty must apply to all and continue to do so over time. The correlative duty implied by a right to climatic stability, in other words, is ongoing and makes no distinction between emissions that will cause harm immediately and those that will cause harm only in the future. If this generation has a duty to maintain climatic stability, then it makes little difference whether its unsustainable emissions violate rights now or violate them in the future, since nothing enjoined by the latter would be allowed by the former.

If we examine, *contra* Parfit, the effects of our actions on our contempo-raries and immediate successors, we can readily find justification for an obliga-tion to conserve, or to ensure that our current actions and policies do not contribute to climate change. The duty of conservation that must therefore be acknowledged by this generation originates in the rational capacity of *foresight*, which involves one simple idea: We can often make reasonably accurate predic-tions regarding the consequences of our actions for others in the future, as well as about the nature of our likely future obligations. Negligence, then, may be regarded as the offense of a failure of foresight, and recklessness the disregard of its warnings. Although I do not currently owe anything to my landlord, I can reasonably predict that I will at the beginning of next month. If I spend all of my paycheck this week, I will have no problem meeting my financial obliga-tions in the immediate future, but problems will arise when the rent again comes due. While I may have no current debts and my landlord has no current claim to that amount of my rent, I can reliably foresee that claim arising in the future. The fact that I *can* anticipate this ought to guide my financial choices between now and the time my rent is due, or I am likely to fail in obligations that, even though I do not have them now, I can expect to have in the future. Foresight draws the salient distinction (overlooked by Parfit) between current obligations and those duties that will predictably be incumbent on existing per-sons at some point in the future but whose discharge depends in some mea-sure on their present acts. The fact that we can now foresee having these obligations has moral consequences for us.

In the case of climate change, many of the consequences of present rates of GHG emissions are already well known, and much of the predictable harm that will likely result in the future is based on fairly firm scientific evidence. As has been pointed out several times in recent theoretical discussions of obliga-tions regarding the environment, the difficulty is not in figuring out *how* to conserve existing resources or even *how much* of them to conserve, but is rather in convincing ourselves *why* we are required to do so. As Barry notes, "It is not terribly difficult to know what needs to be done, though it is of course immensely difficult to get the relevant actors (governmental and other) to do it."[27] When it comes to the consequences of current GHG emission rates for future climatic stability and their related effect on the welfare of future generations, the argument from foresight offers a justification for the imperative to sustainably manage the atmosphere. In this sense, it provides the missing theoretical defense for the right to climatic stability, or for the correlative duty to act now in order to ensure that we avoid violating that right in the future.

This capacity of foresight involves the moral duty to avoid causing predictable harm to others conjoined with a basic principle of equality that refuses to discount harm simply because it accrues in the future, and requires that we take just as seriously problems that our current actions cause tomorrow (or the next day, month, or year) as those that they cause immediately after the offending actions. Because of the problematic nature of establishing obligations to future and therefore nonexistent persons, foresight instead considers present and foreseeable future duties we have, and will come to have, to actually existing persons, including those that will actually exist in the future. If we can foresee that our current actions will, in the future, cause harm to or violate the rights of some future person, or if they are highly likely to do so, then we should refrain from engaging those actions. Although we may not now be amiss in any duty to others in that we do not immediately cause anyone harm or violate anyone's rights, if we are now at the point of decision after which either of these outcomes is likely, we ought to act as if we are now duty-bound to respect those rights and refrain from harm. As noted above, a future person's right to clean water may not be violated at the time that I poison their well since they can have no such right until they come to exist, but the fact that it will *later* be violated ought to be sufficient reason for me to keep the poison out of the well.

Given this understanding of agreeing to a practice of conservation based on rational foresight, the pitfalls associated with Parfit's nonidentity problem are avoided, since a decision to be bound through time to conservation does not entail that the present generation know the actual identity of those they seek to avoid harming by conserving natural resources. Similarly, the other uncertainty problems associated with claims by future others are likewise avoided. What is next needed, then, is an elaboration of the claim that foresight might demonstrate the necessity of conservation, if equal rights are to be recognized and protected, thus giving rise to binding obligations of justice for present generations. In order to establish this point, it must be shown that present individuals are obligated to conserve, without assuming that nonexistent future persons have no morally relevant claims to make on present persons, and that only actual persons can make actual claims, even if they do so backward through time. To do otherwise is to assume a crucial premise, as others have done in taking as given a concern with future persons. Following the common practice in philosophical arguments of this sort, this point is illustrated through a logically possible case involving a desert island community that is completely isolated yet contains residents who are perfectly rational and well educated in contemporary moral and political philosophy.

The Desert Island Case

Suppose, for example, that a self-sufficient island community with a stable population base relies, for some significant measure of necessary utility, on the trees in a forest on the island. On this island, it is not uncommon for people to live into their nineties, but nobody ever makes it to ninety-six years (human warranties, let's say, expire on the ninety-fifth birthday). Suppose further that the island's trees are not self-regenerating, but must be replanted by people if they are to replace those trees harvested for use. Finally, suppose that the only utility gained by persons from trees comes from their use as lumber, which requires a mature tree that is at least 100 years old. As long as usable trees remain, the island community prospers (these are a simple people), but should the mature trees in the forest ever completely disappear, the people will quickly follow them into oblivion. In this case, can any moral obligation of conservation be assumed?

Each year, 1 percent of the original forest is cut down and used for timber. During the first year (t_1), it is clear that every currently living person will have timber available for use throughout his or her lifetime without any replanting program. Furthermore, persons alive when a tree is replanted are assured that it will be of no value whatsoever during their lifetimes. The only possible justification for replanting would appear to be through the assumption of an obligation to future generations, which as Parfit and others point out, cannot exist. Although in possession of perfect foresight into the consequences of their decision, the islanders follow the philosophical advice they receive from Parfit—his *Reasons and Persons* washes up on shore and is afterward taught in schools—and do not replant the trees they have removed.

Five years later (t_5), having depleted 5 percent of the forest, it is clear to the islanders that some of their newborn infants will be alive the year the last tree is cut down. While all of the adults capable of rational decision making on the island are assured of a constant supply of trees throughout their lifetimes, the fact of the appearance of these new moral subjects forces them to reconsider their policy of not replanting the trees they remove. All are in full knowledge that, on complete deforestation, the remaining islanders will retreat briefly to a Hobbesian state of war of all against all, as resource plentitude is necessary for maintaining civilization, before vanishing completely. Do they begin to replant now, for the sake of their children? As was the case at t_1, any tree planted at t_5 will be of no value to anybody currently alive at t_5. Since moral obligation cannot attach to those not yet born—those who might enjoy the benefits of a planted tree—there can be no moral duty to replant, despite full knowledge of the grisly consequences inevitably waiting for their youngest fellows. It is already too late to change the replanting policy. Doomsday awaits the islanders at t_{99}, when the last remaining tree will be felled and not replanted.

Clearly, every year after t_5 contains the same fatalistic resignation that nothing can be done to avert the pending disaster. Could this outcome have been avoided? In year t_4 the replanting decision would be rejected, since not only would no currently living persons be affected, but also the decision in t_1 made deforestation inevitable, regardless of any future actions. As in Garrett Hardin's parable describing the logic behind "The Tragedy of the Commons," the rational basis of the replanting decision rushes the islanders headlong into ruin, despite their full knowledge of the consequences of their actions. Perhaps, in the final human years on the island, Parfit will be demonized for his contributions to the island's Armageddon, but unfairly so, since every islander fully accepts the truth of his claims about duties to future generations.

This scenario contains some obvious simplifications that fail to hold in the real world. Even if no substitutes for trees were available, and even if per capita consumption of trees could not be reduced,[28] the islanders could undergo voluntary population reductions in order to reduce rates of consumption, delaying the inevitable exhaustion of the forest. Even so, the decision to replant will be dictated by the ability of those efforts to benefit some currently living person, and the islanders will eventually perish, maybe in year t_{115} instead. The trees, although commonly held, could be subject to market distribution, where the price ratchets upward every year as supply decreases, delaying the onset of severe scarcity. Without available substitutes or alternative suppliers of trees, the market would only make trees more expensive as scarcity increased, so the final years, in addition to the anxiety regarding the coming catastrophe, would be wracked by inflation. If trees were privately held, the end would come just as surely, although with additional profiteering for the forest owner and cruelty inflicted on those forced to pay monopoly prices to stave off an earlier-than-otherwise-possible death. Short of some breakthrough by the island's genetic engineers that allows for the production of trees that can mature in a period of less than 95 years (the life span of humans), and unless this breakthrough is made in time to prevent complete deforestation, the outcome in year t_{100} (or t_{115}, or whenever it eventually occurs) is determined by the decision in year t_1, and every subsequent year, that replanting is morally unjustifiable.

Since Parfit, let's say, objects to genetic engineering in some later-suppressed apocrypha to which only the islanders are privy, is there anything else that might save the islanders from their own self-destructive logic? As long as trees take longer than a human lifetime to mature, they will never be replanted and will eventually be exhausted. If, however, a kind of futures market in trees were established, and shares in tree futures could be traded, then the islanders may be able to stave off deforestation. In year t_1, let's say, trees are planted by the islanders as part of a for-profit scheme that involves the selling of shares of the future value of the tree. While nobody alive in t_1 could hope to redeem a share of the mature tree in year t_{100}, that share might nonetheless be valuable if it could be held and traded. Beginning in year t_5, some new parents might want to buy these shares in tree futures to assure their children of available wood in their final years. As the years pass, these futures become more and more valuable, since more and more actual persons would be willing to pay for future shares in a tree that they might need in their lifetime. Although they could not benefit from the actual redemption of the futures share, speculators in year t_1 would nonetheless rationally be interested in the trees planted that year because gains from the transfer of that share could be realized during their lifetimes.

The point of the above example is not to argue that free market economics can save the world. Instead, it is to suggest a way out of the dilemma raised by the problem of future generations. The islanders have a rational interest in resource conservation, even without considering the interests of future persons, because the continued availability of trees is valuable *to them*. Even without the futures market scheme, they can through foresight recognize that conservation is a rational practice, since only by present adoption and future adherence to such a policy can disaster be averted. Choosing to deplete the trees today by consuming them without replanting is functionally equivalent to condemning to death all those islanders who might be born next year. That they do not know the identities of these future persons or that they might themselves not have any more children is not relevant. The failure to conserve will, all must realize, affect those who will be born and will suffer as a direct result of present decisions. To return to Parfit's example, if they know that they can prevent certain harm by consenting to the enforcement of a particular practice, they are obligated to do so. They must choose Conservation rather than Depletion because they do not want to be responsible for making the choice that leads to the avoidable suffering of others.

To be bound to the practice of conservation requires not only that people limit their consumption this year, but that they agree to do so in perpetuity, else the game theory solution be lost. Only if an agreement were binding across time would people now be motivated to adopt and adhere to one. It does little good to conserve in t_1 if in t_3 people fail to do so, or even if there is suspicion that they might do so. If, therefore, we have obligations in t_1 to conserve the natural resource base, then those obligations by logical necessity must continue in t_2, and so on. And while in t_1 we may only have obligations to benefit those currently alive, some of them will have obligations in t_{25} toward those born over the upcoming quarter century, and so on. In this way—sometimes described as a "zipper" because it binds together a long string of persons by binding them to their immediate neighbors—our obligations can extend out across generations, including those whom we will never live to meet, though we can affect their welfare by our present actions. Through being a party to this ongoing obligation of conservation, rationally consented to because of rational foresight into the consequences of an alternative decision, arises an indirect obligation to future generations that is every bit as compelling as a direct one.

Conclusion

Once we consider the nature of the capacity of foresight, with its ability to predict the future consequences of or present acts and policies, we must reject the notion that our harmful acts are benign if their effects are felt only in the future. Moreover, once we consider the nature of a duty of conservation, which might be based on a right to climatic stability, we can see that it requires an ongoing practice of sustainable environmental policies, including those that aim to stabilize atmospheric concentrations of GHGs. Construed in this way, there is nothing in such a duty that requires for its justification the consideration of any unique effects on future generations; the same actions or policies that cause distant-future climate-related harm affecting only future persons also cause near-future harm affecting existing persons. Between these two observations and the notion—expressed in Rawls's first principle of justice—that society owes as a matter of justice the most extensive set of rights and liberties compatible with their equal allocation, we can establish a defensible foundation for the right to climatic stability (further explored in chapter 7) as well as a solution to the future generations problem, at least insofar as it might undermine the case for a prudent provision for futurity expressed in the climate convention. That is, if people's interests count equally, and if the continued availability of natural resources affects welfare in the ways suggested previously, then persons with a sense of justice and fair play through foresight ought rationally to commit themselves and their societies to conservation as an ongoing practice. Importantly, this defense of conservation does not depend on the identities of affected persons, nor does it rely on the Rawlsian condition that principles accepted in the original position apply also to previous generations. Instead, it is a decision that can also be made by rational persons with full knowledge of existing conditions and without regard to reciprocity (at least, in this sense).[29]

5

Moral Responsibility and Greenhouse Gas Emissions

The question of who should pay the costs of climate change—that is, of how the burdens of greenhouse gas (GHG) emission reduction efforts and adaptation or compensation costs for victims of climate-related harm should be assigned among nations—looms large in the design of a fair and effective global climate regime. Allocating these costs fairly, as discussed in preceding chapters, involves principles of distributive justice, since at least part of the declared goal of the climate convention is to promote equity through GHG abatement efforts and adaptation programs. Along with those equity-based standards already examined, a second criterion of fairness must be used to inform the design of a global climate regime: the responsibility-based model of fairness identified in the "common but differentiated responsibilities" language of the *UNFCCC* embodied within fault-based liability. Responsibility is a complex philosophical concept since it contains several distinct senses in which persons or groups may be held responsible for some act or outcome, but relies on the same general term to describe these various meanings. This chapter examines the concept of responsibility in its variety of distinct but related senses with an eye toward answering the question of how the various costs of a global climate regime should be assigned.

We might begin by briefly distinguishing the two most basic senses of responsibility examined in this chapter and the next one: between *causal* and *moral* responsibility. Causal responsibility describes relations of cause and effect, involving matters of fact from which no prescriptive implications necessarily follow. When scientists observe atmospheric concentrations of CO_2 that had been stable for millennia suddenly begin to rise, leading to myriad other effects, their interest is in responsibility of this kind; they seek to explain the phenomenon's *causes* and not to attach moral blame to particular persons or policies. On the other hand, observing that developing nations have not contributed toward the climate-related harm that they are projected to suffer and that industrialized nations have been causing that harm, and concluding from these two empirical observations combined with a normative principle of responsibility that industrialized nations ought therefore to bear the greatest climate change mitigation burdens and/or compensate developing nations for the harm they are likely to suffer, employs the concept of responsibility in quite a different sense. The first sense describes a related between observed phenomena, while the second prescribes appropriate responses. One sense is empirical and the other normative.

Although these two senses are distinct, moral responsibility is often assumed to rely on causal responsibility as a necessary if insufficient condition, but the relation between the two is sufficiently nuanced to warrant further analysis. This chapter examines the various ways in which we might hold a person—or, in the case of collective responsibility, a group of persons—responsible for some harmful act, including a variety of related but distinct varieties of moral responsibility. In addition, this chapter examines the normative *principle of responsibility*, on which many of our assessments of national liability for the costs of climate change are based. As Brian Barry articulates this principle: "A legitimate origin of different outcomes for different people is that they have made different voluntary choices…[and] bad outcomes for which somebody is not responsible provide a prima facie case for compensation."[1] As a principle that applies the concept of moral responsibility to issues of distributive justice, Barry's formulation highlights the role of what is often termed the *control condition*, which holds that the extent to which agents can control outcomes through their voluntary acts and choices determines the extent to which they may be held responsible for them, setting up several conceptual quandaries with significant implications for global climate policy. Throughout this chapter and the next, this principle is challenged and, should it survive these challenges, is applied to several of the problems surrounding the design of a global climate regime.

Another problem to be considered below concerns attributing collective responsibility to entire nations for harm resulting from anthropogenic climate change. The normative sense of responsibility used here requires moral agency, and typically only individual persons, and not groups, can be regarded as moral agents. In addition, holding entire groups responsible for the actions of only some of their members appears to violate the principle of responsibility, because outcomes for which some are held responsible lie outside of their control. It might be objected here that the claim "industrialized nations are responsible for climate change" is merely a kind of shorthand for attributing responsibility to large groups of individual persons and that collective responsibility reduces to individual responsibility, but several observations weigh against such an objection. First, the attribution of responsibility might reference national culture or policy, and these are inherently collective products rather than the sort of thing that can be attributed to individuals separately. Second, the design of a global climate regime must allocate emissions caps to nations themselves and not to particular individuals, and assess liability at the national rather than individual level. Finally, many of the predicted impacts of climate change involve ecosystem disruption, political and economic instability, and heightened social and international conflict, and these are inherently collective rather than individual costs. If groups are to be held responsible for the actions of only some members, then some cogent account of collective responsibility is needed, given the objection above.

What Is Responsibility?

While our practical question concerns legal responsibility, because a climate regime must hold parties liable for climate-related harm, our desire to construct a fair and effective climate regime requires that we begin with a philosophical account of responsibility in order to ensure that our legal attributions of responsibility rest on sound normative foundations. Joel Feinberg, whose interest in responsibility likewise seeks to join the legal and moral theories of the concept, offers a fivefold classification of responsibility, accounting for the various ways in which the term is used descriptively, ascriptively, and prescriptively, and these shall assist us in making some relevant preliminary distinctions:

(1) *Straightforward ascriptions of causality* entail no moral agency, no fault, and no liability. In this sense (using Feinberg's examples), a high-pressure system over the Great Lakes may be responsible for today's weather, or Smith may be responsible for the toilet seat being left up; we merely mean that one phenomenon caused another. (2) *Ascriptions of causal agency* can but need not necessarily entail fault or liability, as they attribute authorship of actions to persons and describe morally complex actions. For example, a straightforward ascription of causality might have Peter turn a key, open a door, raise a knife, and stab Paul in the chest—each of these being relatively simple acts in themselves—but an ascription of causal agency would have Peter murdering Paul, where the latter describes a morally complex action and attributes agency

to its author. (3) *Ascriptions of simple agency* involve simple actions that cause nothing further; they may have consequences, but they are not parts of more complex acts, so while moral agents might commit these kinds of acts, they cannot generate other kinds of responsibility. (4) *Imputations of fault* ascribe agency "for a somehow defective or faulty action" and so typically depend on causal agency along with a moral judgment of culpability. Most such judgments are "defeasible" in that fault is prima facie but may be defeated by a sufficiently plausible justification for the act, though some acts always entail fault (they are "indefeasible"). (5) *Ascriptions of liability* entail assignments of responsibility for some further response to an earlier harm, typically through the imposition of compensatory or punitive damages for some faulty act. These latter two are often confused, as Feinberg notes, but they are not the same: One might be at fault for an action for which she is not liable if, for example, one's faulty action doesn't result in harm, and one may be liable for an action for which she is not at fault if, for example, liability is assessed according to one's ability to remedy. Liability, unlike fault, can be transferable, as when persons designate powers of attorney to others; vicarious, as when parents are held responsible for acts of their children; or strict, or independent of actual fault.

From Feinberg's fivefold classification of responsibility, we might begin to connect the two senses of responsibility noted above. The first three kinds of responsibility are descriptive and empirical and aim to establish cause and effect relations between separate events. We might say, for example, that fossil fuel combustion is responsible for climate change, or that Smith driving his Hummer for fifty miles to work each day is responsible for increasing atmospheric GHG concentrations. Neither of these statements imputes fault or ascribes liability, and both are claims that can presumably be established as true or false. When we say that Smith produces too much GHG pollution or find that he owes compensation to the victims of climate change for his excessive emissions, our claim is normative and prescriptive rather than empirical and descriptive and so lacks the truth value of the first three kinds of responsibility. This is not to say that persons cannot be held responsible in the latter two senses, but instead that some form of normative argument, typically combined with empirical claims about causal responsibility, is required in order to establish moral responsibility. While most of the theoretical problems to be addressed through the concept of responsibility concern moral rather than causal responsibility, it is to the latter that we first turn, in order that we may better understand the former.

In attempting to establish empirical causes in order to arrive at normative prescriptions, Feinberg aptly notes that "the meaning we assign the word 'cause' is likely to vary with our purposes."[2] If we wish to produce some new effect, we need to know the *sufficient cause* of that effect, which includes all of the variables necessary for bringing that effect into existence. If instead we wish to avoid some effect, we typically are concerned with identifying *necessary causes*, or those individual variables that, when taken together, make up the effect's sufficient cause. Since most social or environmental problems are the products of highly complex causal chains, public deliberation about how best to address those problems tends to concentrate on identifying necessary causes and then targeting the one that is most readily manipulated, as Feinberg explains: "However much we wish to get rid of defects and infelicities in our bodies, machines, and societies, we never wish to eliminate them at *any price*. What we want when we look for 'the cause' of unfortunate happenings is an *economical* means of eliminating them, the right price being determined by our many implicit underlying purposes."[3] Although social and environmental problems may have multifarious causes, the one attached to liability is likely to depend on an independent judgment concerning the most efficient means of reducing or eliminating the problem or of assigning remedial costs.

Thus, in looking for "the cause" of climate change, we might identify the discovery of coal-based steam power or the invention of the internal combustion engine, the Green Revolution that increased world agricultural output and consequently global population, the design of cities around the automobile that led to longer commutes, American campaign finance laws that allow carbon-intensive industries to dominate the political process and undermine effective climate policies, the advertising industry that promotes unsustainable consumption, the failure of public schools, or any one of a number of relevant variables that together account for the high emission rates in the contemporary United States or elsewhere. Feinberg's point is that it would be an "oversimplification" to identify any one of these single causes for such a complex phenomenon as global climate change to the exclusion of all others. We are interested in causes because we seek solutions to problems, and the identification of *the* cause to address through public policy involves a calculation about the most appropriate means for solving the problem. Attributions of causal responsibility as precursors to moral responsibility thus contain implicit judgments about our future ability to manipulate those variables, not claims about sufficient causes.

Obviously, some of the above "causes" of climate change would be unsuitable targets for an effective climate policy approach. Past scientific or technological discoveries cannot simply be intentionally forgotten, and intermediate causes for contributing variables such as population growth cannot now be reversed without fomenting a humanitarian catastrophe. Past and current emissions cannot now be undone, and conversion from high- to low-emissions technologies or practices involves a considerable time lag between policy initiation and effect. Ultimately, the question of "the cause" of high emissions rates in the

United States, as elsewhere, shall be an issue for policy makers in national, state, and local governments charged with designing and implementing policies that meet their assigned emission reduction targets. Whether the most "economical" policy approaches involve carbon taxes, individual GHG emissions quotas, public investment in emissions-reducing infrastructure, or development and dissemination of efficient technologies makes for an important part of national climate policy debates but is tangential to the design of a global climate regime, which is concerned with what level of emissions various nations ought to be allowed and how they might be allowed to count such measures, but leaves such questions of policy implementation for national governments to decide within the constraints set by the global regime. Hence, although the causes of global climate change are multiple and contestable, in our analysis of causal responsibility for climate change we shall assume the necessary causes to be individual and national GHG emission rates as well as the government policies that enable these rates, leaving other causes to other levels of analysis.

Causal versus Moral Responsibility

How is moral responsibility related to causal responsibility? Suppose, for example, that Smith kills Jones, by which we mean that some act by Smith was both necessary and sufficient to bring about Jones's death. While we may clearly find him to be causally responsible for Jones's death, under what circumstances may we also find Smith to be morally responsible for it? Jones may have been killed by a pure accident—unforeseen by Smith and not due to negligence or other recklessness, although his act was a necessary cause—in which case he bears causal responsibility but neither fault nor liability for the death. Suppose instead that Smith unintentionally kills Jones through a reckless act, where Smith consciously disregards the risks to which he exposes Jones. Here, we find that Smith not only caused Jones's death, but that he is also liable for it. That is, Smith's recklessness was at fault for the death of Jones, and for this recklessness Smith owes compensation to Jones's survivors for having killed him. We might now, in this case, hold Smith to be morally responsible for killing Jones, despite the fact that the death was unintentional and in significant measure a matter of luck, because only a fraction of reckless acts wind up causing harm to others, and luck alone determines which do and which do not. Obviously, we would likewise hold Smith morally responsible if he intentionally killed Jones, and we might treat this as a more serious offense than a reckless killing. From these cases, we can infer that causal responsibility for some bad outcome is often a necessary but never a sufficient condition for attributing moral responsibility for that outcome. Also necessary is some imputation of fault on Smith's behalf.

Moral responsibility, then, refers to a family of distinct but related normative concepts that are worth distinguishing from one another at the outset. Assigning compensatory or punitive costs to a person or group for some harm suffered by another person is to attribute *liability* to them for remedying this harm, and is the form of moral responsibility of primary interest here. As Feinberg notes, the standard conditions for attributing individual liability are threefold:

> First, it must be true that the responsible individual did the harmful thing in question, or at least that his action or omission made a substantial causal contribution to it. Second, the causally contributory conduct must have been in some way *faulty*. Finally, if the harmful conduct was truly "his fault," the requisite causal connection must have been directly between the faulty aspect of his conduct and the outcome. It is not sufficient to have caused harm *and* to have been at fault if the fault was irrelevant to the causing.[4]

Although not the only valid type of liability, this standard case is based in *contributory fault*, for it requires both causal responsibility and moral fault, where the faulty action contributes to the harm in question. Several nonstandard cases of liability are considered below in which one or more of these conditions may not be satisfied, including collective responsibility, where at least some who are held liable may not have directly contributed to the harm in question, and assessments of liability that do not depend on the existence of fault.

What, then, makes an act faulty? Although contributory fault limits its purview to faulty acts that contribute to harm, an act can be faulty without causing harm if, for example, an agent is found to have been *negligent* but avoids causing some harm by a stroke of luck. Since fault admits of degrees, persons can commit faulty acts that contribute, if only in a minor way, to some harm without being liable for that harm. As Feinberg notes, "A person can be morally at fault in what he does without being morally responsible for some given harm, even when the harm would not have happened but for his 'fault.' The harm can be properly ascribed to him only when his 'fault' is sufficiently 'serious' and makes a sufficiently 'important' contribution to the harm."[5] I attempt to further parse these distinctions below, but note for now that moral fault entails that a person is also liable for some act, but that persons can be held liable for acts for which they are not at fault, as in vicarious liability, and even sometimes for harm to which they have not contributed, as in capability-based ascriptions of liability. The various degrees of responsibility can get confusing when allowed to proliferate in this way, so let us confine our purview to a practical question for designing a global climate regime: Under what circumstances may liability be attributed to agents, whether nations or persons, that are found to be causally responsible for some harm?

Our question, then, draws on the legal concept of responsibility in that it is essentially asking whether the relevant agents may be ordered to pay the costs of the harm that they cause. In many ways, legal responsibility is analogous to moral responsibility, as the use of such terms as "fault" and "liability" suggest. Legal responsibility, in which persons are punished for their actions or ordered to pay compensation for harm that results from them, depends on its correspondence with judgments of moral responsibility for its legitimacy, else the coercive use of state power against persons who had done no wrong would raise obvious objections. But the two are not always identical, for reasons that are mostly practical: Assessments of moral responsibility rely on an agent's state of mind, intentions, knowledge, and beliefs, and these are not readily ascertainable by the institutions charged with determining legal responsibility, which instead rely more heavily on the observed consequences of acts, along with any aggravating or mitigating circumstances surrounding them—including evidence concerning the mental state or *mens rea* of the accused—as the basis for determinations and degrees of responsibility.

Insofar as legal and moral responsibility inhabit different spheres—one mostly external and the other mostly internal—several interesting problems arise for the theory of responsibility in general. Sometimes, moral and legal responsibility come to divergent judgments concerning the existence of fault and the assignment of liability, as in the problem of *moral luck*, examined further below. Since our inquiry is based on the problem of assigning costs within a global climate regime, this divergence between legal and moral responsibility may present a problem: Like legal institutions generally, a global climate regime lacks reliable access to those mental states that determine moral responsibility, and so must rely on that external evidence on which legal responsibility is based. If the climate regime is to be fair, however, it cannot attribute fault or assign liability to agents unless they are also responsible in the moral sense. While in most cases legal responsibility and moral responsibility do not diverge in this way, those several cases in which they may do so in the context of our climate inquiry require some further examination.

Positive versus Negative Responsibility

Can we hold persons responsible for consequences that result from their omissions in the same way that we hold them responsible for their actions? This question remains a controversy within ethics as different plausible ethical theories offer contrasting answers. Consequentialist theories base judgments about right and wrong acts on resulting good or bad consequences, making no distinction between consequences resulting from acts and those from omissions. According to consequentialist theories, should I fail to warn you that you were about to eat a poisonous mushroom that would kill you if ingested, my omission, when I could easily have prevented your death, would be just as wrong as if I had poisoned you myself. Deontological ethical theories, on the other hand, attribute less importance to the consequences of acts, and so they often treat consequences resulting from acts differently from those following from omissions. Since the project of this chapter is not to say which ethical theory is the correct one, I raise this distinction here only to note the philosophical controversy involving the moral difference outcomes of acts and those of omissions, or between positive and negative responsibility.

In practice, many moral decisions blur the distinction between positive and negative responsibility, since it is not always clear what constitutes an act and what an omission. For example, we can attribute responsibility to industrialized nations for their high rates of GHG emissions, but are these high rates a kind of act or a kind of omission? On one hand, emissions result from activities that people voluntarily do—driving cars, flying on airplanes, heating large buildings with fossil fuels, and so on—and since these activities are possible to avoid and known to contribute toward climate change, they appear to be more like acts than omissions. Note that persons are held causally responsible for consequences of acts that they commit even if those consequences are secondary or even unintended—they need not drive cars *for the purpose* of polluting the atmosphere in order to be responsible for so doing—because these are irrelevant to the question of what caused some effect. On the other hand, we might think that they are a kind of omission, since within nations that industrialized long ago and that consequently had high per capita emission rates prior to the widespread recognition that these caused anthropogenic climate change, continued high rates of emissions owe to the failure to take active steps to reduce those emissions. Again, the facts that increasing concentrations of atmospheric GHGs are caused by a failure to modify unsustainable behavior or to enact adequate climate policies is not relevant to the question of causal responsibility: We can explain the continuing contribution to climate change by the industrialized nations in terms of either positive or negative responsibility, and neither diminishes our confidence in the judgment that these nations or those residing in them are, in fact, responsible for causing climate change.

The distinction between positive and negative responsibility is often parsed in terms of the difference between killing and letting die, where the former describes agents taking an active role in bringing about some death while the latter refers to a more passive, if equally deliberate, role with the same effect. As noted above, consequentialist ethics makes no distinction between the two, in effect attributing moral responsibility to agents for any bad outcome for which they are found to be causally responsible, whether through their acts or omissions, but in doing so it runs roughshod over considerations (e.g., knowledge, intentions, and motives) that loom large in assignments of legal responsibility. Bad consequences that result from accidents, for example, are typically treated differently under law than similarly bad consequences intentionally brought about, and justifiably so. Given our concern with holding persons or nations legally as well as morally responsible for their contributions to climate change, a more nuanced examination of such considerations is warranted.

An instructive analysis of the ethics of responsibility, which draws on the distinction between positive and negative responsibility in connecting causal with moral responsibility, can be found in Onora O'Neill's essay "Lifeboat Earth," which is ostensibly about world hunger but contains several insights that may readily be applied to some of the philosophical problems surrounding climate change, as well. Consider, she proposes, two lifeboats with six passengers each: one (the "well-equipped lifeboat") with adequate supplies for all to survive until rescue, and another (the "underequipped lifeboat") without adequate supplies. Assuming that all passengers have a prima facie right not to be killed, she asks: Under what circumstances may one or more passengers justifiably cause the death of another passenger on either of these two lifeboats? On the well-equipped lifeboat, she argues, self-defense may be invoked if A threatens to jettison needed drinking water and the others kill him in order to preserve their own lives, provided that killing is the minimum force necessary for self-defense, but B–F cannot be justified in withholding food from A. To do so would be to wrongfully kill, even though the effect is indirectly brought about. On the underequipped lifeboat, by contrast, with enough water for four but not all six passengers, some killing may be justified since two deaths are unavoidable, and "those who did not survive were killed justifiably if the method by which they were chosen was fair."[6] In at least some circumstances on each lifeboat, then, some killing may be justified, and some is unjustified.

When none deliberately attempts to jettison needed supplies from the well-equipped lifeboat, though, might killing ever be justified? Supposing that there exists exactly enough for all six passengers to survive if each consumes the minimally necessary quantity of food and water, would the overconsumption of food or water by one or more passengers be considered to be an unjustified killing, violating the rights of those who, as a result, no longer have access to adequate food or water? Though even less direct in its causation than withholding food, O'Neill thinks so, claiming: "Aboard a well-equipped lifeboat any distribution of food and water which leads to a death is a killing and not just a case of permitting a death. For the acts of those who distribute the food and water are the causes of a death which would not have occurred had those agents either had no causal influence or done other acts."[7] In contrast to the underequipped lifeboat, on which at least two deaths are unavoidable, allowing some to die of starvation or thirst on the well-equipped lifeboat is an act of wrongful killing since those deaths would be avoidable with another distribution of food and water. The fact that none of the passengers intends the deaths, that they occur indirectly as the result of a failure to adequately ration essential supplies rather than through active killing, or that they result from acts (eating and drinking) that are not normally thought to be wrong are not relevant to our moral assessment of them. In this case, we treat a distribution of food and water that causes someone to starve or die of thirst in exactly the same way that we would treat the intentional withholding of food or water from them, despite the fact that one appears to be a kind of act and the other a kind of omission.

O'Neill's argument, of course, is meant as an analogy for the complex causes of famine, which likewise results in deaths on what is essentially a well-equipped lifeboat in that sufficient food and water are produced worldwide to feed all persons on the planet. Her aim is to discredit the case for failing to come to the aid of those suffering from famine by basing principles for the global distribution of food on a negative duty not to kill rather than positive duty to assist, and to dissociate obligations with respect to the distribution of essential goods such as food and water from larger questions about distributive justice. Even with significant global inequality and if all were entitled to their unequal shares of the earth's resources, O'Neill claims, it would be wrong to distribute the world's food resources in such a way that some died from famine. Notably, she claims that this is the case regardless of property rights, rejecting the basis of libertarian claims against positive duties to assist: Even if B is entitled to a much larger share of natural resources than is A, she suggests, "it does not follow that B's exercise of his property rights can override A's right not to be killed."[8] By framing food distribution issues in terms of rights, a defensible rights hierarchy would give priority to more basic rights, such as the right not to be killed, over ones that are less basic, such as the right to acquire or transfer property.

Three general observations about moral responsibility follow from O'Neill's example. First, the issue of distribution of goods that comprise basic needs is directly associated with basic and negative moral rights such that food distribution, and by extension, distribution of all other basic goods, becomes an issue with significant normative implications. Rights are sometimes thought to be unrelated to distributive justice, but this need not be so. One person's excessive consumption of a scarce resource can therefore be seen as a morally objectionable violation of another person's basic rights, and one that overrides nonbasic rights such as those surrounding property, transforming that otherwise private act into a public concern. Similarly, one nation's overconsumption of basic goods such as atmospheric absorptive capacity likewise might be regarded as violating the rights of those forced to consume less as a consequence, and must therefore be treated as an issue of global concern rather than left as purely an internal matter subject to the principle of state sovereignty.

Second, O'Neill's emphasis on the consequences of acts or decisions while invoking a rights-based ethics downplays the distinction between positive and negative responsibility, the roles of intention and uncertainty, and the importance sometimes given to geographic proximity or interpersonal affection. These are not unimportant considerations—no rights would be violated by purely accidental deaths, nor would they be if fair procedures were used to determine which passengers must die on the underequipped lifeboat—but what matters most in assigning fault for causing a death is that persons could have acted otherwise and at costs less significant than those associated with the loss of life. Causal responsibility for avoidable harm, whether positive or negative, here forms the cornerstone of moral responsibility and thus obligation, not the myriad other rationalized forms of selfishness that are often invoked against pleas for the world's affluent nations to do more to relieve the want-related suffering of the impoverished. While most assessments of fault are defeasible, they are not easily voided by the considerations listed above.

Finally, O'Neill raises a salient issue about moral responsibility in climate ethics with her discussion of self-sufficiency and interdependence. Given the interdependence of the global economy, it is possible that economic policies set thousands of miles away might be sufficient causes of want-related suffering and, indeed, that economic policies might violate basic rights in ways that may be indirect and unintentional, but no less deadly. She explains:

> When persons die because of the lowered standard of living established by a firm or a number of firms which dominate a local economy and either limit persons to employment on their terms or lower the other prospects for employment by damaging traditional economic structures, and these firms could either pay higher wages or stay out of the area altogether, then those who establish these policies are violating some persons' rights not to be killed.[9]

O'Neill notes further that lowered commodity prices resulting from agricultural overproduction resulting from domestic subsidies, which harm overseas food production, might likewise cause wrongful deaths. While her analysis relies on a fairly complex causal chain, the larger point is that, given global economic interdependence, very few economic transactions can be truly isolated from their potentially harmful indirect effects. She notes that "modern economic causal chains are so complex that it is likely that only those who are economically isolated and self-sufficient could know that they are part of no such systems of activities."[10] Since persons residing in industrialized nations cannot be economically isolated from the harmful global effects of domestic economic policies, they have a rights-based duty to support policies designed to avoid causing harm worldwide. The same applies to acts and policies affecting the atmosphere: Since none is ecologically isolated from the effects of worldwide GHG emissions, all are by O'Neill's analysis potentially responsible for the harmful effects of their acts and choices and so have a duty not only to reduce individual emissions to that point where sufficient atmospheric capacity is available to all, but also to support policies that guarantee a fair allocation of atmospheric capacity.

Moral Luck

As described above, the principle of responsibility requires that persons be held responsible for the consequences of their voluntary acts and choices, but not for those resulting from circumstances that are beyond their control. In the context of a global climate regime, the questions of who pays and how much they are to pay also turn on this distinction: Assigning liability without contributory fault may be defensible on other grounds, but it cannot rest on the conventional theory of responsibility, because this would entail attributing liability to an agent for redressing some harm for which the agent cannot be held responsible. The requirement of contributory fault as a necessary condition for assessments of liability rests on an intuition that Thomas Nagel describes in his analysis of an ethical problem known as *moral luck*. This moral intuition, based in a standard referred to above as the *control condition*, holds that "people cannot be morally assessed for what is not their fault, or for what is due to factors beyond their control."[11] According to this intuition, we can praise or blame persons for their voluntary acts or choices, but not for consequences that result from luck alone. As Nagel notes of this condition, "a clear absence of control, produced by involuntary movement, physical force, or ignorance of circumstances, excuses what is done from moral judgment."[12]

The problem of moral luck lies in the fact that many good and bad consequences result from a combination of both voluntary acts and choices and the uncontrollable contingencies of circumstance, challenging the intuition behind the control condition. In such cases, the intuition that Nagel describes comes into conflict with another intuition: that persons should be blamed or punished only for those acts that cause harm, and praised or rewarded only for acts that do good. The problem of moral luck forces us to choose one intuition over the other, although neither seems mistaken. He offers an example of Smith and Jones, who each drive home from a cocktail party while slightly intoxicated. Neither should have driven, because both were impaired, so both recklessly endanger others by their ill-chosen behavior. While Smith makes it home without incident, Jones strikes and kills a pedestrian on his way home. Smith may be guilty of a lesser legal offense than is Jones, but do their respective moral offenses also differ? Most probably share Nagel's intuition that there is a morally significant difference between reckless driving and manslaughter, but the only difference between the acts of Smith and Jones owes entirely to elements outside their control. Had the pedestrian attempted to cross the street in front of Smith rather than in front of Jones, their offenses would have been reversed. Whereas Smith was "morally lucky" that no one was in his path as he drove home drunk, Jones was unlucky, but "his recklessness is exactly the same."[13]

Nagel identifies and names this conflict between two intuitive judgments: "Where a significant aspect of what someone does depends on factors beyond his control, yet we continue to treat him in that respect as an object of moral judgment, it can be called moral luck."[14] At first, the problem appears paradoxical: It seems that we must either abandon the control condition, and with it Barry's principle of responsibility, or else admit that there exists no morally significant difference between the acts of Smith and Jones. It would not help to posit that Smith and Jones are both guilty of the same initial offense (reckless driving) but that only Jones was guilty of the additional offense (manslaughter), because this additional crime lies entirely outside of the control of either Smith or Jones. Moreover, the bad outcome for which Jones is blamed results from a combination of intentional action and luck—we would not blame Jones at all if the pedestrian's death was the result of a pure accident rather than his faulty decision to drive while impaired—but the same could be said of the benign outcome of Smith's identical decision. We cannot blame Jones for his bad luck without a reference to his faulty decision, but Smith made the same faulty decision. Holding Jones guilty of an offense for which Smith is innocent relies exclusively on causal responsibility in one moral judgment, holding that Jones *caused* something while Smith did not, while ignoring it altogether in another, holding that both are equally guilty of the alleged offense of reckless driving, though this caused no harm in itself.

The problem of moral luck is pervasive in ethics, since many of those acts that call out for moral assessment involve both external contingencies and internal volitions, motives, and intentions. Insofar as we treat as morally relevant those consequences resulting from luck either alone or in combination with voluntary acts or choices, we must concede that moral judgment cannot be prospective or determinate at the time of decision, but must instead be retrospective, depending on the eventual consequences of acts. When we commit an act, we do so under at least some uncertainty about its eventual consequences, even if we intend to produce certain outcomes and may foresee possible others. Given this uncertainty, our culpability for some act may well depend on what happens after we make the decision to commit it; its rightness or wrongness may not be evident at the time of decision. Although consequentialist ethics cannot evaluate acts until their consequences are known, we can see the moral verdict in advance of our knowledge of which outcome will obtain. As Nagel notes: "If one negligently leaves the bath running with the baby in it, one will realize, as one bounds up the stairs toward the bathroom, that if the baby has drowned one has done something awful, whereas if it has not one has merely been careless."[15]

The problem of moral luck manifests as what appears to be a conceptual gap between moral and legal responsibility, where persons are held morally responsible for all faulty actions but only legally responsible for those faulty acts that result in harm. In cases of recklessness, that is, persons are held legally responsible only for those bad outcomes to which they contribute by their morally faulty action, and can be exonerated or held responsible for a lesser offense for reckless acts that, by luck alone, harm no one. As Feinberg explains:

> One man shoots another and kills him, and the law holds him
> responsible for the death and hangs him. Another man, with exactly
> the same motives and intentions, takes careful aim and shoots at
> his enemy but misses because of a last-minute movement of his
> prey or because of his own bad eyesight. The law cannot hold him
> responsible for a death because he has not caused one; but, from the
> moral point of view, he is only luckier than the hanged murderer.[16]

Not only would the law treat these two cases differently, but consequentialist ethics would seem to, as well. Absent some bad consequences, utilitarian ethics cannot condemn some act as wrong (or so it would seem), even if the act was committed with the *intention* of bringing about those bad consequences, failing to do so only as the result of luck. As discussed in chapter 6, *prospective* consequentialism avoids this problem with moral luck, but this apparent paradox afflicts the *retrospective* evaluation of acts.

In Feinberg's example, we have two choices in our moral assessments of these two cases: We can treat them identically, condemning both men for attempted murder and treating the actual killing in the first case as morally irrelevant, or we can treat them differently, where successful attempts at murder are treated as either uniquely wrong or morally worse than unsuccessful ones. If we treat the two cases identically, then we concede that actual consequences of acts are irrelevant to moral judgment, contradicting a strong moral intuition, and that only motives and intentions matter in moral assessment. If we treat them differently, regarding attempted murder as a lesser offense than success-ful murder, then we must admit that actual consequences of acts *do* matter, regardless of intentions, even where luck alone is responsible for the disparate outcomes in otherwise similar cases, and must therefore abandon the principle of responsibility for its rejection of luck as a morally relevant consideration.

In order to isolate the effects of luck from our moral judgments, we may invoke what Feinberg calls "the doctrine of the internality of morals," claiming that moral and legal theories of responsibility have a different jurisdiction. Here, morals are held to "constitute a kind of internal law, governing those inner thoughts and volitions which are completely subject to the agent's con-trol," while "the external law governs a man's relations with his fellows, to which both other persons and outer nature can make unexpected and uncon-trolled contributions."[17] This solution to the moral luck problem supposes that judgments of responsibility can be made more precisely and persuasively if the contingencies of luck can be controlled and a person's will or volition made the sole object of assessment. Judgments concerning legal responsibility require observations of external consequences of acts since they cannot have direct access to internal motives and intentions, and so are inevitably subject to the arbitrariness of luck. Although they may aim to *approximate* moral responsibil-ity, as based on external evidence about an agent's motives or intentions, assess-ments of legal responsibility cannot depend on a person's mental states alone, and so must include consequences as among the relevant variables distinguish-ing more from less serious offenses.

Invoking such a doctrine, as Feinberg notes, cannot rescue moral respon-sibility from the inescapable arbitrariness associated with legal responsibility. Basing moral judgments on internal mental states rather than external circum-stances might appear to mitigate the influence of luck on moral judgments, but this solution is not as compelling as it might at first appear. Luck seems to be an entirely external phenomenon, but this solution to the problem of moral luck and the criticism of the control condition that it implies fails to eliminate arbitrariness from moral judgment insofar as it still leaves a causal role for luck in determining mental states. Feinberg illustrates this causal role in another example in which two agents are similarly provoked, but one is distracted by some noise at the precise moment at which he would otherwise have formed the intention to commit a violent act, preventing that intention from forming. Since he would have been held responsible for the intention as well as the violent act that it motivated and bad outcome that it produced, luck alone distinguishes the faulty agent from the faultless one, despite this purely internal standard of moral assessment. Luck enters the picture in myriad ways, and the alleged "complete control and independence of luck" to be found in an internal domain moral of responsibility, relying on intentions alone in moral assessment, cannot rescue the control condition from the arbitrariness problem observed above.

This problem, however, need not be fatal either for the principle of responsibility or for the congruence between moral and legal responsibility. As Feinberg notes of such problematic cases, legal responsibility "is something to be *decided*, not simply *discovered*."[18] Although pragmatic considerations often demand that courts reach determinations of legal responsibility, assignments of liability are neither more nor less capable of controlling for all vagueness or contingency than are judgments of moral responsibility, on which they ought to be based. We can find it unfair to reward or penalize someone based on factors that lie outside of their control while admitting that the distinction between what is and what is not within their control is not always clearly determinable. Hard cases exist in both law and ethics, but we need not abandon useful principles every time they fail to yield uncontroversial judgments. The mere facts that we are sometimes impelled not to punish negligent acts that by luck alone avoid causing harm, as in Nagel's example, or to treat unsuccessful malicious acts as less serious than successful ones, as in Feinberg's, cannot refute the control condition, for in neither case do we completely excuse the lucky agent. Both cases underscore the commonsense intuition that consequences do matter, but both also emphasize the extent to which the control condition remains intuitively plausible. Attributing responsibility and assessing liability, in the case of climate as in other problematic cases, must be the product of rational decision making that is based on good reasons after weighing all relevant facts, where both an agent's mental states and the external consequences of acts that follow may be relevant to such decisions.

Moral Responsibility and Moral Mathematics

Multifarious individual acts and choices contribute, often imperceptibly, to the causal chain that is expected to produce profound changes to the planet's climatic system unless significant mitigation efforts begin soon. Persons, that is, through various individual acts, *cause* climate change—they are *causally* responsible for the problem—but are they *morally* responsible for the harm that is expected to result? Since many of the acts that contribute GHGs into the atmosphere are common activities in which no harm is either intended or anticipated, nor is any adverse effect even perceptible, few of the acts for which persons are causally responsible for contributing to climate change exhibit the obvious characteristics of moral fault. Attributing moral responsibility for these predicted harmful consequences is further complicated by failures to correctly assess the import of various individual contributions to collectively produced harm, or errors in attributing causal responsibility that Derek Parfit calls "mistakes in moral mathematics." The conceptual difficulty in disaggregating minute and discrete individual contributions from aggregate phenomena such as global climate change complicates assessments of fault and therefore also liability, and so warrants further attention here.

Supposing that anthropogenic climate change will, as is predicted, cause significant harm to persons in both the near and distant future, to what extent can that harm be attributed to faulty individual emissions of GHGs, released through such mundane activities as driving automobiles, using electrical appliances, or eating beef raised in deforested subtropical areas? Connecting an aggregate effect such as climate change to its individual causes is complicated by the countless tiny point sources of GHG emissions, threshold considerations, and other problems of disaggregating large cumulative consequences into apparently negligible discrete acts. Given the nature of an aggregative harm such as air pollution, there exists a kind of paradox of small effects: It appears to be true of no one that their acts by themselves cause any palpable harm to anyone, and yet the combined like acts of many cause significant harm. In view of consequences, it seems paradoxically to be the case that a morally significant harm has resulted from a series of morally insignificant acts; some bad outcomes appear to have been caused by entirely blameless acts.

One solution to be further considered below comes through the concept of collective responsibility, from which we might hold individual GHG-producing acts faultless but aggregate national emissions at fault for the harm of climate change. Here, attributions of fault for climate change would be what Feinberg terms *contributory group fault: collective but not distributive*, where the group as a whole is at fault for some harm, but no member is held to be individually responsible for it. Consider, Feinberg suggests, Jesse James robbing a trainload of passengers, where the group could have easily overwhelmed him and saved their property, but instead all submit to the robbery. Here, "no individual

in the group was at fault for not resisting," since the individual failure to perform the supererogatory act of a hero cannot be faulted even though its performance would be praiseworthy, but the group as a whole can be faulted "for not
producing a hero when the times require it."[19] Even if no passengers were
faulty in their inaction, all must individually be held vicariously liable for some
harm for the group's failing. In standard cases of vicarious individual liability,
one person may be held liable for the fault of another, but in this example there
is no individual person at fault. Thus, the fault must lie elsewhere, in the collective acts or omissions of the entire group, but not in any single one of its
members.

The problem of attributing responsibility to individual polluters is similar
in form to the *voter's paradox*: Given the vanishingly small chances of a single
vote altering the outcome of a national election, participation by each is thought
to be irrational, since the expected costs of voting outweigh any expected benefits from the activity. Assuming one additional vote to make no difference in
the election's outcome, each individual vote is assumed to be inconsequential.
Yet, *in combination*, individual votes may make a difference. Here, some act
that apparently has no effect on its own may have a significant effect as part of
a set of similar acts, leading to the apparent paradox that individual acts simultaneously do and do not make a difference. While quantitative social scientists
estimating the expected costs and benefits of voting may be correct in claiming
that the chances of being seriously injured or killed on the way to the polls are
higher than those of altering the outcome of a national election with a single
vote,[20] it does not follow that the expected consequences of voting are zero, only
that they are very small.

Indeed, single votes in large elections and single GHG emission-producing
acts among seven billion humans sharing an atmosphere both appear
insignificant in comparison with either aggregated votes or emissions, but this
appearance is deceptive. As Parfit has shown, the sort of accounting on display
in the so-called voter's paradox involves not a paradox but a "mistake in moral
mathematics." This mistake consists in what he terms "ignoring small chances"
of a single act. The *effects* of altered electoral outcomes may not be small, but
the *chances* of a single vote altering those effects certainly are. Nonetheless, we
must consider those very small chances against their large potential effects.
Parfit here argues by analogy: We would ordinarily treat a one-in-a-million
chance of killing a person as an acceptable level of risk, but would not so readily
dismiss the same odds, faced by a nuclear engineer, of killing a million people.
"When the stakes are very high," he suggests, "no chance, however small,
should be ignored."[21] Since we cannot vote with the benefit of hindsight and so
cannot know at the time of decision whether or not our single vote may make

a difference, we must estimate the expected value of the vote by discounting the effects of altered electoral outcomes by the chances of our altering them. While our resulting value is likely to be microscopic, it will be slightly above zero, assuming the altered electoral outcome to have positive value.

While both involve small acts and large outcomes, the case of minute and multifarious individual contributions to climate change is distinct in that it involves not the small *chances* of individual acts causing significant harm that creates the apparent paradox, but instead the very small and often imperceptible *effects* of individual actions that cause, in combination with other like actions, significant harm. A great many actions have small, almost immeasurable effects on environmental quality, yet no single one of them may have a perceptible effect on any person. Taken collectively, though, billions of tiny point sources of pollution do cause perceptible harm. Whereas it is highly likely that a single vote will make no difference in the outcome of a national election, a single GHG emission does have some effect on climate change, even if this effect is so tiny as to be imperceptible. In both cases, though, the moral value of each tiny contribution to a large aggregate phenomenon is related to its expected value, which is tiny but not zero, despite any mistaken inference to the contrary.

May we conclude from this disaggregation of small contributions from large effects that each polluting emission indicates an act that indeed causes some harm, albeit a tiny fraction of a significant problem, and that can therefore be treated as a faulty act by a regulatory regime? Must we treat these micro-offenses as constituting acts of palpable harm, though their individual effects are imperceptible, warranting state interference?[22] If so, the upshot is a ban on nearly all human activity, including the exhaling of CO_2, insofar as such acts release GHGs into the atmosphere. Such a conclusion would obviously be absurd. But does the rejection of this absurd conclusion justify its opposite: that we should not regard any small act of pollution or resource degradation as harmful? Although this conclusion may be adopted by policy makers, such an inference does not follow necessarily and at least requires further argument before its implication for environmental regulation can be accepted.

One obvious mistake in the above inference concerns *threshold effects*, in which the many individual contributions to an aggregate harm are individually insufficient to produce some harmful consequence but jointly become sufficient to cause harm. Consider a chemical such as fluoride, which has neutral or even beneficial effects below some threshold concentration in drinking water but becomes toxic once that threshold is exceeded. Suppose further some group of would-be assassins, each of whom puts a small amount of this chemical in their intended victim's well on successive days (they could also be would-be opponents of tooth decay, since their intention is not relevant to the example), but for the first several weeks the threshold is not exceeded. Then one day, the addition of a few more drops of the chemical into the well brings the concentration in the water over the toxic threshold; the victim drinks it and consequently dies. Not realizing this, several additional assassins show up in the days following the fatal dosage, each dumping their droplets of chemical into the now-deceased victim's former water supply. Which, if any, of the assassins is at fault?

Individually, no assassin contributed a sufficient amount of the chemical into the victim's water supply to individually cause the harmful outcome, but it would be counterintuitive to hold that none of the assassins was responsible for the victim's death. We might think that the only one responsible was the assassin whose contribution exceeded the threshold, but this act was functionally identical to all like acts that occurred both before and after. Presuming that none knew the exact concentrations of the chemical within the water, the earlier assassins could not have known that their contributions were individually insufficient. The only difference between the act that finally made the difference and those coming before or after was a matter of pure luck, and as noted above, such luck normally cannot distinguish between the faultless and faulty. Parfit argues that, in such a case, all of the assassins, including those whose contributions came after the threshold was exceeded, acted wrongly and should be held to be equally responsible.

Individual GHG emissions cause harm in much the same way as the above example of threshold effects. Not only are individual emissions exceedingly small contributions to a large aggregate effect, causing us to make one kind of mistake in moral mathematics, but it is also true of each that their individual contributions would be entirely faultless if not for the similar contributions of a sufficient number of others, causing another mistake. After all, humans were for millennia able to engage in activities that released GHGs into the atmosphere without the atmospheric concentration of CO_2 rising above 280 ppm, so not affecting the global climate in the way that humans have in the past half century. At much lower than present per capita emissions rates, preindustrial concentrations might have been maintained even with the rapid population growth rates of the past century. And at today's much higher per capita emission rates, it would be possible to sustain a smaller global population's fossil fuel combustion without exceeding the planet's capacity to reabsorb those gases. Only after a threshold is exceeded—in population or per capita emissions, or some combination of the two—do further emissions begin to cause harm. Thus, some act that once was entirely benign, and would still be given smaller global population, *became* harmful once some threshold level of population or emissions was exceeded. Literally, the wrongness of some act may depend on how many other people are able to benignly commit that same act, an observation that challenges both conventional ethical theory and entrenched moral norms.

In analyzing the effects of individual GHG-producing acts, we must avoid the mistake of thinking that such acts are benign because they are only a very small part of an aggregate phenomenon, but we cannot therefore assume that all individual emissions necessarily harm. Parfit refers to the difficulties surrounding this threshold problem as the mistake of "ignoring the effects of sets of acts," in which it is sometimes falsely inferred from the benign nature of individual acts when committed in isolation that they must remain benign when committed as part of a set of similar acts. Since many desirable outcomes require thresholds of contributions among groups of people, and in the absence of such cooperation those individual acts fail to bring about even a fraction of the desired outcome, some notion of the role of individual participation in a group endeavor, Parfit aptly notes, is needed. Likewise, some kinds of actions do not appear to cause harm individually, but taken together with other similar acts they do cause measurable harm beyond some threshold. Under what circumstances may we find those acts to be either blameless or faulty?

Where pollution displays threshold effects—when the environment can safely assimilate a pollutant up to some level of production, beyond which that pollutant begins to cause harm—we have difficulty distinguishing between harmful and benign acts. While the first emission beyond the threshold triggers the harmful effect, this cannot be the first faulty emission, since without all previous releases of that pollutant into the atmosphere, the hazardous effect would not have obtained. Similarly, it cannot be the last emission before the threshold was the morally reprobate one, even though this made it impossible for anyone else to safely release any more pollutants, since this fact depends on all those pollutants previously released. The same can be said for the second-to-last emission, the third-to-last, as well as all before them, since it is true of each that it contributes toward some concentration of pollution that either causes harm in combination with other like acts or else prevents others from enjoying the benefits of polluting acts in avoidance of that harm. Likewise for those emissions produced after the threshold is crossed: although the harm already obtains, these further contributions to a hazardous concentration of pollutants are part of a set of acts that together cause harm, even if they are individually neither necessary nor sufficient contributors to that harm. Relevant to moral assessment is not the order in which some agents contributed to some set of jointly harmful acts, but rather the facts of contribution and harm.

The problem is one of disaggregating individual contributions from aggregate acts and their effects, and the ethical principle that Parfit offers for overcoming this mistake in moral mathematics is that "even if an act harms no one, this act may be wrong because it is one of a *set* of acts that *together* harm other people. Similarly, even if some act benefits no one, it can be what someone ought to do, because it is one of a set of acts that together benefit other people."[23] The benefit or harm of a cooperative endeavor must be disaggregated so that individual acts can properly be assigned responsibility for their contributions to the overall outcome, and the above principle does just that. Where joint contributions to a collective harm involve thresholds, the relevant fact is not the order in which each contributed—whether, for example, their contribution came before or after the threshold was exceeded—but rather the fact that theirs was one of a set of acts that caused some good or bad outcome. Even if individual GHG-producing acts appear to have no effect and therefore appear to be entirely faultless, we must recognize that this false appearance is due to a mistake in disaggregating individual contributions from group-based harm.

Although individual responsibility for aggregate phenomena such as climate change need not be equally distributed, and Parfit's principle does not yield a precise formula for determining each person's share of responsibility, it does suggest how individual persons may be held responsible for problems that do not appear to be caused by any person's individual acts but yet *collectively* cause harm. Collective responsibility may reduce to individual responsibility when the harmful consequences of group activities, including very large groups such as nations, can be disaggregated into jointly sufficient individual acts, even if none of these individual acts is a necessary cause. If a thousand people simultaneously throw rocks through a glass window that cannot be broken by a single rock but is shattered when struck by several, all one thousand people are responsible for breaking the window; the alternative to finding all causally responsible is to find none so. The fact that none of the individual acts is either necessary or sufficient to produce the harm is irrelevant to the assessment of fault or liability, because the group endeavor clearly caused harm, and each person equally contributed to that harm.

A similar mistake, though one that does not involve thresholds, follows from "the belief that imperceptible effects cannot be morally significant." This mistake is based on the false assumption that persons cannot be harmed in fact unless they can perceive each discrete instance of harm, and is compounded by the problems associated with small contributions being parts of larger sets of harmful acts. Even if one's share of a collective act that causes either harm or benefit is so small that the effects of each individual contribution cannot be perceived by a beneficiary or sufferer, those effects, Parfit claims, are morally relevant in that the contributor is morally responsible for that harm. Environmental harm is especially prone to this mistake in moral mathematics, because of the very small contributions that individual point sources of pollution make to aggregate pollution levels. Likewise with the depletion of natural resources, including the overuse of atmospheric absorptive capacity: Isolated individual contributions to larger aggregate problems may appear to be trivial, and yet the countless occurrences of such seemingly trivial acts together add up to quite serious harms. As Parfit puts it, "Each of our acts may be *very* wrong, because of its effects on other people, even if none of these people could ever notice any of these effects. Our acts may *together* make these people very much worse off."[24] As before, the mistake is caused by the failure to adequately disaggregate individual contributions from cumulative phenomena.

To illustrate, Parfit proposes a "commuter's dilemma" in which persons commuting into a city must decide whether to drive, thus contributing a small amount of pollution, or take public transportation, yielding a much smaller share. The latter option has a convenience cost that most people are unwilling to bear, at least in the absence of a significant countervailing benefit. Like many other coordination problems involving groups, this dilemma leaves each potential driver weighing the trivial cost of pollution (shared by all) against the seemingly higher convenience cost of using public transportation (borne by each). Each may recognize air pollution to be a significant public health issue and acknowledge that automobile emissions are a prime cause of such pollution, but individual commuters regard their own contribution to the problem as insignificant, further reasoning that their own "sacrifice" in taking public transit will have an imperceptible effect on the overall pollution problem, given the likelihood that others will continue to drive. As game theory predicts in such dilemmas, they all choose to drive. But should they? Can the state legitimately discourage them from doing so? Are they, in thinking their acts benign, committing a mistake in moral mathematics?

Parfit, rejecting the mistaken intuition that holds imperceptible effects to be insignificant, answers that they should not. In the past, he notes, when most resided in small communities, the consequences of making such mistakes in moral mathematics were far less serious. Relatively small groups of persons where each makes trivial contributions to air pollution may never harm anyone, insofar as that pollution remains dispersed and falls within the capacity of the natural environment to cleanse itself. With urbanization, these mistakes began to take on far more serious consequences when carrying capacity was exceeded, and many more apparently trivial contributions to aggregate problems such as pollution became more insidious. Judgments concerning the significance of small contributions to large problems cannot be made in isolation from such considerations as population density and the number of other persons committing similar acts within a limited ecosystem, although the social norms on which many such judgments are made in practice often fail to keep pace with such changes.

Increasingly concentrated populations dramatically intensify individual contributions to problems of pollution, especially once carrying capacity is exceeded, but large populations do nothing to disperse those harms or diminish their effects. Each person may contribute only a tiny fraction of the overall levels of pollutants in the environment, but each suffers from the whole of that accumulated pollution. A single person inhaling carbon monoxide does almost nothing to cleanse the air of that pollutant. Anthropogenic climate change might be regarded as resulting from the widespread failure to correctly disaggregate individual acts from much larger sets of similar acts, such that all persons falsely believe their individual contributions to climate change to be entirely benign—a belief that once may have been true, given threshold effects, or may have been falsely inferred from the fact that their individual acts had only very small or even imperceptible effects—thereby failing to see how they may be morally responsible for a problem that their actions continue to cause. While perhaps true that society in the past could safely ignore small or imperceptible harms, such is no longer the case. "It now makes a great difference whether we continue to believe that we cannot have greatly harmed or benefited others unless there are people with obvious grounds for resentment or gratitude," Parfit urges. "If this is what we think, what we do will often be much worse for all of us."[25]

Collective Responsibility

Thus far, we have understood responsibility in terms of individual acts and choices, but another sense of responsibility is necessary if we are to make sense of the notion that national emissions caps reflect relative responsibility for global climate change. Since responsibility is usually understood in individualistic terms—that is, persons are held responsible for their acts and choices qua individuals—we might notice several preliminary obstacles to holding entire nations responsible for their aggregate GHG emissions. Insofar as assessments of fault rely in part on an agent's knowledge and intentions at the time he or she commits an act, and since only individual persons and not groups can have such mental states, attributing fault to group actions becomes considerably more complicated than with individuals. Moreover, when entire groups are held liable for some problems toward which they have contributed through their faulty acts, as in required compensation to the victims of climate change, a blanket assessment of group liability belies a potentially wide variation in levels of individual responsibility within the group. Some Americans produce very high levels of annual emissions while others emit far less, but all are held to be equally responsible when the nation itself is assessed responsibility based on its aggregate emissions. It seems unfair to assign equal remedial burdens between Americans with widely disparate individual contributions, but collective national responsibility implies, though it need not entail, undifferentiated group fault. Finally, collective responsibility may hold some to be vicariously liable for some harm, despite their having no causal role in it. Assessing liability in the absence of causal responsibility appears to violate Barry's principle of responsibility and so requires further exploration before it can be accepted as part of a fair global climate regime.

Assessments of national responsibility determine the relative national burdens assigned to various countries in their emission caps and are reflected in the "common but differentiated responsibilities and respective capacities" language of the *UNFCCC*. Those nations with higher past emissions bear greater historical responsibility for climate change, because past GHG emissions accumulate in the atmosphere and continue to affect climate for decades after they are first released. Those with higher current emissions might likewise be said to bear greater current responsibility, and in assessing overall responsibility for the purpose of assigning differential caps, both sorts of national responsibility must be taken into consideration. The Kyoto Protocol, for example, distributes its worldwide average reduction of 5 percent from the 1990 baseline unevenly among nations, based partly though imperfectly on relative assessment of national responsibility. Bearing greater national reduction burdens, in terms of the higher costs associated with a larger percentage decrease in national emissions from current levels, depends on the claim that some nations are more responsible for the problem than others, and this relies on a notion of collective rather than individual responsibility.

Can we justifiably assert collective national responsibility for climate change, though, rather than reducing national responsibility down to individual emissions? Recall that standard attributions of responsibility entail contributory fault, where persons cause some harm through their faulty acts, making them individually responsible. In collective responsibility, by contrast, members of groups are sometimes held responsible in the absence of individual contributory fault. Do these and other problems surrounding collective responsibility undermine the fairness of nation-based assessments of responsibility such as the Kyoto Protocol, which assign caps on aggregate annual emissions rates to nations rather than to individuals? Insofar as assigned emissions reductions entail costs to be distributed among individual citizens within a society, do caps based on average emissions unfairly implicate those with individual emissions well below those of their fellow citizens, and so wrongly attribute guilt merely by association? Is it unfair to make some citizens bear costs of remedial compensation for climate-related harm caused by others, including their departed forebears, even though they are not individually responsible for causing the harm from which the compensatory claims originate? To such questions we now turn.

The most common philosophical approach to determining the moral status of groups is *methodological individualism*, which denies that there are any actions, interests, or intentions of organizations that cannot be reduced to those of their constituent members. By this account, on which this inquiry relies, groups do not cause harm; only individuals do, even if they may do so qua members of groups. When individuals cause harm through their participation in groups, as when one person's act is insufficient to bring about some harm but is jointly sufficient when performed along with other like acts, the appropriate locus of responsibility is by this account the individual and not the group. Here, speaking in terms of collective responsibility provides a kind of shorthand for references to sets of responsible individuals. Anything done by a group can be reduced to the various discrete acts of its members, with no remainder of group responsibility beyond the sum of individual responsibilities. Methodological individualism thus challenges the idea of holding nations responsible for their emissions, at least insofar as this means something other than that its citizens are also held individually responsible for those emissions. Collective responsibility at least sometimes holds individuals responsible for harm toward which they have not contributed, as when all members of a group are blamed for some harm caused by only some of its members, so Barry's individualistic principle of responsibility appears to be violated in such cases. In justifying a nation-based remedial climate regime, can attributions of collective responsibility withstand the individualist challenge?

In the sense in which collective responsibility is applied to the design of a global climate mitigation regime, the individualist objections to collective responsibility may not undermine the case for assigning targets on a national level, since national governments may in turn implement those targets through policies that affect individual acts and choices. Responsibility simply enters the picture at two different levels of analysis simultaneously: Aggregate global emissions are seen as being the product of all aggregate national emissions, and national emissions are seen as being the product of all individual emissions. While there may be intermediate levels above and below national emissions— the European Union as a supranational body with its own emissions cap under the Kyoto Protocol or individual states or provinces with their own emissions standard, for example—these multiple levels need not suppose that some discrete agent (the nation) emits GHGs that are not somehow produced by some individual within it. While nations make policies that affect their ability to comply with emissions caps and so can be held responsible for noncompliance, the operational account of collective responsibility at work here need not suppose the ontological existence of the nation in a manner objectionable to methodologically individualist accounts of collective responsibility.

Even if we are not precluded from conceiving of the collective responsibility of nations for anthropogenic climate change, there remain several difficulties surrounding the relationship between individual and national responsibility. The principle of responsibility, which holds that agents are responsible for the consequences that follow from their voluntary acts and choices but not those that are the result of luck alone, relies on a core individualist premise that appears to contradict the notion of collective responsibility. As previously observed, being the citizen of a particular nation must be regarded as the epitome of the "natural lottery" for which persons are not responsible, yet imposing costs on persons based on their nation of residence—as national emissions caps would seem to do—appears to assign burdens on the basis of characteristics for which persons cannot be responsible. Liberal egalitarians are especially concerned with this individualistic conception of responsibility, so they ought to be particularly troubled by the imposition of costs on persons based solely on their unchosen national membership, and one can conceive of national emissions caps as doing exactly that. Writing about national responsibility, David Miller identifies this problem as a core concern with protecting the individual liberty and the autonomy of persons, urging that "as far as possible we want people to be able to control what benefits and burdens they receive, but we also want to protect them against the side effects, intended or unintended, of other people's actions."[26]

The primary reason for holding any group responsible for its actions or decisions matches our reason for holding individuals responsible: After the fact, we need to know who to punish for some harmful action (the punitive component) and/or who must compensate the victim for the wrong received (the compensatory component). When persons are harmed by one or more others, they incur costs for which they are not responsible, and justice demands that those responsible for committing that harm are either punished or required to compensate their victim for the misdeed. Here, our concern with the normative justification for holding persons or groups responsible for their emissions is grounded in the practical need to assign differential burdens to the world's nations based on some assessment of their responsibility for past, current, or future climate-related harm, but we must ensure that in so doing we do not violate the principle of responsibility, which vicarious assessments of liability based in group membership appear to do.

Thus, the core objection to be considered in collective responsibility concerns holding some persons responsible for the harmful actions of others by imposing on them a punitive or compensatory burden, which would seem to violate a basic precept of retributive justice that limits punishment to those at fault. This worry has been expressed, for example, in objections against the idea of holding contemporary white Americans responsible for slavery or contemporary Germans responsible for the Holocaust, where reparations are demanded of the descendants of those perpetrating some harm, to be paid to the descendants of its victims. Official national apologies for past atrocities committed by nations against their indigenous populations likewise encounter similar objections. Part of these objections is based on the temporal distance between the events and the eventual assignment of responsibility—no American now asked to pay for slavery reparations has ever owned slaves—but part is also based on the problems associated with attributing responsibility to all of a group's members regardless of their individual contributions to its harmful actions.

Miller uses an example of an angry mob that vandalizes a neighborhood with the intent of "teaching them a lesson," where the actions of some are clearly more destructive than those of others. Does it makes sense in this circumstance, he asks, to hold the entire mob responsible for the group's actions by, for example, requiring the entire group to bear financial responsibility for cleaning up the damage? Miller thinks that it does, given that the mob is a "like-minded group" where members share common purposes, since all took part with the same general attitude and all made some causal contribution to the final outcome. Consider, he suggests in an example of the difficulties in dissociating individual from group responsibility, the case of several persons simultaneously throwing bricks through a plate glass window: "We cannot say that any particular brick thrower was (causally) responsible for smashing the window, but we can say that the group as a whole is outcome responsible for the damage they brought about."[27] Internally to the group, some members may bear greater responsibility for its actions (e.g., ringleaders), so the group may internally assign differential liability to individual members based on their differential causal roles, but in requiring the entire group to repair the damage, the responsibility is collective rather than individual. Justice requires that responsibility be assigned in cases with bad outcomes that demand remedial measures, Miller suggests, but practical and epistemic reasons often weigh in favor of assigning responsibility collectively, because "it may be impossible to assign specific shares of responsibility for what happened to individual members of the mob. We may not even know what causal contribution each made to the final outcome, and even if we did, it might still be controversial how responsibility should be divided."[28]

Notice that, in Miller's example, justice is applied at two different levels of analysis. He argues that it is up to the group itself to decide to how responsibility may be divided up internally among group members, suggesting that justice may demand greater responsibility for those with a larger causal role, but the internal division of responsibility within the group "is irrelevant from the point of view of achieving a fair distribution of costs and benefits between the rioters and their victims." Justice at this level requires that the group itself repair the damages done by the group as a whole or remedy its victims through compensation, but is indifferent as to the internal division of responsibility within the group. Against the contrary supposition made by the above objection, Miller's example does not insist that group members all be held equally responsible for group actions, and so does not advance a conception of collective responsibility that is not reducible to individual responsibility. Ultimately, it is individuals that are held responsible for their actions qua members of the group, but based on their individual contributions to the group's actions.

Miller's second example is more controversial and presents a closer analogue to the problems of assessing national responsibility for climate change. In groups displaying what he terms "cooperative practices" characteristics, an internal division of responsibility is much more difficult to assign. Consider, for example, a polluting firm in which a dissenting minority of its employees opposes that pollution, favoring instead the purchase of some costly antipollution controls in order to avoid it. Although they oppose the group's final decision by voting against it, can they be held responsible for it anyway? Miller thinks that they can, at least under some circumstances, insofar as

> they are the beneficiaries of a common practice in which participants are treated fairly—they get the income and other benefits that go with the job, and they have a fair chance to influence the firm's decisions—and so they must be prepared to carry their share of the costs, and in this case the costs that stem from the external impact of the practice.[29]

Insofar as members have meaningful opportunities to influence the group's actions—for example, decisions are not made by a small clique of elites against the will of the majority—the mere fact that some oppose the group's final decision does not exonerate them from responsibility, as long as they benefit from the cooperative endeavor of the group. Miller argues, in what he intends to apply also to social and political decisions in democracies, which are also cooperative endeavors where members benefit from the group, that "participating in the practice and sharing in the benefits may be sufficient to create responsibility."[30] Thus, he suggests, the more open and democratic the group, the more each member must be held responsible for its actions and decisions, regardless of whether or not they personally supported them in their role as citizens.

Here, collective responsibility is stretched quite far, since some group members are held responsible for actions or decisions that they oppose but are powerless to stop. Given that Miller elsewhere rejects the attribution of responsibility to persons for outcomes that they are powerless to avoid, how does he reconcile these apparently contradictory positions? The resolution may lie in the functional difference between individual and collective decisions. When I as an individual decide to do X, the vote is always 1–0 with my choice in the majority. While consequences may be affected by contingencies that lie outside of my control or beyond my knowledge, I remain fully in control of my decisions and so can be held responsible for them. On the other hand, if a group to which I belong collectively decides democratically to do X, it is possible that I may find myself in the minority, opposing X. Even if I benefit by my membership in the group, am I necessarily responsible for its decision? Suppose that the group is a polity to which I belong and X is the decision to wage aggressive war against another state, and I vigorously oppose the collective decision but find myself in the minority. Must I be held equally responsible for X, alongside its most ardent supporters? Is there any way to escape from this sort of responsibility, short of exercising my exit option from society? Must I go beyond the standard avenues of democratic participation before my opposition to X can be regarded as adequately sincere, and would such measures release me from responsibility even if it is ineffective? The issue concerns the shares of individual responsibility for collective decisions in a democracy, including those to allow ongoing GHG pollution, and to this problem we now turn.

Democracy and Collective Responsibility

One of the most common uses of vicarious liability concerns the hierarchal relationships of authority in the military, and just war theory contains one of the best developed philosophical analyses of collective responsibility. In terms of vicarious responsibility, it is generally assumed that soldiers in the field are obligated to follow orders without question, within reasonable limits, so while they may be at fault for their wartime atrocities, the moral blame and legal liability are typically attributed to commanding officers issuing the orders or failing to control the conduct of those under their command. Indeed, soldiers under the command of military officers are often used as the quintessential example of principal–agent relations where the principal is at fault while the agent vicariously bears liability for his actions. However, military commanders rarely make the decision to wage wars, so may this vicarious liability that is transferred from soldiers to their commanders be transferred in turn to those citizens of democratic states, in whose name and presumably with whose consent the war is being waged? Generally, can citizens of a democracy be held responsible for the actions of their government, as Miller claims? Under what, if any, circumstances may they be released from this responsibility, in instances when they oppose the actions or policy decisions undertaken by their government?

Michael Walzer, in considering the case for reparations for the victims of aggressive wars, notes that such reparations are generally paid for through taxation of all a nation's citizens, not just the active supporters of the war, and over time, such that many who had nothing to do with the decision to wage war may continue to bear collective responsibility for it. This does not, he thinks, pose a particularly difficult philosophical problem as long as they are only held liable and not guilty for the war's atrocities. Of liability following from citizenship in a nondemocratic state that wages unjust wars, he writes:

> In this sense, citizenship is a common destiny, and no one, not even its opponents (unless they become political refugees, which has its costs, too) can escape the effects of a bad regime, an ambitious or fanatic leadership, or an overreaching nationalism. But if men and women must accept this destiny, they can sometimes do so with a good conscience, for the acceptance says nothing about their individual responsibility. The distribution of costs is not the distribution of guilt.[31]

As Feinberg notes, attributions of liability (as in reparations) are not necessarily attributions of legal or moral guilt, but are rather judgments based on the existence of harm, the finding of fault, and the demand of justice to compensate the victims for their injuries. Making such responsibility collective rather than individual, even if this implicates a war's opponents along with its supporters, acknowledges the causal role of citizenship in a state's decision to wage an aggressive war. Yet, Walzer's observation seems unsatisfactory from the perspective of the principle of responsibility, for it holds persons liable (if not guilty) for decisions over which they as citizens of nondemocratic states have no control.

Of course, citizenship confers far greater responsibility in a democratic state that it does in an authoritarian one. Although it is difficult to find an example of a perfectly democratic state waging aggressive wars, even if cases of nominally democratic ones doing so abound, Walzer proposes the example of one doing so from open and democratic processes. Who, he asks, should be held responsible for that decision? He quite plausibly claims that those "who voted for it and who cooperated in planning, initiating, and waging it" must be held responsible, including those soldiers who, in their capacities as citizens though not in their capacities as soldiers, shared in the decision to wage the war. Those who voted against the war, he argues, cannot be blamed for it. But what about those citizens who did not vote? Walzer suggests that they are blameworthy for their "indifference and inaction" in failing to do what they could have done to oppose an unjust policy, "though they are not guilty of aggressive war." Suppose further that the antiwar minority could have won the decision, had they staged marches and demonstrations, rather than merely voting, but they opted not to. Would they then bear responsibility? Walzer thinks so, "though to a lesser degree than those slothful citizens who did not even bother to go to the assembly." Given the magnitude of the injustice of aggressive war, the democratic citizen is obligated, he argues, to "do all he can, short of frightening risks, to prevent or stop the war."[32]

Democracy is best regarded, as Walzer suggests, as "a way of distributing responsibility," and to the extent that citizens have control over their collective decisions, they must also be held responsible for them. Collective responsibility in wartime and its aftermath therefore sometimes extends even to those citizens that opposed the war at the ballot box or public forum, insofar as they did not do all they could reasonably have done to stop it. In this sense, citizens are the principals that collectively bear responsibility for the decisions of the state, which is their agent. In a democracy, such responsibility is collectivized, just as guilt for aggression is made collective among soldiers in wartime, such that self-defense may justify a soldier's killing any enemy combatant and not merely the one that is actively threatening them at the time. Collective responsibility thus serves a valuable social role in expressing and strengthening the solidarity of groups that share mutual interests or bonds of affection, and serves a useful role in strengthening norms and encouraging cooperation. But it also raises issues for the principle of responsibility, because the fault of the group does not readily reduce to the faults of all individual members held liable for group actions and decisions.

In his discussion of national responsibility, Miller defines the collectivity of a nation as "a community of people who share an identity and a public culture, who recognize special obligations to one another and value their continued association, and who aspire to be politically self-determining."[33] His aim is in part to distinguish nations from states—while nations often act *through* states, they are distinct from them—but he means also to emphasize the importance of common culture, group solidarity, and self-determination in attributing collective responsibility for national decisions. Solidarity is a key ingredient for collective responsibility, as can be seen in the vicarious pride and shame felt by some group members for the actions of others, but it is self-determination that plays the larger role for Miller. Only policies adopted by democratic states can be assumed to be authentic expressions of a national culture, he argues, even if some citizens disagree with them. Hence, he claims, it is only in democracies that "the policies pursued by the state can reasonably be seen as policies for whose effects the citizen body as a whole is collectively responsible, given that they have authorized the government to act on their behalf in a free election."[34]

Climate change may be caused by individual actions, but significant contributing causes of those actions are state policies and the norms of the larger society, and in the contemporary United States neither norms nor policies prohibit individual GHG emissions at levels that are well above those that are globally sustainable. Despite the democratic deficits of its public policy processes, the U.S. government remains answerable to its citizens in periodic elections and through interelection pressure groups, so the citizenry must shoulder at least some share of the responsibility for the failure of its government to make adequate domestic climate change mitigation policy, and perhaps also for its continued obstruction of global climate policy efforts, given the widespread passive support for the government's active opposition to global efforts to reduce emissions. But the failure of the U.S. government to adequately address global climate change is not merely an institutional shortcoming, in that American social norms are plainly too permissive to generate genuinely democratic support for taking the necessary policy steps to avoid dangerously high GHG concentrations from accumulating, much less to achieve those aims in the absence of coercive policies. Part of the problem is an identity and public culture constructed around the personal automobile, large living spaces, high resource consumption, and little regard for their consequences for the world's less fortunate. Democratic decisions ultimately reflect this public culture, and the shared values and common identity it fosters both create the necessary conditions for attributing collective responsibility and generate the preferences for which such attributions are necessary. Prior to those political decisions lies a culture that is inimical to meaningful action to reduce emissions, and that culture can only be the product of society taken as a collectivity, and irreducible to individuals.

One might plausibly identify the lack of any effective domestic climate policy, rather than the many individual GHG-producing acts that are thereby allowed, as the cause of high U.S. per capita contributions toward climate change, and in turn attribute this inadequate policy to the democratic politics in which all participate. Here, citizens may still be held responsible for the harm that climate change entails, but for different reasons. They contribute to the problem qua citizens of the nation that is responsible for more than 30 percent of global emissions, and due to their collective failure to adopt effective GHG-limiting policies. Viewing each person's share of responsibility for national policy in this way, may we (following Walzer) still hold all citizens who voted for the government that withdrew the nation from the Kyoto Protocol and continues to obstruct global climate policy development responsible for national contributions to climate change, but exonerate those who voted against it? Do citizens incur vicarious liability only for those policy decisions that they support—or, following Walzer, fail to oppose—or is responsibility for national policies in a democracy (as Miller claims) to be distributed more evenly throughout a citizenry, regardless of expressed preferences in such avenues of participation as elections?

In vicarious liability, contributory fault is ascribed to one party but liability to another. For example, principals authorizing agents to act on their behalf incur liability for the faulty acts of those agents, and within a military hierarchy vicarious liability is applied to commanding officers for the fault of their subordinates. In general, we can hold some persons vicariously liable for the faulty actions of others based on some prior arrangement to which both parties have consented. Collective liability is another form of *noncontributory fault*, or assignment of liability to some persons for whom contributory fault cannot be ascribed, when entire groups are held responsible for the actions of only some of their members, while some group members cannot be held to be at fault qua individuals. As in the case of individual vicarious liability, it will often be the case with collective responsibility that those held responsible qua members of groups are ascribed liability for consequences that result from the fault of others. When all citizens of a democracy are held responsible for the policies adopted by their government, even when only some can be held to be causally responsible for that rather than another government being in power, this kind of noncontributory fault appears to be involved, raising objections based in the principle of responsibility.

Where groups are held collectively responsible for some harm, may some group members extricate themselves from liability incurred through association with the group? Must they exit the group in order to avoid this association, or can they also exercise a voice option? In another example of the same kind of collective responsibility, Feinberg considers the deeply ingrained racism practiced by whites in the postbellum South, where only some group members took part in acts of violence against blacks but where "99 percent of them, having been shaped by the prevailing mores, whole-heartedly approved of them."[35] Though the vast majority actively or passively reinforced a hostile environment for blacks—faulty acts for which they may be held responsible—what about that 1 percent that disapproved? According to Feinberg, the extent to which they could be implicated in the group's fault—with the community's passive supporters guilty of abetting those actually undertaking violent attacks—depends on the pains they took to distance themselves from the acts of the majority. One might plausibly oppose this racism, he suggests, but to do so would "totally alienate" a person from the white Southern community, and such total alienation would be "unlikely to be widely found in a community that leaves its exit doors open." Commenting on the same example, Miller argues that one cannot escape collective responsibility merely by speaking out or voting against such practices, but rather "must take all reasonable steps to prevent the outcome occurring."[36]

Here, the more demanding standard for extricating oneself from responsibility for harm caused by group actions, separately endorsed by Walzer, Feinberg, and Miller, is more plausible, requiring democratic citizens to take all reasonable and prudent steps to avoid individually contributing to a problem and not merely to vote against some candidate or harmful policy, since merely speaking or voting against something that finds support not only from other citizens but also through prevailing social norms amounts to too meager an attempt to avoid personally contributing to the problem. Especially given the fact that Americans contribute toward climate change both through their roles as citizens, failing to support adequate climate policies or to elect governments willing to adopt them, and as consumers, through their excessive individual levels of GHG emissions, which indicts most but not all, one cannot merely vote for a losing candidate or ballot measure, return to one's oversized home, park the SUV in the three-car garage, and reasonably expect to be exonerated from causal responsibility or liability for the harm associated with climate change. One must, as Miller argues, "take all reasonable steps" to prevent climate change from occurring—not only at the ballot box or public forum, but also in one's everyday consumer decisions that likewise contribute, though in a different way, to the problem. Although government policy may enable continued high per capita emissions in the United States, its citizens are nonetheless able to control (to some extent, at least) their individual contributions to the problem and so can by the principle of responsibility be held liable for them.

In addition to the kinds of responsibility for climate change that persons bear in their roles as citizens and members of society, one might also identify their causal role as consumers in the chain that contributes excess GHGs into the atmosphere. Were it not for the consumption patterns of those residing in the industrialized world, environmental regulations such as those necessary for stabilizing climate would be unnecessary. Perhaps consumers should bear the liability costs for climate-related harm directly, as through a carbon tax. As

Iris Young suggests, the responsibility attributed to owners and managers of sweatshops for the harm to workers that results is distinct from that properly attributed to those consumers who purchase sweatshop-made garments. The former, she suggests, can be held liable, but the latter bear *political responsibility*, which requires consumers "to reflect morally on the normal and hitherto acceptable market relationships in which they act."[37] Similarly, Ken Conca argues that moral responsibility for environmental problems such as climate change should be assigned not to nations or individuals but to global commodity chains,[38] recognizing a process-centered rather than agent-centered form of causal responsibility and so rejecting the methodological individualism of Barry's principle. Alternative loci of responsibility are available to a global climate regime; the decision to base responsibility on actions and policies that can be attributed to nations can be justified by appeal to practical aims of implementation as well as individualistic egalitarian justice principles. Basing it directly on consumer purchases or indirectly through commodity chains obscures the sense in which persons are responsible for causing climate change in multiple roles, which can be amalgamated as collective national responsibility in the sense discussed above.

Thus, the sort of collective responsibility involved in anthropogenic climate change comes closest to what Feinberg terms *contributory group-fault: collective and distributive*, where there exists contributory fault on the part of all members of a group, so no one's fault is vicarious because all are somehow at fault. Fault need not be distributed equally among group members—more liability may be attributed to bigger contributors—but all members are held to be responsible in some way for the harm in question, and can be held liable for it. As an example of this kind of collective responsibility, Feinberg suggests a man shouting for help on a public beach with no lifeguard within audible distance of a thousand accomplished swimmers, who all leave him to drown. Though the common law would not hold those thousand potential rescuers liable, Feinberg suggests, they are all at fault for their collective failure to assist, since "each has a duty to attempt rescue so long as no more than a few others have already begun their efforts."[39] It may be that each potential rescuer is equally faulty or that some are more so than others—those closest to the water, and thus in the best position to help, may be at slightly greater fault than those far away—but the responsibility accrues to the group itself, with none held vicariously liable for some harm for which he or she was not at some fault. Thus, all group members would, as a consequence of their responsibility for the drowning, owe the man's survivors some compensation for their liability.

From such examples, a preliminary picture emerges concerning each person's share of the collective responsibility that attaches to being a citizen of the nation with the world's highest overall and per capita rates of GHG emissions. Even though national per capita averages obscure a wide range within individual emissions, the aggregate rate of fossil fuel combustion within the United States is plainly too high to avoid collective fault (collective and distributive), yet those patterns of behavior that generate such high emissions are supported by community norms in the same way that white racism in the postbellum South was the product of such norms. As is the case in Feinberg's racism example, some may be more responsible than others for contributing to climate change, and so might be assessed greater liability for compensating those harmed by it, but there are none who escape some fault altogether. Justice requires that, insofar as the United States as a nation owes compensation to the victims of climate change for its collective responsibility for contributing to that problem, justice also requires that those who are at greater fault owe greater compensation than those at lesser fault. Nothing in the general claims of collective responsibility diminishes the sense of individual responsibility discussed above.

Conclusions

Once we understand the mistake in moral mathematics that tempts us to see individual GHG-emitting acts as faultless where they are faulty in fact, we can see that attributing collective responsibility to entire nations does not hold anyone vicariously liable for the faulty acts of others. By viewing aggregate national luxury emissions as a faulty contribution to global climate change, we can more easily see how the individual acts that comprise that aggregate set of acts might plausibly confer fault among all group members and, when combined with the allocation of responsibility to citizens in democracy for the consequences of national policies, thus why all might defensibly be held liable for the expected harmful consequences of global climate change. Collective responsibility, then, can sometimes serve as a useful construct for identifying a responsible party when all individual acts appear faultless. A global climate regime that aims to assess fault and assign liability for climate change based on the relative moral responsibility of various agents, whether nations or persons, must take into account not only the relative causal responsibility of agents, avoiding the various mistakes and unjustified exemptions from fault noted above, but also the respective roles played by both individual emissions and the national policies that enable them.

6

Knowledge, Beliefs, and Responsibility

How much must we know about a predicted hazard before costly preparations designed to mitigate that hazard are warranted? To what extent must we be knowledgeable about the consequences of our actions before we can be held morally responsible for them? Can we be held morally responsible for bad outcomes that we did not intend, or that we failed to anticipate? In assessing liability, how much of a determining role owes to an agent's mental state and how much to the consequences of his or her actions? To what extent does scientific uncertainty affect these judgments, and what policy responses are justified under conditions of such uncertainty? These questions are central to current debates about the appropriate policy response to the looming crisis of global climate change, as well as to the relative assessment of national responsibility necessary for assigning remedial burdens within a global climate regime.

Recall that in the *UNFCCC*'s "common but differentiated responsibilities" model of fairness, moral responsibility determines liability for GHG abatement costs and compensation for victims of climate change, and depends primarily on assessments of causal responsibility combined with attributions of fault. When measured in terms of each nation's historical emissions, causal responsibility can now be readily determined and straightforwardly assessed, because such historical data are available. Following this model, liability would be assessed for each nation in proportion to its share of accumulated atmospheric GHGs, provided that each country can also be shown to be at fault for them. Recall also one major exception to this formula: Nations can be held responsible for their historical luxury emissions but not their survival emissions, since only the former can be regarded as voluntary in the relevant sense and hence culpable. Although the responsibility-based model of fairness cannot determine each nation's share of atmospheric space for current and future emissions allocations, it does offer a parsimonious formula for assigning remedial costs for redressing climate-related harm. While parsimony is often a virtue, it sometimes obscures relevant considerations, and this chapter examines several further objections to allocating national climate-related remedial costs in proportion to historical emissions which suggest that it does exactly that.

One could simply avoid these difficult philosophical questions by holding nations to a standard of strict liability, where fault is irrelevant to assessments of national liability. Agents would by this standard held liable for all damages they cause, regardless of such complicating considerations. Strict liability in this case would violate the principle of responsibility, holding persons or nations responsible for some consequences that are not the result of their voluntary acts or choices, so we shall presume against ruling out the possible mitigating or defeating considerations that are the subjects of this chapter, but we must also keep open the possibility that the principle of responsibility itself is invalid and that strict liability may yet be the most defensible standard for this case. This chapter examines three main complications for the straightforward assignment of liability based on each nation's historical emissions, in the interest of preserving fault-based liability and ensuring that norms of justice are incorporated into the design of a global climate regime.

The first issue complicating assessments of moral responsibility on the basis of historical emissions alone concerns the role of knowledge, which is sometimes taken to be a necessary epistemic condition for attributing fault. In some cases, agents can be excused from moral responsibility for causing harm that they did not anticipate—for example, when their ignorance concerning the harmful effects of their actions is held to be reasonable—but ignorance cannot excuse the harm that agents unknowingly cause in others cases. Here, their actions are regarded as faulty, and they are held liable for harm that results from them if they *should* have anticipated the harmful consequences of their actions, whether or not they did so in fact. In evaluating national responsibility for historical emissions, the question thus arises of whether nations ought to be held liable for all of their historical luxury emissions, only some of them, or none of them. If relevant parties did not in fact know that their all or part of their historical emissions may lead to environmental harm, and unless it can be shown that they should have anticipated such harm, then some portion of a their historical emissions must be exempted from fault-based liability. But can ignorance about climate-related harm undermine culpability and justify such exemptions?

Further complicating this epistemic problem is the role of scientific uncertainty in establishing causal connections between emissions-producing acts and the predicted hazards of climate change. Given current and past degrees of scientific uncertainty surrounding the causes and likely effects of climate change, can nations plead ignorance concerning their contributions to the problem by citing a lack of adequate evidence about those causes and effects, thereby exonerating themselves from responsibility for it? Can they be held responsible for their luxury emissions released prior to the point when the scientific basis of climate change was well established and widely disseminated? If not, at what point can we identify the end of reasonable ignorance concerning the causes and effects of anthropogenic climate change? Does ongoing scientific uncertainty concerning some aspects of climate science constitute a defense for past or current contributions to climate change, insofar as agents cannot be certain that their acts or omissions will actually cause some predicted harm? Does it matter whether relevant agents actually believe that their emissions-facilitating actions are harmless?

The second issue complicating assessments of fault and liability for contributing to climate change concerns an agent's intentions, which are often related to but distinct from their knowledge of the likely effects of their actions. As the moral luck examples from chapter 5 illustrate, a person can cause harm without intending it or intend harm without causing it, and this disjunction between intention and outcome complicates attributions of fault. Causation without intention presents the more salient problem for assessing moral responsibility for climate change, since most GHG-emitting acts are likely committed without the intent to cause climate change. More contestably, those chiefly responsible for blocking U.S. participation in the Kyoto Protocol may not intend harm by their obstructionism, possibly even believing from a kind of ignorance that they are saving their constituents immense resources by preventing the state from joining an expensive scheme that is merely a "hoax" perpetrated upon the public. Here, agents have access to the relevant information linking actions and harmful effects but opt to disregard that information, sometimes calling its accuracy publicly into question, and so act in ways that are expected to cause harm, albeit unintentionally. Can agents be held liable for harm that is both unintended and unanticipated, especially if caused with the motive of preventing another kind of harm? Given the difficulty in discerning another's mental states, such as intentions, can we reliably know whether publicly stated intentions are sincere, and can we infer to the contrary by their related actions? And if we cannot reliably know an agent's intentions, can they be used as mitigating or defeating factors in finding fault and assessing liability?

A third issue concerns the role of deception in the formation of knowledge and beliefs about the causes and effects of climate change. While we may sometimes excuse a harmful act that is committed from ignorance of its effects or when those consequences are unintended, there must be limits to the fault-canceling powers of ignorance and benign intentions. One such limit concerns the role of deception, where one attempts to manufacture false beliefs in the mind of another, usually in an attempt to manipulate the second person into acting in ways beneficial to the first. We sometimes blame the deceived for failing to exercise prudential skepticism in the face of a deceiver and so hold that person liable for acts committed from blameworthy gullibility, while at other times the act of deception transfers both fault and liability from the deceived to the deceiver, because the former is the proximate cause of some harm but the latter manipulates the former into action and so incurs fault and liability for it. Given the existence of what appears to be a coordinated campaign to deceive the American public on issues related to climate change, we must consider whether this excuses from liability those who might be successfully deceived by it, whether the public should be faulted for failing to see through that campaign, and whether those engaged in the deception incur greater liability for the harm that they facilitate through their efforts to manufacture false beliefs concerning the effects of GHG-producing acts.

Knowledge, Ignorance, and Culpability

Given the nature of individual contributions to aggregative problems such as climate change and the massive public relations effort designed to discredit the scientific basis for the causal link between human activities, increasing atmospheric concentrations of GHGs, and their predicted consequences, it should not be surprising that many Americans do not feel at all responsible for the consequences of their emissions-producing acts.[1] People do *cause* climate change through a wide variety of otherwise innocuous acts but are largely ignorant about the effects of these acts. Does this ignorance in any way diminish their culpability as individuals? Does it diminish the national responsibility of the United States or other countries similarly plagued by ignorance insofar as individual citizens may have been unaware of the harmful consequences of their actions? On the other hand, should such ignorance be dismissed as unreasonable, given the wide dissemination of scientific evidence linking human activities to climate change? Under what circumstances might such ignorance affect attributions of fault and assignments of liability in a climate regime?

At issue here is not what causes climate change—the Intergovernmental Panel on Climate Change (IPCC) has established the relevant causal links with a high level of certainty[2]—but under what circumstances persons or groups can be held morally responsible for their contribution to the problem. Normally, disjunctions between findings of causal and moral responsibility depend in some way on an agent's mental states, including his or her knowledge and intentions concerning the harmful effects of their actions, so this question concerns the states of mind under which persons commit those acts that contribute to climate change. Must they be cognizant of the causal connection between their act and the resultant harm at the time of decision? Must they intend to produce that harm? Since persons are sometimes held causally but not morally responsible for harm based on their mental states at the time of decision, our examination of culpability might begin with two such cases.

The first case in which causal responsibility does not entail moral responsibility concerns unavoidable acts or consequences: *Ought* implies *can*, so it cannot be that all GHG emissions trigger moral blame or legal liability unless persons could plausibly be expected to refrain from exhaling CO_2. No act that is unavoidable or essential for basic human functioning can be morally faulty, so none triggers liability for harm that results. Implied in the claim that persons ought to commit or refrain from committing certain acts is the condition that obedience to such commands is possible. Since some emissions are the unavoidable product of human life, releasing these "survival emissions" into the atmosphere cannot entail fault or trigger liability, so these generate causal but not moral responsibility. While it would be absurd to blame a person for exhaling CO_2, it does not follow that all individual emissions are therefore faultless. As observed in chapter 2, agents may be held responsible for their luxury emissions, because these are avoidable and causally responsible for climate change. Some threshold sets the limit for faultless individual emissions, where further emissions beyond this level constitute a morally faulty failure to remain within the bounds of sustainability. As considered in chapter 7, persons have a right to produce survival emissions, but emissions beyond this threshold trigger moral fault and compensatory liability.

The second case where persons are not held morally responsible for bad consequences that they cause involves reasonable ignorance about those consequences. As observed above, many Americans do not regard their everyday polluting acts to be causally related to global climate change, despite widely disseminated IPCC reports linking fossil fuel combustion, changing land use patterns, and climate-related problems. Although based in a mistake in ascertaining facts, such widespread ignorance nonetheless complicates attributions of moral responsibility, because the harmful effects in question result not from individual malevolence but rather from adherence to widely accepted social norms, which offer no prohibitions against such acts. Can we hold persons or nations morally responsible for harm that results from acts that they do not think are wrong or believe do not violate existing ethical norms? Can one be faulted for an act that is not uncommon, legally prohibited, or even discouraged, when they are also unaware that the act causes any significant harm? Although ignorance is not always a defeating condition for assessments of fault, there are certain conditions under which agents' mental states excuse them from moral responsibility for harm they cause, and these we must consider further.

Ordinarily, we do not hold persons responsible for bad consequences that result from accidents, where an accident is defined as a consequence that could not reasonably have been anticipated at the time of decision. Notice that accidents involve causal responsibility; persons do, in fact, cause their consequences, but they are not held to be culpable for those unintended consequences. This divergence between causal and moral responsibility, however, applies only to some acts that produce unintended consequences. If persons fail to anticipate that their acts might cause some bad consequences but reasonable and prudent persons would have anticipated those consequences, then the resulting harms can no longer be regarded as accidentally caused and so become the products of negligence. The relevant question in assessing such cases, then, is what persons *ought* to have known or expected at the time of decision, not what they knew or expected in fact, where the reasonableness of ignorance distinguishes between pure accidents and negligent acts. Against the view (originating in Aristotle's *Ethics*) that knowledge or anticipation of bad consequences is a necessary epistemic condition for attributions of moral responsibility, the notion from legal philosophy that persons can be held responsible for negligent acts weighs against treating all instances of factual ignorance as blameless. By this standard, agents are to be held morally responsible for their acts or omissions insofar as they can reasonably be expected to anticipate their consequences, whether or not they do in fact anticipate them.

Negligence involves inadvertently caused harm, making the agent causing it less culpable than with recklessness, which involves the conscious disregard for the dangers of a situation, but morally and legally faulty nonetheless. Harm resulting from negligence, then, connotes a level of culpability greater than that resulting from pure accidents but less than either recklessly or intentionally caused harm. One problem with defining negligence in terms of what a reasonable person would anticipate, however, is that such a standard relies on prevailing social norms, and a "reasonable" American may well not regard GHG-producing acts as wrong. The common law tradition from which negligence has conventionally been defined is confounded by problems such as anthropogenic climate change, in which once-innocuous actions begin to cause harm at some point, once thresholds are crossed and further GHG emissions accumulate in the atmosphere and begin to cause harm. Social norms can also fail to keep pace with advances in knowledge, where the empirically established causal links between certain acts and future harm may experience a considerable lag time before they are fully incorporated into action-guiding norms. In such cases, norms lag behind the factual bases of our obligations to others, and the genuinely reasonable and prudent persons necessary for defining negligence may be difficult to find. Hence, reliance on social norms for defining reasonable ignorance and assessing fault and liability is a perilous approach, because it tacitly allows the ongoing occurrence of harmful acts well after they are widely known to cause harm.

In many cases, the evolution of norms can be accelerated when normative standards that reflect the current state of knowledge are embodied within public policy. Building codes provide an illustrative example of this effect: The process of social learning would eventually, through a gradual and extensive process of trial and error, coalesce around certain materials and practices that are safer and more cost-effective than others, creating a set of nonmoral norms. But this long and slow process would necessitate a large number of avoidable mistakes. Alternatively, by relying on the best available knowledge, regulatory standards could be established, accelerating the development of norms through coercion at first but eventually through common practice, and many mistakes could be avoided. The same holds for climate policy, only the stakes here are much higher: By the time the social learning process of norm evolution catches up to the factual basis of climate change, too much damage will have already been done and remedies will be far more difficult and expensive. Rather than relying on fault-based assessments of liability in which reasonable ignorance is defined by factually mistaken and hence obsolete norms concerning the innocuous nature of unlimited GHG emissions, we ought to assess fault and liability on the basis of currently available knowledge, holding persons responsible for their luxury emissions regardless of whether or not either they or some "reasonable" person might comprehend the effects of these actions. Not only would such a standard provide a more defensible account of responsibility, but it would also speed the process of norm evolution, easing the transition to a more sustainable society and bolstering an effective source of positive behavioral change.

Such a standard would also hold persons responsible for their false beliefs, at least when those beliefs are unreasonably held and acted upon. In order to avoid cognitive dissonance, many people may be tempted to ignore reports linking bad consequences to their everyday actions, since internalizing the relevant knowledge requires difficult and often costly value reassessments as well as changes in habits and practices, through the process of social learning described above. Many people cling with tenacity to such unjustified beliefs, based not in any rational assessment of the facts in question but rather in the desire to avoid such reassessments or the guilt that accompanies the failure to perform them. Such willful ignorance is psychologically understandable, but this does not make it morally defensible.

Holding persons responsible for what they should know, based on the best available scientific knowledge, rather than what they know in fact or prefer to believe, has several significant advantages. Holding persons responsible for acting on their unreasonable false beliefs provides an incentive to avoid this willful ignorance and thus to avoid contributing to known problems. Anticipating issues discussed further below, it also neutralizes the incentive for either government or industry to engage in disinformation campaigns aiming to create false beliefs and thereby to avoid regulation that might curb known hazards, because no liability advantage would follow from such cultivated ignorance. As noted above, internalizing relevant knowledge about some phenomenon speeds the process of norm evolution while reinforcing defensible norms of harm-avoiding action. Finally, it supports the idea of environmental rights by underscoring the notion that persons are entitled to an adequate environment, free from anthropogenic climatic instability, regardless of whether threatened by ignorance or malice.

Some conception of reasonable ignorance is instructive for assessments of national liability based on historical emissions. Now, more than a decade after the Rio Declaration committed most nations to GHG abatement, and with four scrupulously researched and widely disseminated IPCC assessment reports, claims to reasonable ignorance concerning the causes or consequences of anthropogenic climate change are fully unreasonable. Most industrialized nations have scientific societies that are charged with verifying knowledge for its use in public policy, and all have held unequivocally that anthropogenic climate change is real and ongoing. Even if the predictions about the harmful consequences of climate change made by nearly every national academy of science turn out to be overstated or mistaken, ignoring the considered judgments of the vast majority of the world's scientific community amounts at least to gross negligence and, plausibly, to recklessness when it comes to national failures to act, because national governments are now surely aware of the harmful consequences of their policies, even if they consciously disregard them. Here, as above, any remaining ignorance can only be willful and therefore unreasonable, and so can no longer exonerate agents from moral responsibility and liability for harm that results from their ongoing luxury emission producing acts or policies.

Thus far, we have equated each nation's responsibility for the harms of climate change with their historical luxury emissions, but this formula fails to take into account the role that developing knowledge about the causes and likely effects of climate change has played on the culpability of those causally responsible for significant shares of those GHGs now accumulated in the atmosphere. Even if we accept the above claim that nations and persons are now liable for their luxury emissions because causal ignorance concerning their harmful effects is no longer reasonable, there remains the problem of historical ignorance about these effects. Since our finding of fault and assessment of liability for ongoing luxury emissions is based on the claim that persons or governments should know their harmful effects, the same cannot be said for the whole of each nation's historical luxury emissions. If we go back far enough, a plausible case may be made that a nation's luxury emissions, while no less causally responsible for climate change, were faultless, because neither individual citizens nor the government could reasonably have been expected to be aware of their harmful effects. Relying on a standard of fault-based liability, where reasonable ignorance is taken to be a defeating condition for attributions of fault, there must have been some point in the past prior to which ignorance concerning the causes and effects of climate change was still reasonable, during which nations and persons could not be held morally responsible for their emissions. If they could not be held to be morally responsible for them at the time they were produced or allowed, then they cannot be liable for them now.

But when was this historical end of reasonable ignorance, and what does this observation entail for assessments of liability now? Prior to the 1990 release of the IPCC's first assessment report, it might seem unreasonable to have expected national governments to have developed and enforced policies limiting GHG emissions, for the relevant officials in those governments could not have been expected to take seriously a problem about which most had little knowledge. Before the 1988 Toronto Conference on the Changing Atmosphere, the "greenhouse effect" was a phenomenon that was largely unknown to the general public, even though scientists had accumulated fairly convincing evidence demonstrating its existence and had formed reasonable hypotheses concerning its effects, so expectations for government action or changes in individual behavior may have then been unreasonable. Prior to the 1958 release of the "Keeling curve" showing increases in atmospheric concentrations of CO_2, no scientific evidence yet existed that could demonstrate the effect of fossil fuel combustion on climate, so none could plausibly be faulted for failing to recognize the urgency of the problem. And yet, each nation's historical emissions stretch back well beyond 1958, when no government could reasonably have been faulted for it failure to enact GHG abatement policies. Is it unfair to now hold those nations responsible for acts or policies that predate that point at which we might begin to find them to be faulty? If so, how much of their historical emissions are nations culpable for emitting? At what point did moral responsibility begin to coincide with causal responsibility?

Following strict liability, nations would be held responsible for all of their historically accumulated emissions, regardless of such considerations. Henry Shue implicitly defends such a standard by distinguishing between punishment and responsibility, suggesting that responsibility be seen as distinct from punishment and not necessarily based in moral fault. "It is not fair to punish someone for producing effects that could not have been avoided," he writes, "but it is common to hold persons responsible for effects that were unforeseen and unavoidable."[3] At least in cases where fairness demands that some party be held responsible in order that victims may be compensated, assessing of strict liability in the absence of fault may be preferable to the denial of compensatory claims of restorative justice. But in such cases, one kind of unfairness is being traded off against another. If holding nations liable for causing climate change involves the obligation to compensate those harmed by it, the decision to assign faultless liability is based in a judgment that by holding those nations responsible in this way, the worse outcome of making victims bear responsibility for their predicament can be avoided. Justice demands that if liability can be based in contributory fault, with responsible parties held liable so that victims can be compensated for their injury, then it ought to be so assessed, for fault-based liability relies on morally relevant distinctions between acts that may be similar in their consequences but vary in their culpability. The problem here lies not in determining contributory fault, since recent luxury emissions are plainly faulty in the relevant sense, but in ascertaining at what point to begin counting historical luxury emissions.

In examining historical national GHG emissions, the timeline described above does not offer any compelling point before which ignorance concerning the causes and likely effects of climate change would be entirely reasonable and after which entirely unreasonable, but some points for a cutoff are more defensible than others. The most defensible starting point for assessing moral responsibility for historical emissions is the year 1990, with the publication of the IPCC's first assessment report. By then, most national governments were fully aware of the likely effects of various kinds of human activity on global climate and could have initiated emission abatement programs, as they later pledged to do in the 1992 *UNFCCC*. Continued luxury emissions after 1990, allowed under full knowledge of their consequences for global climate and despite pledges to reduce them, ought to affect the assignment of compensatory burdens. Since the principle of responsibility holds nations morally responsible for harm resulting from their voluntary acts and choices and a plausible case can be made that luxury emissions after 1990 were allowed under knowledge conditions where reasonable persons would have anticipated their harmful effects, fault most clearly begins to attach to luxury emissions then.

Of course, there may be other relevant considerations that ought to be included in assessments of national liability. Shue, for example, defends assessing national liability for all historical emissions based on equity combined with some pragmatic observations concerning the historical effects of unequal national emissions. Modifying the polluter-pays principle, he claims:

> If whoever makes a mess receives the benefits and does not pay the costs, not only does he have no incentive to avoid making as many messes as he likes, but he is also unfair to whoever does pay the costs. He is inflicting costs upon other people, contrary to their interests and, presumably, without their consent.[4]

Because industrialized nations not only cause climate change through their relatively high historical emissions but also through many of the same processes exacerbate global inequality, Shue argues that "the minimum extent of the compensatory burden we are justified in assigning is enough to correct the inequality previously unilaterally imposed."[5] Similarly, Peter Singer implies that industrialized nations ought to be assessed responsibility not only from climate change, but for the immense global inequity in which the problem is bound:

> And since the wealth of the developed nations is inextricably tied to their prodigious use of carbon fuels (a use that began over 200 years ago and continues unchecked today), it is a small step from here to the conclusion that the present global distribution of wealth is the result of the wrongful expropriation by a small fraction of the world's population of a resource that belongs to all human beings in common.[6]

Both of these authors advance a similar set of claims: Since industrialized nations became enormously wealthy and contributed disproportionately to climate change as a direct result of their high rates of fossil fuel combustion, they might be faulted for two harmful consequences rather than one. By consuming more than their share of global resources, they exacerbated scarcity and increased global inequality, both at the expense of the world's poor. Even if they cannot be faulted for having willfully caused climate change by their entire historical emissions, the acts by which they did so can be faulted on other grounds, and therefore must be in this case.

While there are compelling reasons to fault industrialized nations for the consequences of their excessive and inequitable appropriation and consumption of the world's resources other than consequences for climate, a global climate regime cannot be expected to remedy all such historical injustices. In assessing national fault and liability for contributions to climate change, what matters are each nation's causal responsibilities for *that* problem in terms of historical emissions and the extent to which each nation may be at fault in so doing. Americans, for example, might be at fault for a range of harmful effects resulting from their seemingly insatiable appetites for oil, including support for brutal governments in oil-producing nations, air and water pollution from fuel combustion, urban sprawl caused by excessive reliance on car travel, and decreased biodiversity from oil drilling in and transportation through ecologically sensitive areas, but the salient harm for which liability is in question here must be limited to their effects on climate. Fault for these other harmful consequences may begin to follow causal responsibility at an earlier or later point than fault for climate change, and some historical actions that are faultless for their contributions of GHGs may be faulted for emitting other air pollutants, but these are grievances to be redressed elsewhere.

In restricting the attribution of fault to those circumstances in which persons or nations can be held liable for their contributions toward climate change, fault-based liability is reserved for those cases in which reasonable ignorance cannot validly be claimed. Restricting ourselves to those cases alone, industrialized nations would still be held primarily liable for the remedial costs associated with climate change, because they are responsible for the vast majority of luxury emissions since 1990, albeit slightly less so than for luxury emissions before then. On the other hand, a standard of strict liability would impose significant remedial costs on large developing nations such as India and China, since no distinction could be made between survival and luxury emissions under strict liability, though their per capita emissions remain far below those of industrialized nations. One cannot acknowledge the unfairness of finding these nations to be at fault for climate change without abandoning strict liability for a fault-based standard, but with the latter necessarily come the various difficulties that are the subject of this chapter.

Scientific Uncertainty, Deception, and Responsibility

One might respond to this contention that ignorance concerning the causes and effects of climate change is no longer reasonable by claiming that since even scientists are uncertain about these causes and effects, no lay person can reasonably be expected to draw causal links between actions and consequences when these continue to befuddle highly trained experts. In assessing fault-based liability, the problem of scientific uncertainty affects the reasonableness of ignorance concerning harm for which persons are causally responsible, but is complicated by the assertion that it is unreasonable to expect persons to anticipate harmful consequences of their actions when these consequences have not yet been conclusively proven to result from the acts in question with the requisite degree of certainty. At first, this objection seems plausible, since lay persons cannot reasonably be expected to understand natural phenomena such as climate as well as scientific experts, and—according to popular media coverage of the "controversy" over the existence of anthropogenic climate change—even the experts cannot agree that humans are now contributing toward climate change. Even if there are more experts on one side of the alleged "controversy" than the other, the fact that some climate skeptics continue to challenge the mainstream view within the field exonerates members of the lay public from fault based on the expectation that they should anticipate the harmful consequences of their acts. Given ongoing disagreement among experts concerning the reality of climate change, it cannot be unreasonable for persons to regard their GHG-producing acts as entirely harmless.

This invocation of scientific uncertainty in the service of building an ignorance-based defense against assessments of liability for contributing to climate change raises several challenges for applying the concept of responsibility to the design of a global climate regime. First and least onerous is the empirical claim concerning the existence of ongoing scientific uncertainty about the causes and likely effects of climate change. Because the sort of genuine scientific uncertainty that might excuse GHG-producing acts from liability for climate-related harm does not in fact exist—rather, its alleged existence is "manufactured" as part of a political strategy to avoid GHG regulation—two further questions arise concerning fault and liability. If this campaign to produce the appearance of uncertainty within the scientific community is one of deception, can fault or liability be transferred from citizens that are manipulated into thinking their GHG-emitting acts harmless to those who are manipulating them? Recall the discussion of vicarious liability from chapter 5, where some are held liable but not at fault for the harmful acts of others, because this question involves a similar transfer of liability from one person to another. On the other hand, should citizens who are manipulated into falsely believing their acts to be harmless be faulted for their failure to exercise prudent skepticism against the false claims issuing from industry-sponsored disinformation campaigns, in which figures in government may also be complicit, when the consensus view of reputable climate scientists is widely available?

Climate science is a sophisticated field of research, drawing on a vast network of data collection, advanced computer models, and well-organized and well-funded research institutes. For well more than a decade, published scientific findings have been collected, subjected to further analysis and additional processes of peer review, and then widely and carefully disseminated by the IPCC, which represents the best available assessment of the scientific consensus on the issue. The panel's reports and the research on which they are based have not been without elements of uncertainty. Climate is the product of highly complex processes, and the mathematical models used to predict future climate patterns rely on a vast array of variables and possible scenarios, and so issue predictions of likely causes and effects within confidence intervals and with graduated levels of certainty. While the IPCC is committed to consensus-based conclusions, scrupulously documenting those findings on which experts cannot agree or where key uncertainties remains, some disagreement has appeared among IPCC contributors, and some conclusions are reached at higher levels of certainty than are others. Such disagreement and uncertainty are endemic to the sort of long-range forecasts that climate science entails, but most in the field are not troubled by it, conceiving of their work as minimizing and "managing" uncertainty rather than the impossible task attempting to eliminate it entirely.[7]

Although uncertainty remains around several questions of the nature, extent, and impact of climate change, there remains no reasonable uncertainty about several basic facts of climate change. Atmospheric CO_2 concentrations have increased from their preindustrial equilibrium of 280 ppm to 383 ppm today, with the vast majority of that increase occurring since 1950, very likely due to changes in land use and fossil fuel combustion. Largely as a result, average surface temperature increases during the twentieth century were the largest of the millennium, and the 1990s was the warmest decade of the century. These facts are undisputed. Where scientific uncertainty does exist, it is over the extent and impacts of global climate change, not over its existence or primary causes. Scientists expect average global surface temperatures to increase by between 1.4°C and 5.8°C in the period 1990–2100, with a consensus coalescing around 3°C,[8] a projected rate of warming that would be unprecedented in more than 10,000 years. Global temperatures and weather patterns have already been altered, although the worst climatic effects are expected to manifest in the future. Consequences of climatic changes include increasingly severe weather, increased threats to human health, diminished ecological productivity and biodiversity, decreased crop yields, and increasing water shortages, along with the economic, social, and political problems that accompany increased resource scarcity and ecological stress. Despite the uncertainty that

surrounds much of their work, all of these predictions are made with medium
to high confidence (or 90 percent certainty) with the consensus of all IPCC
scientists.[9]

The IPCC's third assessment report, published in 2001, carefully notes the
key uncertainties remaining in various areas of climate science. The "magnitude and character of natural climate variability" and the "climate forcings due
to natural factors and anthropogenic aerosols" remain uncertain, as do the
effects of climate feedbacks in modeling the carbon cycle. In projecting future
climatic changes, probability distributions related to temperature and sea level
changes, the "mechanisms, quantification, time scales, and likelihoods associated with large-scale abrupt/nonlinear changes," and difficulties in quantifying
and projecting climate models to local and regional climate scales likewise
remain uncertain. Climate impacts similarly contain key uncertainties, including the reliability of local detail in projected local and regional effects, assessment and prediction of the responses of ecological, social, and economic
systems to the combined effects of climate change and other related stresses,
and "identification, quantification, and valuation of damages associated with
climate change." In terms of mitigation, key uncertainties include the interac-
tions between climate change and other environmental issues with their socioeconomic implications, the future price of energy and development of
low-emissions technologies, the social and political means for reducing the
barriers to implementing low-emissions technologies, and the quantification
of the relative mitigation costs of various approaches and of adaptation costs to
climate changes.[10] Concerning the existence, the causes, and the likely effects
of climate change, however, there remains no genuine uncertainty within the
scientific community.

Uncertainty of the kind purported to exist by climate skeptics, where the
very existence of anthropogenic climate change is alleged to be a mere *theory*—
a term that is itself supposed to connote uncertainty and even doubt, allegedly
unsupported by empirical evidence or as likely to be beneficial as harmful—
cannot credibly be inferred from the available evidence and using defensible
standards of inquiry. Although uncertainties remain, one simply cannot characterize the state of knowledge as uncertain concerning the essential basic
facts. Setting aside for the moment the likely ulterior motives of climate skeptics and their sponsors, we might first try to understand the source of the widespread belief that the scientific basis of climate change remains unsettled. As
noted in chapter 1, well-funded public relations campaigns that feature climate
skeptics in a variety of roles and media contribute to this mistaken perception,
as do ideological think tanks, pundits, and politicians that have joined the skeptical chorus. Likewise, as Richard Wolfson and Stephen Schneider note, the

U.S. mass media, in "attempting to be fair to both sides has given the 'contrarian' view publicity vastly disproportionate to its support in the community of climate scientists."[11]

The public itself must also be held partially responsible for preferring to hear a message, and choosing beliefs based on that preference, that reassures them that their everyday acts are not causing the problems predicted by reputable scientists, filtering out contrary information that indicts those actions and either creates cognitive dissonance or justifies significant restrictions on activities that persons would prefer to continue in their guiltless enjoyment. For a host of reasons and based in a range of contributing factors, the message that has been disseminated by those opposed to GHG regulation both in and out of government has resonated with some members of the public. To the extent that they should have known better, however, the skepticism that they imbibe from its primary sources must be seen as faulty, factually and morally.

Part of this mistaken perception owes also to the climate scientists charged with writing reports disseminated to the public, for failing to adequately explain the observed uncertainties and what they represent. When probabilities for various scenarios are not included with warming impact estimates, or when some quantifiable levels of uncertainty are not attached to the various predictions in a scientific report, it is easier for various groups to use uncertainty to advance their own agendas. Skeptics use admissions of uncertainty to cast doubt on identified causes or projected impacts, while environmental groups often seize upon numbers that are at the high end of estimated impacts in order to draw publicity to possible dangers.[12] Many lacking scientific literacy mistakenly assume—encouraged in this false belief by skeptics—that since anthropogenic climate change is only a "theory," it must not yet be something that is accepted as fact and thus cannot serve as the basis of reasonable expectations for consequences of actions. Wolfson and Schneider attempt to clarify the nature of scientific theories:

> A scientific theory is a coherent set of principles put forth to explain aspects of physical or biological or social reality. Decades of testing confirm a theory as providing the best available explanation for the phenomena at hand. It's always possible that an established theory may someday be proved wrong (or at least incomplete), but that possibility diminishes every time events in the real world live up to the theory's predictions.[13]

While climate change is "merely" a theory, as are many other scientific precepts that are widely accepted as true, and while it relies on some speculation, it would be false to dismiss its predictions as merely speculative. As confusing as this may be to members of the general public, many of whom subscribe to false dichotomies between immutable facts and mere conjecture and who are barraged with messages that aim to discredit other scientific "theories" such as evolution, the lack of scientific literacy among the public surely plays a role. As Wolfson and Schneider note, "The public needs to recognize that established theories represent solidly confirmed bodies of scientific principles with broad explanatory powers and that, absent unlikely, radical new discoveries, such theories are the closest we can get to claiming we know the truth about physical reality."[14]

Manufacturing Uncertainty

While the above factors may explain much of the evident fact that, despite the abundance of widely disseminated information to the contrary, many people cling to the now-unreasonable belief that scientists do not yet know whether climate change is real or what might cause warming patterns that exist, one major casual explanation for this ignorance requires further examination. The false belief in ongoing scientific uncertainty concerning the causes and likely effects of climate change would be philosophically uninteresting were it not for the deliberate effort to manipulate the mass public into accepting that belief as true, or at least into rejecting the known facts of climate change as speculative and unsettled. As suggested above, much of this perceived uncertainty is neither accidental nor purely the product of widespread scientific illiteracy; rather, it has been in some way manufactured, and its chimerical existence owes to a deliberate campaign to create the false appearance that some set of scientific questions remain unsettled when in fact such uncertainty does not exist. Some of the alleged "uncertainties" are entirely manufactured, while others have been deliberately and grossly exaggerated for the same effect, taking some genuine uncertainty and then misrepresenting it in order to lead the public into believing that some theories or conclusions are much less widely accepted than they are in fact. In both cases, the accusation imputes fault to those engaged in distorting the truth, and may also entail some fault on the part of those taken in by such campaigns.

Both are serious allegations: In both cases, the accused seeks to mislead the public into rejecting some set of conclusions that are either known to be true or widely accepted as such. By itself, the effort to manipulate public opinion might be condemned for its dishonesty, even if the accused has nothing to gain and the public nothing to lose by this falsification of reality. When the stakes are high—when those engaged in manipulating public opinion stand to significantly gain or the public to significantly lose by the latter's acceptance of the disseminated falsehoods as true—the offense increases, with simple dishonesty becoming serious fraud or exploitation. When the stakes are high and the accused is a public official, the offense is even greater. We may often excuse such deception in the service of profit when it is used to sell unneeded consumer products that would otherwise not be purchased, but we cannot so readily excuse it when used to sell some public policy that the public would never accept if the truth were widely known. When political actors manufacture and exaggerate scientific uncertainties surrounding climate change in order to mislead the public into falsely believing that the problem has yet to be accepted as real by the relevant specialists and therefore that GHG regulations are unjustified, its actions are straightforwardly deceptive and deeply troubling.

The desire to ensure that government policies are justified by well-established scientific facts before undertaking major reforms or issuing costly regulations cannot in itself be faulted and, indeed, characterizes a virtue among those policy makers who are genuinely concerned with protecting or advancing the public interest. With many public policy issues, ongoing scientific controversies, unsettled questions, or significant uncertainties surrounding the existence or causes of some problem may constitute legitimate reasons for delaying actions on those issues. The need for a prudent caution in policy making cannot be disputed, and examples illustrating the need for such prudence may readily be found, where policy makers have rushed to judgment prior to the adequate study of a problem, unnecessarily acting in costly ways or causing regrettable harm. Like virtues generally, this sort of caution is best exercised in moderation, as examples are also readily available of regrettable failures to act in time to prevent a predicted problem, owing to the excessive timidity of policy makers in possession of sufficient information to justify action but who fail to prevent some predicted and avoidable harm.

The inquiry in this section focuses on the assessment of what appears to be deliberate exaggeration or outright fabrication of scientific uncertainty, along with suppression of evidence and intimidation of researchers, as a means of advancing a policy agenda that depends on the public's ignorance of the science in question. Since it is at least possible that those involved in climate science disinformation campaigns act from a sincere belief that the current scientific consensus is mistaken, the following section considers whether the actual beliefs of those engaged in such campaigns matter in the assessment of their actions.

Part of the insidious nature of campaigns of "manufactured uncertainty" owes to what is commonly assumed to be its underlying motive. As public relations strategy, claims of scientific uncertainty have been advanced as rhetorical ploys in the service of deregulation or continued nonregulation and as a legal subterfuge for deflecting tort liability claims.[15] For example, the tobacco industry for decades denied any causal connection between smoking and adverse health effects, despite knowledge from both internal and external studies confirming that connection—a legal and political strategy that, while successful, constitutes an ethically repugnant campaign of deception, for reasons examined below. Attempts to regulate tobacco have repeatedly been frustrated on the false premise that no conclusive evidence links smoking and health problems, while compensatory lawsuits brought on behalf of those killed by tobacco have been denied on three mutually contradictory grounds: that causal responsibility cannot be established since smoking is not adequately certain to be hazardous to health, that the smoker should have known about the widely disseminated health risks and therefore assumed them by taking up smoking or not quitting, or that the smoker is deceased and therefore lacks legal standing to sue the producer of the product that killed him or her. Uncertainty, in this case, is merely the first line of defense in a broader legal and political strategy, with the same elements on display in current campaigns to discredit the scientific basis of climate change.

Claims about uncertainty, in the cases of both GHG emissions and tobacco, are often intended to obfuscate the scientific facts in order to "manage" concerns about the public health effects of smoking and the causes and likely consequences, as well as the very existence, of climate change. The tobacco industry continues to call for further study regarding the causal links between smoking and the resulting adverse health effects that have long been established in the scientific literature, and the U.S. government along with its allies in industry appears to be following a similar strategy on climate change. In 1998, the *New York Times* published a leaked memo from the American Petroleum Institute, outlining the oil industry's strategic effort to "maximize the impact of scientific view consistent with ours with Congress, the media, and other key audiences" and its prediction that "victory will be achieved when recognition of uncertainty becomes part of the 'conventional wisdom.'"[16] Similarly, a leaked strategy memo about winning "the environmental communications battle" from the Republican political consultant Frank Luntz to the George W. Bush White House advised: "Should the public believe that the scientific issues are settled, their views about global warming will change accordingly. Therefore, you need to make scientific certainty a primary issue in the debate."[17] Accordingly, the administration's 2002 *Economic Report of the President* claims:

> We are uncertain about the effect of natural fluctuations on global warming. We do not know how much the climate could or will

change in the future. We do not know how fast climate change will occur, or even how some of our actions could affect it. Finally, it is difficult to say with any certainty what constitutes a dangerous level of warming that must be avoided.[18]

The first objective of this legal and public relations strategy of manufactured uncertainty is to forestall carbon regulation as long as possible, and to do so it seeks to discredit the science on which the IPCC's reports are based. Also useful in delaying the onset of regulation is the implied need for further study, which might presumably reduce those uncertainties to the point where public policy may be guided by sufficiently well-established scientific fact, but which also creates a convenient pretext for further inaction. In what does not appear to be a coincidence, the Bush administration and ExxonMobil—a staunch opponent of the Kyoto treaty and a major source of funding for climate skeptics[19]—both recently announced significant grants to further study climate change, including provisos that regulatory action be reconsidered when studies are completed in 2010.[20] Proposals to further study problems such as smoking and climate change are not inherently insidious, but become so when accompanied by requests to delay meaningful policy responses to serious problems about which reasonable scientific certainty already exists. Insofar as the goal is avoiding regulation, the strategy has worked brilliantly in the United States, where the denial of complicity in this impending crisis provides a comforting narrative for a populace that appears all too willing to accept any pretext for its unabated consumption.

Such campaigns may plausibly be described as ones of deception. A charge of deception is an especially serious one to make against public officials because it implies a culpable disregard for the truth, and possibly worse, given the public trust with which they have been invested, and so warrants several prefatory remarks. Deception involves the intentional distortion of the truth in order to mislead others, where the deceived are led by a deceiver to act or think in ways that they would not otherwise, typically to serve the interests of the deceiver and often against the interests of the deceived. Thus, its status as a moral offense turns on more than the falsity of statements made or ideas implied, because *intent* to mislead is an essential element. One can unknowingly convey false information to others without displaying this intent to mislead, and false information intentionally conveyed that does not aim to mislead (as in a work of fiction) is not deceptive. It is possible to mislead another in the relevant sense without saying or writing something that is literally false, since nominally true statements can readily be enlisted to create false impressions. To be guilty of deception, persons must intentionally convey information that they know to be false with the aim of creating false beliefs in the minds of others so as to alter their actions, opinions, or behavior. Thus, it is a form of lying, though deception need not involve spoken or written language; persons can deceive through actions, gestures, symbols, and even silence. As long as ideas or information are communicated from one person to another, deception is possible.

Deception can be more or less serious, depending on the harmful consequences to which it contributes and its causal role in bringing those consequences about. When deception causes others to act in ways that are harmful to themselves or others and when the deceived are held to be entirely faultless for acting on the basis of information obtained through deception, the fault as well as liability for the resulting harm transfers from deceived to deceiver; whereas when victims of deception are partially to blame for their gullibility and the culpable manipulability that results, less of the fault and liability transfers. However, deception is always faulty, even if the fault is sometimes shared with the deceived, whether or not it is successful in its insidious objective, for its offense lies in the intent to mislead. A dishonest but inept telemarketer who fails in his or her effort to prey upon gullible elderly victims cannot be held blameless merely because he or she displays so little skill in manifesting malevolence or because those potential victims should have known better than to trust their money to someone that they had never met. Moreover, deceivers need not benefit by the deception in order to be faulted, as long as they mislead persons into acting in ways harmful to themselves or others. Here, deception differs from exploitation.

Thus, deception connotes fault insofar as it is causally responsible for harmful acts, as well as moral blame for its insidious motive. It need not be a sufficient cause of those acts—hence attributing fault for unsuccessful deception and shared fault between deceiver and deceived—but fault can transfer from one committing the harmful act to another only if the latter is somehow causally connected with the act's commission, which is why liability but not fault transfer in principle–agent cases of vicarious liability. In deception, multiple agents are involved in the causal chain, because neither the deceiver nor the deceived are individually sufficient causes of the act in question, but fault and moral responsibility are attributed to the deceiver and not to the deceived unless the latter can be shown to be at fault for falling victim to deception; insofar as they *should* have known better, deceived persons can be held partially liable for those harmful acts that they would not have committed but for the false or misleading claims of a deceiver. Overly gullible persons who fail to exercise adequate precaution and who are as a result too easily manipulated into acting in ways that are harmful to themselves or others may sometimes be required to bear some of the costs of their deception, but *some* moral responsibility must be attributed to persons who deceive others into causing harm, even if, like Iago to Othello, the deceived must share in that responsibility.

Within the context of climate politics, many of the false statements made and inaccurate information conveyed fall well short of deception, for they do not meet the above criteria of intentional efforts to mislead others. It is quite possible, for example, that Republican Senator James Inhofe, described in chapter 1, actually believes that climate change is a "hoax," in which case he would not be guilty of intentionally distorting the truth in order to mislead others. Similarly, those climate skeptics whose research is sponsored by energy companies and who coincidentally reach conclusions about the existence of climate change that their sponsors desire may be exonerated from any charge of intentionally misleading, as long as they were selected on the basis of the conclusions that they were already predisposed to reach rather than reaching them as quid pro quo for their industry sponsorship. These acts may not be entirely faultless, but they lack the moral offense endemic to deception. On the other hand, if "experts" should knowingly falsify data or otherwise alter their own or others' findings in order to reach a preordained conclusion, or if a politician should knowingly ignore or suppress credible scientific findings in order to protect an interested patron, advance an opposing political agenda, or protect a culpable colleague, then deception appears to be a warranted accusation. In perhaps the clearest example, when an oil industry lobbyist with no scientific training alters the substantive content of a completed and approved scientific report in order to make it seem to support the policy goals of the oil industry, the act is straightforwardly deceptive. When done by a former oil industry lobbyist while head of the White House Council for Environmental Quality, as described in chapter 1, the insidious act takes on an added dimension of offense for its blatant violation of the public trust.

The salient question for this chapter, then, involves the extent to which persons or nations can be faulted for their GHG-producing acts when these may be partly the product of deception rather than mere ignorance. Insofar as fault in such cases transfers away from the deceived and to a deceiver, wholly or in part, does this transfer of fault diminish the degree to which persons can be held liable for their emissions? Does their ignorance concerning the consequences of their actions become more reasonable when it results in part from deliberate campaigns to distort the truth? And if so, what might this entail for national assessments of liability for climate change? The first two of these questions are not possible to answer generally, since they depend in large measure on the particular facts of the episode in question. One can certainly imagine cases in which persons deceived into committing harmful acts ought to be completely exonerated from any form of moral responsibility for them, but one can equally well imagine other cases in which considerable fault attaches to the deceived. In climate politics, there probably exists a range of different plausible divisions of fault between deceiver and deceived for acts contributing toward climate change, depending on the facts of the case. The answer to the third, however, is more straightforward: Assessments of national liability for GHG emissions cannot be diminished by ignorance resulting from campaigns of deception. Whether or not public officials are directly involved in such campaigns, government has a responsibility to counter them when they appear, and exempting a nation from liability for environmental harm that it helps to cause when its residents are made to be sufficiently ignorant of the causes or effects of those problems would create a serious moral hazard, encouraging rather than discouraging such campaigns.

When governments are either actively complicit in campaigns of deception or else fail to adequately counter their manipulative effects, some fault for the harm that results may also be justifiably applied to them. But as discussed in chapter 5, citizens are fully at fault for the actions of their government if it is perfectly democratic, but cannot be held at all responsible for the actions of their perfectly autocratic government. Between these extremes, actual governments and citizenries must share responsibility for their nation's acts and policies, with the share of fault assigned to government being inversely proportional to the extent that citizens exert democratic control over state policy. In assessing U.S. culpability for those acts that contribute to climate change, there is plainly enough fault to share between citizens and the state. Chapter 5 considers the extent to which individuals might be held responsible for contributing toward climate change, but the concern here is which factors aggravate or mitigate a government's share of national responsibility—specifically, whether government campaigns to discredit climate science as instrumental to defeating meaningful climate policy increases its share of moral responsibility, or whether citizens themselves are to blame for their unreasonable acceptance of false information disseminated by their government.

As implied above, a government's share of responsibility for a harmful public policy, or lack of policy that might avoid the harm, is significantly increased when that policy results not from open and deliberative democratic processes in which citizens have access to accurate information, but instead from ignorance produced by deception. This is so even when the government is not itself directly responsible for the deception, insofar as states have normative commitments to transparency and its consequence is the subversion of the democratic process. When a harmful policy results from deception committed by the government itself, nearly all of the responsibility for that harm may be attributed to the government itself.

More complicated are cases where a harmful policy results from inaccurate information disseminated by government, but where the public officials who convey it do so unintentionally, or without knowledge that it is indeed false. In such cases, we still attribute some fault to the government, for a perfectly democratic process in which fault is attributed entirely to citizens requires that citizens have accurate information that is relevant to the issue under consideration. In other cases, public officials may convey false or inaccurate information to citizens in a way that contributes to the adoption of a harmful policy, and while that official might not realize that the information is indeed false, they might be found to be at fault for using the influence of their office to cause citizens to adopt false beliefs when they should have ascertained the falsity of the information they disseminated. Along a continuum, government bears more fault for a harmful policy to the extent that it participates in the spread of inaccurate information that leads to that policy's adoption, and to the extent that it should have identified that information as inaccurate before disseminating it. At one end of this continuum is a culpably uninformed public causing or failing to avert significant harm, and at the other, a government actively participating in deception in order to adopt or maintain a policy that it knows to be harmful and against the hypothetical will of an informed public.

The inquiry here focuses on various points along this continuum, rather than on either pole. Given the government's prominent endorsement of climate skepticism, which is the primary driver of false beliefs among citizens about the causes and effects of climate change, we can disregard the possibility that U.S. climate policy (or lack thereof) is merely the product of a culpably uninformed public. We shall also set aside the possibility that public antipathy toward the predicted hazards of climate change is entirely the result of government- or industry-led deception, for this possibility entails a dim view of the democratic competence of citizens and raises no philosophically interesting issues. Instead, we shall consider how various intermediate positions along the continuum may depend on the existing state of knowledge within climate science as well as the mental states of public officials. Where the policy results from free and open public debate on the merits of various policy alternatives and in light of knowledge about the problem in question and the likely effects of the various alternatives, and is the result of fair procedures based in principles of political equality and majority rule, the adoption of a harmful policy is the responsibility of the public that supports it. Had the current U.S. climate policy been adopted in such a fashion, the public would be wholly responsible for any resulting harm, and government would bear no unique responsibility for a policy that represents the public will.

United States climate policy development has not proceeded in this manner. At no point has there been an open, informed, and empowered public debate over national climate policy—the Bush administration's decision to withdraw from the Kyoto Protocol was unilateral and in no way the product of any remotely democratic process, and little genuine public deliberation surrounded either the 1997 Byrd-Hagel Resolution or the 2003 Climate Stewardship Act. Indeed, the issue has been largely kept off the national policy agenda by opponents of GHG regulation, and the various ongoing disinformation campaigns have probably undermined the possibility of any near-future informed public debate. Besides the largely elite-driven policy process that has thus far dominated U.S. climate policy and the lack of open and informed public debate about policy alternatives, a campaign finance system that allows corporate contributions to narrow the field of viable candidates for federal office and to keep issues such as GHG regulation off of the national policy agenda, in a phenomenon described by Peter Bachrach and Morton Baratz as involving an oft-unseen face of power,[21] likewise impugns the democratic nature of climate policy development, violating norms of political equality and majority rule as political influence is distorted by money through campaign finance, leading majorities in government to oppose policies such as U.S. participation in the Kyoto Protocol while substantial majorities of citizens favor it.[22] If the public's share of fault and responsibility for a harmful policy is assessed in proportion to the genuinely democratic nature of that policy's development, then the American public cannot be held all that responsible for its current climate policy.

Or can it? Recall that in some cases, an entire group can be held collectively responsible for the actions or decisions of only some of its members. In the collective decision to wage unjust war, according to Michael Walzer's argument examined in chapter 5, those citizens that oppose the war at the ballot box are held liable along with the war's supporters and those too indifferent to vote for harm that results from it as long as they fail to do enough to stop it. One might make a similar claim about responsibility for climate change, particularly since its consequences are expected to be as serious as many historical examples of aggressive war, and since opportunities to meaningfully affect climate policy have thus not been offered through normal political processes. Similarly, one might blame the public for failing to express its support for meaningful policy action to curb GHG emissions at the ballot box and for failing to hold elected politicians accountable for their intransigence on the issue. As Walzer suggests, democracy is a way of attributing responsibility, so democratic citizens must be held responsible for the harmful policies of their government, even when those policies result in part from deception in which that government is complicit. Even if they are not fully responsible for endorsing policies about which they have been deceived, citizens are responsible for their government's policy decisions because they are ultimately responsible for their government. Any fault that can be attributed to the actions of government entails the (sometimes vicarious) liability of its citizens, insofar as they are principals authorizing the government to act as their agent.

In the end, the division of responsibility between a government and its populace over their harmful rates of GHG emissions makes little practical difference, because any liability assessed to the government would simply be borne by the populace anyway. Were it possible for victims of climate-related harm to bring lawsuits against those causing the problem for the recovery of damages, any liability assessed to a government would simply transfer the nation at large. While a nation's government may merely be the decision-making apparatus for the nation itself, it must be assumed to be authorized to act on behalf of the entire nation in a principle–agent relationship. Whether assessments of liability hold Americans collectively responsible for their contributions to climate change in their role as consumers for releasing excessive GHGs into the atmosphere or as citizens for electing a government that allows this to continue and opposes every effort to curb such harmful behavior, in either case their liability is based in some contributory fault.

Moreover, fully exonerating citizens for the policies and actions of their governments creates a moral hazard similar to the one noted above, since this fails to hold citizens responsible for their political choices and undermines the incentive for the watchdog and accountability functions assigned to a democratic electorate. If each nation is required to pay into a climate change compensation fund in proportion to its luxury emissions, this would create a powerful incentive not only for proactive policy to curb such emissions, but also for governments to crack down on and refrain from participating in campaigns of deception designed to maintain high rates of national luxury emissions and, more generally, for citizens to better educate themselves concerning contemporary policy issues and to grant higher salience to the externality costs of national policies in their voting decisions. Where harmful policies result from democratic deficits rather than expressions of popular will, a responsibility-based liability scheme would encourage citizens in flawed democracies to demand more accountability for public officials and thus more popular control over potentially high future damage assessments. In this sense, a global climate regime that holds nations responsible for their luxury emissions not only looks backward in basing liability on the extent to which various parties contributed to the problem, but also looks forward by encouraging better performance in the future, and may be justified either way.

Beliefs, Motives, and Fault

Do a person's motives matter in assessing fault for their harmful acts? When persons should anticipate contributing toward some harmful phenomenon such as climate change through their actions and would do so if in possession of relevant facts, but act from ignorance and so without the motive or intention of causing such problems, can they still be faulted for them? Our deferred question about whether or not climate skeptics could be faulted for their campaigns against climate science if they sincerely believe in the skepticism that they publicly advance turns on the related question about the role of intentions in assessments of fault, because it presents a case in which a bad consequence is neither anticipated nor intended. In assessing such cases, we might recall that negligence involves actions for which persons improperly fail to anticipate the harmful consequences that are likely to follow, while recklessness involves the conscious decision to disregard anticipated harmful consequences of actions. Following this graduated culpability scale, it would seem that persons must be held morally responsible for harmful acts whether or not they intend or anticipate them; they act negligently if they fail to anticipate the harmful effects of their actions, and recklessly if they anticipate but disregarded them. In the context of climate ethics, however, this standard reply seems premature, for it condemns as faulty many acts in which persons unintentionally contribute toward climate-related harm.

Some maintain that an agent's motives or intentions play a significant role, even the defining one, in moral responsibility. Kant, for example, claims that the only morally good acts are those that result from a moral motive or obedience to the moral law, thus distinguishing between autonomous and heteronymous actions and reserving moral praise for the former alone. Elsewhere in ethics, motives play a much less important role in moral assessment. Utilitarianism, for example, bases its judgments of right and wrong acts in their consequences, not the mental states of agents at the time of decision. Motives, it would seem, are here entirely irrelevant, because actions are retrospectively evaluated in terms of the consequences that they actually bring about, not those that their authors may have intended. Retrospectively, utilitarians describe an act in which the agent meant well but unintentionally caused harm as having been wrong, and the agent's motive does nothing to affect our retrospective judgment. However, even utilitarianism takes account of motives and intentions in *prospective* judgment: In practical ethics, we need to know if an act is right or wrong before we commit it. Waiting until their consequences obtain and then retrospectively evaluating past choices yields little of practical value. Prospective moral judgment requires an estimate of likely consequences of alternative acts in advance of a decision, and utilitarianism requires persons to act in the way that can reasonably be expected to produce the best overall outcome, identifying the morally right action at the time of decision even it later turns out to have adverse consequences that could not have been reasonably anticipated.

Since we are primarily concerned with attributions of fault and assignments of liability, such distinctions between these two ethical theories—which are instead concerned with moral blame—may not make a difference to our main inquiry. Clearly, consequences are often relevant to liability given its concern with providing a remedy for those made to suffer some harm for which they are not responsible. Moral blame, by contrast, is not remedial and so need not depend on prerequisite bad consequences. If consequences alone were relevant to assessments of liability, we would have to jettison fault-based liability in favor of a strict liability standard, holding persons or nations liable for their actual contributions to the harm in question. But as the examples of moral luck illustrate, a purely consequentialist assessment of fault is often arbitrary, basing fault and liability on factors that are outside of an agent's control, thereby violating the principle of responsibility. To ensure that a climate regime holds nations or persons responsible, but does so justly, it must sometimes be required to decide rather than simply discover instances of fault, and to do so it must consider whether or not the standards used to distinguish faultless from faulty acts can themselves be justified. An agent's lack of intention to cause harm presents another case with clear application to the assessment of responsibility in a global climate regime where such a decision is needed.

Setting aside the issue of ignorance, persons often act with the knowledge that their actions may, in some small way, contribute toward larger problems, but not from the motive of causing or contributing toward those problems. Perhaps this disjunction between knowledge and motive or intention is partially the result of one or more of the "mistakes in moral mathematics" surveyed in chapter 5, since persons may well realize that GHGs contribute toward climate change, and that climate change is expected to be harmful, but nonetheless not regard their own actions are themselves harmful. At any rate, it seems safe to say that most individual acts that contribute to climate change do so unintentionally, and are motivated instead by distinct and often benign considerations. Driving a personal automobile, for example, is widely known to contribute to a range of problems besides the emissions produced through fossil fuel combustion, yet few drive cars with the express intention of contributing toward such problems. Instead, they need to get from here to there, lack convenient alternatives to automobile transport, and so opt to drive, sometimes consciously aware of the harm caused by driving but so acting in spite of rather than because of such awareness. Describing such behavior as reckless, defined as the conscious disregard of harm one might be causing, seems like hyperbole in such cases, because individual contributions toward larger problems are small and the alternatives to driving limited.

The doctrine of double effect—a relic of medieval casuistry that is sometimes applied to several contemporary moral problems—holds that an act may be permissible, even if it is known to cause harm, provided that it is committed with the intention of bringing about some other outcome whose good outweighs the bad of the foreseen but unintended harm. In this way, the doctrine is used as an argument to overcome the principle of non-maleficence, which prohibits the intentional causing of harm. In just war theory, for example, the doctrine is used to defend the use of high-altitude air strikes or other insufficiently discriminatory ordinance that can be expected to kill some noncombatants as "collateral damage" along with the legitimate military targets whose death or destruction is the intended outcome. From this example, the primary case against the doctrine of double effect can readily be seen: It allows agents to sacrifice the good of one person for the sake of another, allowing willful harm and thus violating Kant's imperative to treat persons as ends in themselves. If allowed as an exception to prohibitions against harm, it risks abuse since it can be used disingenuously to rationalize a variety of ordinarily repugnant acts, such as intentionally killing the innocent.

Nonetheless, something like the principle of double effect's emphasis on intention offers a sensible conceptual frame for evaluating acts such as those contributing to climate change. Many acts contribute in a small way to that problem, because they release GHGs into the atmosphere. Surely, we would not want to describe all of these acts as morally wrong, for the harmful nature of individual acts is insufficient to warrant the strong social disapprobation that the language of morality invokes, and lumps a large number of otherwise innocuous acts alongside genuinely wrong ones in a manner that risks diluting the force of moral norms. Recall, however, that attributing fault and assessing liability are not moral judgments; they are merely ways of assigning remedial responsibility to persons for harm that they might cause. Persons can be held liable for acts that are not morally wrong, as long as those acts are in some way faulty as well as being causally responsible for some harm.

Here, the role of intention returns. In criminal law, a lack of intent to cause harm does not always exonerate persons from culpability for harmful actions, but it is often a mitigating factor in assessing the degree of guilt that attaches to harmful acts, and thus the degree of punishment or restitution that is required. The doctrine of double effect, on the other hand, may be taken to imply the lack of fault as well as a lack of moral guilt, since it is typically used to justify some action in light of its anticipated harmful effects, implying against the standard view of fault that agents should not have acted otherwise. But can the combination of an intended good or benign effect with an unintended yet foreseen bad effect serve as a defeating condition for attributions of fault and liability? If so, the limits on any remedial global climate regime would be profound.

Suppose that a national government defends its policy of allowing its citizens and industries unlimited GHG emissions on grounds that it does not intend to cause climate change in so doing, although it knows or should know this to be a likely consequence, but rather intends to maximize economic growth and GHG regulations would reduce that growth. Can we then excuse the policy's harmful effects, committed with the requisite knowledge but in the absence of malicious intentions? Clearly, we cannot. To see why such a defense fails, we must separate two distinct claims that are being conflated above. First is a claim about total utility, which holds that it is sometimes permissible to act in such a way that some persons are made worse off as long as these effects are outweighed by corresponding benefits to others. This claim, which often comes into conflict with norms of justice and individual rights that reject its reasoning, does not depend on intentions at all. The second claim asserts critical importance to intentions in moral assessment, suggesting (as in Joel Feinberg's doctrine of the internality of morals, described in chapter 5) that persons are to be judged by their intentions alone, not the outcomes of their acts. Because outcomes are often outside the control of agents, we can hold them morally responsible only for what they intend, not what they actually do.

These are incompatible claims. According to the first, right action is determined by outcomes alone, and the motives or intentions of agents are wholly irrelevant. According to the second, outcomes are set aside as irrelevant, and intentions alone are allowed to reign supreme. If we accept the first, then agents can be justified in their GHG-producing acts only if they do more good than harm, and a defense of everyday polluting acts must therefore proceed through a utility comparison in which some but not all such acts might be justified on the basis of their net beneficial effects. If, on the other hand, we accept the second claim, we must reject the first, because it would not matter whether the intended good outcome actually outweighs the harmful unintended but expected effect, as judgment turns on intentions alone and not outcomes.

As is suggested in chapter 5, where a purely internal domain of morals stands in contrast with the external domain of law, a system of legal responsibility based on intentions alone would be impossible, given the lack of reliable access of legal institutions to a person's true intentions, let alone those of entire nations. If intending some other outcome than the one produced was allowed as a defense of harmful acts, none could ever unwillingly be found guilty, for this defense would always be available. The problem of intention collapses into one of knowledge when persons exhibit the requisite *mens rea* for unintended bad consequences in cases of recklessness or negligence, but access to a person's knowledge is practically limited for the same reasons as with intentions. Since external behavioral standards by which malicious intentions are measured in criminal proceedings can only approximate a defendant's intentions, and then only through a fairly labor-intensive process, requiring intention in assessing liability for climate-related harm would be practically untenable as well as unnecessary. For obvious practical reasons, this process would be unavailable for assessments of intent for every GHG-producing act, but it is also unnecessary as long as the relevant questions are not what persons knew or intended in fact, but whether their actions caused harm and whether a reasonable person would have anticipated this outcome.

For such reasons, we may be able to distinguish between intentional deception and unintentional distortions of the truth in assigning moral blame—deception seems to be uniquely blameworthy, given its insidious motive—but we cannot readily distinguish between the two in our attribution of fault and assessment of liability. Given the nature of deception, it would be difficult to infer from someone's behavior any reliable evidence of deception, because successful deception depends in part on keeping one's true intentions a secret. We have instead only their actions, the effects of those actions on others, and the harm that results from which to assess their fault and assign liability, and deception often appears behaviorally identical to the unintentional dissemination of falsehoods.

The science fiction writer Michael Crichton, who in his novel *State of Fear* sets forth a narrative of climate scientists and environmentalists conspiring to shake down frightened donors, maintain research agency budgets, and ultimately to subject the United States to the authority of world government, may well believe this narrative to be true. Likewise, Senator Inhofe—who in Senate hearings cited with approval Crichton's "compelling presentation of the scientific facts of climate change," denounced anthropogenic climate change as possibly the greatest "hoax" to be "perpetrated on the American people," and in 2005 invited Crichton to advise his Committee on Environment and Public Works on the scientific facts of climate change[23]—probably does believe in this conspiracy theory. If we assume their public statements to be sincere, neither has engaged in deception and both may have acted from the honorable if misguided intention of sparing the country from a costly and unnecessary GHG-abatement effort. If their representations of fiction as truth were based in simple ignorance rather than willful deception, then neither deserves moral blame for his actions, but this cannot exonerate them from fault. Insofar as either is causally responsible for the U.S. failure to enact effective climate policies, the false beliefs on which their sincere efforts to spare the nation from this conspiracy can be faulted for their unreasonable ignorance. While neither intended or anticipated that harm would result from their public acts, both should have known that the disinformation campaigns in which they continue to engage contribute to climate-related harm. Neither bears any unique liability for ongoing U.S. emissions, however, because it would be unreasonable for anyone to accept the authority of the Crichton/Inhofe conspiracy theory over the widely disseminated consensus of the world's most respected climate scientists.

Assessments of moral guilt and not mere fault may be useful for some aspects of a global climate regime, however, insofar as the regime is given authority to punish offenders or is in some other way based in retributive rather than restorative justice. For example, civil lawsuits such as torts can combine compensatory and punitive awards, and a global climate regime may want to include both kinds of authority in order to ensure that its standards are adequately enforced. If some nation fails to comply with its assigned emissions caps and this appears to result from a blatant disregard for fairly assigned standards through a process in which the offending nation had adequate opportunity to voice its grievance and seek relief, then some sort of punitive damages may be warranted on top of the liability assessments based on its luxury emissions. In civil law, such punitive damages are based on an assessment not only of one's causal responsibility combined with fault but also in a kind of moral guilt, and the same judgments may in principle also be made against nations.

Insofar as nations can be found guilty and not merely liable for causing climate-related harm, knowledge and intentions may matter in moral and legal assessment. For example, a legislator taking a bribe in exchange for voting against GHG regulation may be guilty of more than simply contributory fault for climate change; some punitive sanction for their corruption may also be appropriate. Similarly, a government that engages in ongoing campaigns of deception in order to diffuse public pressure for climate legislation and suppressed or alters evidence about the effects of current policies may be guilty of an offense that warrants additional punishment beyond what is required of liability. The punitive component does not aim to restore justice by compensating the victims of climate change, but rather aims to encourage good faith compliance with the policy's terms. Such crimes, of course, are not unique to climate policy, and for this and other practical reasons ought not to be within the jurisdiction of a global climate regime, but they do speak to the need for an effective system with international judicial capacity, to allow the community of nations to bring such sanctions in order to bring outliers and free riders back within the fair terms of international cooperation.

In this sense, punitive sanctions might comprise a separate component of global climate policy, complementing those concerned with assessing liability. Since liability can be easily routinized within many of the activities that contribute toward climate change—through, for example, a carbon tax—it requires far less institutional capacity to assess and enforce than do judgments concerning guilt. Since judgments of liability involve moral responsibility but not moral wrongness or guilt, one could be instantly and completely absolved of any further moral responsibility for their emissions by their having paid their liability in advance at the pump, and determinations of knowledge or intentions would be entirely unnecessary. From the perspective of a global climate regime, the manner in which nations implement their prescribed reductions in policy is largely a matter of national priorities and subject to the principle of sovereignty. Some may choose to rely on hard caps that in violation would raise questions of guilt and not mere liability, but many problems associated with ascertaining the mental states of polluters can be avoided by focusing on fault rather than blame and developing climate policies accordingly.

Policy Making under Conditions of Uncertainty

Genuine uncertainty continues to exist in climate science, raising questions not only about the requisite levels of knowledge and certainty for validly attributing fault and liability, but also concerning the appropriate responses to ongoing scientific uncertainties. The assumption implied within campaigns to manufacture uncertainty—that the existence of any uncertainty, defined as lack of unanimity among experts, warrants further study but not costly action—is unfounded, but how should policy makers proceed while working under conditions of scientific uncertainty? Since nearly all public policy that aims to address the future consequences of present actions involves some kinds of uncertainty, this question has implications beyond climate policy, although that is our focus here.

Scientific uncertainty either can result from a lack of data or other information, or can be the product of disagreement among experts concerning the accuracy of models or the validity of various assumptions built into them. Depending on which of these two better describes the cause of ongoing uncertainties in climate science, different responses may be warranted. As Schneider and Kristen Kuntz-Duriseti suggest, uncertainty cannot be eliminated, but it can be *mastered*—scientists can "reduce the uncertainty through data collection, research, modeling, simulation, and so forth," which aims to "overcome the uncertainty–to make known the unknown"—or it can be *managed*, integrating that uncertainty into policy making.[24] In some cases, such as when lack of data is the primary cause of uncertainty, the appropriate strategy would be to attempt to master uncertainties before embarking on policy formulation dealing with the scientific issue at hand. As Schneider and Kuntz-Duriseti note, however, "the daunting uncertainty surrounding global environmental change and the need to make decisions before the uncertainty is resolved make the first option difficult to achieve." For this reason, many urge the *precautionary principle* as a response to ongoing uncertainty in problems such as climate change, but more might first be said about how policy makers could manage the uncertainties remaining in climate science.

In order to guard against uncertainty being disingenuously used in the service of political agendas, whether by environmental groups aiming to exaggerate climate-related threats or by the industry or ideological groups seeking to deny them, Schneider and Kuntz-Duriseti suggest, scientists should clearly define and quantify any noted uncertainties so that users of scientific reports may accurately convey to others the degree of uncertainty that surrounds their various predictions. In formulating policy, the use of expected value analysis in risk assessment can build uncertainty into cost–benefit estimates, and these must anticipate all possible scenarios, together with their probabilities, including within estimates "imaginable surprises" (high-cost but low-probability outcomes) in order to properly estimate both climate-related costs and the value of ecosystem services. While analysts are often tempted to ignore unlikely scenarios and values such as those of ecosystem services that are difficult to quantify and instead to concentrate on the most likely outcomes of various policy alternatives, this can result in underestimating the possible negative effects that occur at low probability, leaving policy makers ill-prepared should worst cases obtain. Uncertainties must be acknowledged, but built into such estimates.

In addition, a rational policy response to scientific uncertainty involves what Schneider and S.L. Thompson call "anticipatory adaptation" to climate change. To prepare for possible future outcomes about which uncertainty remains, policy makers should anticipate requirements for adapting to those outcomes if they do obtain, and take proactive steps now toward easing the adaptation process down the road. For example, policy makers might anticipate the need to significantly reduce national GHG emissions and begin investing significant amounts in research and development of low-carbon technologies, anticipating their future necessity.[25] If technology could be developed before mandates for sharp reductions in national GHG budgets begin, such proactive anticipatory efforts would make compliance considerably cheaper and easier, and such research may have ancillary benefits even if such mandates never appear. Schneider and Kuntz-Duriseti illustrate co-benefits policy strategies, which stabilize climate in addition to other goals, with the example of tropical forest protection policies: Since tropical deforestation accounts for 20 to 30 percent of global carbon emissions through the combination of destroyed sinks and the oxidation of biomass in slash-and-burn logging, rainforest protection policies not only are a relatively cheap means of reducing atmospheric GHG concentrations, but also advance biodiversity interests and protect the other ecosystem services that such forests provide, increasing political support for such policies and increasing the value of climate policies.[26]

Energy conservation policies, despite Vice President Dick Cheney's infamous quip to the contrary, form the basis for rational policies in the face of uncertainty, since not only does the reduction in fossil fuel combustion have clear benefits for GHG abatement efforts and thus climatic stability, but also reduced domestic dependence on foreign oil has the potential to significantly reduce the trade deficit and offers significant strategic benefits. Reduced consumption of oil and coal would significantly benefit consumers in two ways unrelated to climate: directly through reduced energy-related expenditures as reduced demand lowers prices, and indirectly through reduced air and water pollution. Additionally, creating market incentives for research and development of energy-efficient vehicles, appliances, and other technologies could have a significant economic stimulus effect that could result in long-term economic gains as innovations come on line. Reducing demand for energy would eliminate the need for most of the new power plants proposed by the Cheney energy task force, making future compliance with GHG targets much less expensive than they would be if those 1,300 new plants were constructed, as described in chapter 1. Reduced dependence on fossil fuels could likewise promote the "fuel diversity" that President Bush nebulously invoked in defense of further reliance on oil and coal, lessening the nation's dependence on supplies of energy coming through the Gulf Coast, thereby decreasing the nation's vulnerability to weather-related supply disruptions in an era of increasing and more intense storms. In short, a rational policy response to uncertainty in climate science would be precisely the opposite of what the Cheney task force recommended: more energy conservation, less reliance on fossil fuels, and more development of renewable and low-emissions energy sources. Even if the consensus predictions of climate science turn out to be mistaken or overstated, these measures would be justified on the strength of their ancillary benefits.

While genuine scientific uncertainty exists in many areas, it cannot be allowed to be used as a subterfuge that serves to protect offenders in their harmful acts. Justice demands impartiality between the parties to a dispute, and the rules of procedure that govern the adjudication of those disputes must be neutral with respect to the parties in order to produce an outcome that is untainted with either personal or institutional bias. This procedural neutrality, however, cannot entail that merely producing a single contrary "expert" counters the consensus view of an entire community of experts, setting the standard of proof so high that it undermines the principle of responsibility and produces patently nonneutral outcomes. If unreasonable ignorance is sufficient to exonerate a polluter from responsibility, then the outcome will invariably be to favor the offender and hurt the victim. That is, it would be a nonneutral procedural rule disguised as a neutral one, turning the very idea of impartiality on its head.

In cases of environmental harm, this problem is especially acute, since deferral of action to some future point at which uncertainty disappears not only vastly exacerbates the problem during the time in which less costly remedies are denied, but often also makes future remedies impossible. GHGs, for example, remain in the atmosphere for centuries, trapping heat and altering weather patterns, and the window of opportunity for mitigating the worst effects of those changes will eventually close, and may do so in the near future. As in the case of tobacco liability defense, where offenders seek to delay a remedial or compensatory order until a victim dies, at which point the case is dismissed for lack of standing, a climate remedy that is delayed is a remedy denied. For this reason, many have urged a commitment to the precautionary principle, holding an alternative set of presumptions as necessary for policy making under conditions of uncertainty and given the nature of environmental harm.

The Precautionary Principle

The precautionary principle, which exists as both an ethical norm and as a nascent justiciable legal standard, declares that significant environmental risk justifies preventative or remedial action even in the absence of full scientific certainty. Although there is no universal formulation of the principle, one example containing its main elements can be found in Principle 15 of the 1992 Rio Declaration:

> In order to protect the environment, the precautionary approach shall
> be widely applied by States according to their capabilities. Where
> there are threats of serious or irreversible damage, lack of full
> scientific certainty shall not be used as a reason for postponing
> cost-effective measures to prevent environmental degradation.

The principle as articulated here asserts a standard of evidence in which "full scientific certainty" is not needed before preventative measures are taken, and so aims to reverse the presumptions that would otherwise require those advocating environmental protection policies to establish an unimpeachable case for preventative action. Support for the principle has arisen in large part because of the difficulty in establishing causation for environmental harm in civil actions, where the burden of proof is on the plaintiff, who must demonstrate that the injury would not have occurred but for the defendant's action—an extraordinarily difficult requirement given the complex causal chains involved in most kinds of environmental harm.

In one sense, then, the precautionary principle is merely a commitment to social risk aversion, where society is urged to avoid subjecting its members and others to risks of serious and irreversible harm. Where individual risk aversion is usually treated as a mere preference that may differ among persons, with some wagering potentially large losses for the prospect of greater gains while others prefer smaller gains for the assurance of smaller maximum losses, the principle can be seen as urging risk avoidance for society at large in the formulation of public policy. In a more expansive sense, however, it takes on further normative implications, arguing against one set of norms and urging another. As Tim Hayward describes the principle, "it embodies a presumption in favor of ordinary citizens' right to protection from environmentally hazardous activities, and places the burden of proof on proponents of a new technology, activity, process, or chemical to show that it does not pose a serious threat."[27] By making the case for precaution a prima facie one, it strengthens the notion that citizens are entitled to protection from environmental degradation and refuses to trade off long-term environmental stability for short-term economic gain, and it diffuses the strategy of using scientific uncertainty as a pretext for delaying or avoiding regulation of environmentally hazardous activities such as GHG emissions.

Kristen Shrader-Frechette suggests that the precautionary principle is in part an ethical response to problems of scientific uncertainty, since the essential tradeoff that the principle addresses concerns the economic interests of polluters, who stand to lose in a more risk-averse society that would sharply curtail polluting acts, and the basic negative rights of potential victims of pollution, which the precautionary principle aims to protect. In the absence of full scientific certainty, a risk-tolerant society may favor polluters by, for example, allowing the use of a pesticide about which questions exist concerning its safety, but where that safety is uncertain, while a risk-averse or precautionary society would prohibit the use of the pesticide until it could be proven safe. She poses the question: Is it worse to reject a true null hypothesis (e.g., failing to use some pesticide that is, in fact, safe) or to fail to reject a false null hypothesis (e.g., using some unsafe pesticide)? In the first case, potential polluters would be prevented from using a pesticide that may or may not be unsafe, presumably incurring costs in so doing, while in the second case, potential victims of that pollution incur the risk of harm.

As Shrader-Frechette notes, scientists are often biased in favor of the precautionary principle, since "pure scientists often attach a greater loss to accepting a falsehood than to failing to acknowledge a truth," but this does not yet justify the principle. Rather, a justification would take the form of a harm principle, since failing to avert a possible harm in the face of uncertainty exposes persons to risk without their consent, and without, in most cases, the upside potential rewards of risk, which accrue primarily to polluters and not to society. "In cases of uncertainty," she notes, "it is impossible to obtain free, informed consent of potential victims because, by definition, the risks are uncertain and we have inadequate information about them."[28] Allowing innocent persons to be harmed in order to protect the welfare interests of polluters would violate their rights. In deciding where to place the burden of proof, the precautionary principle aims to protect negative rights against being harmed by environmental hazards, placing the burden of proof under conditions of uncertainty on polluters, whose basic rights are not at stake and who can bear the costs of that tradeoff. In this sense, it protects the security rights of potential victims of pollution and promotes equity by refusing to allow polluters, who are often more advantaged and less vulnerable in such conflicts of interest, from transferring externality costs onto potential victims of pollution, who are typically among society's least advantaged. Hence, it can be based either in a priority of basic over nonbasic rights such as that sketched above, or in a conception of justice similar to the Rawlsian difference principle, as discussed in chapter 2. The precautionary principle need not be prohibitory, necessarily regulating all possible if uncertain hazards, and it would be mistaken to interpret its objective as treating merely possible hazards as certain ones in the absence of conclusive evidence to the contrary. Nor is it, as Cass Sunstein claims, "a presumption in favor of regulatory controls."[29] However, the principle quite justifiably aims to undermine the "ignorance defense" examined previously, where the lack of full scientific certainty—understood in terms of dissemination of organized climate skepticism or the ongoing existence of areas of uncertainty within a phenomenon that is otherwise reasonably well understood in its causes and effects—is taken as sufficient reason to avoid taking any costly steps to mitigate a predicted hazard. In opposing the Kyoto Protocol on grounds that its likely costs exceed its likely benefits, Sunstein does not intend to elevate manufactured uncertainty to the level of fact, nor does he disingenuously aim to protect big GHG polluters or rationalize the undeserved advantages of the world's affluent. Rather, he observes that the modest effects on atmospheric GHG concentrations achieved through compliance with the protocol's prescribed 5 percent reduction on Annex B emissions by 2012 would likely fail to avert the worst predicted consequences of climate change, yet would be costly for those nations required to comply with the treaty's terms. As noted in chapter 1, stabilizing atmospheric concentrations at a level sufficient to avoid dangerous climatic instability would require global caps and prescribed reductions of more than 50 percent from the 1990 baseline.

Sunstein advocates an approach to managing risk in which the precautionary principle is replaced by a form of cost–benefit analysis combined with an incentive structure that he terms "libertarian paternalism,"[30] but missing from his analysis is the recognition that climate change is not merely a prudential problem of maximizing expected benefits. The precautionary principle focuses attention on the risks and uncertainties of causing avoidable harm, but it is essential to see the fundamental problem as one of avoiding adequately certain injustice if serious climatic instability is allowed, not merely one of rational utility maximizing. So regarded, precaution can be seen as a value that applies to a narrow part of climate policy—that of policy making under conditions of uncertainty—but not as the underlying justification for the entire effort. Sunstein may be correct in suggesting that the Kyoto Protocol's costs exceed its benefits, as well as in implying that the resources devoted to climate change mitigation could do more good if deployed elsewhere, but neither of these provides a decisive case against taking meaningful action to reduce GHG emissions. The protocol may be a useful step on the way to a genuinely fair and effective global climate regime, based on the imperatives of promoting equity and responsibility, but its purpose must be seen as centrally concerned with distributing and not merely maximizing, else its justice dimension is dissolved into a narrowly instrumental prudence that misunderstands the true nature of the problem.

Conclusions

Relying on a standard of fault-based liability for assessing each nation's respective share of moral responsibility for contributing toward climate change, this chapter considers the roles of knowledge and beliefs, motives and intentions, and campaigns of disinformation and deception in their effects on our initial judgment that nations should be assigned liability based on their historical emissions. Although a standard of strict liability cannot withstand scrutiny in this application, because it would violate the principle of responsibility, only two exceptions to an assessment of fault based on each nation's historical emissions were found to be defensible: Nations cannot validly be held to be responsible for their historical emissions prior to 1990, and they cannot be held liable for their survival emissions. While uncertainty continues to surround some important issues within climate science, this uncertainty cannot justify inaction and cannot excuse persons or nations from liability based in claims of reasonable ignorance. For reasons that are practical and principled, nations must be held liable for their continuing contributions to climate change, regardless of the mental states under which relevant acts are committed, and may even be found morally guilty for some extraordinary causal contributions to climate-related harm, such as campaigns of deception. Since the overarching aim of a responsibility-based conception of fairness is to ensure justice, redressing undeserved harm suffered by the victims of climate change and assigning costs for such remediation to those who are responsible for causing problems, we must carefully consider the possible arguments for exempting nations or persons from liability but must ensure that liability is nonetheless assessed, and done so in the most defensible manner possible. That such assignments may also serve other worthy aims—creating incentives for democratic accountability, avoiding moral hazards, and so on—simply underscores the justification of the standards urged above.

7

Equity, Responsibility, and Climate Change Mitigation

Having considered the roles of equity and responsibility in developing a fair and effective global climate regime, we now turn to the question of what such a regime might look like in practice. Chapter 2 considers the allegation that the Kyoto Protocol is unfair because it exempts developing countries from the first round of emission cuts, and showed that objection to be wanting. This chapter considers several additional challenges to the fairness of that treaty, and these shall assist in our design of an alternative regime that might successfully answer the charges of unfairness that stick when levied against some of Kyoto's terms. In so doing, two alternative proposals are considered in the *equal burdens* and *equal shares* approaches, paying attention to what might be fair or unfair in each of them. Since the larger objective is to design a global climate regime that is both fair and effective and that might thus meet the normative aims declared in the climate convention, the critical examination of policy alternatives in light of the claims and observations surveyed in chapters 1–6 should illuminate at least the main features of such a proposal. Since we are interested in both the intrinsic value of fairness and the conditions for bringing about a fair global climate regime, the requirements of procedural fairness are also sketched under which the terms of an international climate treaty might justly be negotiated.

Before examining alternative schemes for allocating climate-related burdens, let me summarize the conclusions thus far. Concerns for justice are aptly declared within the climate convention, since no agreement is likely to be effective unless it is fair in the way that it allocates the costs of climate change mitigation and adaptation, and no regime can truly be fair, especially once the rights and interests of future persons are considered, unless it is also effective in stabilizing atmospheric greenhouse gas (GHG) concentrations, because the failure to do so would require ongoing and increasing adaptation and compensation expenses, culminating perhaps in global economic collapse and an uninhabitable planet. Based on ideals expressed in the climate convention, fairness can be understood in terms of two primary normative criteria or models: equity and responsibility. Regarding the third standard identified within the *UNFCCC*, a capabilities-based model in which climate-related burdens are assigned in proportion to each nation's ability to reduce its emissions is either based on efficiency rather than fairness and becomes superfluous once flexible compliance measures are included within the climate regime, or else collapses into national equity and responsibility, so the focus in this chapter is on the application of these two primary normative ideals or models of fairness.

In addition to these two conceptions of fairness, the design of a fair global climate regime requires the allocation of two categories of costs or burdens among the world's nations: the costs associated with emissions abatement efforts, assigned through a system of mandatory caps that includes all nations, and the costs of adaptation to a changing climate for those forced to suffer its deleterious effects, assigned through assessments of national liability for contributing toward climate-related harm. Hence, we have two distinct categories of burdens to allocate among the world's nations and two models of fairness by which to allocate them. Each model of fairness is particularly well suited to guiding one of these distributive issues—equity for the allocation of emissions shares, and responsibility for the allocation of costs of compensation and adaptation—so our design of a climate regime will be based on the fitness of each distributive principle for each allocation issue.

The equity model is forward-looking, justifying departures from equal allocations based on the incentive effects of such inequality for the least advantaged, so is more appropriate for determining each nation's relative shares of total allowable annual emissions. In applying equity-based principles of justice to assigning emissions shares, all persons are presumed to be moral equals and thus to have equal claims to the atmosphere's absorptive services. As this equality is generally interpreted, equal claims translate to a default position of equal per capita emissions shares, with unequal shares in principle justified only by their benefits for the least advantaged. The responsibility model, conversely, looks backward at an agent's past actions or choices in attributing fault and assessing liability, restoring justice that has been or will be disturbed by climate change insofar as liability burdens are applied to remedy undeserved harm suffered by the victims of climate change and are borne by those responsible for contributing to that harm in proportion to their contributions. Hence, it is more appropriate for allocating compensation and adaptation costs for those harmed by climate change. Together, these equity- and responsibility-based models can, if implemented into the design of a global climate regime, realize aims of fairness in climate change mitigation.

Cosmopolitan Justice and National Emissions Shares

If the equity-based model of fairness is to be applied to allocations of national emissions shares, it must build on the ideal of cosmopolitan justice advocated by Charles Beitz (see chapter 3), where egalitarian principles of distributive justice are applied only to the assignment of national shares of the atmosphere's emission absorptive capacity. Since John Rawls rejects the international application of the difference principle (see chapter 4), this section considers again the case for cosmopolitan justice, this time paying particular attention to the problem of allocating national emissions shares. We also consider whether or not something like the maximin rule of the difference principle can be applied to this problem, possibly justifying unequal shares, or whether cosmopolitan justice instead justifies equal per capita emissions shares.

Recall that Beitz defends a resource redistribution principle that would subject the world's natural resources to redistribution in accordance with egalitarian principles of justice. The case for egalitarian distribution of natural resources relies on the strong causal role of natural resource wealth in national prosperity, which in turn produces the requisite material conditions for establishing institutions of justice and bringing about what Rawls terms a well-ordered society. Following the logic of the Rawlsian original position, Beitz correctly points out that the current distribution of resources is morally arbitrary and cannot be justified by claims of moral desert on the part of resource-rich or resource-poor nations, so justice demands that these be redistributed according to principles that might be generated behind a Rawlsian veil of ignorance in which persons are unaware of their nation of residence, and thus their respective national shares of the world's natural resources. From such a position, could they endorse the de facto global distribution of resources? Plainly, they could not, for the maximin rule requires that they be attentive to the relative position of the least advantaged in evaluating various distributive principles, and the status quo distribution of resources leaves some nations desperately poor and with little chance of becoming well ordered or developing institutions of justice, while others are undeservedly wealthy and with no concomitant benefits for those least advantaged. In no sense does the current, radically unequal allocation of global resources benefit the world's least advantaged when compared against their more equal allocation, and as the problem of anthropogenic climate change illustrates, it often does the opposite.

From an international original position and in seeking a rule that applies only to the global distribution of natural resources, Beitz makes a compelling case for a much more equal allocation of the world's natural resources, in the interest of promoting justice and on the basis of defensible claims about what persons deserve according to something like the principle of responsibility. Based on Beitz's limited case for cosmopolitan justice made on behalf of his resource redistribution principle, a compelling claim for greater global natural resource equity, and one with implications for global climate policy, can be found. Since the capacity of the atmosphere to absorb GHG emissions is a kind of natural resource, its allocation ought to be based in egalitarian distributive principles, such as the Rawlsian difference principle, rather than being left to the anarchic inegalitarianism of current unsustainable de facto claims. If the world was to start following Beitz's resource redistribution principle, the vast current disparities in wealth and opportunity among the world's persons would significantly diminish, though they would not disappear altogether, for as Rawls notes, material conditions are not the only relevant variable in national development, and other differences among nations—culture, for example— would remain. Even this limited cosmopolitanism, though, would go a long way toward reducing global inequality.

While Beitz's case for the resource redistribution principle is compelling and Rawls's reply to it inadequate, one might posit a still more limited cosmopolitanism in which the only natural resource to be subjected to egalitarian distributive principles is atmospheric absorptive capacity, and where only the allocation of emissions shares follows the difference principle. Here, all territorial claims to a nation's other natural resources would be set aside, because the principle would not apply to any resources that are physically located within national borders, and only the common global resource of the planet's atmospheric absorptive capacity is subject to redistribution from those current claims on it that exist in the form of national emissions. Plainly, these current claims cannot be defended by appeal to norms of justice, for they are based purely on historical use patterns, where widely disparate de facto claims on the atmosphere represent little more than squatters claims on an increasingly scarce resource, and none can validly be held to deserve their nation's current (or any historical baseline) level of emissions shares. Indeed, they cannot be defended by appeal to conventional property rights, riparian law, or any other existing system of resolving disputes over shared resources, for their truly global nature defies conventional analysis. The atmosphere presents a rare example of a pure public good, where no one has a valid claim to larger shares of the good than anyone else.

How might egalitarian distributive principles be applied to the allocation of shares of the atmosphere's absorptive capacity? Egalitarian principles are individualistic: They maintain that no person is entitled to a larger share of a finite good than any other, for this would be to ascribe greater value to the lives of those allowed to emit more GHGs than those required to emit fewer. National emissions caps would therefore be set on the basis of population only, assigning them equally per capita, because all persons are presumed to be equally entitled to use the common global resource of the atmosphere. The philosophical case for this position is largely negative: Given that no defensible claim justifies unequal allocations, no departure from the default case for equality appears warranted. This equal per capita allocation—hereafter referred to as the *equal shares* approach—is grounded in the egalitarian premise of moral equality, but still must apply the logic of the difference principle to the allocation of national emissions shares. Might some nations be allowed larger shares, based on the advantages that such an allocation offers to others? Initially, it seems unlikely that granting larger emissions shares to some nations could somehow improve the material conditions of the world's least advantaged, since the aggregate global cap on emissions cannot be increased through the entrepreneurial incentives that Rawls allows through the difference principle, because the atmosphere's capacity to absorb GHG emissions is finite. Insofar as the allocation of national emissions shares is a zero-sum game—higher emissions for some requires lower caps for others—it seems that the unequal shares justified by the maximin rule cannot apply to this case.

However, there are several ways in which nations can increase the planet's atmospheric absorptive capacity, and these might justifiably be encouraged through the allocation of national emissions shares. Nations can, for example, increase the size and CO_2-absorbing capacity of carbon sinks, whether within their own borders or elsewhere, through reforestation efforts and other ecological restoration projects. Since such projects allow for slightly higher aggregate annual global emissions, the logic of the difference principle would allow those nations that sponsor them a larger share of total allowable emissions provided that they are undertaken on a sufficient scale that they can at the same time allow all nations slightly higher per capita caps as a result. Sustainable development projects undertaken through Joint Implementation and the Clean Development Mechanism (CDM) of the Kyoto Protocol (see chapter 1) allow nations to count toward compliance such emissions-reducing or sink-enhancing projects in developing countries, in effect allowing sponsoring nations higher gross emissions—subtracting from net emissions the effects of sinks and emissions-reducing projects—in return for their investments. In such cases, however, nations would still be assigned equal per capita caps but would be allowed to meet part of those requirements each year through such projects. Such flexible compliance mechanisms follow the difference principle in that they allow limited inequality in gross (but not net) emissions in return for funding projects that increase overall atmospheric absorptive capacity and include ancillary benefits for the less advantaged regions in which they are undertaken. These compliance mechanisms operate within, rather than challenging, the equal shares approach.

A number of commentators (myself included[1]) have called for some version of the equal shares approach, defending this proposal from an egalitarian perspective. Generally, the defense starts from the premise of moral equality and proceeds to challenge various potential arguments for unequal shares, showing them to rely on untenable claims about desert or indefensible assumptions about the respective values attached to the lives of persons from different nations. As Paul Baer notes, "The central argument for equal per capita rights is that the atmosphere is a global commons, whose use and preservation are essential to human well being."[2] No person or nation has a valid claim for larger shares on the basis of historical use, and no person or nation has any territorial ownership claims that might likewise justify unequal shares. Or as Peter Singer succinctly puts the same point, "Everyone has the same claim to part of the atmospheric sink as everyone else,"[3] a claim that he finds to be "self-evidently fair" and in need of no further justification than moral equality itself. Hence, a defense of the equal shares approach turns on considering and rejecting alternative formulas for assigning nations unequal per capita shares. Starting from egalitarian premises, the case for some version of equal per capita shares may be a compelling one, but the next section considers several arguments against it.

First, though, consider several criteria that weigh in favor of allowing limited inequality in per capita emissions shares in what might be called a *modified equal shares* model for national emissions allocations. As observed in chapter 3, survival emissions levels are likely to vary among and within nations, so the portion of available global emissions to be subject to egalitarian distribution ought to be luxury emissions, not total emissions. Provision for transfers of wealth from affluent to poor nations, as through an emissions trading regime, may satisfy the maximin imperative of the difference principle, because trades of emissions rights for other resources may benefit the least advantaged, although again, this would not justify inequality in emissions shares as initially allocated and prior to trading, since the trading regime depends on some nations needing to purchase unused credits in order to meet their assigned targets.

Since these various mitigating circumstances upset the parsimony of the equal shares proposal, they must be defended on the basis of their coherence with egalitarian premises, not from their departures from them. As Leigh Raymond suggests, the criteria sometimes proposed for justifying unequal shares can "look morally arbitrary" and "threatens to undermine its initial advantages of clarity and simplicity as a basic human right."[4] However, egalitarian premises have elsewhere included such impact measures within distributive principles—hence the focus on all-purpose resources such as primary goods rather than any single good within the literature on distributive justice—and the same measures might be included here within a national index of survival emissions levels. As Ronald Dworkin argues, nations cannot be awarded larger per capita GHG emissions shares merely because of preferences for consumption over which they have control, or in what he terms the problem of *expensive tastes*,[5] but differences in circumstance that lie outside of an agent's control can form the basis for valid claims for unequal resources, and must do so insofar as these affect opportunities for welfare.

Having previously observed the justification for and limits of this control condition in chapter 5, it should by now be clear that such distinctions are not easily made. How, for example, should the decision by the United States to build its cities around the automobile be treated by the assignment of national emissions shares? While such decisions were in principle within the control of urban planning agencies, most were made prior to that point at which ignorance concerning the causes and effects of climate change became unreasonable, so should they now be treated as within the control of governments and hence subject to the principle of responsibility, or as a matter of luck and so immune from it? All such cases are likely to be the subject of contestation, so candidates for deserved inequality must be kept to a minimum, and the total inequality that all such considerations might warrant must likewise be kept relatively small enough that the descriptive label *modified equal shares* does not become misleading, but note also that equity need not necessarily entail equality.

Once we reject the untenable assumption that industrialized nations are entitled to their high per capita rates of GHG emissions, the ideal of equity points squarely to a modified equal shares approach in which national emissions caps reflect an entitlement to equal per capita luxury emissions, subject to considerations noted above. All nations seek to use atmospheric absorptive capacity to accommodate their GHG emissions, which allows for industrialization, consumption, and other activities associated with national welfare, but finite capacity entails that unlimited national demands for its services be strictly limited through assignments of national emissions shares that, taken together, avoid destabilizing the global climate through excessive emissions. If climate change could be avoided altogether, the only national burdens to be allocated would be those associated with meeting these assigned emissions shares. Insofar as some climate change is unavoidable and as some persons or peoples are harmed by it, then an additional compensatory burden must also be allocated among nations.

The first burden treats all claimants to the atmospheric services of the common resource equally, in which case, as Singer urges, "everyone has the same claim to part of the atmospheric sink as everyone else."[6] Prior use levels, economic power, and military might are irrelevant to the fair assignment of emissions shares, because the distributive problem is one of fairly dividing a shared resource among many parties with competing claims. Unequal shares, insofar as these allow for unequal opportunities for development and ultimately unequal life chances for the residents of nations allowed unequal per capita emissions, cannot be justified in this way, even if these other sources of inequality among nations led to the highly unequal allocation of emissions shares in the Kyoto Protocol.

Not only does the premise of equality among the international parties weigh in favor of the equal shares proposal, but so also does the analysis of the atmosphere as a commons. As Baer notes of common resources and the collective action problems that affect their management:

> In a commons, individuals typically gain much more from their use of the resource than they suffer from the degradation their use causes; thus one can increase one's own well-being by overconsuming and harming the other users. Furthermore, restricting one's own use does not ensure protection against the harms caused by others' use of the resource. In these ways, a common resource establishes a moral community. To protect the resource and to protect themselves, the parties must grant each other the right to a fair share, and accept enforcement of a mutually agreed limit.[7]

Despite the temptation of all nations to free ride, refusing emissions limits even while others abide by them, the need for a cooperative solution with binding and enforceable limits is evident in the structure of the dilemma. No nation can afford to allow the atmospheric commons to become degraded by overuse, so all have an incentive to participate in a global climate regime with the goal of maintaining the shared resource. The price of such a solution is, as Baer notes, that all must be granted a fair share, which is likely to be less than powerful nations might otherwise prefer. However, the downside costs of failure to agree on a cooperative scheme are worse, at least when the long-term costs of climate change are included within the cost–benefit equation. Hence, fairness in allocation of national emissions shares can be justified by practical considerations as well as principled ones.

Alternatively, one might view the allocation of emissions shares as needing to take into account past as well as current and future claims on the atmosphere. One might, for example, argue for equal national per capita shares over a lifetime, so that bigger historical polluters are now and into the near future assigned smaller per capita emissions caps as a result. Baer calls this the "historical accountability" formula, and finds some support for it in that "countries are assumed to have benefited permanently (as by increased wealth and infrastructure) from that overuse and to have a debt to repay."[8] Similarly, Anil Agarwal suggests that the biggest historical polluters ought now to bear the vast majority of climate-related burdens, since

> with such high levels of GHG emissions, industrialized countries are holders of natural debt, borrowing from the assimilative capacity of the environment by releasing waste gases faster than they can be removed naturally. These countries therefore should not think of resources devoted to curbing climate change as a sudden extra cost being imposed on them but as the inevitable need to repay the ecological debt that has helped them enjoy their present wealth.[9]

Singer makes a similar case, suggesting that, even with an equal shares approach, "for at least a century the developing nations are going to have to accept lower outputs of greenhouse gases than they would have had to, if the industrialized nations had kept to an equal per capita share in the past."[10] Holding developing nations responsible for the historical emissions of industrialized ones through the lower per capita shares made necessary by past GHG emissions violates the principle of responsibility, and yet results from setting aside historical emissions in assignments of national emissions shares on an equal per capita basis. The justification for this "historical accountability" claim is fairly straightforward: The effects on climate of GHG emissions are cumulative—gases in the atmosphere that were released in 1900 have essentially the same effect on climate in 2007 as do those emitted in 2000—so the allocation of national emissions shares must take into account the ongoing effects of past national emissions in its current and future assignments. If each nation is allowed the same per capita claim on the atmosphere this year, then those nations with high past emissions must now be assigned lower per capita emissions caps, as past emissions continue to make claims on atmospheric space long after they are initially released, and those with lower past emissions can now be allowed higher ones.

As Baer notes, this historical accountability approach may be criticized for "holding living persons responsible for the activities of their ancestors," in violation of the principle of responsibility, given "the fact that it hasn't been known for long that overuse was causing a problem" and that "not everyone in wealthy countries has contributed equally or benefited equally from their cumulative emissions."[11] These objections are considered elsewhere and the force of each of them is incorporated into the responsibility-based model of remedial climate burdens where appropriate. Neither the first nor the third objections holds against assignments of fault-based liability, because, as observed in chapter 5, nations can be held collectively responsible for the acts of only some of their members, and collective historical benefits may now entail collective remedial burdens. Baer's second objection is structurally similar to an ignorance claim considered in chapter 6, which concluded that emissions prior to 1990 cannot count in the allocation of responsibility-based burdens, but incorporating this objection into allocations of current and future national caps mistakenly conflates these two distinct distributive problems.

While "historical accountability" may be appropriate for responsibility-based allocations under strict liability, it is complicated by knowledge problems under fault-based liability and is entirely inappropriate for equity-based allocation issues that are properly based on egalitarian distributive principle and grounded in current rather than past claims. Hence, Baer is justified in claiming that "parties that have exceeded their fair share have obligations to parties that will therefore get less,"[12] but these obligations must be met by the responsibility-based component of the climate regime, not the assignment of national emissions shares themselves. Big historical GHG polluters may have affected the total amount of global emissions available for allocation in the present and near future since their historical emissions remain in the atmosphere for generations, but this unequal historical responsibility can be adequately instantiated in assignments of liability rather than being factored into current or future national emissions allowances. Responsibility for excessive prior appropriations of atmospheric space may more readily and fairly be assessed in the other distributive component of the climate regime, guided by the other model of fairness.

Responsibility and the Global Climate Regime

According to the principle of responsibility, those who now stand to be most severely affected by climate change deserve compensation for their injuries, present and future, because they bear little responsibility for causing the problem, and this compensation may be used either to adapt to adverse climatic changes or to relocate if adaptation is not possible. Relying on fault-based liability, compensatory costs should be assigned in proportion to each nation's share of historical luxury emissions, with the biggest historical polluters paying the largest amounts into a remedial fund established to compensate victims for climate-related harm. A version of a compensatory polluter pays principle was considered during the conferences leading up to the Kyoto Protocol but was rejected in favor of the "common but differentiated responsibilities" language and a system that essentially eschews compensation altogether. Brazil's proposal for a punitive and compensatory Clean Development Fund, which would have based remedial responsibility on historical emissions by requiring big national polluters to contribute into a development fund in proportion to their emissions and would have used these funds to finance sustainability projects in developing countries, was replaced with the noncompensatory CDM, which takes no account of historical or current emissions. In the end, nothing included within the protocol assessed responsibility for historical emissions.

Rather than incorporating responsibility-based measures, the treaty did almost exactly the opposite by grandfathering 1990 GHG pollution levels into the protocol's assigned emissions caps. Whereas big historical polluters would have borne much greater abatement burdens under a responsibility-based model, they were assigned smaller ones under the protocol. Calculating caps from the 1990 baseline rather than following an equal shares approach meant that the United States, which had significantly higher per capita emissions that year than did either Europe or Japan, was allowed to maintain that wide disparity in average pollution levels, paying less for each unit of GHG reduction, having started with significantly less efficient infrastructure and therefore being more easily able to improve from the baseline and even to increase that disparity in allowable emissions; the European Union was assigned an 8 percent emissions reduction under Kyoto, compared to the 7 percent reduction assigned to the United States. Rather than holding the bigger historical polluters responsible for their greater contributions to the problem by assessing them greater remedial burdens, the protocol in effect rewarded them by grandfathering their historical pollution rates, allowing those nations that had done the least to minimize pollution in the past to continue polluting at significantly higher levels than those nations that had lower historical emissions rates, largely as a result of proactive antipollution and energy efficiency measures.

If we suppose that contemporary Americans, for example, have obligations of justice to non-Americans and future people, what is implied for the design of a global climate regime? Both obligations can be captured by two imperatives:

Current and near-future climate policy efforts must attempt to minimize the impacts of climate change across national borders and on future generations, and must assist in adaptation or provide compensation for the victims of those climatic changes that occur as a consequence of current actions. The first imperative requires significant GHG reduction programs, implemented through a global climate regime that includes all nations and that assigns and enforces national emissions caps, along with a program of technical assistance in order to assist in meeting emissions reduction goals. Since it is now too late to eliminate altogether negative climatic effects in both the near and further future, the questions remain at what level emissions are to be stabilized and what this entails in the way of annual global emissions caps, but these do not concern us here. The second imperative takes these inevitable consequences and aims to remediate them, following the normative directives of the principle of responsibility. Insofar as persons elsewhere and in the future are not responsible for the problems associated with anthropogenic climate change, they should not have to suffer its adverse consequences. Some fund must be established to assist them in adapting to a changing climate, along with one for compensating those who are unavoidably harmed or displaced by climatic changes, with contributions to the fund based on an assessment of responsibility for the problem. Americans, that is, can take responsibility by taking all reasonable steps to avoid causing harm to others in the first place, and then compensating for harm that is unavoidable. The same is true for all other peoples responsible for faultily contributing toward climate change.

Such a fund is unlikely to be small, because the costs of climate-related harm are already high and are widely expected to escalate in coming years and decades. The damage costs from Hurricane Katrina in the summer of 2005 reached into the tens of billions of dollars, and this was just a single climatic event. Such natural disasters—a misnomer that obscures the anthropogenic contribution to such phenomena—are expected to become increasingly frequent and severe as a consequence of warming oceans and other climatic disturbances. Since the responsibility-based component of the climate regime complements the equity-based assignment of national emissions shares, and since the allowance of excessive global emissions in the latter entails greater liability assessments in the former, the relative costs of each of these components depends significantly on the efficacy of current and near-future emissions abatement efforts. As more time elapses before a genuinely effective global climate regime is implemented, the size of this remedial fund—and thus also the prominence of the responsibility-based model of fairness in the larger climate justice scheme—will increase. Concerns of justice are not indifferent between the respective roles of prevention and compensation burdens, because it is always preferable to avoid causing others undeserved harm, but justice also demands that both components be present in the design of a global climate regime.

How might the proper mix between mitigation and compensation be calculated, if not based on the ethical principle of non-maleficence, which enjoins agents against causing others unnecessary and undeserved harm? Economists conceive of the level of "optimal pollution" as that point where marginal abatement burdens equal marginal damage costs and, in doing so, contravene the demands of this ethical principle, as I have argued elsewhere.[13] Laws mandating zero luxury emissions would be inefficient because prohibitively expensive, so by this account should aim instead for that point where one extra dollar invested in abatement technology would result in less than one dollar in avoided costs. According to the Intergovernmental Panel on Climate Change, the optimal level of atmospheric CO_2 concentration is somewhere between 400 and 450 ppm—a level considerably lower than would result from global compliance with the Kyoto Protocol but high enough to produce significant adverse effects, particularly on developing countries. At this "optimum" level, damage costs would roughly equal mitigation costs, with both estimated at approximately 1 percent of gross world product (GWP). The damage costs would be inequitably distributed, however, with the North bearing costs ranging from 0.7 to 1.2 percent of gross national product (GNP), with the South suffering costs ranging from 1.8 to 8 percent.[14] Reliance on such calculations for determining optimal emissions, which affects the balance of compliance and damage costs to be borne by this and later generations, is compatible with the equal shares approach, even if its manner of justifying costs exists in tension with some of its underlying egalitarian premises.

Given that those nations with high current and historical emissions stand to be assessed significant burdens by both components of the climate regime, it might appear as though the world's affluent industrialized nations are being subjected to a kind of double jeopardy by this proposal, being assessed much more costly GHG abatement burdens, based on their higher current emissions, as well as being attributed much greater remedial liability, based on their larger historical luxury emissions. Given the unequal assignment of both kinds of costs, one might anticipate the objection that such burdens are unfair to these nations, that one or the other of these categories of mitigation costs might be fair to assign so disproportionately to affluent nations, but that both of them together amount to an undue burden. Two observations may suffice in response to this objection: First, this conflates the high assigned costs with analyses of fairness, where the two are distinct considerations; and second, the two categories of costs are symbiotic in that reductions in a nation's annual emissions result in decreases in both categories of costs in the next year. The fact that some nation or person may prefer an unfair allocation or may benefit by it relative to a fair one does not indict its fairness.

The Equal Burdens Model and Its Discontents

The primary alternative to the equal shares approach entails a grandfathering of existing national emissions levels, and the basing of future national emissions caps on a roughly equal allocation of mitigation costs: the *equal burdens* approach. In cases involving global problems such as climate change, where international cooperation is essential but the absence of a strong centralized global authority makes the authoritative allocation of costs impossible, the most politically expedient solution to cost allocation issues is often to distribute remedial costs equally, since the politically contentious issues of justifying unequal costs, such as unique national needs or circumstances, variable levels of responsibility, unequal impacts, and so on, can thereby be avoided. When all members of a group jointly contribute to some problem that affects them all, even if their contributions are unequal, an easier solution is to set aside the hotly contested issues examined in chapters 5 and 6 in favor of an allocation system that absolves all parties of any historical responsibility for causing the problem, and simply asking all to contribute equally toward that problem's solution. While such equality is not always equitable—equity ideals are often sacrificed in the interest of expedience when costs are shared equally—the advantages of expedience sometimes outweigh those of equity. Requiring that all responsible parties shoulder an equal burden toward the problem's solution need not entail that each party bear the same costs—larger parties could be asked to pay more and smaller parties less, as by the assignment of costs on a per capita basis—but it entails that the burdens be divided equally among all members of the group.

The Kyoto Protocol relied on a modified version of this approach, basing its assigned emissions caps on 1990 baseline emissions and requiring participating nations to reduce their national emissions by an average of 5 percent from that level by 2012, where variation around that 5 percent mean was supposed to be based on the "common but differentiated responsibilities and respective capacities" criteria, although as described in chapter 1, they were in fact based primarily on political expedience rather than stated criteria. Nations were assigned percentage reductions from their 1990 baseline emissions, but the use of a baseline essentially grandfathered each nation's 1990 emissions rates and assigned roughly equal mitigation burdens from those historical figures, disregarding both historical emissions and the wide variations that marked per capita emissions in 1990. Because national per capita emissions in 1990 were highly unequal among nations, the grandfathering approach of the protocol allowed each Annex B country to retain roughly the same share of aggregate global allowable emissions each year, rather than reducing inequalities among those nations in their per capita emission rates, even if each nation's total would decrease slightly between 1990 and 2012.

As a result, those nations that had the highest per capita emissions in 1990 would be allowed to maintain that distinction throughout the protocol's compliance period, and those with the lowest per capita rates would likewise be required to keep them relatively low through the treaty's lifetime. Herein lies one source of the unfairness inherent in the equal burdens approach: Those nations that had done the most to reduce their emissions or keep them low through proactive antipollution or energy efficiency efforts undertaken before 1990 were, in effect, penalized for that prudential effort, while those nations that had done the least in this regard were, in effect, rewarded for their past indifference toward such concerns. Moreover, since the most cost-effective GHG-reducing projects are usually those undertaken first, the nations that had proactively begun such ecological modernization efforts had already exhausted the cheapest GHG reduction projects before they could receive credit for them, and so would be required to spend more to achieve an equivalent reduction in comparison with those nations that had done little upgrading of their most inefficient facilities by the time the treaty was put into force. As noted above, to the extent that a grandfathering approach can be defended at all, its defense is generally based in expedience, not in fairness or equity. As Baer notes, "It is rare for anyone to make an ethical argument for pure grandfathering" at all, since the sort of objections noted above constitute a decisive indictment of its fairness.[15] The Kyoto Protocol, in taking an equal burdens approach, ignored its declared ideals of equity and responsibility in the interest of securing consent for a weak agreement rather than risking none at all.

Grandfathering historical emissions raises another problem, because any baseline year used to calculate future emissions limits appears arbitrary, and different baselines create different advantages and disadvantages for different nations. At the climate meetings in Kyoto, for example, a major political quagmire opened over the problem of what to do with the Annex B countries of the former Soviet Union, whose economic output and emissions had significantly declined in the early 1990s due to economic collapse. Collectively, their emissions since the 1990 baseline year had plummeted nearly 40 percent by the 1997 Conferences of the Parties, and for reasons that had little to do with concern for the global environment. Given the existence of an emissions trading market, Russia and Ukraine would stand to gain significantly by selling their excess emissions shares, prompting vocal complaints from representatives of Annex B nations that would be required under a cap-and-trade system to purchase these "hot air" shares from them. Should Russia and Ukraine benefit by emissions reductions that were unintentionally generated? Some thought that they should not, and indeed, one might be tempted to this conclusion by the principle of responsibility: Insofar as their emissions reductions came about as a result of luck,[16] one can imagine a claim for their being exempted from the kind of credit given to, for example, the European Union, which achieved its gains from a more deliberate and purposive effort. After all, there seems to be a worthy distinction between proactive pollution prevention and accidental gains, and incentives built into the climate regime can promote the former but not the latter. Following this critique, Russia and Ukraine's emissions baselines could be adjusted in order to reflect the unintentional nature of these reductions. But would this be fair? The Annex B country economic collapse cannot be regarded as a matter of brute luck[17] and thus completely dissociated from responsibility such that their resulting "hot air" emissions credits must be discounted. Although the economic collapse experienced by those countries was surely unplanned, the relevant distinction is between unplanned acts and their consequences and those consequences resulting from luck alone, where luck connotes consequences for which none are responsible. The Annex B economic collapse, in which Russia's emissions declined by 29 percent and Ukraine's by 49 percent, may not have itself been the product of voluntary choices, but its beneficial ecological effects cannot to be written off as beyond the responsibility of those who bore the costs of those involuntary emissions reductions. Residents suffered consequences from those nations' significant declines in economic production and consumption, and thus in one sense were held responsible of that phenomenon.

While their intention was surely not to reduce national emissions, can this lack of a specific motive or intention be counted against them? Must we demand that only those emission reductions achieved through conscious and deliberate efforts count toward Kyoto targets? What if the motives for such reductions are mixed, as between mitigating climate change and the myriad other benefits of reduced fossil fuel combustion? Many of the same actions or policies that reduce GHG emissions also conserve energy, reduce air pollution, relieve road congestion, and save money for consumers. Such ancillary benefits of emission reduction efforts, rather than consequences for global climate, are often the strongest motives for undertaking climate-friendly policies. Should their beneficial consequences for climate be thereby disqualified?

Such a conclusion would obviously be absurd. Although there are more and less effective ways of reducing a nation's GHG emissions without significantly reducing affecting the welfare of its current residents—few would be tempted to follow Russia's and Ukraine's examples in this regard—compliance with GHG targets and calculations of unused emissions shares available for trading on a market cannot be based on such considerations as whether or not those emissions reductions were intended; not only would this kind of micromanaging of domestic policy be prohibitively difficult, given problems already noted in ascertaining intentions of collective entities such as nations, but it would intrude on state sovereignty in a manner that is unnecessary and objectionable. As discussed in chapter 6, an agent's intentions cannot by themselves affect assessments of national liability in the responsibility-based components of the climate regime, as long as the consequences could reasonably have been anticipated. While Russia's and Ukraine's economic collapse may itself not have been either intended or foreseen, its effect on GHG emissions could readily have been predicted once it began. Moreover, the fault-based standards applicable to allocating national liability cannot apply to the equity-based concerns of allocating national emissions shares. Each is informed by a distinct model of fairness, and intentions play no direct role in either model.

An element of hypocrisy accompanies the suggestion that Russia and Ukraine not be allowed to trade their "hot air" credits to nations such as the United States, Canada, and Australia, all of which lodged objections to awarding Annex B countries "hot air" credits. Since 1997, delegates from these nations have insisted on the crediting of their large forested areas as carbon sinks toward emission reduction targets. The more densely populated nations in Europe and Asia that lack such huge sinks unsuccessfully objected to this proposal, since they would serve as a de facto reduction in abatement burdens for the relatively sparsely populated nations advocating them, diminishing as well the global carbon reductions given existing targets. The hypocrisy, though, comes through the assertions that emission reductions resulting from the prolonged economic recessions in Russia and Ukraine ought not to count toward their assigned reduction targets, ostensibly because these resulted from luck rather than voluntary choices, but that the abundant forests in North America and Australia ought to count toward compliance as somehow the product of deliberate human planning and voluntary effort. In effect, this combination of arguments has the effect of further punishing the unfortunate for their misfortune, and further rewarding the fortunate for their good luck.

Complaints lodged by Kyoto opponents about the emission reductions counted under the European Union's compliance record resulting from the cleanup of former East German factories and power plants illustrate another problem with the equal burdens approach. These emissions reductions cannot be considered as the products of luck, since Germany spent billions of dollars modernizing older industrial infrastructure in order to achieve the reductions that largely account for Europe's movement toward compliance. Yet, there remains a troubling problem with the emissions credit that resulted from the one-time event of German reunification. The use of the 1990 baseline results in a benefit for the European Union, and one factored into their relatively onerous joint emissions cap under the Kyoto Protocol, following from the existence of high-emissions East German factories and power plants in that year—a state of affairs that resembles luck—and that may partially undermine claims of responsibility for its cleanup. Likewise, Russia and Ukraine gained by virtue of the fact that their emissions were at an historical peak in 1990. Those nations that were the largest polluters at the time the baseline was established thereby received a kind of reward for this. Meanwhile, nations that accounted for much less pollution at the time the baseline was established were limited in their future emissions for this reason.

Starting points for the various participants thus become highly relevant under any scheme that prescribes reductions from an historical baseline, because this approach essentially grandfathers those historical patterns. The equal burdens approach of the Kyoto Protocol, despite its claim to follow the "common but differentiated responsibilities" formula for allocating costs, fails to compensate for the unfairness of these widely disparate starting points. Those countries that polluted more in 1990 were entitled to pollute more into the indefinite future, and vice versa. The United States, with per capita national emissions more than twice as high as the European Union or Japan, five times as high as China, and ten times those of India, would under the protocol be grandfathered into a substantially higher emissions allowance than its economic competitors. These disparities from 1990 emissions, which would be impossible to justify by any standard of international fairness, would be legitimated by the protocol, establishing de facto pollution rights that are distributed in a highly inequitable manner and locked in over time. In following an equal burdens approach, this climate regime violates the ideals of equity and responsibility that are expressed within the climate convention; not only would the variable historical responsibility or climate change be entirely disregarded, but it would serve as the basis for inequitable future pollution rights.

Had developing countries been included in the initial round of mandatory caps, they would have been locked in near their 1990 emissions levels, freezing the world economic hierarchy by denying them the ability to industrialize by capping future GHG emission increases. As soon as those nations are brought under the regulatory framework of the treaty, if they are, their growth potential may be frozen in a way that the earlier developing Annex B countries were not.

The problem here is not that binding emissions limits are inherently unfair—indeed, they are a necessary feature of an effective climate regime that *could* be assigned fairly—but is rather with the widely disparate caps that allow more pollution from historically bigger polluters, thereby undermining the principle of responsibility, which requires that all bear a share of the abatement burden in proportion to their contribution to the problem. The problem, in other words, is not with the design of any particular equal burdens approach, but is the approach itself. The objection raised regarding the "hot air" emissions credits awarded to Russia and Ukraine results not from the lack of an intent-based standard for distinguishing between those emissions reductions worthy of reward and those judged to be unworthy, but in the reliance on any kind of historical baseline in allocating costs of GHG abatement. Critics are half correct in asserting that Russia's 1990 emissions cannot be used as the basis for a claim to a larger share of the atmosphere, since unequal past emissions connote no defensible claim for unequal future emissions, but they are also half wrong in suggesting that its 1997 emissions justify a smaller share.

Hence, the protocol's basic strategy of relying on a modified equal burdens approach is indeed "fatally flawed," as both George W. Bush and the Global Climate Coalition asserted, though not for the reasons they cite. Another shortcoming of the equal burdens approach is revealed in trying to identify what constitutes an equal burden in climate change mitigation efforts. Any given per capita dollar expenditure will amount to a greater burden for a poor nation than for a wealthy nation, just as a $500 tax constitutes a far greater burden on a poor person than on a millionaire, so mitigation costs themselves cannot be the burden that is to be divided equally. Baer writes: "If we accept a principle of equal sacrifice, and we believe that it is a greater sacrifice for a poor person to pay a dollar than it is for a rich person—in economic terms, the declining marginal utility of income—we might define a person's or country's fair share based on ability to pay."[18] Per capita units of emissions reductions likewise cannot count as the measure of equal burdens, for a metric ton of annual per capita GHG reductions would be a more costly assignment for a nation with an average per capita emissions rate of 1.5 metric tons than for one with an average of 8 metric tons, because the most wasteful emissions are easiest to reduce. Likewise, a fixed percentage reduction from a baseline constitutes less of a burden for a nation that starts at 8 metric tons per capita than one now emitting 1.5 tons, although these burdens will be less unequal than per capita unit reductions. The measure of the respective burden imposed on various nations to reduce their emissions will be a product of their capacities to reduce emissions, which in turn are based on their national wealth along, current emissions rates, and the cost-effectiveness of efficiency improvements. A true equal burdens approach must take account of relative national capacities to reduce emissions and assign caps on that basis.

Two similar formulas for assigning national emissions shares are worth brief mention, because both are based loosely on the equal burdens standard but neither offers a defensible formulation of the relevant index on which emissions allocations might be equally assigned. One might, as the Bush administration has implicitly proposed with its Kyoto "alternative," base GHG shares on economic production, allocating emission shares equally by GNP. This could be done in one of two ways: Each nation might be allowed a share of some global emissions cap based on its GNP's percentage of GWP, or it could follow the Bush proposal of limiting nations to a cap on emissions intensity so that their emissions could not exceed some percentage of their GNP. Both proposals are obviously unfair, although for slightly different reasons. The first relies on an implausible entitlement claim—that those residing in nations with higher economic productivity deserve further rewards for that fortunate attribute—and poses an onerous barrier to development for those countries whose relative shares of GWP are now quite low, again freezing the world's economic order by grandfathering existing inequality into assignments of national emissions shares. The second proposal is also unfair to developing countries, since nations in the early stages of industrialization necessarily have higher rates of emissions intensity, advantaging late-stage industrial and postindustrial economies and disadvantaging developing countries in allocations of emissions shares. Moreover, the Bush plan places no cap on aggregate emissions, allowing them to rise indefinitely along with GNP, and so would be ineffective as well as unfair.

Environmental Rights

While the ideals of justice, equity, and responsibility may be entrenched in the design of a global climate regime, their formal recognition in law and public policy can more effectively be accomplished by substantiating them as environmental rights, which provide the necessary legal and political support for assisting rights holders in having their claims recognized. Since rights connote valid claims to either provision in the case of positive rights or noninterference with negative rights, they offer a robust form of protection for the interests that they are designed to advance by providing potential claimants an avenue of appeal against rulings or shortcomings of the climate regime, allowing for a quasi-judicial check on its administration as well as having a powerful effect on the formation of social norms. As Tim Hayward notes of instantiating aims of environmental protection through legal or constitutional rights, "It entrenches a recognition of the importance of environmental protection; it offers the possibility of unifying principles for legislation and regulation; it secures these principles against the vicissitudes of routine politics, while at the same time enhancing possibilities of democratic participation in environmental decision-making processes."[19]

Given the trumping power of constitutional rights, Hayward makes the case for them by comparing environmental rights to the set of recognized universal human rights, noting the intuition that "an adequate environment is as basic a condition of human flourishing as any of those that are already protected as human rights."[20] The right to an adequate environment meets the standard test for a genuine human right, he argues, since it protects human interests that are "of paramount moral importance," given that "environmental harms can threaten vital human interests." Moreover, he suggests, such a right would also be genuinely universal, since "the interests it is intended to protect are common to all humans."[21]

Although many formulations of this right exist in law and the academic literature on human rights, the most encompassing formulation of the range of interests to be protected by environmental rights posits the right to an adequate environment, which protects the necessary physical conditions for human flourishing. An exemplary version can be found in the Stockholm Declaration from the 1972 U.N. Conference on the Human Environment:

> Principle 1: Man has the fundamental right to freedom, equality, and
> adequate conditions of life, in an environment of a quality that
> permits a life of dignity and well-being, and he bears a solemn
> responsibility to protect and improve the environment for present
> and future generations.[22]

Essential to the expression of the right to an adequate environment are several features that are instructive to the case for a right to climatic stability, which are considered below. First, the environmental conditions that the right aims to secure are set alongside basic human ideals of freedom and equality in order to emphasize that all three ought to have the status of fundamental rights and are mutually reinforcing and jointly necessary. Second, all three of these rights are associated with human dignity and well-being, which aims to undercut the common assertion that environmental protection trades off against human welfare. Finally, the resolution associates this right to a "solemn responsibility" or set of correlative duties of environmental protection to which persons are obligated from cosmopolitan and intergenerational justice.

The right to an adequate environment is intended to encompass a broad range of anthropocentric duties of environmental protection, and the right to climatic stability appears to be an obvious corollary of such a right. While climate change is only one of many ongoing threats to the maintenance of an adequate environment, it must be regarded as among the most serious threats. Therefore, the duty to maintain climatic stability, or to refrain from excessive GHG emissions, is a necessary but insufficient condition for meeting the general obligation to maintain an adequate environment, making this a subsidiary right to the general right sketched above. Whether the right to climatic stability is sufficiently distinct or inherently weighty to require separate legal or constitutional mention or whether, by contrast, it ought to be considered as a necessary part of a more general fundamental right to an adequate environment, need not concern us here. Suffice to observe that the two are very closely associated and share a similar form, so the case for the more general right for which Hayward argues entails the recognition in some form of a right to climatic stability.

The case for establishing a fundamental right to climatic stability as among the set of universal human rights is further explored below, but first consider how an equally basic interest that can be protected as a right might also be incorporated into sustainability obligations. Recall that a central debate within the international climate policy development process concerns the supposed right to sustainably develop, which can be violated by a climate regime that places excessively restrictive caps on the emissions limits assigned to those non-Annex B nations not currently assigned binding caps under the Kyoto Protocol. Chapter 2 examines a related right that supposes that all persons are entitled to some basic level of survival emissions; the right to development would presumably build on this minimum per capita GHG allowance by claiming a larger per capita share than is necessary for meeting basic needs, because it implies a claim to further luxury emissions. If a right to develop—or, more specifically, the right to sufficient atmospheric space to accommodate per capita emissions rates that allow for development—is to be recognized alongside the right to an adequate environment as something to which are persons are entitled, then these two rights must somehow be brought into balance. Recognizing the latter right connotes a correlative duty to protect against dangerous anthropogenic interference with the planet's climatic system, while the former requires increasing emissions allowances among the world's poor, threatening climatic stability unless contracting them elsewhere. The next section explores these rights along with a proposal for balancing their competing claims.

Greenhouse Gas Emissions Rights

Rather than beginning with the more ambitious claim that residents of developing nations have a right to develop—or, in what comes to the same thing, that all persons have a fundamental right to some level of luxury emissions—let us begin with the more modest claim that all persons are entitled as a matter of basic rights to survival emissions, or a level of emissions sufficient to allow for their basic human functioning. (Recall the distinction between survival emissions and luxury emissions, or the amount of each person's emissions beyond those required for meeting basic needs.) In examining a nation's historical and current emissions, we have distinguished between these two in a manner compatible with a rights analysis: Since none can be held morally responsible for their survival emissions but all can be assessed liability for harm resulting from their luxury emissions, the former warrants the status of a basic right while the latter does not so clearly qualify for the sort of protection that rights entail. Persons' survival emissions cannot be attributed to their voluntary acts or choices, but persons can and do elect to further emit beyond that threshold. Insofar as all have a vital interest in the necessary conditions for human survival, all have a vital interest to survival emissions; insofar as they have a less basic but still important interest in flourishing or emissions beyond this threshold, they have a strong, if not vital, interest in luxury emissions.

We might put this observation in a slightly different way in order to illuminate the role of rights in the design of a fair and effective climate regime: Persons have a *basic right* to their survival emissions, but they have lesser rights, or no rights at all, to their luxury emissions. Basic rights are strong claims of entitlement that trump nonbasic rights or interests, so no right to luxury emissions can be allowed to threaten another's right to survival emissions. Several implications follow from formulating this distinction in terms of rights. First, all persons have valid claims to emit GHGs up to the survival threshold, so assessments of liability cannot be made against acts to which persons are entitled as a matter of right. Second, this right entails a valid claim for remedial state assistance when others threaten the practical ability of persons to exercise the right, so a global climate regime may curb luxury emissions in order to allow sufficient atmospheric space for survival emissions. Finally, survival emissions maintain their priority over luxury emissions even in the context of significant global inequality, since basic right claims to survival emissions trump those based in the lesser property right claims usually wielded in defense of inequality. For example, governments of poor nations cannot be allowed to sell their "unused" survival emissions in GHG markets to affluent nations seeking more luxury emissions, regardless of the price offered in return.

Although environmental rights have not been legally recognized as among the set of universal human rights to which all are entitled, several national constitutions and international agreements have declared versions of the right to an adequate environment, or to the procedural rights necessary for persons to participate in environmental decision making. For an example of procedural rights, the 1998 Aarhus Convention, intended as an exposition of principle 10 of the Rio Declaration (holding that "environmental issues are best handled with the participation of all concerned citizens, at the relevant level"), grants broad transparency and participatory rights to persons affected by environmental policy decisions, declaring its objective:

> Principle 1: In order to contribute to the protection of the right of every person of present and future generations to live in an environment adequate to his or her health and well-being, each Party shall guarantee the rights of access to information, public participation in decision-making, and access to justice in environmental matters in accordance with the provisions of this Convention.[23]

Although the convention establishes no substantive rights of environmental protection such as those found in the Stockholm Declaration, Hayward lauds it as "probably the most important step yet taken toward environmental rights protection,"[24] given this stated commitment to guaranteeing procedural rights as instrumental to realizing "the right of every person of present and future generations to live in an environment adequate to his or her health and well-being." Why should interests in environmental protection be instantiated in a rights framework? Why should rights such as those suggested above be regarded alongside the widely recognized set of universal human rights, to which all are entitled? Perhaps the most compelling case for environmental rights follows from Henry Shue's work on subsistence rights. He argues against the conventional distinction between security rights, which are often regarded as more fundamental and so tend to enjoy better protection under law, and economic rights, which are considerably less protected, suggesting that the more salient distinction supporting a priority system for weighing competing rights claims is between basic and nonbasic rights. Basic rights, he suggests, "specify the line beneath which no one is to be allowed to sink" and so constitute "everyone's minimum demand on the rest of humanity." A right that is genuinely basic trumps those rights that assist in the further development of human potential but that are not essential for basic functioning when the two kinds of rights conflict, Shue argues, and ought to be given priority in deploying scarce resources. The justification for this priority system is built into the idea of a basic right itself: "When a right is genuinely basic, any attempt to enjoy any other right by sacrificing the basic right would be quite literally self-defeating, cutting the ground from beneath itself."[25]

Although security rights—for example, those against harm, wrongful arrest, or excessive punishment—have long been enshrined within law and protected by states, social and economic rights, such as the right to public education or to organize a labor union, have more recently begun to be added to legal and political documents alongside these security rights, engendering at least some controversy about whether or not they belong there. The standard view holds security rights to be more fundamental than are social or economic rights in that they protect the most basic human interest not to be harmed, and for this reason gives these priority over less important rights. Following this distinction, societies may elect to provide social and economic rights after all security rights have been provided for, but the former are optional and clearly of a lesser priority. Moreover, the standard criticism equates security rights with negative rights, which are thought to be more cheaply and easily provided by the state since they correspond only with the duty to refrain from certain acts, whereas social and economic rights are usually equated with positive rights, regarded as more costly to provide. To illustrate, if you have a negative right against harm, then I have an easily met correlative duty to refrain from harming you, but if you have a positive right to something, such as a public education, then I have a correlative duty to help pay for it through my taxes. Taken together, the standard criticism maintains that new economic or social rights should not be added to the already lengthy lists of individual or human rights until security rights have been fully guaranteed, and then only after considering the opportunity costs of providing them.

Against these prevailing distinctions between economic and security rights, Shue points out that many security rights are partially positive in character, requiring provision rather than mere restraint, and actually are quite expensive to maintain, including the costs of domestic law enforcement and the military, along with the judicial and penal systems, while many economic rights are largely negative and cost relatively little for the state to provide. Workplace safety laws, for example, protect economic rights but function much as do many negative security rights. Insofar as the conventional case against them rests on the mistaken assumption that they are more costly for a state to guarantee, Shue offers the basic/nonbasic distinction as a more defensible priority system for weighing conflicting claims and deploying scarce state resources. Rather than relying on false generalizations about economic rights being more expensive to maintain combined with cost–benefit analysis that supposes rights protection to be justified only when it is cost-effective for the state to do so, he argues for a priority system based on the extent to which a given right protects activities essential to meeting human needs or safeguard those that are instrumental to human flourishing. According to Shue, the protection of basic rights is a matter of basic justice and ought therefore to be secured before attempts are made to provide for less basic rights.

Once we think of rights in this way, environmental rights become more plausible. As Shue notes, basic rights protect vital human interests in physical security as well as minimal economic security, or *subsistence*, including "unpolluted air, unpolluted water, adequate food, adequate clothing, adequate shelter, and minimal preventative health care."[26] In contrast to global efforts that have treated poverty and hunger as problems of charity rather than issues of justice or basic rights, he urges that subsistence be socially guaranteed as a matter of right, or else "attempts to actually enjoy the other rights remain open to a standard threat like the deprivation of security or subsistence."[27] Since the priority of basic over nonbasic rights is based on the parallel distinction between vital and nonvital interests, Shue argues that the world's affluent are required to sacrifice, in increasing order of importance, their preference satisfaction, cultural enrichment, and nonbasic rights—and are permitted, but cannot be required, to sacrifice some of their basic rights—in order to secure the basic rights of the world's poor.

According to Shue, this duty of justice is based on the *vital interests principle*, which holds that "it is unfair to demand of people actions the very performance of which would preclude for themselves a way of protecting a vital interest while failing to provide some other protection for that interest, when it is possible to protect it by means that do not threaten the vital interests of anyone."[28] Failing to act in order to protect threatened basic rights when this can be accomplished without the sacrifice of anyone's basic rights is essentially to fail to regard persons as equals; it is to give priority to the nonvital interests of some over the vital interests of others. It is, in other words, a violation of a fundamental premise of egalitarian justice: that no person is intrinsically more valuable than another. This entails a duty on the part of national governments, which are uniquely capable of securing basic rights and as "powerful institutions capable of causing severe deprivations when they do not restrain themselves," to avoid depriving others of their basic rights, whether through a negative act of restraint in avoidance of harm or through positive acts of provision.

In addition to the environmental rights that Shue lists above, one might also suppose that a stable climate may be considered as among the basic rights of humans, and that anthropogenic climate change therefore not only threatens to transfer substantial costs onto the world's poor, indirectly affecting their subsistence rights, but also directly affects their subsistence by reducing crop yields, diminishing water availability and quality, and in some cases threatening the territorial integrity of entire peoples. In June 2005, for example, the representatives of the Inuit—a people of 155,000 residing in Arctic regions of Canada, Alaska, Greenland, and Russia—filed a petition with the

Inter-American Commission on Human Rights alleging that the United States was violating their human rights by exacerbating global warming, since the warming trends caused by increasing GHG concentrations have already had profound thinning effects on Arctic ice sheets, threatening those species on which Inuit hunters depend and so, in effect, threatening the cultural preservation of the entire Inuit people. Since climate change is widely expected to threaten wildlife and shift species habitats, myriad other potential threats to traditional cultures may likewise be affected, elevating the prominence of such right claims in the climate debate.

The idea of a right to survival emissions finds some theoretical basis in Shue's work on subsistence rights, which may also lend support to the idea of a right to develop on the part of poor countries that have difficulty meeting the basic needs of their citizens. Classifying the atmosphere's "emission absorptive capacity" as a basic right, he suggests that persons ought to be entitled to a basic minimum level of per capita GHG emissions as a matter of right, entailing that provision of this entitlement ought therefore to trump the exercise of other nonbasic rights:

> For practically everyone at present, and for the immediate future,
> survival requires the use of GHG emissions absorptive capacity. No
> reasonable, immediate alternative exists. Strange as it might initially
> sound, emission absorptive capacity is as vital as food and water
> and, virtually everywhere, shelter and clothing.[29]

Insofar as basic or subsistence rights can be understood as protecting vital interests, where one cannot enjoy other rights unless these basic rights are first protected, then supposing that survival emissions count among a person's basic rights clearly follows. Since persons literally cannot survive without them, they are as basic as physical security and the standard set of subsistence rights such as those to food, water, and shelter. As Shue suggests, attributing a right to survival emissions generates a distributive principle that applies to the assignment of national emissions shares: that "the only morally permissible allocations of emissions are allocations that guarantee the availability of the minimum necessary emissions to every person, which entails reserving adequate unused absorptive capacity for those unused emissions."[30]

Development Rights

It is one thing to suppose that all persons are entitled as a matter of basic right to survival emissions, but quite another to assert that they are entitled to equal per capita emissions shares. While the argument for the former can be grounded in subsistence rights, the latter requires a more difficult argument for equality rather than one simply based in the avoidance of harm or protection of basic rights. In the distributive justice literature, this contrast is often referred to as between equality and sufficiency, or between an egalitarian distribution and a one guaranteeing basic minimum. The case for a universal human right to a level of survival emissions is more easily made than the case for a human right to development, but the latter has been nonetheless asserted, and may be implied by the equal shares proposal. Having now surveyed the case for the more limited right defended by Shue, from a distinction between survival and luxury emissions, how might the latter argument on behalf of a right to considerable luxury emissions go?

From classical liberalism, a longstanding constraint on inequality comes from the proviso that Locke attaches to his labor theory of property in the *Second Treatise*, in which persons are allowed to appropriate natural resources—much as they now appropriate atmospheric absorptive capacity—only insofar as they leave "enough, and as good" for others. Since the appropriation by some of any finite resource can harm others by diminishing their opportunities to do the same, Locke's proviso can be read as a harm principle limiting appropriation under conditions of scarcity. Given the finite and increasingly scarce capacity of the atmosphere to absorb GHGs, its overappropriation by some countries violates this Lockean proviso, leaving too little atmospheric space for others to develop. Hence, Locke recognizes a key limit on appropriation of resources such as atmospheric space and claims based in rights of property or prior use; opponents of GHG regulation that ground their arguments in a Lockean "nightwatchman state" must realize that the seminal figure in the libertarian tradition long ago laid the groundwork for justifying a global regulatory regime designed to allocate emission shares in a manner that avoids the overuse problem that Locke identifies. If nothing else, his proviso stresses that the appropriation of natural resources must be subject to some distributive principle, not left the laissez faire nonregulation that contemporary neo-Lockeans recommend.

Going from justified limits on appropriation to equal shares requires additional steps, however, and draws on the idea of cosmopolitan justice discussed in chapter 3. As noted above, Beitz's resource redistribution principle argues for the egalitarian allocation of natural resources, based on the Rawlsian logic of the original position. Even if we reject his plausible contention that this principle applies to the allocation of all natural resources now geographically located within national borders and instead apply it only to the territorially unbounded resource of atmospheric absorptive capacity—the weakest possible interpretation of

Beitz's argument for cosmopolitan justice—his analysis nonetheless makes a strong case for the equal per capita allocation of emissions shares, subject only to several side constraints concerning population growth and variations in survival emissions. Given equal per capita emissions shares, no nation would be allowed any greater capacity to industrialize than any other, nor would any be granted the license to consume more than any other, which can prohibit social as well as economic development. This equal shares approach would amount to the guarantee of a right to develop, at least as long as the absorptive capacity of the atmosphere can accommodate *any* development.

How does a right to develop emerge from the analysis of atmospheric absorptive capacity as a shared resource combined with Beitz's principle? Insofar as residents of developing nations are understood to have a right to develop, as is claimed by the climate convention and elsewhere, then there exists a correlative duty on the part of the world's affluent nations not only to refrain from interfering with that development, but also to provide certain kinds of positive assistance in order to facilitate it. A right to develop, that is, has both positive and negative dimensions. In the context of a global climate regime, that assistance includes at least the allowance of the requisite atmospheric capacity for increased social and economic development, which is a negative duty that requires industrialized nations to yield some of the atmospheric space that they now claim through their larger per capita emissions, thus allowing developing countries sufficient space to accommodate the emissions growth that accompanies development. To prevent aggregate global emissions from rising as increasing proportions originate within developing nations, not only must per capita emissions shares among developing nations be allowed to rise from current levels, but per capita emissions in industrialized nations must be correspondingly decreased.

This "contraction and convergence" scenario offers an alternative normative foundation for the equal shares approach to assigning national emissions caps. Due to the nonexistence of any formal limits on emissions during those periods in which the world's affluent nations developed economically, their processes of industrialization were uninhibited in ways that can no longer tenably be allowed for those that have yet to undergo such processes of transformation. Should the industrialized nations now impose emissions caps on developing countries that inhibit their ability to industrialize, they would in effect be interfering with their right to develop. In order to accommodate this interest in development, sufficient atmospheric space must be freed up under a global emissions cap to allow for GHG emissions increases by developing countries, and this space can come only at the expense of decreased emissions from industrialized nations. As Baer argues, some equivalent to a right to develop may be practically necessary if developing countries such as Brazil, India, and China are to be voluntarily brought into a system of binding emissions caps, since "everyone in the developing world cannot emit at the high rates of the North, but why should developing countries agree to restrictions that bind them to their current, much lower per capita rates or that restrict their economic growth?"[31] As observed in chapter 3, the South cannot agree to such restrictions, and the climate regime must be fair to all if it is to be effective, because universal participation under a system of caps is essential.

Along with this negative duty to refrain from overappropriating atmospheric space by limiting GHG emissions, a positive duty to assist developing countries in human and economic development comprises a vital component to the right to develop. It is here that those sustainable development incentives built into the climate convention take on a crucial dual role, in allowing Annex B nations to meet part of their emission reduction burdens by undertaking CDM projects outside of their own borders and by promoting ecological modernization through investment in high-efficiency infrastructure development in poorer countries. Merely refraining from placing a legal prohibition on luxury emissions is insufficient to promote sustainable development, so some positive component is necessary if the right is to acquire any meaningful substance, and these provisions built into the climate convention create the proper incentives for the interests that such a right aims to advance to be realized. In addition to the development assistance that accompanies CDM projects, economic and human development might be promoted by requiring developing countries to dedicate some percentage of their sales of unused emissions shares toward such campaigns.

The CDM program, as it currently exists within the climate convention, is not without its flaws or critics, but a modified version of the program may well serve these development goals. Originally proposed by Brazil as a punitive device to be based on national responsibility rather than a flexibility mechanism that allows affluent nations to meet their Kyoto targets with lesser domestic GHG reductions, the program morphed into a market-based policy tool that ostensibly promotes economic efficiency rather than moral responsibility, a shift that leads to the program's greatest strength and most serious flaw. The efficiency incentives negate the need for basing national burdens on relative capabilities, because the flexible compliance mechanisms included within the climate convention direct expenditures toward the greatest potential gains regardless of which nations are required to pay for the projects that they involve. As a result, the most efficient projects can be undertaken first, freeing the climate regime to assign national climate-related burdens based on defensible normative principles of equity and responsibility, whether in the assignment of national emissions shares or in remedial liability.

The upside to CDM is that it directly promotes efficiency and sustainable development, and indirectly promotes international equity by shifting resources from rich to poor nations. In the short run, these advantages appear compelling, though its long-term downside effects are more worrying. As Ellen Wiegandt notes, the incentives that allow Annex B counties to undertake the most cost-effective emission reduction projects first also entails "leaving the costs of more expensive ones to developing countries should they take on commitments at some later date."[32] Especially since developing countries are not currently included under mandatory emissions caps, the most cost-effective projects are likely to be claimed by affluent nations in the short term, leaving much less cost-effective ones for developing countries, including those within their own borders, for that future point at which they have mandatory caps of their own. Projects that now cost $10 to $25 per ton of carbon reduction are estimated to cost as much as $200 to $300 per ton after the end of the Kyoto Protocol's first compliance period, at which time developing countries may be assigned mandatory caps. According to Agarwal, the more insidious side of CDM efficiency incentives encourages "the North to buy up the cheap emission reduction options available today, leaving the South to pay a heavy price tomorrow," which offers those "cash-strapped developing country governments an opportunity to discount the future" by selling off their most efficient GHG abatement projects now, despite these predictable future consequences.[33] Moreover, CDM incentives encourage Annex B nations to target investments toward industrializing countries such as China and India, where opportunities for emissions abatement of most lucrative, ignoring most of the world's poorest regions merely because their emissions rates, as a measure of both human and economic development, remain stagnant. As Agarwal notes of this structure of incentives, "Africa can be meaningfully integrated into the Kyoto Protocol only if the principle of emission avoidance is incorporated."[34]

If a meaningful right to develop is to be effectively recognized and advanced by a global climate regime, it must avoid structuring incentives in such a way that developing countries are encouraged to sacrifice long-term economic viability for short-term gain. Rather, it must promote long-term human and economic development aims in a manner that is socially, economically, and environmentally sustainable, and following *UNFCCC*'s expressed goals of promoting equity and responsibility. Concern for equity and responsibility should not be dismissed as secondary to the primary goal of avoiding catastrophic climate change, for as previously noted, the environmental problem of anthropogenic climate change is also a problem of justice and so cannot be genuinely remedied unless the international response aims to promote justice while limiting global GHG emissions. The right to develop is likewise a right grounded in ideals of justice, which seek to guarantee that the "natural lottery" of birth not continue to dictate the radically unequal life prospects that currently attach to one's nation of residence. Global climate may be only part of the complex causal chain that produces this unjust inequality, but it is a significant part, as resource exploitation patterns that contribute to climate change have led to and continue to widen global inequality, and the predicted effects of climate change include the imposition of externality effects that significantly exacerbate that inequality. Given the interrelation between inequality and environmental degradation—the Brundtland Report aptly identifies global inequality as a primary cause of stress on environmental resources and ecological degradation as a primary cause of that inequality[35]—a right to sustainably develop is grounded in the nature of anthropogenic climate change itself. Global justice and climate change must be addressed simultaneously, and as manifestations of the same set of problems.

Since rights exist in order to protect interests, a strong case can be made from the critical importance to human welfare of climatic stability for a right to an adequate environment with the corollary that the right includes a claim to climatic stability, which entails duties to ensure that this claim is met as well as a system of compensation when it is not. Given the further interest in human flourishing, we can also posit that persons have other universal human rights that guard against other threats or constraints on that interest, including a right to human and economic development. While such a right cannot be unlimited—the right to economic development does not entail a permission to deplete resources or befoul the environment, for example—it must trump rights or other claims that are less basic to human flourishing, including those implicitly made by or on behalf of those residents of industrialized nations whose desire to continue producing excessive luxury emissions entails that development restrictions be imposed on poor countries. As Shue argues, more basic interests outweigh less basic ones, so more basic rights must also trump less basic ones. While the right to develop cannot trump the right to survival emissions, the former must be recognized as making a more compelling claim on limited atmospheric space than do those de facto claims now being made on that space by the relatively affluent residents of industrialized nations, who selfishly seek to protect or enlarge their undeserved advantages by denying to the less advantaged a prerogative on which their present prosperity is largely based.

Why Procedural Fairness?

How fair has the current climate convention negotiation process been to various affected parties? The *UNFCCC* process has been heavily weighted toward the most powerful nations and largest GHG polluters, both in the negotiating sessions and in its formal policy provisions. Despite rhetorical gestures toward inclusive processes, Agarwal describes climate negotiations as largely exclusive affairs where "the United States and EU have sorted out their differences and presented developing countries with a take-it-or-leave-it deal on climate change."[36] Even in those cases in which developing nations have been allowed to participate in policy development, the vast power differentials among nations have created bargaining situations in which rich nations such as the United States have an effective veto over almost all aspects of climate policy, despite American nonparticipation in the Kyoto Protocol, while poor nations, which cannot threaten to pull out of and therefore cripple the effort if they do not get their way, struggle to have their voices heard at all, let alone allow their interests to be reflected in policy. The result is, as Shue notes, "precisely the kind of procedure most likely to produce outcomes that merely reflect the enormous power differentials among the bargainers."[37] Bad process begets bad policy, and allowing such power disparities to permeate the climate policy-making process virtually guarantees policy outputs that benefit the powerful and cost the powerless. A recipe for generating a fair and effective climate policy this is not.

Why, though, should we concern ourselves with procedural fairness when we have already identified the substantively fair policy by reference to philosophical theories of justice? Fairness in process seems unnecessary given that we have made the case for a substantive policy outcome on independent grounds, and we have no guarantee that a reasonably fair climate policy-making process would endorse the proposal sketched above. The answers to these questions are threefold. As a practical matter, the international climate policy development process requires legitimacy if its terms are to be endorsed by all as fair and followed by participants in the absence of a strong set of global executive institutions. Policy processes in which political equality is denied and opportunities for meaningful participation by affected parties are undermined are sure to be regarded by those excluded as unfair, and this judgment is bound to carry over to the policies yielded by those processes. Although the imperfect procedural justice of improved climate policy processes cannot guarantee a substantively fair outcome, they can significantly increase the probability that the policies adopted through fair, open, and inclusive deliberative processes really are fair, in addition to appearing so. Finally, bad process not only begets bad policy, but as the Cheney task force illustrates, it also breeds distrust, and trust is essential to any international agreement that depends on the willing cooperation of participants.

To illustrate the importance of good faith negotiations in climate policy development, consider the following analysis of the role of *perception* in negotiations over a policy such as a climate regime when it comes to the credibility of an actor such as the United States in urging substantive fairness in policy outcomes. When one party refuses to participate in a cooperative scheme because that party sees it as unfair and denounces it as such, there are two possible interpretations of what is meant by this explanation: One assumes a sincere desire of fairness in which the holdout genuinely desires a fair arrangement for all and would immediately join the scheme if such an arrangement could be produced, and the other makes a cynical reading of the party's motives for nonparticipation in which the holdout is merely using the pretext of fairness in order to press for a greater advantage than other participants in the scheme are willing to grant. When the holdout is sufficiently important to the cooperative scheme's success that its refusal to participate can undermine any benefits that the group might produce without it, the holdout acquires tremendous power that might be used either to press a *sincere case for fairness* that can be used to overcome resistance to dropping the scheme's unfair provisions, or to press a *cynical case for fairness* in which unfair terms are urged through a discourse of fairness. In the latter case, the less powerful parties face a dilemma: Accept terms that unfairly advantage the holdout at the expense of the other participants in the scheme, or else lose the benefits of cooperation altogether. When a dominant holdout threatens nonparticipation in this way, the other participants hope that the threat is based on a sincere case for fairness rather than on a cynical one, but often fear that the opposite is true.

It would be useful to be able to determine, based on the holdout's behavior, whether its case for fairness was sincere or cynical. If sincere, the others would be well advised to work with the holdout in order to seek a fair agreement. None can reasonably reject an agreement that is genuinely fair, even if worse for them than some alternative, because fairness is widely understood as a prerequisite for participation by the holdout and its participation is vital to the success of the cooperative scheme. On the other hand, if the holdout was merely using the discourse of fairness as a pretext for seeking even greater advantage from the cooperative scheme than initially offered, then the others may be better off not cooperating with the holdout at all. Since all know that the holdout is merely invoking fairness in this cynical way, they cannot trust its expressed desire to allow others a fair share of the cooperative scheme's benefits, since precisely the opposite is true. If they yield a small amount of their own expected benefits from the cooperative scheme in order to enlarge the share to potentially be enjoyed by the holdout in order to entice its participation, they may still benefit from the scheme but less so than if benefits were fairly divided. Knowing this, and seeking maximum advantage, the holdout will demand greater and greater concessions, continuing to threaten nonparticipation up until that point at which no further concessions are possible, because the others no longer stand to receive any more benefit from the cooperative scheme than without it. Once this point is reached, at which point the rational holdout would finally agree to participate, the others could join the scheme only with profound regret and resentment, for none but the cynical holdout would benefit by it.

The question is, then, how the others might know if the holdout was sincere in making its participation conditional on a fair agreement being reached. Are there observable behavioral indices that might allow others to distinguish between a sincere holdout and a cynical one? How would a sincere holdout behave if its expressed desire to reach a fair agreement was genuinely sincere? How would a cynical holdout behave, if differently from a sincere holdout? To these questions, we can venture only tentative and untested but commonsense hypotheses. Given its genuine desire for a fair agreement, the sincere holdout would specify explicitly to the others exactly what it understands fairness to require, taking care to articulate and justify the conception of fairness on which these requirements are based. It does so, of course, not so that it can persuade others to agree with it, but from a sincere desire to discover the nature of fairness itself, at least as it might be applied to the cooperative scheme. Since it is aware that its unequal power within the group does not necessarily grant it a monopoly on wisdom, the holdout recognizes its fallibility, and since its commitment to fairness also includes a desire to avoid mistakenly pressing for an unfair agreement, it engages in a critical discussion about the nature of fairness with others, not in order to persuade them to agree to unfair terms—something that, at any rate, is more easily accomplished by threats than by persuasion—but to ensure that the conception of fairness sought by the holdout in the agreement is indeed fair. In the end, all would thus be able to clearly see how the various unfair alternatives that others might prefer to the fair one depart from fairness in some way. Although the others need not assent to the fair scheme from a sincere desire for fairness, since they realize that the sincere holdout will disallow any unfair agreements and they prefer a fair scheme to none at all, there exists only one agreement that all can endorse: the fair one.

The cynical holdout will not be so forthcoming or cooperative. Knowing that critical examination and discussion of the nature of fairness will make it difficult or impossible to defend its preferred scheme, which is based on maximizing its own advantage rather than achieving genuine fairness, and since open discussion would expose an indefensible conception of fairness for all to see and spoil the pretext of a sincere desire for a fair agreement, the cynical holdout may invoke the language of fairness in its ploys for advantage but will refuse to articulate, much less discuss, the conception of fairness on which its proposed arrangements are based. Not only will it not engage in critical discussions about the nature of fairness with others, but it will also refuse to discuss alternative arrangements, preventing others from proposing alternatives to its favored scheme. The cynical holdout knows that open, democratic deliberation where all are allowed to participate on equal terms might result in alternative proposals that appear intuitively to be more fair than the holdout's preferred one, requiring it to explain to others why this intuition is mistaken, at which point it might be drawn into a discussion of the nature of fairness itself, which it aims to avoid. Hence, the holdout will seek to limit or avoid altogether any such debate over alternative proposals, perhaps even prohibiting others from discussing the holdout's favored proposal among themselves, which might foment rebellion if the intuition about fairness that the others possess leads them toward the conclusion that the holdout is indeed a cynical one. Rather, the cynical holdout will make its demand, threatening nonparticipation if others do not agree to it, perhaps making some perfunctory remarks about fairness but without elaboration, and require others to either accept or reject its terms, with no opportunities for debate or amendment. The cynical holdout, in other words, will behave as the United States has in the context of global climate policy development.

The point of the preceding analysis is not to accuse the United States of cynically cloaking its case for advantage in the discourse of fairness, but rather to urge openness and inclusion in genuine deliberation over the meaning and implications of justice and fairness as applied to the design and implementation of a global climate regime. It has been a central objective of this book to examine this application of normative ideals with some care, and it remains my hope that the problem of anthropogenic climate change can be addressed in such a way that a genuine and robust consensus may first be formed around a set of normative ideals and objectives to be achieved through the policy-making process, and then to the policies themselves. While some would surely deride such hopes as unrealistically utopian—as perhaps they are—the practical shortcomings inherent in actual democratic practices should not be used as a rationalization for policy-making processes that are known to be much worse. As I have taken considerable pains to try to demonstrate, the normative questions on which the fairness of the climate regime can be constructed are complex, controversial, and certain to elicit further debate rather than ensure instant and lasting consensus. But they are nonetheless answerable, and some answers are based in more defensible reasoning or grounded in more justifiable objectives than are others. Insofar as we may aspire to address this looming global problem justly—and we must, if we are to address it effectively over the long term—we must start by the earnest examination of the very ideals on which the global response to anthropogenic climate change is to be constructed. Genuine deliberation over these issues and their implications, which has thus far been absent in the halls of power, is certainly the best and perhaps the only hope for realizing the expressed ideals of the climate convention and for avoiding an environmental catastrophe.

Notes

INTRODUCTION

1. Michael McCarthy, "This *Is* Global Warming, Says Environmental Chief," *Independent* (online edition, September 23, 2005).

2. P.J. Webster, G.J. Holland, J.A. Curry, and H.R. Chang, "Changes in Tropical Cyclone Number, Duration, and Intensity in a Warming Environment," *Science* 309 (September 16, 2005): 1846.

3. Richard Kerr, "Is Katrina a Harbinger of Still More Powerful Hurricanes?" *Science* 309 (September 16, 2005): 1807.

4. The term "climate change" offers the more inclusive account of the various weather-related effects of increasing atmospheric concentrations of heat-trapping greenhouse gases (GHGs) and so is the one used throughout this book to refer to the phenomenon that some call global warming.

5. Gerald Meehl and Claudia Tebaldi, "More Intense, More Frequent, and Longer Lasting Heat Waves in the 21st Century," *Science* 305 (August 13, 2004): 994–97.

6. Evan Mills, "Insurance in a Climate of Change," *Science* 309 (August 12, 2005): 1040.

7. Stephen H. Schneider and Kuntz-Duriseti, "Uncertainty and Climate Change Policy," in *Climate Change Policy: A Survey*, ed. Stephen H. Schneider, Armin Rosencranz, and John O. Niles (Washington, DC: Island Press, 2002): 53–88, p. 61.

8. Mills (2005), pp. 1041–42.

9. Intergovernmental Panel on Climate Change, *Climate Change 2001: A Synthesis Report. A Contribution of Working Groups I, II, and III to the Third Assessment Report of the IPCC*, ed. R.T. Watson and the Core Writing Team (New York: Cambridge University Press, 2001), p. 12.

10. John Rawls, *A Theory of Justice* (Cambridge, MA: Belknap Press, 1971), p. 3.

CHAPTER 1

1. Svante Arrhenius, "On the Influence of Carbonic Acid in the Air upon the Temperature of the Ground," *London, Edinburgh, and Dublin Philosophical Magazine and Journal of Science*, 5th ser. (April 1896): 237–76, as cited in Gale Christianson, *Greenhouse: The 200-Year Story of Global Warming* (New York: Penguin Books, 1999), pp. 113–14.

2. Quoted from Christianson (1999), p. 115.

3. Roger Revelle and Hans Suess, "Carbon Dioxide Exchanges Between Atmosphere and Ocean and the Question of an Increase of Atmospheric CO_2 During the Past Decades," *Tellus* 9 (1957): 18–27, as quoted in Christianson (1999), pp. 155–56.

4. J.W. Anderson, "A 'Crash Course' in Climate Change," in *The RFF Reader in Environmental and Resource Management*, ed. Wallace Oates (Washington, DC: Resources for the Future, 1999), p. 215.

5. Intergovernmental Panel on Climate Change, *Climate Change 2001: A Synthesis Report. A Contribution of Working Groups I, II, and III to the Third Assessment Report of the IPCC*, ed. R.T. Watson and the Core Writing Team (New York: Cambridge University Press, 2001), pp. 4–10.

6. Intergovernmental Panel on Climate Change (2001), pp. 10–16.

7. Intergovernmental Panel on Climate Change (2001), p. 12.

8. See Charles Lindblom, "The Science of 'Muddling Through,'" *Public Administration Review* 19 (1959): 79–88. Though the rational-comprehensive model provides an ideal for well-informed and far-reaching policy change, by far the most common process involves what Lindblom calls "muddling through"—restricting analysis to a narrow range of solutions, making incremental rather than wholesale changes from the status quo, and focusing on what is politically feasible rather than what is best.

9. United Nations, *United Nations Framework Convention on Climate Change* (1992).

10. Anderson (1999), p. 219.

11. Available at UNFCCC.int/essential_background/kyoto_protocol/status_of_ratification/items/2613.php.

12. Amanda Griscom Little, "Pact or Fiction?" *Grist* (August 4, 2005), available at grist.org/news/muck/2005/08/04/little-pact/?source=muck.

13. Executive Office of the President, *Economic Report of the President* (February 2002), p. 247.

14. Intergovernmental Panel on Climate Change (2001), pp. 25–27.

15. Robert T. Watson, "Climate Change: The Political Situation," *Science* 302 (2003): 1925–26.

16. Executive Office of the President (2002), p. 247.

17. See the report by the Union of Concerned Scientists, *Drilling in Detroit* (2002), available at www.ucsusa.org/clean_vehicles/fuel_economy/drilling-in-detroit.html.

18. On the relationship between economic growth and quality of life, see Eric Davidson and George Woodwell, *You Can't Eat GNP: Economics As If Ecology Mattered* (Reading, MA: Perseus Books, 2001).

19. See Bjorn Lomborg, *The Skeptical Environmentalist* (New York: Cambridge University Press, 2001), especially pp. 305–15.

20. Executive Office of the President (2002), p. 218.

21. "Blowing Smoke," *Economist* (February 14, 2002).

22. Pew Center on Global Climate Change, "Analysis of President Bush's Climate Change Plan" (February 2002), available at www.pewclimate.org.

23. See, e.g., Carl Pope and Paul Rauber, *Strategic Ignorance: Why the Bush Administration Is Recklessly Destroying a Century of Environmental Progress* (San Francisco: Sierra Club, 2004); and Robert S. Devine, *Bush Versus the Environment* (New York: Anchor, 2004).

24. Bill McKibben, "Crossing the Red Line," *New York Review of Books* (June 10, 2004): 32–36, p. 32.

25. Bill Moyers, "Welcome to Doomsday," *New York Review of Books* (March 24, 2005): 8–10, p. 10.

26. While Moyers's hypothesis concerning the role of some Christian fundamentalists invoking theology in opposing meaningful climate policy efforts is probably accurate, many evangelical and other Christians have also taken a strong advocacy role in support of such policy. E.g., the U.S. Conference of Catholic Bishops has called on followers to practice good planetary stewardship that includes reducing GHG emissions, and the Evangelical Environmental Network has likewise called for action to protect climatic stability, organizing several initiatives in support of the Kyoto Protocol and in criticism of the Bush administration's opposition to it. See, e.g., Blain Harden, "The Greening of Evangelicals," *Washington Post* (February 6, 2005): A1.

27. Richard Hofstadter, "The Paranoid Style of American Politics," *Harper's* (November 1964): 77–86, p. 81.

28. Senator James M. Inhofe (R-OK), "An Update on the Science of Climate Change," *Congressional Record* (January 4, 2005), p. S18.

29. Quoted from Jeremy Leggett, *The Carbon War: Global Warming and the End of the Oil Era* (New York: Taylor & Francis, 2001), p. 250.

30. Joseph Kahn, "Cheney Promotes Increasing Supply as Energy Policy," *New York Times* (May 1, 2001), p. A1.

31. Natural Resources Defense Council, "Slower, Costlier, and Dirtier: A Critique of the Bush Energy Plan" (May 2001), available at www.nrdc.org/air/energy/scd/scdinx.asp.

32. Counting prima per capita energy consumption (commercial and noncommercial) and relying on 1995 data, the average American consumes nearly 340 gigajoules (compared with 140 in Western Europe). See World Energy Council, *World Energy Assessment: Energy and the Challenge of Sustainability* (2003).

33. Union of Concerned Scientists, *Energy Security: Solutions to Protect America's Power Supply and Reduce Oil Dependence* (February 2002).

34. Natural Resources Defense Council (2001), p. 3.

35. Interlaboratory Working Group, *Scenarios for a Clean Energy Future* (Oak Ridge, TN: Oak Ridge National Laboratory and Berkeley, CA: Lawrence Berkeley National Laboratory, November 2000), available at www.ornl.gov/sci/eere/cef/.

36. Natural Resources Defense Council, "Environmentalists Had Limited Access to the White House Energy Task Force," available at www.nrdc.org/air/energy/taskforce/bkgrd2.asp.

37. Natural Resources Defense Council, "Data Shows Industry had Extensive Access to Cheney's Energy Task Force" (press release, May 21, 2002), available at www.nrdc.org/media/pressreleases/020521.asp.

38. U.S. General Accounting Office, *Energy Task Force: Process Used to Develop the National Energy Policy*, GAO Report to Congressional Requesters (August 2003), available at www.gao.gov/cgi-bin/getrpt?GAO-03-894.

39. Elizabeth Drew, "Selling Washington," *New York Review of Books* (June 23, 2005): 24–27, p. 25.

40. Leggett (2001).

41. The term refers to a small group of scientists that have accepted the role of public opponent to the prevailing scientific view that anthropogenic climate change is real in order to provide political cover for politicians opposed to GHG regulation on other grounds and to confuse the public into believing climate change to be an unsettled scientific controversy or even an outright hoax.

42. Quoted from Ross Gelbspan, *The Heat Is On* (Reading, MA: Perseus Books, 1997), p. 34.

43. Gelbspan (1997), p. 37.

44. William Clay Ford, Jr., Speech to the fifth annual Greenpeace Business Conference, London (October 5, 2000), available at media.ford.com/article_display.cfm?article_id=6217.

45. Lester E. Brown, "The Rise and Fall of the Global Climate Coalition" Earth Policy Institute (July 25, 2000), available at www.earth-policy.org/Alerts/Alert6.htm.

46. Business Environmental Leadership Council, available at www.pewclimate.org/companies_leading_the_way_belc.

47. Center for Media and Democracy, "Impropaganda Review: Global Climate Coalition," available at www.prwatch.org/improp/gcc.html.

48. For a comprehensive list, see www.exxonsecrets.org.

49. Chris Mooney, "Some Like It Hot," *Mother Jones* (May 2005).

50. Willie Soon and Sallie Baliunas, "Proxy Climatic and Environmental Changes of the Past 1000 Years," *Climate Research* 23 (2003): 89–110, p. 89.

51. Jeff Nesmith, "Three Journal Editors Resign over Flawed Skeptic Paper," Cox News Service (July 29, 2003).

52. Antonio Regalado, "Global Warming Skeptics Are Facing Storm Clouds," *Wall Street Journal* (July 31, 2003).

53. After finding errors in the models used to allegedly demonstrate the lack of tropospheric warming over the past century, several recent studies have conclusively demonstrated a warming pattern, which those climate skeptics that had previously denied such warming now concede. See Andrew Revkin, "Errors Cited in Assessing Climate Data," *New York Times* (August 12, 2005).

54. "Claims by Pro-Bush Think-Tank Outrage Eco-groups," *The Observer/UK* (November 28, 2004).

55. In sworn testimony to the U.K. House of Lords Science and Technology Committee in 2003, Exxon's public affairs director, Nick Thomas, claimed: "I think we can say categorically we have not campaigned with the United States government or any government to take any sort of position over Kyoto." Quoted from John Vidal, "Revealed: How Oil Giant Influenced Bush," *The Guardian* (online edition, June 8, 2005).

56. Vidal (2005).

57. Gelbspan (1997), p. 64.

58. Gelbspan (1997), p. 68.

59. Jeffrey Mervis, "NOAA Loses Funding to Gather Long-Term Climate Data," *Science* 307 (2005): 188.

60. Andrew Revkin, "Climate Research Faulted over Missing Components," *New York Times* (online edition, April 22, 2005).

61. The report begins: "Greenhouse gases are accumulating in Earth's atmosphere as a result of human activities, causing surface air temperatures and subsurface ocean temperatures to rise. Temperatures are, in fact, rising." National Academy of Sciences, Commission on Geosciences, Environment, and Resources, *Climate Change Science: An Analysis of Some Key Questions* (2001), available at www.nap.edu/books/0309075742/html.

62. The report begins: "Human activities are increasingly altering the Earth's climate. These effects add to natural influences that have been present over Earth's history. Scientific evidence strongly indicates that natural influences cannot explain the rapid increase in global near-surface temperatures observed during the second half of the 20th century." American Geophysical Union, "Human Impacts on Climate" (2003), available at www.agu.org/sci_soc/policy/climate_change_position.html.

63. Naomi Oreskes, "The Scientific Consensus on Climate Change," *Science* 306 (2004): 1686.

64. U.S. Department of State, *U.S. Climate Action Report* (May 2002).

65. Katherine Q. Seelye, "President Distances Himself from Global Warming Report," *New York Times* (online edition, June 5, 2002).

66. See www.epa.gov/airtrends.

67. U.S. Environmental Protection Agency, *Report on the Environment* (June 23, 2003), available at www.epa.gov/indicators/roe/index.htm.

68. A.C. Revkin and K.Q. Seelye, "Report by EPA Leaves Out Data on Climate Change," *New York Times* (online edition, June 19, 2003).

69. Union of Concerned Scientists, *Scientific Integrity in Policymaking* (2004), available at www.ucsusa.org/global_environment/rsi/page.cfm?pageID=1641.

70. Andrew C. Revkin, "Bush Aide Softened Greenhouse Gas Links to Global Warming," *New York Times* (online edition, June 8, 2005).

71. Revkin, "Bush Aide Softened" (2005).

72. Joel Connelly, "Ill Wind Swirling Around Climate Science," *Seattle Post-Intelligencer* (August 3, 2005).

73. Connelly(2005).

74. John McCain and Peter Likins, "Politics Versus the Integrity of Research," *Chronicle of Higher Education* (September 2, 2005).

75. David Michaels, "Doubt Is Their Product," *Scientific American* 292, no. 6 (June 2005).

76. Available at earth.usgcrp.gov/usgcrp/nacc.

77. "Suit Challenges Climate Change Report by U.S.," *New York Times* (August 7, 2003).

78. Office of Maine Attorney General Steven Rowe, "AGs: White House, Right Wing Group Conspired to Stifle Science" (August 11, 2003)

CHAPTER 2

1. See Alan Wertheimer, *Exploitation* (Princeton, NJ: Princeton University Press, 1996).

2. While some in the Marxist tradition, e.g., G.A. Cohen, also place normative ideals of equality at the center of their theorizing about justice, most rely on the conventional Marxist theory of exploitation, which defines justice in different terms. For an illustration of this contrast, see Cohen, *Self-Ownership, Freedom, and Equality* (New York: Cambridge University Press, 1995); and John Roemer, *A General Theory of Exploitation and Class* (New York: Cambridge University Press, 1982).

3. John Rawls, *A Theory of Justice* (Cambridge, MA: Belknap Press, 1971), p. 62.

4. Dworkin develops this theory in a two-part series of articles: "What Is Equality? Part I: Equality of Welfare," *Philosophy and Public Affairs* 10, no. 3 (summer 1981): 185–246; and "What Is Equality? Part II: Equality of Resources," *Philosophy and Public Affairs* 10, no. 4 (fall 1981): 283–345.

5. Such is Robert Nozick's claim in *Anarchy, State, and Utopia* (New York: Basic Books, 1977).

6. John Rawls, *Justice as Fairness: A Restatement* (Cambridge, MA: Belknap Press, 2001), p. 64.

7. The 1987 report of the World Commission on Environment and Development titled *Our Common Future* (New York: Oxford University Press; commonly called the Brundtland Report after the commission chair, Gro Harlem Brundtland) popularized the term "sustainable development," causally linking environmental protection and social justice efforts. Describing the causal connections between social inequality and environmental degradation, the report announced, "Poverty is a major cause and effect of global environmental problems. It is therefore futile to attempt to deal with environmental problems without a broader perspective that encompasses the factors underlying world poverty and economic inequality" (p. 3).

8. Terrence Ball ("Democracy," in *Political Theory and the Ecological Challenge*, ed. Andrew Dobson and Robyn Eckersley [New York: Cambridge University Press, 2006], pp. 131–47) argues that the interests of animals and future generations could be represented by proxies in democratic institutions, giving at least some voice to their interests, though it is doubtful that such schemes could ever grant more than token representation to these groups, since they would necessarily remain a legislative minority.

9. George W. Bush, "Text of a Letter from the President to Senators Hagel, Helms, Craig, and Roberts," available at www.whitehouse.gov/news/releases/2001/03/20010314.html.

10. Centre for Science and Environment, "George Bush: 'I Oppose the Kyoto Protocol': The Leader of the Most Polluting Country in the World Claims Global Warming Treaty Is 'Unfair' Because It Excludes India and China" (press release, March 16, 2001), available at www.cseindia.org/html/au/au4_20010317.htm; emphasis original.

11. Thomas Athanasiou and Paul Baer, *Dead Heat: Global Justice and Global Warming* (New York: Seven Stories Press, 2002), p. 75.

12. Athanasiou and Baer (2002), p. 128.

13. Eileen Claussen and Lisa McNeilly, *Equity and Global Climate Change* (Arlington, VA: Pew Center on Global Climate Change, 2000).

14. Energy Information Administration, *International Energy Outlook 1998* (Washington, DC: U.S. Department of Energy, 1998).

15. United Nations Development Programme, *Human Development Report 2001* (New York: Oxford University Press, 2001), p. 144.

16. Athanasiou and Baer (2002), pp. 73–74.

CHAPTER 3

1. Intergovernmental Panel on Climate Change, *Climate Change 2001: A Synthesis Report. A Contribution of Working Groups I, II, and III to the Third Assessment Report of the IPCC*, ed. R.T. Watson and the Core Writing Team (New York: Cambridge University Press, 2001), p. 12.

2. Allen Buchanan, "Theories of Secession," in *Social and Political Philosophy: Contemporary Readings*, ed. George Sher and Baruch Brody (New York: Harcourt Brace, 1999): 402–15, p. 409.

3. See, e.g., Will Kymlicka, *Liberalism, Community, and Culture* (Oxford: Clarendon Press, 1989); David Miller, *Citizenship and National Identity* (Malden, MA: Polity Press, 2000); and Yael Tamir, *Liberal Nationalism* (Princeton, NJ: Princeton University Press, 1993).

4. John Rawls, *The Law of Peoples* (Cambridge, MA: Harvard University Press, 1999), p. 81.

5. In 2004, eight U.S. states and New York City brought suit against five of the country's largest power companies in an effort to force them to reduce their GHG emissions, in 2005 four cities joined Friends of the Earth and Greenpeace in suing the Export-Import Bank and Overseas Private Investment Corporation for funding overseas oil development projects without considering their climate impacts, and in 2007 California sued six automobile manufacturers to accomplish the same. Perhaps the most successful climate lawsuit was brought by Massachusetts against the U.S. Environmental Protection Agency, in which the Supreme Court ruled that the agency (against protests from the George W. Bush administration) has the authority to regulate GHG emissions. Such lawsuits, which typically involve transboundary pollution issues, have aimed to press forward responsible climate policy in the regulatory vacuum left by a Congress and president that have refused to act.

6. David Held, "Regulating Globalization? The Reinvention of Politics," *International Sociology* 15 (June 2000): 394–408, p. 399.

7. Thomas Hobbes, *The Leviathan*, ed. Richard Tuck (New York: Cambridge University Press, 1991), p. 188.

8. Robert Kagan, "Power and Weakness," *Policy Review* 113 (2002): 1–20, p. 1.

9. Charles R. Beitz, *Political Theory and International Relations* (Princeton, NJ: Princeton University Press, 1979), p. 33.

10. Marshall Cohen, "Moral Skepticism and International Relations," in *International Ethics*, ed. Charles Beitz, Marshall Cohen, T.M. Scanlon, and John Simmons (Princeton, NJ: Princeton University Press, 1985): 3–52, p. 12.

11. Richard Ned Lebow, *The Tragic Vision of Politics* (New York: Cambridge University Press, 2003), p. 237.

12. David Miller, "Justice and Global Inequality," in *Inequality, Globalization, and World Politics*, ed. Andrew Hurrell and Ngaire Woods (New York: Oxford University Press, 1999): 187–210, p. 190.

13. Andrew Hurrell, "Global Inequality and International Institutions," in *Global Justice*, ed. Thomas W. Pogge (Malden, MA: Blackwell, 2004): 32–54, p. 42.

14. Hurrell (2004), pp. 49–51.

15. Beitz (1979), p. 127.

16. John Rawls, *A Theory of Justice* (Cambridge, MA: Belknap Press, 1971), p. 102.

17. Beitz (1979), p. 138.

18. Beitz (1979), p. 141.

19. Beitz (1979), p. 144.

20. Beitz (1979), pp. 148–49.

21. Beitz (1979), p. 151.

22. Rawls (1999), pp. 116–17.

23. See Adam Przeworski, Michael Alvarez, José Antonio Chiebub, and Fernando Limongi, *Democracy and Development: Political Institutions and Well-Being in the World, 1950–1990* (Cambridge University Press, 2000). The authors conclude that "there is no doubt that democracies are more likely to be found in the more highly developed countries. Yet the reason is not that democracies are more likely to emerge when countries develop under authoritarianism, but that, however they do emerge, they are more likely to survive in countries that are already developed." (p. 106).

24. Derek Parfit, *Reasons and Persons* (Oxford: Clarendon Press, 1994), p. 61.

25. Paul Baer, "Equity, Greenhouse Gas Emissions, and Global Common Resources," in *Climate Change Policy: A Survey*, ed. Stephen H. Schneider, Armin Rosencranz, and John O. Niles (Washington, DC: Island Press, 2002): 393–408, p. 396.

26. Eileen Claussen and Lisa McNeilly, *Equity and Global Climate Change* (Arlington, VA: Pew Center on Global Climate Change, 2000).

CHAPTER 4

1. Nicholas Stern, *The Stern Review: The Economics of Climate Change* (New York: Cambridge University Press, 2006), p. vi.

2. Stern (2006), p. 33.

3. E.g., Brian Barry ("Sustainability and Intergenerational Justice," in *Fairness and Futurity*, ed. Andrew Dobson [Oxford University Press, 1999], pp. 93–117) begins his

discussion of sustainability with the "simple thought" that "as temporary custodians of the planet, those who are alive at any given time can do a better or worse job of handing it on to their successors" (p. 93).

4. John Rawls, *A Theory of Justice* (Cambridge, MA: Belknap Press, 1971), p. 285.

5. Rawls (1971), p. 291.

6. Rawls (1971), p. 288.

7. Rawls (1971), p. 290.

8. Rawls (1971), p. 115. Such duties, Rawls argues, "are owed not only to definite individuals, say to those cooperating together in a particular social arrangement, but to persons generally."

9. Rawls (1971), p. 289.

10. John Rawls, *The Law of Peoples* (Cambridge, MA: Harvard University Press, 1999), p. 119.

11. Rawls (1971), p. 289.

12. Rawls (1971), p. 274.

13. Rawls (1971), p. 287.

14. Derek Parfit, *Reasons and Persons* (Oxford: Clarendon Press, 1984), p. 377.

15. Parfit (1984), p. 366.

16. Parfit assumes in his argument that the higher standards of living that are likely to result from the higher consumption rates under Depletion will lead to more rapid population growth. This claim, however, may be empirically false. Rising standards of living have the effect of decreasing rates of reproduction, since number of children is an economic function of families and the need for parents to have support from children in their old age. If true, this observation complicates Parfit's contention that the policies of Conservation and Depletion lead to Different-Number Choices. Depletion may not only reduce the natural resources available to future persons, but also reduce their number (harming them, by Parfit's logic). For this point, I am indebted to Erik Olin Wright.

17. For an example of this strategy for refuting the future generations problem, see Edith Brown Weiss, *In Fairness to Future Generations: International Law, Common Patrimony, and Intergenerational Equity* (Dobbs Ferry, NY: Transnational Publishers, 1989).

18. See Alan Carter, "Can We Harm Future People?" *Environmental Values* 10 (2001): 429–54.

19. Parfit (1984), p. 378.

20. Joel Feinberg, "The Rights of Animals and Unborn Generations," in *Rights, Justice, and the Bonds of Liberty* (Princeton, NJ: Princeton University Press, 1980), p. 167.

21. Feinberg (1980), p. 181.

22. Feinberg (1980), p. 182.

23. Feinberg (1980), p. 182.

24. Parfit (1984), p. 357.

25. Brian Barry, "Justice Between Generations," in *Law Morality and Society: Essays in Honor of H.L.A. Hart*, ed. P.M.S. Hacker and Joseph Raz (Oxford: Clarendon Press, 1977): 268–84, p. 268.

26. Indeed, Parfit endorses intertemporal equality, which treats persons as moral equals regardless of generational membership.

27. Barry (1999), p. 116.

28. Suppose instead that trees could be used more efficiently, so that consumption could be reduced. By the same logic, consumption could only be reduced for the sake of currently living persons (and not for nonexistent persons), so such efforts could not begin until t_5. That year, and every year after, consumption could be reduced by 1/95th of its original t_5 level. If possible, complete deforestation could be indefinitely delayed by such a strategy, but alas, this is not possible. By year t_{100}, this would amount to zero consumption, which is beyond the parameters of the original assumption (that use of trees was necessary for life). Far before this, however, natural limits to how efficiently a tree can be used would be reached; e.g., houses built from wooden beams that are too thin would begin to collapse. Rescuing the islanders through more efficient use of trees is impossible.

29. There is a kind of reciprocity involved in this transaction, since each person (after the generation that practices conservation) both receives benefits from and incurs costs for adhering to conservation guidelines, but it is not strict reciprocity where there are exactly two actors exchanging obligations for benefits.

CHAPTER 5

1. Brian Barry, "Sustainability and Intergenerational Justice," in *Fairness and Futurity*, ed. Andrew Dobson (New York: Oxford University Press, 1999): 93–117, p. 97.

2. Joel Feinberg, "Action and Responsibility," in *Doing and Deserving* (Princeton, NJ: Princeton University Press, 1970), p. 144.

3. Feinberg (1970), p. 145.

4. Feinberg (1970), p. 222.

5. Feinberg (1970), pp. 32–33.

6. Onora Nell (O'Neill), "Lifeboat Earth," *Philosophy and Public Affairs* 4 (Spring 1975): 273–92, p. 278.

7. Nell (1975), p. 281.

8. Nell (1975), p. 282.

9. Nell (1975), p. 283.

10. Nell (1975), p. 286.

11. Thomas Nagel, "Moral Luck," in *Mortal Questions* (New York: Cambridge University Press, 1979), p. 25.

12. Nagel (1979), p. 25.

13. Nagel (1979), p. 29.

14. Nagel (1979), p. 26.

15. Nagel (1979), pp. 30–31.

16. Feinberg (1970), pp. 31–32.

17. Feinberg (1970), p. 33.

18. Feinberg (1970), p. 27.

19. Feinberg (1968), p. 687.

20. See Robert Stubbings and Edward Carmines, "Is It Irrational to Vote?" *Polity* 23 (Summer 1991): 629–40.

21. Derek Parfit, *Reasons and Persons* (Oxford: Clarendon Press, 1984), p. 75.

22. John Stuart Mill ("On Liberty," in *Utilitarianism, on Liberty, Considerations on Representative Government*, ed. H.B. Acton [Rutland, VT: Everyman's Library, 1972], pp. 78–83) famously argues for interference in individual liberty if (and only if) the act in question causes harm to others, but rejects the application of his harm principle to acts that produce "imperceptible" effects.

23. Parfit (1984), p. 70.

24. Parfit (1984) p. 83.

25. Parfit (1984), p. 86.

26. David Miller, "Holding Nations Responsible," *Ethics* 114 (January 2004): 240–68, p. 245.

27. Miller (2004), p. 250.

28. Miller (2004), p. 251.

29. Miller (2004), p. 253.

30. Miller (2004), p. 253.

31. Michael Walzer, *Just and Unjust Wars* (New York: Basic Books, 1977), p. 297.

32. Walzer (1977), pp. 300–301.

33. Miller (2004), p. 243.

34. Miller (2004), p. 260.

35. Feinberg (1968), p. 686.

36. Miller (2004), p. 255.

37. Iris Marion Young, "Responsibility and Global Labor Justice," *Journal of Political Philosophy* 12 (December 2004): 365–88, p. 378.

38. Ken Conca, "Beyond the Statist Frame: Environmental Politics in a Global Economy," in *Nature, Production, Power: Towards an Ecological Political Economy*, ed. Fred P. Gale and Michael M'Gonigle (Cheltonham, UK: Edward Algar, 2000): 141–55.

39. Joel Feinberg, "Collective Responsibility," *Journal of Philosophy* 65 (1968): 674–88, p. 683.

CHAPTER 6

1. According to a 2002 Harris Poll, 74 percent of Americans believe that "increased carbon dioxide and other gases released into the atmosphere will, if unchecked, lead to global warming and an increase in average temperatures," but it is likely that any even smaller percentage consider their own GHG emissions as responsible for the problem, perhaps due to the "mistakes in moral mathematics" surveyed in chapter 5. See "Majorities Continue to Believe in Global Warming and Support Kyoto Protocol," Harris Poll No. 56 (October 23, 2002), available at www.harrisinteractive.com/harris_poll/index.asp?PID=335.

2. Intergovernmental Panel on Climate Change, *Climate Change 2001: A Synthesis Report. A Contribution of Working Groups I, II, and III to the Third Assessment Report of the IPCC*, ed. R.T. Watson and the Core Writing Team (New York: Cambridge University Press, 2001).

3. Henry Shue, "Global Environment and International Inequality," *International Affairs* 75, no. 3 (1999): 531–45, p. 535.

4. Shue (1999), p. 533.

5. Shue (1999), pp. 533–34.

6. Peter Singer, *One World: The Ethics of Globalization* (New Haven, CT: Yale University Press, 2002), p. 31.

7. The Intergovernmental Panel on Climate Change's (2001) disclaimer on uncertainty: "Decision making has to deal with uncertainties including the risk of non-linear and/or irreversible changes and entails balancing the risk of either insufficient or excessive action, and involves careful consideration of the consequences (both environmental and economic), their likelihood, and society's attitude toward risk" (p. 39).

8. The temperature range is based on a variety of emissions scenarios that stabilize atmospheric concentrations of CO_2 at between 540 and 970 ppm. The most significant uncertainty variable driving the range of emissions scenarios is the global political response to mitigate climate change.

9. Intergovernmental Panel on Climate Change (2001), p. 12.

10. Intergovernmental Panel on Climate Change (2001), pp. 31–32.

11. Richard Wolfson and Stephen Schneider, "Understanding Climate Science," in *Climate Change Policy: A Survey*, ed. Stephen H. Schneider, Armin Rosencranz, and John O. Niles (Washington, DC: Island Press, 2002): 3–52, p. 41.

12. For an account of the problems that have arisen around estimating scientific uncertainty, and of the campaign to make more precise estimates of such uncertainty as a way of avoiding such problems, see Jim Giles, "Scientific Uncertainty: When Doubt Is a Sure Thing," *Nature* 418 (August 2002): 476–78.

13. Wolfson and Schneider (2002), p. 42.

14. Wolfson and Schneider (2002), p. 43.

15. Both the anti-Kyoto effort and the campaign by the tobacco industry to avoid regulation employed similar public relations strategies and, in some cases, similar organizations. See Sheldon Rampton and John Stauber, *Trust Us, We're Experts! How Industry Manipulates Science and Gambles with Your Future* (New York: Putnam, 2000).

16. See Chris Mooney, "Blinded by Science," *Columbia Journalism Review* 6 (November/December 2004), available at www.cjr.org/issues/2004/6/mooney-science.asp.

17. Andrew Gumbel, "U.S. Says CO_2 Is Not a Pollutant," *Independent* (online edition, August 31, 2003).

18. Executive Office of the President, *Economic Report of the President* (February 2002), p. 245.

19. Rampton and Stauber (2000).

20. See Andrew Revkin, "Exxon-Led Group Is Giving a Climate Grant to Stanford," *New York Times* (online edition, November 22, 2002).

21. Peter Bachrach and Morton Baratz, "The Two Faces of Power," *American Political Science Review* 56, no. 4 (December 1962): 947–52.

22. See, e.g., Pew Research Center, "Americans Support Action on Global Warming" (November 21, 1997), available at people-press.org/reports/display.php3?ReportID=100; and Chicago Council on Foreign Relations and the German

Marshall Fund of the United States, *Worldviews 2002 Survey*, available at www. worldviews.org.

23. Michael Janofsky, "Michael Crichton, Novelist, Becomes Senate Witness," *New York Times* (September 29, 2005).

24. Stephen Schneider and Kristen Kuntz-Duriseti, "Uncertainty and Climate Change Policy," in *Climate Change Policy: A Survey* (2002): 53–88, p. 55.

25. S.H. Schneider and S.L. Thompson, "Future Changes in the Atmosphere," in *The Global Possible*, ed. R. Repetto (New Haven, CT: Yale University Press, 1985): 397–430.

26. Schneider and Kuntz-Duriseti (2002), p. 75.

27. Tim Hayward, *Constitutional Environmental Rights* (New York: Oxford University Press, 2005), p. 168.

28. Kristen Shrader-Frechette, "Environmental Ethics, Uncertainty, and Limited Data," in *Ethics and Agenda 21*, ed. Noel J. Brown and Pierre Quiblier (New York: United Nations Publications, 1994): 77–89, p. 79.

29. Cass Sunstein, *The Laws of Fear* (New York: Cambridge University Press, 2005), p. 24. As suggested in the text discussion, the precautionary principle, when properly invoked, aims to manage uncertainty rather than risk by urging defensible standards of scientific evidence rather than presuming harm where it does not exist.

30. Sunstein (2005), pp. 175–203.

CHAPTER 7

1. Steve Vanderheiden, "Justice in the Greenhouse: Climate Change and the Idea of Fairness," *Social Philosophy Today*, 19 (2004): 89–101.

2. Paul Baer, "Equity, Greenhouse Gas Emissions, and Global Common Resources," in *Climate Change Policy: A Survey*, ed. Stephen H. Schneider, Armin Rosencranz, and John O. Niles (Washington, DC: Island Press, 2002): 393–408, p. 401.

3. Peter Singer, *One World: The Ethics of Globalization* (New Haven, CT: Yale University Press, 2002), p. 35.

4. Leigh Raymond, "Cutting the 'Gordian Knot' in Climate Change Policy," *Energy Policy* 34 (April 2006): 655–58.

5. See Ronald Dworkin, "What Is Equality? Part 1: Equality of Welfare," *Philosophy and Public Affairs* 10 (1981): 185–246.

6. Singer (2002), p. 35.

7. Baer (2002), p. 396.

8. Baer (2002), p. 402.

9. Anil Agarwal, "A Southern Perspective on Curbing Global Climate Change," in *Climate Change Policy: A Survey*, ed. Stephen H. Schneider, Armin Rosencranz, and John O. Niles (Washington, DC: Island Press, 2002): 375–91, p. 377.

10. Singer (2002), p. 44.

11. Baer (2002), p. 402.

12. Baer (2002), pp. 395–96.

13. Steve Vanderheiden, "Missing the Forests for the Trees: Justice and Environmental Economics," *Critical Review of International Social and Political Philosophy* 8, no. 1 (March 2005): 51–69.

14. Intergovernmental Panel on Climate Change, *Climate Change 2001: A Synthesis Report. A Contribution of Working Groups I, II, and III to the Third Assessment Report of the IPCC*, ed. R.T. Watson and the Core Writing Team (New York: Cambridge University Press, 2001), pp. 108–122.

15. Baer (2002), p. 400.

16. Their luck was both good and bad—good for the benefits that it might bring under a trading scheme, but bad in most other respects. It might nonetheless be called luck because of the disparity between actual and intended outcomes.

17. The case of Russian and Ukrainian economic collapse comes closest to the kind of luck known as circumstantial luck (or "luck in the kind of problems or situations that one faces") or resultant luck (or "luck in the way one's actions and projects turn out"), both of which involve at least some moral responsibility. Unlike brute luck, both of these forms of luck (i.e., circumstances in which good or bad fortune plays a role in determining outcomes) involve some element of control over outcomes, albeit less than in those cases in which luck plays no role in determining outcomes. See Thomas Nagel, *Mortal Questions* (New York: Cambridge University Press, 1993), p. 60.

18. Baer (2002), p. 395.

19. Tim Hayward, *Constitutional Environmental Rights* (New York: Oxford University Press, 2005), p. 7.

20. Hayward (2005), p. 11.

21. Hayward (2005), pp. 47–48.

22. *Declaration of the United Nations Conference on the Human Environment* (1972).

23. U.N. Economic Commission for Europe, Aarhus Convention on Access to Information, *Public Participation in Decision-Making and Access to Justice in Environmental Matters* (1998).

24. Hayward (2005), p. 57.

25. Henry Shue, *Basic Rights* (Princeton, NJ: Princeton University Press, 1980), pp. 18–19.

26. Shue (1980), p. 23.

27. Shue (1980), p. 34.

28. Shue (1980), pp. 126–27.

29. Henry Shue, "Climate," in *A Companion to Environmental Philosophy*, ed. Dale Jamieson (Malden, MA: Blackwell, 2001): 449–59, p. 451.

30. Shue (2001), p. 454.

31. Baer (2002), p. 394.

32. Ellen Wiegandt, "Climate Change, Equity, and International Negotiations," in *Climate Change Policy: A Survey*, ed. Stephen H. Schneider, Armin Rosencranz, and John O. Niles (Washington, DC: Island Press, 2002): 127–50, p. 139.

33. Agarwal (2002), p. 385.

34. Agarwal (2002), p. 386.

35. World Commission on Environment and Development, *Our Common Future* (New York: Oxford University Press, 1987), pp. 5–6.

36. Agarwal (2002), p. 378.

37. Shue (2001), p. 454.

Bibliography

Agarwal, Anil. "A Southern Perspective on Curbing Global Climate Change." In *Climate Change Policy: A Survey*, edited by Stephen H. Schneider, Armin Rosencranz, and John O. Niles. Washington, DC: Island Press, 2002: 375–91.

Anderson, J.W. "A 'Crash Course' in Climate Change." In *The RFF Reader in Environmental and Resource Management*, edited by Wallace Oates. Washington, DC: Resources for the Future, 1999.

Arrhenius, Svante. "On the Influence of Carbonic Acid in the Air upon the Temperature of the Ground." *London, Edinburgh, and Dublin Philosophical Magazine and Journal of Science*, 5th ser. (April 1896): 237–76.

Bachrach, Peter, and Morton Baratz. "The Two Faces of Power." *American Political Science Review* 56, no. 4 (December 1962): 947–52.

Baer, Paul. "Equity, Greenhouse Gas Emissions, and Global Common Resources." In *Climate Change Policy: A Survey*, edited by Stephen H. Schneider, Armin Rosencranz, and John O. Niles. Washington, DC: Island Press, 2002: 393–408.

Barry, Brian. "Justice Between Generations." In *Law Morality and Society: Essays in Honor of H.L.A. Hart*, edited by P.M.S. Hacker and Joseph Raz. Oxford: Clarendon Press, 1977: 268–84.

Barry, Brian. "Sustainability and Intergenerational Justice." In *Fairness and Futurity*, edited by Andrew Dobson. New York: Oxford University Press, 1999: 93–117.

Beitz, Charles R. *Political Theory and International Relations*. Princeton, NJ: Princeton University Press, 1979.

Buchanan, Allen. "Theories of Secession." *Philosophy and Public Affairs* 26 (Winter 1997): 31–61.

Carter, Alan. "Can We Harm Future People?" *Environmental Values* 10 (2001): 429–54.

Christianson, Gale. *Greenhouse: The 200-Year Story of Global Warming.* New York: Penguin Books, 1999.

Claussen, Eileen, and Lisa McNeilly. *Equity and Global Climate Change.* Arlington, VA: Pew Center on Global Climate Change, 2000.

Cohen, G.A. *Self-Ownership, Freedom, and Equality.* New York: Cambridge University Press, 1995.

Cohen, Marshall. "Moral Skepticism and International Relations." In *International Ethics,* edited by Charles Beitz, Marshall Cohen, T.M. Scanlon, and John Simmons. Princeton, NJ: Princeton University Press, 1985: 3–52.

Conca, Ken. "Beyond the Statist Frame: Environmental Politics in a Global Economy." In *Nature, Production, Power: Towards an Ecological Political Economy,* edited by Fred P. Gale and R. Michael M'Gonigle. Cheltenham, UK: Edward Elger, 2000: 141–55.

Davidson, Eric, and George Woodwell. *You Can't Eat GNP: Economics As If Ecology Mattered.* Reading, MA: Perseus Books, 2001.

Devine, Robert S. *Bush Versus the Environment.* New York: Anchor, 2004.

Dobson, Andrew, and Robyn Eckersley, editors. *Political Theory and the Ecological Challenge.* New York: Cambridge University Press, 2006.

Drew, Elizabeth. "Selling Washington." *New York Review of Books* (June 23, 2005): 24–27.

Dworkin, Ronald. *Sovereign Virtue: The Theory and Practice of Equality.* Cambridge, MA: Harvard University Press, 2000.

Executive Office of the President. *Economic Report of the President,* February 2002.

Feinberg, Joel. "Collective Responsibility." *Journal of Philosophy* 65 (1968): 674–88.

Feinberg, Joel. *Doing and Deserving.* Princeton, NJ: Princeton University Press, 1970.

Feinberg, Joel. "The Rights of Animals and Unborn Generations." In *Rights, Justice, and the Bonds of Liberty.* Princeton, NJ: Princeton University Press, 1980.

Gardiner, Stephen. "Ethics and Global Climate Change." *Ethics* 114 (April 2004): 555–600.

Gardiner, Stephen. "The Global Warming Tragedy and the Dangerous Illusion of the Kyoto Protocol." *Ethics and International Affairs* 18 (2004): 23–39.

Gelbspan, Ross. *The Heat Is On.* Reading, MA: Perseus Books, 1997.

Hardin, Garrett. "The Tragedy of the Commons." *Science* 162 (1968): 1243–48.

Hayward, Tim. *Constitutional Environmental Rights.* New York: Oxford University Press, 2005.

Held, David. "Regulating Globalization? The Reinvention of Politics." *International Sociology* 15 (June 2000): 394–408.

Held, David, and Anthony McGrew. *Globalization/Anti-globalization.* Cambridge: Polity Press, 2002.

Held, David,. *Models of Democracy.* Stanford, CA: Stanford University Press, 2006.

Hofstadter, Richard. "The Paranoid Style of American Politics." *Harper's* (November 1964): 77–86.

Hurrell, Andrew. "Global Inequality and International Institutions." In *Global Justice,* edited by Thomas W. Pogge. Malden, MA: Blackwell, 2004: 32–54.

Intergovernmental Panel on Climate Change. *Climate Change 2001: A Synthesis Report. A Contribution of Working Groups I, II, and III to the Third Assessment Report of the IPCC*, edited by R.T. Watson and the Core Writing Team. New York: Cambridge University Press, 2001.

Kagan, Robert. "Power and Weakness." *Policy Review* 113 (2002): 1–20.

Kymlikca, Will. *Liberalism, Community and Culture*. Oxford: Clarendon Press, 1989.

Lebow, Richard Ned. *The Tragic Vision of Politics*. New York: Cambridge University Press, 2003.

Leggett, Jeremy. *The Carbon War: Global Warming and the End of the Oil Era*. New York: Taylor & Francis, 2001.

Lindblom, Charles. "The Science of 'Muddling Through.'" *Public Administration Review* 19 (1959): 79–88.

McKibben, Bill. "Crossing the Red Line." *New York Review of Books* (June 10, 2004): 32–36.

Michaels, David. "Doubt Is Their Product." *Scientific American* 292, no. 6 (June 2005): 96–101.

Mill, John Stuart. "On Liberty." *Utilitarianism, on Liberty, Considerations on Representative Government*, edited by H.B. Acton. Rutland, VT: Everyman's Library, 1972: 78–83.

Miller, David. *On Nationality*. New York: Oxford University Press, 1995.

Miller, David. "Justice and Global Inequality." In *Inequality, Globalization, and World Politics*, edited by Andrew Hurrell and Ngaire Woods. New York: Oxford University Press, 1999: 187–210.

Miller, David. *Citizenship and National Identity*. Malden, MA: Polity Press, 2000.

Miller, David. "Holding Nations Responsible." *Ethics* 114 (January 2004): 240–68.

Mooney, Chris. "Some Like It Hot." *Mother Jones* (May 2005): 36–43.

Moyers, Bill. "Welcome to Doomsday." *New York Review of Books* (March 24, 2005): 8–10.

Nagel, Thomas. *Mortal Questions*. New York: Cambridge University Press, 1979.

O'Neill, Onora. "Lifeboat Earth." *Philosophy and Public Affairs* 4 (spring 1975): 273–92.

Oreskes, Naomi. "The Scientific Consensus on Climate Change." *Science* 306 (2004): 1686.

Parfit, Derek. *Reasons and Persons*. Oxford: Clarendon Press, 1994.

Pogge, Thomas. "Cosmopolitanism and Sovereignty." *Ethics* 103 (October 1992): 48–75.

Pogge, Thomas. "An Egalitarian Law of Peoples." *Philosophy and Public Affairs* 23 (Summer 1994): 195–224.

Pope, Carl, and Paul Rauber. *Strategic Ignorance: Why the Bush Administration Is Recklessly Destroying a Century of Environmental Progress*. San Francisco: Sierra Club, 2004.

Rampton, Sheldon, and John Stauber. *Trust Us, We're Experts! How Industry Manipulates Science and Gambles with Your Future*. New York: Putnam Publishing Group, 2000.

Rawls, John. *A Theory of Justice*. Cambridge, MA: Belknap Press, 1971.

Rawls, John. *Political Liberalism*. New York: Columbia University Press, 1993.

Rawls, John. *The Law of Peoples*. Cambridge, MA: Harvard University Press, 1999.

Raymond, Leigh. "Cutting the 'Gordian Knot' in Climate Change Policy." *Energy Policy* 34 (April 2006): 655–58.

Revelle, Roger, and Hans Seuss. "Carbon Dioxide Exchanges Between Atmosphere and Ocean and the Question of an Increase of Atmospheric CO_2 During the Past Decades." *Tellus* 9 (1957): 18–27.

Roemer, John. *A General Theory of Exploitation and Class*. New York: Cambridge University Press, 1982.

Schneider, Stephen H., and Kristin Kuntz-Duriseti. "Uncertainty and Climate Change Policy." In *Climate Change Policy: A Survey*, edited by Stephen H. Schneider, Armin Rosencranz, and John O. Niles. Washington, DC: Island Press, 2002: 53–88.

Schneider, Stephen H., and S.L. Thompson. "Future Changes in the Atmosphere." In *The Global Possible*, edited by Richard Repetto. New Haven, CT: Yale University Press, 1985: 397–430.

Shrader-Frechette, Kristen. "Environmental Ethics, Uncertainty, and Limited Data." *Ethics and Agenda 21*, edited by Noel J. Brown and Pierre Quiblier. New York: United Nations Publications, 1994: 77–89.

Shue, Henry. *Basic Rights*. Princeton, NJ: Princeton University Press, 1980.

Shue, Henry. "Global Environment and International Inequality." *International Affairs* 75, no. 3 (1999): 531–45.

Shue, Henry. "Climate." In *A Companion to Environmental Philosophy*, edited by Dale Jamieson. Malden, MA: Blackwell, 2001: 449–59.

Singer, Peter. *One World: The Ethics of Globalization*. New Haven, CT: Yale University Press, 2002.

Sunstein, Cass R. *Laws of Fear: Beyond the Precautionary Principle*. New York: Cambridge University Press, 2005.

Tamir, Yael. *Liberal Nationalism*. Princeton, NJ: Princeton University Press, 1993.

United Nations. *United Nations Framework Convention on Climate Change*, 1992.

U.S. Department of State. *U.S. Climate Action Report*, May 2002.

Vanderheiden, Steve. "Justice in the Greenhouse: Climate Change and the Idea of Fairness." *Social Philosophy Today* 19 (2004): 89–101.

Vanderheiden, Steve. "Knowledge, Uncertainty, and Responsibility: Responding to Climate Change." *Public Affairs Quarterly* 18 (April 2004): 141–58.

Vanderheiden, Steve. "Missing the Forests for the Trees: Justice and Environmental Economics." *Critical Review of International Social and Political Philosophy* 8, no. 1 (March 2005): 51–69.

Vanderheiden, Steve. "Climate Change and the Challenge of Moral Responsibility." In *Ethics and the Life Sciences*, edited by Fred Adams. *Journal of Philosophical Research* special issue, 2007: 85–92.

Vanderheiden, Steve. "Conservation, Foresight, and the Future Generations Problem." *Inquiry* 49, no. 4 (August 2006): 337–52.

Victor, David G. *Climate Change: Debating America's Policy Options*. New York: Council on Foreign Relations, 2004.

Walzer, Michael. *Just and Unjust Wars.* New York: Basic Books, 1977.

Watson, Robert T. "Climate Change: The Political Situation." *Science* 302 (2003): 1925–26.

Weiss, Edith Brown. *In Fairness to Future Generations: International Law, Common Patrimony, and Intergenerational Equity.* Dobbs Ferry, NY: Transnational Publishers, 1989.

Wertheimer, Alan. *Exploitation.* Princeton, NJ: Princeton University Press, 1996.

Whiteside, Kerry H. *Precautionary Politics: Principle and Practice in Confronting Environmental Risk.* Cambridge, MA: MIT Press, 2006.

Wiegandt, Ellen. "Climate Change, Equity, and International Negotiations." In *Climate Change Policy: A Survey,* edited by Stephen H. Schneider, Armin Rosencranz, and John O. Niles. Washington, DC: Island Press, 2002: 127–50.

Wolfson, Richard, and Stephen Schneider. "Understanding Climate Science." In *Climate Change Policy: A Survey,* edited by Stephen H. Schneider, Armin Rosencranz, and John O. Niles. Washington, DC: Island Press, 2002: 3–52.

World Commission on Environment and Development. *Our Common Future.* New York: Oxford University Press, 1987.

Young, Iris Marion Young. "Responsibility and Global Labor Justice." *Journal of Political Philosophy* 12 (December 2004): 365–88.

Index